510.76 HP2

FOUNDATION MATHEMATICS FOR GCSE

A complete course for the Foundation Tier

Written for AQA specifications A & B

Kevin Evans

Brian Speed

Keith Gordon

Collins

D1387092

Published by Collins Educational
An imprint of HarperCollins*Publishers* Ltd
77–85 Fulham Palace Road
Hammersmith
London W6 8JB

Browse the complete Collins catalogue at
www.harpercollins.com

© HarperCollins*Publishers* Ltd 2001
First published 2001

Reprinted 10 9 8 7 6

ISBN 0 00 711508 3

Kevin Evans, Brian Speed and Keith Gordon assert the
moral right to be identified as the authors of this work.
All rights reserved. No part of this publication may be
reproduced, stored in a retrieval system, or transmitted in
any form or by any means, electronic, mechanical,
photocopying, recording or otherwise, without the prior
permission of the Publisher or a licence permitting
restricted copying in the United Kingdom issued by the
Copyright Licensing Agency Ltd, 90 Tottenham Court
Road, London W1P OLP.

British Cataloguing in Publication Data
A catalogue record for this book is available from the
British Library

Edited by John Day
Typesetting by Derek Lee
Expert Reader: Peter Clarkson
Illustrations by Moondisks, Cambridge
and Illustrated Arts, Sutton
Cover by Sylvia Kwan
Index by Susan Leech
Production by Kathryn Botterill
Printed and bound by Printing Express, Hong Kong

Acknowledgements

We are grateful to the following Examination Groups for
permission to reproduce questions from their past
examination papers and from specimen papers. Full
details are given with each question. The Examination
Groups accept no responsibility whatsoever for the
accuracy or method of working in the answers given,
which are solely the responsibility of the authors and the
publisher.

Assessment and Qualification Alliance (AQA)
EDEXCEL Foundation (formerly ULEAC)
Midland Examining Group (MEG)
Northern Examinations and Assessment Board
    (NEAB)
Northern Ireland Council for the Curriculum
    Examinations and Assessment (NICCEA)
Oxford, Cambridge and RSA examinations (OCR)
Southern Examining Group (SEG)
Welsh Joint Education Committee (WJEC)

Every effort has been made to contact all copyright
holders. If any have been inadvertently overlooked, the
publisher would be pleased to make full
acknowledgement at the first opportunity.

You might also like to visit:
www.harpercollins.co.uk
The book lover's website

Contents

Contents

Introduction

This book is the title's second edition, specifically tailored to meet the requirements of the GCSE mathematics specifications which come into force in September 2001, to be first examined in June 2003.

All the changes to content for examination from 2003 onwards are covered, including the non-calculator component (which first appeared as a separate examination paper in June 2000).

Non-calculator questions

Throughout the book, the non-calculator questions are flagged by the non-calculator icon. The icon indicates that the numerical demands of the question are such that it could appear in Paper 1, which is the non-calculator paper. Questions not flagged may be solved with the help of a calculator.

Syllabus changes

Coursework

All specifications now have a coursework component. There is no end-of-course examination paper to test coursework. A minimum of two coursework tasks must be done. One of these can be on Number and Algebra or Shape, Space and Measures (or a combination of them), and the other must be on Handling Data.

Throughout the book, at the end of each chapter, appropriate investigations are suggested. These can be done by the students as coursework tasks, and marked by their teachers. However, all boards will be setting their own tasks, which will be marked by the boards. Whichever way coursework is marked, it is assessed by the same criteria.

Content

The content of Number and Algebra has been slightly expanded but the extent of Handling Data which is to be examined has been reduced. This accounts for the introduction of the coursework task on handling data.

In the previous syllabuses, Using and Applying Mathematics (UAM) was tested by coursework in school, or in the end-of-course coursework paper. Some questions on UAM are now included in the end-of-course examinations. Generally, these will test a student's ability to think a problem through and may expect the student to use his or her mathematical skills in an unfamiliar context.

Other matters

As in the first edition, each chapter opens with a 'What you should already know' section and closes with a list of skills which the chapter should have imparted to the students.

At the end of each chapter is a selection of questions from recent foundation-tier examination papers of the various boards. Where possible, these are arranged in order of difficulty.

Using the internet

Through the internet, students have access to a vast amount of data which they could use in a variety of activities, particularly their coursework on Handling Data.

Chapter 22 contains a survey activity involving use of the internet, for which several well-established websites are listed as sources of data. Addresses of other appropriate website sources are available from the Collins maths website:

> www.**Collins**Education.com
> Online Support for Schools and Colleges

We hope that everyone who uses this book enjoys it, and we wish them the best of luck with any examinations!

Kevin Evans, Brian Speed, Keith Gordon.

1 Basic number

This chapter is going to ...

remind you of the basic number skills that you should have already done. You should be able to do the exercises without the use of a calculator.

What you should already know

✔ Times tables up to 10×10
✔ Addition and subtraction of numbers less than 20
✔ Simple multiplication and division
✔ How to multiply numbers by 10 and 100

Activity

Adding with grids

You need a set of cards marked 0 to 9:

| 0 | 1 | 2 | 3 | 4 | 5 | 6 | 7 | 8 | 9 |

Shuffle the cards and lay them out in a 3 by 3 grid. You will have one card left over.

3	5	0
7	6	4
8	2	9

Copy this on paper. Then add up each row and each column and their totals:

3	5	0	8
7	6	4	17
8	2	9	19
18	13	13	44

Look out for things which help. For example, in the first column,
3 + 7 make 10 and 10 + 8 = 18

In the last column, 9 + 4 = 9 + 1 + 3 = 10 + 3 = 13

Reshuffle the cards, lay them out again and copy the new grid. Recopy the new grid on a fresh sheet of paper, leaving out some of the numbers.

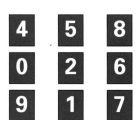

4	5	8	17
0	2	6	8
9	1	7	17
13	8	21	42

4	☐	8	17
☐	2	☐	8
9	☐	7	☐
☐	8	21	42

Pass this last grid to a friend to work out the missing numbers. You can make it quite hard because you are using only the numbers from 0 to 9. Remember: once a number has been used, it **cannot be used again** in that grid.

Example Find the numbers missing from this grid:

☐	☐	9	17
☐	2	☐	11
8	☐	☐	☐
19	3	17	☐

Clues The two cards missing from the second column must add up to 1, so they must be 0 and 1. The two cards missing from the first column add to 11, so they could be 7 and 4 or 6 and 5. Now, 6 or 5 won't work with 0 or 1 to give 17 across the top row. That means it has to be:

7	1	9	17
4	2	☐	11
8	0	☐	☐
19	3	17	☐

giving

7	1	9	17
4	2	5	11
8	0	3	11
19	3	17	39

as the answer.

EXERCISE 1A

WHOLE EXERCISE

1 Find the row and column sums of each of these grids.

a
```
1  3  7  □
9  2  8  □
6  5  4  □
□  □  □  □
```

b
```
0  6  7  □
8  1  4  □
9  5  3  □
□  □  □  □
```

c
```
0  8  7  □
1  6  2  □
9  3  4  □
□  □  □  □
```

d
```
2  4  6  □
3  5  7  □
8  9  1  □
□  □  □  □
```

e
```
5  9  3  □
6  1  8  □
2  7  4  □
□  □  □  □
```

f
```
0  8  3  □
7  2  4  □
1  6  5  □
□  □  □  □
```

g
```
9  4  8  □
7  0  5  □
1  6  3  □
□  □  □  □
```

h
```
0  8  6  □
7  1  4  □
5  9  2  □
□  □  □  □
```

i
```
1  8  7  □
6  2  5  □
0  9  3  □
□  □  □  □
```

2 Find the numbers missing from each of these grids. Remember: the numbers missing from each grid must be chosen from 0 to 9 without any repeats.

a
```
1   7  □ | 16
□   3  6 | 9
5   □  2 | 11
6  14 16 | 36
```

b
```
1  □  3  | 6
□  5  4  | 15
7  8  □  | 24
14 15 16 | 45
```

c
```
9  3  □  | 18
4  □  5  | 9
□  2  8  | 11
14 5  19 | 38
```

d
```
□  □  □  | 16
2  □  4  | 13
8  5  0  | 13
19 13 10 | 42
```

e
```
2  □  6  | 17
□  1  □  | □
5  □  8  | 13
11 □ 17  | 38
```

f
```
1  □  □  | 16
□  2  4  | 12
□  9  3  | □
12 □ 15  | □
```

g
```
0  2  □  | 3
9  □  □  | □
□  4  5  | 17
17 □ 13  | 42
```

h
```
□  □  3  | 4
□  7  4  | □
9  6  □  | 20
18 □ 12  | □
```

i
```
□  □  4  | 10
□  2  □  | □
8  □  □  | 15
15 □  □  | 36
```

Activity

Special table facts

You need a sheet of squared paper.

Start by writing in the easy tables. These are the 1×, 2×, 5×, 10× and 9× tables.

Now draw up a 10 by 10 table's square before you go any further. (Time yourself doing this and see if you can get faster.)

Once you have filled it in, shade in all the easy tables. You should be left with:

×	1	2	3	4	5	6	7	8	9	10
1										
2										
3			9	12		18	21	24		
4			12	16		24	28	32		
5										
6			18	24		36	42	48		
7			21	28		42	49	56		
8			24	32		48	56	64		
9										
10										

Now cross out **one** of each pair of sums that have the same answer, such as 3 × 4 and 4 × 3. This leaves you with:

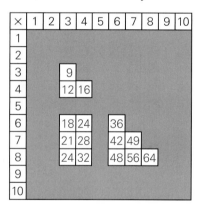

×	1	2	3	4	5	6	7	8	9	10
1										
2										
3			9							
4			12	16						
5										
6			18	24		36				
7			21	28		42	49			
8			24	32		48	56	64		
9										
10										

These are just 15 table facts. Do learn them.

The rest are easy tables, so you should then know all of them. But keep practising!

EXERCISE 1B

WHOLE EXERCISE

1 Write down the answer to each of the following without looking at the multiplication square.

a	4×5	**b**	7×3	**c**	6×4	**d**	3×5	**e**	8×2
f	3×4	**g**	5×2	**h**	6×7	**i**	3×8	**j**	9×2
k	5×6	**l**	4×7	**m**	3×6	**n**	8×7	**o**	5×5
p	5×9	**q**	3×9	**r**	6×5	**s**	7×7	**t**	4×6
u	6×6	**v**	7×5	**w**	4×8	**x**	4×9	**y**	6×8

2 Write down the answer to each of the following without looking at the multiplication square.

a	$10 \div 2$	**b**	$28 \div 7$	**c**	$36 \div 6$	**d**	$30 \div 5$	**e**	$15 \div 3$
f	$20 \div 5$	**g**	$21 \div 3$	**h**	$24 \div 4$	**i**	$16 \div 8$	**j**	$12 \div 4$
k	$42 \div 6$	**l**	$24 \div 3$	**m**	$18 \div 2$	**n**	$25 \div 5$	**o**	$48 \div 6$
p	$36 \div 4$	**q**	$32 \div 8$	**r**	$35 \div 5$	**s**	$49 \div 7$	**t**	$27 \div 3$
u	$45 \div 9$	**v**	$16 \div 4$	**w**	$40 \div 8$	**x**	$63 \div 9$	**y**	$54 \div 9$

3 Write down the answer to each of the following. Look carefully at the signs, because they are a mixture of $\times$, $+$, $-$ and $\div$.

a	$5 + 7$	**b**	$20 - 5$	**c**	3×7	**d**	$5 + 8$	**e**	$24 \div 3$
f	$15 - 8$	**g**	$6 + 8$	**h**	$27 \div 9$	**i**	6×5	**j**	$36 \div 6$
k	7×5	**l**	$15 \div 3$	**m**	$24 - 8$	**n**	$28 \div 4$	**o**	$7 + 9$
p	$9 + 6$	**q**	$36 - 9$	**r**	$30 \div 5$	**s**	$8 + 7$	**t**	4×6
u	8×5	**v**	$42 \div 7$	**w**	$8 + 9$	**x**	9×8	**y**	$54 - 8$

4 Write down the answer to each of the following.

a	3×10	**b**	5×10	**c**	8×10	**d**	10×10
e	12×10	**f**	18×10	**g**	24×10	**h**	4×100
i	7×100	**j**	9×100	**k**	10×100	**l**	14×100
m	24×100	**n**	72×100	**o**	100×100	**p**	$20 \div 10$
q	$70 \div 10$	**r**	$90 \div 10$	**s**	$170 \div 10$	**t**	$300 \div 10$
u	$300 \div 100$	**v**	$800 \div 100$	**w**	$1200 \div 100$	**x**	$2900 \div 100$
y	$5000 \div 100$						

Order of operations and BODMAS

Suppose you have to work out the answer to $4 + 5 \times 2$. You will probably say the answer is 18, but the correct answer is 14.

There is an order of operations which **must** be followed when working out sums like this. The $\times$ is always done **before** the $+$.

This gives $4 + 10 = 14$

Now suppose you have to work out the answer to $(3 + 2) \times (9 - 5)$. The correct answer is 20

You have probably realised that each **bracket** had to be done **first**, giving $5 \times 4 = 20$

So, how do you work out a sum like $9 \div 3 + 4 \times 2$?

To do sums like this, you **must** follow the BODMAS rule. This tells you the **sequence** in which you **must do** the operations:

B Brackets
O Order (powers)
D Division
M Multiplication
A Addition
S Subtraction

For example, to do $9 \div 3 + 4 \times 2$:

First divide	$9 \div 3 = 3$	giving	$3 + 4 \times 2$
Then multiply	$4 \times 2 = 8$	giving	$3 + 8$
Then add	$3 + 8 = 11$		

And to do, say, $60 - 5 \times 3^2 + (4 \times 2)$:

First, work out the bracket	$(4 \times 2) = 8$	giving	$60 - 5 \times 3^2 + 8$
Then the order (power)	$3^2 = 9$	giving	$60 - 5 \times 9 + 8$
Then multiply	$5 \times 9 = 45$	giving	$60 - 45 + 8$
Then add	$60 + 8 = 68$	giving	$68 - 45$
Finally, subtract	$68 - 45 = 23$		

Activity

Dice with BODMAS

You need a sheet of squared paper and three dice.

Draw a 5 by 5 grid and write the numbers from 1 to 25 in the spaces.

The numbers can be in **any order**.

14	13	18	7	24
15	1	16	17	6
23	8	2	12	5
3	22	4	10	19
25	21	9	20	11

Now throw three dice. Record the score on each one.

Use these numbers to make up a sum.

You must use all three numbers, and you must not put them together to make a number like 136. For example, with 1, 3 and 6 you could make:

$$1 + 3 + 6 = 10 \qquad 3 \times 6 + 1 = 19 \qquad (1 + 3) \times 6 = 24$$

$$6 \div 3 + 1 = 3 \qquad 6 + 3 - 1 = 8 \qquad 6 \div (3 \times 1) = 2$$

and so on. Remember to use BODMAS.

You have to make only one sum with each set of numbers.

When you have made a sum, cross the answer off on the grid and throw the dice again. Make a sum up with the next three numbers and cross that answer off. The dice are then thrown again and so on.

The first person to make a line of five numbers across, down or diagonally is the winner.

You must write down each sum and its answer so that they can be checked.

Just put a line through the number on the grid. Do not cross it out so that it cannot be read, otherwise your sum cannot be checked.

This might be a typical game.

14	13	18	7	24
15	1	16	17	6
23	8	2	12	5
3	22	4	10	19
25	21	9	20	11

First set (1, 3, 6) $6 \times 3 \times 1 = 18$
Second set (2, 4, 4) $4 \times 4 - 2 = 14$
Third set (3, 5, 1) $(3 - 1) \times 5 = 10$
Fourth set (3, 3, 4) $(3 + 3) \times 4 = 24$
Fifth set (1, 2, 6) $6 \times 2 - 1 = 11$
Sixth set (5, 4, 6) $(6 + 4) \div 5 = 2$
Seventh set (4, 4, 2) $2 - (4 \div 4) = 1$

EXERCISE 1C

WHOLE EXERCISE

1 Work out each of these.

a $2 \times 3 + 5 =$ **b** $6 \div 3 + 4 =$ **c** $5 + 7 - 2 =$

d $4 \times 6 \div 2 =$ **e** $2 \times 8 - 5 =$ **f** $3 \times 4 + 1 =$

g $3 \times 4 - 1 =$ **h** $3 \times 4 \div 1 =$ **i** $12 \div 2 + 6 =$

j $12 \div 6 + 2 =$ **k** $3 + 5 \times 2 =$ **l** $12 - 3 \times 3 =$

2 Work out each of these. Remember: first work out the bracket.

a $2 \times (3 + 5) =$ **b** $6 \div (2 + 1) =$ **c** $(5 + 7) - 2 =$

d $5 + (7 - 2) =$ **e** $3 \times (4 \div 2) =$ **f** $3 \times (4 + 2) =$

g $2 \times (8 - 5) =$ **h** $3 \times (4 + 1) =$ **i** $3 \times (4 - 1) =$

j $3 \times (4 \div 1) =$ **k** $12 \div (2 + 2) =$ **l** $(12 \div 2) + 2 =$

3 Copy each of these and put a loop round the part that you do first. Then work out each one. The first sum has been done for you.

a $(3 \times 3) - 2 = 7$ **b** $3 + 2 \times 4 =$ **c** $9 \div 3 - 2 =$

d $9 - 4 \div 2 =$ **e** $5 \times 2 + 3 =$ **f** $5 + 2 \times 3 =$

g $10 \div 5 - 2 =$ **h** $10 - 4 \div 2 =$ **i** $4 \times 6 - 7 =$

j $7 + 4 \times 6 =$ **k** $6 \div 3 + 7 =$ **l** $7 + 6 \div 2 =$

4 Work out each of these.

a $6 \times 6 + 2 =$ **b** $6 \times (6 + 2) =$ **c** $6 \div 6 + 2 =$

d $12 \div (4 + 2) =$ **e** $12 \div 4 + 2 =$ **f** $2 \times (3 + 4) =$

g $2 \times 3 + 4 =$ **h** $2 \times (4 - 3) =$ **i** $2 \times 4 - 3 =$

j $17 + 5 - 3 =$ **k** $17 - 5 + 3 =$ **l** $17 - 5 \times 3 =$

m $3 \times 5 + 5 =$ **n** $6 \times 2 + 7 =$ **o** $6 \times (2 + 7) =$

p $12 \div 3 + 3 =$ **q** $12 \div (3 + 3) =$ **r** $14 - 7 \times 1 =$

s $(14 - 7) \times 1 =$ **t** $2 + 6 \times 6 =$ **u** $(2 + 5) \times 6 =$

v $12 - 6 \div 3 =$ **w** $(12 - 6) \div 3 =$ **x** $15 - (5 \times 1) =$

y $(15 - 5) \times 1 =$ **z** $8 \times 9 \div 3 =$

5 Copy each of these and then put in brackets to make each sum true.

a $3 \times 4 + 1 = 15$ **b** $6 \div 2 + 1 = 4$ **c** $6 \div 2 + 1 = 2$

d $4 + 4 \div 4 = 5$ **e** $4 + 4 \div 4 = 2$ **f** $16 - 4 \div 3 = 4$

g $3 \times 4 + 1 = 13$ **h** $16 - 6 \div 3 = 14$ **i** $20 - 10 \div 2 = 5$

j $20 - 10 \div 2 = 15$ **k** $3 \times 5 + 5 = 30$ **l** $6 \times 4 + 2 = 36$

m $15 - 5 \times 2 = 20$ **n** $4 \times 7 - 2 = 20$ **o** $12 \div 3 + 3 = 2$

p $12 \div 3 + 3 = 7$ **q** $24 \div 8 - 2 = 1$ **r** $24 \div 8 - 2 = 4$

6 Three dice are thrown. They give scores of 3, 1 and 4:

A class makes the following sums with the numbers.
Work them out.

a $3 + 4 + 1 =$ **b** $3 + 4 - 1 =$ **c** $4 + 3 - 1 =$

d $4 \times 3 + 1 =$ **e** $4 \times 3 - 1 =$ **f** $(4 - 1) \times 3 =$

g $4 \times 3 \times 1 =$ **h** $(3 - 1) \times 4 =$ **i** $(4 + 1) \times 3 =$

j $4 \times (3 + 1) =$ **k** $1 \times (4 - 3) =$ **l** $4 + 1 \times 3 =$

7 Three different dice give scores of 2, 3, 5. Put ×, +, ÷, − or ( ) in each sum to make it true.

    a   2   3   5 = 11   **b**   2   3   5 = 16   **c**   2   3   5 = 17

    d   5   3   2 = 4   **e**   5   3   2 = 13   **f**   5   3   2 = 30

Place value and ordering numbers

In the number 5348

    the 5 stands for 5 thousands or 5000

    the 3 stands for 3 hundreds or 300

    the 4 stands for 4 tens or 40

    the 8 stands for 8 units or 8

And in the number 4 073 520

    the 4 stands for 4 millions or 4 000 000

    the 73 stands for 73 thousands or 73 000

    the 5 stands for 5 hundreds or 500

    the 2 stands for 2 tens or 20

We write and say this number as

    four million, seventy-three thousand, five hundred and twenty

Note the use of narrow spaces between each group of three digits, starting from the right. All whole and mixed numbers of five or more digits are spaced in this way.

Example 1

Put these numbers in order with the smallest first:

    7031   3071   3701   7103   7130   1730

Look at the thousands column first and then each of the other columns in turn. The order is:

    1730   3071   3701   7031   7103   7130

EXERCISE 1D

WHOLE EXERCISE

1 Write the value of each underlined digit.

    a   3<u>4</u>1   **b**   47<u>5</u>   **c**   <u>1</u>86   **d**   2<u>9</u>8   **e**   <u>8</u>3

    f   83<u>9</u>   **g**   23<u>8</u>0   **h**   1<u>5</u>07   **i**   653<u>0</u>   **j**   2<u>5</u> 436

    k   29 <u>0</u>54   **l**   18 25<u>4</u>   **m**   4<u>3</u>08   **n**   52 9<u>9</u>4   **o**   <u>8</u>3 205

2 Copy each of these sentences, writing the numbers in words.
   a The last Olympic games in Greece had only 43 events and 200 competitors.
   b The last Olympic games in Britain had 136 events and 4099 competitors.
   c The last Olympic games in the USA had 271 events and 10 744 competitors.

3 Write each of the following using just words.
   a 5 600 000   **b** 4 075 200   **c** 3 007 950   **d** 2 000 782

4 Write each of the following using digits only.
   a Eight million, two hundred thousand and fifty-eight.
   b Nine million, four hundred and six thousand, one hundred and seven.
   c One million, five hundred and two.
   d Two million, seventy-six thousand and forty.

5 Write these numbers in order, putting the **smallest** first.
   a 21,   48,   23,   9,   15,   56,   85,   54
   b 310,   86,   219,   25,   501,   62,   400,   151
   c 357,   740,   2053,   888,   4366,   97,   368

6 Write these numbers in order, putting the **largest** first.
   a 52,   23,   95,   34,   73,   7,   25,   89
   b 65,   2,   174,   401,   80,   700,   18,   117
   c 762,   2034,   395,   6227,   89,   3928,   59,   480

7 Copy each sentence and fill in the missing word *smaller* or *larger*.
   a 7 is …… than 5   **b** 34 is …… than 29
   c 89 is …… than 98   **d** 97 is …… than 79
   e 308 is …… than 299   **f** 561 is …… than 605
   g 870 is …… than 807   **h** 4275 is …… than 4527
   i 782 is …… than 827

8 Using each of the digits 3, 6 and 8 only once in each number:
   a Write as many three-digit numbers as you can.
   b Which of your numbers is the smallest?
   c Which of your numbers is the largest?

9 Using each of the digits 0, 4 and 8 only once in each number, write as many different three-digit numbers as you can. (Do not start any number with 0.) Write your numbers down in order, smallest first.

10 Write down in order of size, smallest first, all the two-digit numbers that can be made using 3, 5 and 8. (Each digit can be repeated.)

Rounding off

We use rounded-off information all the time. Look at these examples. All of these statements are using rounded-off information. Each actual figure is either above or below the approximation shown here. But if the rounding off is done correctly, we can find out what the maximum and the minimum figures really are. For example, if we know that the number of matches in the packet is rounded off to the nearest 10,

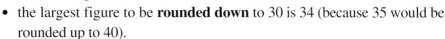
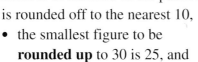

- the smallest figure to be **rounded up** to 30 is 25, and
- the largest figure to be **rounded down** to 30 is 34 (because 35 would be rounded up to 40).

So there could actually be from 25 to 34 matches in the packet.

What about the number of runners in the marathon? If we know that 23 000 people is the number to the nearest 1000,
- the smallest figure to be rounded up to 23 000 is 22 500, and
- the largest figure to be rounded down to 23 000 is 23 499.

So there could actually be from 22 500 to 23 499 people in the marathon.

EXERCISE 1E

WHOLE EXERCISE

1 Round off each of these numbers to the nearest 10.

a	24	**b**	57	**c**	78	**d**	54	**e**	96
f	21	**g**	88	**h**	66	**i**	14	**j**	26
k	29	**l**	51	**m**	77	**n**	49	**o**	94
p	35	**q**	65	**r**	15	**s**	102	**t**	107

2 Round off each of these numbers to the nearest 100.

a	240	**b**	570	**c**	780	**d**	504	**e**	967
f	112	**g**	645	**h**	358	**i**	998	**j**	1050
k	299	**l**	511	**m**	777	**n**	512	**o**	940
p	350	**q**	650	**r**	750	**s**	1020	**t**	1070

3 On the shelf of a sweetshop are three jars like the ones below.

Jar 1   Jar 2   Jar 3

80 sweets (to the nearest 10)

120 sweets (to the nearest 10)

190 sweets (to the nearest 10)

In which jar could each of these numbers of sweets be?
(For example, 76 sweets could be in jar 1.)

a 78 sweets	**b** 119 sweets	**c** 84 sweets
d 75 sweets	**e** 186 sweets	**f** 122 sweets
g 194 sweets	**h** 115 sweets	**i** 81 sweets
j 79 sweets	**k** 192 sweets	**l** 124 sweets

m Which of these numbers of sweets **could not** be in jar 1:
74, 84, 81, 76?

n Which of these numbers of sweets **could not** be in jar 2:
124, 126, 120, 115?

o Which of these numbers of sweets **could not** be in jar 3:
194, 184, 191, 189?

4 Round off each of these numbers to the nearest 1000.

a 2400	**b** 5700	**c** 7806	**d** 5040	**e** 9670
f 1120	**g** 6450	**h** 3499	**i** 9098	**j** 1500
k 2990	**l** 5110	**m** 7777	**n** 5020	**o** 9400
p 3500	**q** 6500	**r** 7500	**s** 1020	**t** 1770

5 Round off each of these numbers to the nearest 10.

a 234	**b** 567	**c** 718	**d** 524	**e** 906
f 231	**g** 878	**h** 626	**i** 114	**j** 296
k 279	**l** 541	**m** 767	**n** 501	**o** 942
p 375	**q** 625	**r** 345	**s** 1012	**t** 1074

6

Welcome to Elsecar
Population 800
(to the nearest 100)

Welcome to Hoyland
Population 1200
(to the nearest 100)

Welcome to Jump
Population 600
(to the nearest 100)

Which of these sentences could be true and which must be false?

a There are 789 people in Elsecar.

b There are 1278 people in Hoyland.

c There are 550 people in Jump.

d There are 843 people in Elsecar.

e There are 1205 people in Hoyland.

f There are 650 people in Jump.

7 These were the crowds at nine Premier Division games on a weekend in September 1995.

Bolton v QPR	17 362
Chelsea v Arsenal	31 048
Coventry v Aston Villa	20 987
Leeds v Sheffield Wednesday	34 076
Middlesbrough v Blackburn	29 462
Notts Forest v Manchester City	25 620
Tottenham v Wimbledon	25 321
Everton v Newcastle Utd	33 080
Manchester Utd v Liverpool	34 934

a Which match had the largest crowd?

b Which had the smallest crowd?

c Round off all the crowds to the nearest 1000

d Round off all the crowds to the nearest 100

8 Give these cooking times to the nearest 5 minutes.

a	34 min	**b**	57 min	**c**	14 min	**d**	51 min
e	8 min	**f**	13 min	**g**	44 min	**h**	32.5 min
i	3 min	**j**	50 s				

Adding and subtracting numbers with up to four digits

Addition

Three things to remember when adding two whole numbers:

- The answer will always be larger than the bigger number.
- Always add the units column first.
- When the total of the digits in a column is more than 9, a digit has to be carried into the next column on the left, as shown in Example 2. It is important to write down the carry digit, otherwise you may forget to include it in the addition.

Example 2

$$
\begin{array}{r}
167 \\
+\ 25 \\
\hline
192 \\
\end{array}
\qquad
\begin{array}{r}
2296 \\
+1173 \\
\hline
3469 \\
\end{array}
$$

Subtraction

Four things to remember when subtracting two whole numbers:
* The bigger number must always be written down first.
* The answer will always be smaller than the bigger number.
* Always subtract the units column first.
* When you have to take a bigger digit from a smaller digit in a column, you must first remove 10 from the next column on the left and put it with the smaller digit, as shown in Example 3.

Example 3

$$8\,{}^6\!7\,{}^1\!4$$
$$-2\ 1\ 5$$
$$\overline{6\ 5\ 9}$$

$$\,{}^2\!3\,{}^9\!\emptyset\,{}^1\!0$$
$$-1\ 6\ 3$$
$$\overline{1\ 3\ 7}$$

EXERCISE 1F

WHOLE EXERCISE

1 Copy and work out each of these additions.

a	365	**b**	95	**c**	4872	**d**	317	**e**	287
	+348		+56		+1509		416		+335
							+235		

f	483	**g**	4676	**h**	438	**i**	175	**j**	562
	+832		+3584		147		+276		93
					+233				+197

2 Complete each of these additions.

a	128 + 518	**b**	563 + 85 + 178	**c**	3086 + 58 + 674
d	347 + 408	**e**	85 + 1852 + 659	**f**	759 + 43 + 89
g	257 + 93	**h**	605 + 26 + 2135	**i**	56 + 8407 + 395
j	89 + 752	**k**	6143 + 557 + 131	**l**	2593 + 45 + 4378
m	719 + 284	**n**	545 + 3838 + 67	**o**	5213 + 658 + 4073

3 Copy and complete each of these subtractions.

a	637	**b**	908	**c**	954	**d**	572	**e**	732
	−187		−345		−472		−158		−447

f	673	**g**	602	**h**	638	**i**	650	**j**	580
	−187		−358		−354		−317		−364

k	6254	**l**	8043	**m**	8432	**n**	8034	**o**	5375
	−3362		−3626		−4665		−3947		−3547

4 Complete each of these subtractions.

a 354 – 226   **b** 285 – 256   **c** 663 – 329

d 506 – 328   **e** 654 – 377   **f** 733 – 448

g 592 – 257   **h** 753 – 354   **i** 6705 – 2673

j 8021 – 3256   **k** 7002 – 3207   **l** 8700 – 3263

5 Copy each of these and fill in the missing digits.

a
```
   5 3
 +2 □
 ─────
  □ 9
```
b
```
  □ 7
 +3 □
 ────
  8 4
```
c
```
  4 5
 +□ □
 ────
  9 3
```
d
```
  4 □ 7
 +□ 5 □
 ──────
  9 3 6
```

e
```
  □ 1 8
 +2 5 □
 ──────
  8 □ 7
```
f
```
  5 4 □
 +□ □ 6
 ──────
  8 2 2
```
g
```
  4 6 9
 +□ □ □
 ──────
  7 3 5
```
h
```
  □ □ □
 +3 4 8
 ──────
  8 0 7
```

i
```
  □ 4 □
 +3 3 7
 ──────
  7 □ 5
```
j
```
  3 5 7 8
 +□ □ □ □
 ────────
  8 0 7 6
```

6 Copy each of these and fill in the missing digits.

a
```
   7 4
 −2 □
 ─────
  □ 1
```
b
```
  □ 7
 −3 □
 ────
  5 4
```
c
```
  8 5
 −□ □
 ────
  2 7
```
d
```
  6 7 □
 −□ □ 3
 ──────
  1 3 5
```

e
```
  □ 1 4
 −2 5 □
 ──────
  3 □ 7
```
f
```
  5 4 □
 −□ □ 6
 ──────
  3 2 5
```
g
```
  4 6 2
 −□ □ □
 ──────
  1 8 5
```
h
```
  □ □ □
 −2 4 7
 ──────
  3 0 9
```

i
```
  □ 4 □
 −5 5 8
 ──────
  2 □ 5
```
j
```
  8 0 7 6
 −□ □ □ □
 ────────
  6 1 8 7
```

Multiplication and division by single-digit numbers

Multiplication

Two things to remember when multiplying two whole numbers:
- The bigger number must always be written down first.
- The answer will always be larger than the bigger number.

Example 4

$$\begin{array}{r} 213 \\ \times \quad 4 \\ \hline 852 \\ \hline {\scriptstyle 1} \end{array}$$

Note that the first multiplication, 3×4, gives 12. So, a digit has to be carried into the next column on the left, as in the case of addition.

Division

Two things to remember when dividing one whole number by another whole number:
- The answer will always be smaller than the bigger number.
- Division starts at the **left-hand side**.

Example 5

$417 \div 3$ is set out as

$$3\overline{\smash)4^11^27}^{\,1\ 3\ 9}$$

This is how the division was done:
- First, we divided 3 into 4 to get 1 and remainder 1. Note where we put the 1 and the remainder 1.
- Then, we divided 3 into 11 to get 3 and remainder 2. Note where we put the 3 and the remainder 2.
- Finally, we divided 3 into 27 to get 9 with no remainder.

EXERCISE 1G

WHOLE EXERCISE

1 Copy and work out each of the following.

a	14	**b**	13	**c**	17	**d**	19	**e**	18
	× 4		× 5		× 3		× 2		× 6

f	23	**g**	34	**h**	42	**i**	53	**j**	85
	× 5		× 6		× 7		× 4		× 5

k	50	**l**	200	**m**	320	**n**	340	**o**	253
	× 3		× 4		× 3		× 4		× 6

2 Calculate each of the following by setting it out in a column.

a 42×7 **b** 74×5 **c** 48×6
d 208×4 **e** 309×7 **f** 630×4
g 548×3 **h** 643×5 **i** 8×375
j 6×442 **k** 7×528 **l** 235×8
m 6043×9 **n** 5×4387 **o** 9×5432

3 By doing a suitable multiplication, answer each of these questions.

a How many days are there in 17 weeks?

b How many hours are there in 4 days?

c Eggs are packed in boxes of 6. How many eggs are in 24 boxes?

d Joe bought 5 boxes of matches. Each box contained 42 matches. How many matches altogether did Joe buy?

e A box of Tulip Sweets holds 35 sweets. How many sweets are in 6 boxes?

4 Calculate each of the following.

a $438 \div 2$ **b** $634 \div 2$ **c** $945 \div 3$
d $636 \div 6$ **e** $297 \div 3$ **f** $847 \div 7$
g $756 \div 3$ **h** $846 \div 6$ **i** $576 \div 4$
j $344 \div 4$ **k** $441 \div 7$ **l** $5818 \div 2$
m $3744 \div 9$ **n** $2008 \div 8$ **o** $7704 \div 6$

5 By doing a suitable division, answer each of these questions.

a How many weeks are there in 91 days?

b How long will it take me to save £111, if I save £3 a week?

c A rope, 215 metres long, is cut into 5 equal pieces. How long is each piece?

d Granny has a bottle of 144 tablets. How many days will they last if she takes 4 each day?

e I share a box of 360 sweets between 8 children. How many sweets will each child get?

Investigation checklist

During your GCSE course, you will be required to do several mathematical investigations. This work will either be assessed by your teacher or will be marked by your examination board through coursework tasks.

The example on this page and the next shows you how to set out the solution to an investigation. Also, throughout the book there are many investigations for you to try.

When you do an investigation, it is helpful to have a checklist to make sure that you follow a method that is appropriate to all coursework tasks. Such a checklist is given below. Note that for some types of task it may not be necessary to follow every stage in the list.

1 Try some simple examples to show that you understand the task.
2 Work in an ordered way by breaking the task down into easy steps.
3 Make a table to record your results.
4 Look for any pattern or rule in your table of results.
5 Use this pattern or rule to try to predict another example.
6 Test this example to see whether your pattern or rule works.
7 If possible, explain why your pattern or rule works by using diagrams, graphs or algebra.
8 Make up a similar problem of your own.

Investigation

The first item, *Stamps*, shows you how to set out the solution to an investigation. Look at the investigation checklist above to remind yourself of the stages you should follow when doing an investigation.

Stamps

Which different amounts can be made using only 2p and 5p stamps?

Solution

1 Simple examples

$4p = 2p + 2p$ $6p = 2p + 2p + 2p$ $7p = 2p + 5p$

2 Break down task

Amount	Stamps required
1p	Not possible
2p	$1 \times 2p$
3p	Not possible
4p	$2 \times 2p$
5p	$1 \times 5p$
6p	$3 \times 2p$

3 Table of results

Amount	Stamps required
1p	Not possible
2p	$1 \times 2p$
3p	Not possible
4p	$2 \times 2p$
5p	$1 \times 5p$
6p	$3 \times 2p$
7p	$2p + 1 \times 5p$
8p	$4 \times 2p$
9p	$2 \times 2p + 1 \times 5p$
10p	$2 \times 5p$ or $5 \times 2p$
11p	$3 \times 2p + 1 \times 5p$
12p	$6 \times 2p$ or $1 \times 2p + 2 \times 5p$

4 Rule

It is possible to make all amounts after 3p by addition and/or multiplication.

6 Test

$$13p = 8p + 5p \qquad\qquad 14p = 12p + 2p \quad \text{or} \quad 7 \times 2p$$
$$ = 4 \times 2p + 5p \qquad\qquad = 2 \times 5p + 2 \times 2p \quad \text{or} \quad 7 \times 2p$$

8 Own problem

The investigation can be extended by using different pairs of values for the stamps. For example, 5p and 8p stamps.

Now try the investigation on page 20.

Units Rule

■ Write down any two numbers less than 10. Add them together but write down only the number in the units column. For example, 4 + 9 = **13** but write down 4, 9 and **3**.

■ Now repeat by adding together the last two numbers: 9 + 3 = **12** Write down 4, 9, 3 and **2**

■ Continue to form a list of numbers: 4, 9, 3, 2, 5, …

■ What happens? Try to explain what you find.

■ Now try your own examples.

Examination questions

1 This machine multiplies all numbers by 7 then subtracts 2.

In → ×7 → −2 → Out

a Complete this table

In	Out
5	33
2	
7	

b 26 comes **out** of the machine. What was put **in**?

NEAB, Question 1, Paper 2, June 1996

2 a i Write down the number **fifty-two thousand, four hundred and six** in figures.

   ii Write down **fifty-two thousand, four hundred and six** to the nearest thousand

b i Write down 10 292 in words.

   ii Write down 10 292 to the nearest hundred.

EDEXCEL, Question 1, Paper 1, June 1999

3 Bethan worked out 2 + 4 × 3 and got 18. Jamie worked out 2 + 4 × 3 and got 14. Explain why they got different answers.

NEAB, Question 10, Specimen Paper 2F, 1998

4 The table has information about the sales of two newspapers.

Newspaper	Sales in September 1996
Sun	4 023 548
Guardian	400 093

a The *Sun* was bought by 4 023 548 people in September 1996. Write the number 4 023 548 in words.

b The *Guardian* was bought by 400 093 people in September 1996. Write the number 400 093 correct to the nearest thousand.

NEAB, Question 1, Specimen Paper 1F, 1998

5 a Here is a list of numbers:

  15   150   1500   15 000   150 000   1 500 000

  Write down the number from this list which is:

  i Fifteen hundred

  ii One hundred and fifty thousand

b Fill in the missing numbers

  i $1500 \div \boxed{} = 150$

  ii $15 \times \boxed{} = 150\,000$

AQA, Question 3, Specimen Paper 1, 2000

6 The map shows the positions and heights of six mountains.

  a Write the names of the six mountains in order of height. Put the highest mountain first.

  b Helvellyn is added to the list of mountains in part **a**. It is fourth in the list. What can be said about the height of Helvellyn?

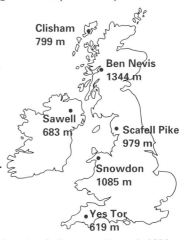

MEG, Question 9, Specimen Paper 1, 1998

7   The size of the crowd at a football match is given as 34 700 to the nearest hundred.

   a   What is the lowest number that the crowd could be?

   b   What is the largest number that the crowd could be?

NEAB, Question 13, Specimen Paper1F, 1998

8   For each of the following, write down whether it is true or false **and** give a reason for your answer.

   a $5 \times 7 \times 6 = 7 \times 6 \times 5$

   b $20 \div 4 = 4 \div 20$

   c $5 \times 2 + 7 \times 2 = 12 \times 2$

AQA, Question 4, Paper 1, June 1999

9   The diagram shows four discs with numbers on.

The number shown here is 1743.

   a   Using all these four discs only, write down

     i   the **largest** number

     ii   the **smallest** number

     iii   the missing numbers in this problem

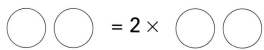

Another **different** disc is needed to complete the problem below..

   b   Write the missing number in the empty disc

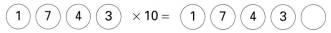

Here is another disc.

The number on this disc is doubled.
Then 3 is added.
The answer is then 15.

   c   What is the number on this disc?

EDEXCEL, Question 3, Paper 2, June 1999

What you should know after you have worked through Chapter 1

✔ How to use BODMAS.

✔ How to put numbers in order.

✔ How to round off to the nearest ten, hundred, thousand.

✔ How to solve simple problems using the four operations of arithmetic: addition, subtraction, multiplication and division.

PUZZLE PAGE

Letter sets

Find the next letters in these sequences.

a   O, T, T, F, F, ...   **b**   A, E, F, H, I, ...

Valued letters

In the three additions below, each letter stands for a digit. But a letter may not necessarily stand for the same digit when it is used in more than one sum.

a   ONE   **b**   TWO   **c**   FOUR
       + ONE   + TWO   + FIVE
       ─────   ─────   ─────
        TWO   FOUR   NINE

Write down each sum in numbers.

Four fours

Make sums to give answers from 1 to 10 using only four 4s and any number of the operations $+, -, \times$ and $\div$. For example:

$1 = (4 + 4) \div (4 + 4)$ $2 = (4 \times 4) \div (4 + 4)$

Heinz 57

Pick any number in the grid on the right. Circle the number and cross out all the other numbers in the row and column containing the number you have chosen. Now circle another number that is not crossed out and cross out all the other numbers in the row and column containing this number. Repeat until you have five numbers circled. Add these numbers together. What do you get? Now do it again but start with a different number.

19	8	11	25	7
12	1	4	18	0
16	5	8	22	4
21	10	13	27	9
14	3	6	20	2

Magic squares

This is a magic square. Add the numbers in any row, column or diagonal. The answer is **always** 15.

8	1	6
3	5	7
4	9	2

Can you complete this magic square using every number from 1 to 16?

2 Fractions

This chapter is going to ...

show you how to add, subtract, multiply and order simple fractions, how to cancel down fractions, how to work out equivalent fractions, how to convert a top-heavy fraction to a mixed number (and the other way), and how to calculate a fraction of a quantity.

What you should already know

✔ What a fraction is
✔ Times tables up to 10×10

Reminder   A fraction is a part of a whole.
The top number is called the **numerator**.
The bottom number is called the **denominator**.
So, for example, $\frac{3}{4}$ means divide a whole thing into 4 portions and take 3 of them.

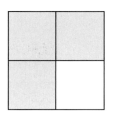

It really does help if you know the times tables up to 10×10. They will be tested in the non-calculator paper, so you need to be confident about tables and numbers.

EXERCISE 2A

1   What fraction is shaded in each of these diagrams?

a 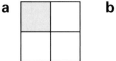   b   c   d

e   f   g   h

i j k l

 m n o  p

2 Draw diagrams as in question **1** to show these fractions.

   a $\frac{3}{4}$ **b** $\frac{2}{3}$ **c** $\frac{1}{5}$ **d** $\frac{5}{8}$ **e** $\frac{1}{6}$ **f** $\frac{8}{9}$

   g $\frac{1}{9}$ **h** $\frac{1}{10}$ **i** $\frac{4}{5}$ **j** $\frac{2}{7}$ **k** $\frac{3}{8}$ **l** $\frac{5}{6}$

Adding and subtracting simple fractions

Fractions which have the same denominator (bottom number) can easily be added or subtracted. For example,

$$\frac{3}{10} + \frac{4}{10} = \frac{7}{10}$$

$$\frac{7}{8} - \frac{2}{8} = \frac{5}{8}$$

Just add together or subtract the top numbers. The bottom number stays the same.

EXERCISE 2B

1 Calculate each of the following.

   a $\frac{1}{4} + \frac{2}{4}$ **b** $\frac{1}{8} + \frac{3}{8}$ **c** $\frac{2}{5} + \frac{1}{5}$ **d** $\frac{3}{10} + \frac{5}{10}$

   e $\frac{1}{3} + \frac{1}{3}$ **f** $\frac{2}{7} + \frac{3}{7}$ **g** $\frac{2}{9} + \frac{5}{9}$ **h** $\frac{1}{6} + \frac{4}{6}$

   i $\frac{3}{5} + \frac{1}{5}$ **j** $\frac{5}{8} + \frac{2}{8}$ **k** $\frac{2}{10} + \frac{3}{10}$ **l** $\frac{4}{7} + \frac{1}{7}$

   m $\frac{3}{5} + \frac{1}{5}$ **n** $\frac{2}{6} + \frac{3}{6}$ **o** $\frac{4}{9} + \frac{1}{9}$ **p** $\frac{2}{11} + \frac{5}{11}$

2 Calculate each of the following.

   a $\frac{3}{4} - \frac{1}{4}$ **b** $\frac{4}{5} - \frac{1}{5}$ **c** $\frac{7}{8} - \frac{4}{8}$ **d** $\frac{8}{10} - \frac{5}{10}$

   e $\frac{2}{3} - \frac{1}{3}$ **f** $\frac{5}{6} - \frac{1}{6}$ **g** $\frac{5}{7} - \frac{2}{7}$ **h** $\frac{7}{9} - \frac{2}{9}$

   i $\frac{3}{5} - \frac{2}{5}$ **j** $\frac{4}{7} - \frac{1}{7}$ **k** $\frac{8}{9} - \frac{5}{9}$ **l** $\frac{9}{10} - \frac{3}{10}$

   m $\frac{4}{6} - \frac{1}{6}$ **n** $\frac{5}{8} - \frac{3}{8}$ **o** $\frac{7}{11} - \frac{5}{11}$ **p** $\frac{7}{10} - \frac{3}{10}$

3 **a** Draw a diagram to show $\frac{2}{4}$.

    b Show on your diagram that $\frac{2}{4} = \frac{1}{2}$.

    c Use the above information to write down the answer to

       i $\frac{1}{4} + \frac{1}{2}$ **ii** $\frac{3}{4} - \frac{1}{2}$

4 **a** Draw a diagram to show $\frac{5}{10}$.

b Show on your diagram that $\frac{5}{10} = \frac{1}{2}$.

c Use the above information to write down the answers to

i $\frac{1}{2} + \frac{1}{10}$ **ii** $\frac{1}{2} + \frac{3}{10}$ **iii** $\frac{1}{2} + \frac{2}{10}$

Activity

Making eighths

You need lots of squared paper and a pair of scissors.

Draw three rectangles, each 4 cm by 2 cm, on squared paper.

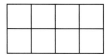

Each small square is called an *eighth* or $\frac{1}{8}$.

Cut one of the rectangles into halves, another into quarters and the third into eighths.

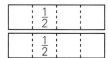 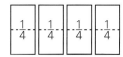 

You can see that the strip equal to one half takes up 4 squares, so

$$\frac{1}{2} = \frac{4}{8}$$

These are called **equivalent fractions**.

1 Use the strips to write down the following fractions as eighths.

a $\frac{1}{4}$ **b** $\frac{3}{4}$

2 Use the strips to answer the following sums. Leave your answers as eighths.

a $\frac{1}{4} + \frac{3}{8}$ **b** $\frac{3}{4} + \frac{1}{8}$ **c** $\frac{3}{8} + \frac{1}{2}$

d $\frac{1}{4} + \frac{1}{2}$ **e** $\frac{1}{4} + \frac{3}{8}$ **f** $\frac{1}{8} + \frac{1}{4}$

g $\frac{3}{8} + \frac{3}{4}$ **h** $\frac{3}{4} + \frac{1}{2}$

▶ *Making twentyfourths*

You need lots of squared paper and a pair of scissors.

Draw four rectangles, each 6 cm by 4 cm, on squared paper.

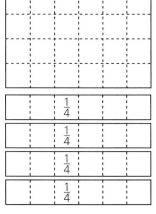

Each small square is called a *twentyfourth* or $\frac{1}{24}$. Cut one of the rectangles into quarters, another into sixths, another into thirds and the remaining one into eighths.

You can see that the strip equal to a quarter takes up 6 squares, so

$$\frac{1}{4} = \frac{6}{24}$$

This is another example of **equivalent fractions**.

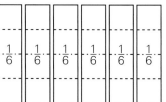

This idea is used to add fractions together. For example,

$$\frac{1}{4} + \frac{1}{6}$$

is changed into

$$\frac{6}{24} + \frac{4}{24} = \frac{10}{24}$$

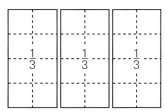

EXERCISE 2C

1 Use the strips to write down each of these fractions as twentyfourths.

a $\frac{1}{6}$ **b** $\frac{1}{3}$ **c** $\frac{1}{8}$ **d** $\frac{2}{3}$ **e** $\frac{5}{6}$

f $\frac{3}{4}$ **g** $\frac{3}{8}$ **h** $\frac{5}{8}$ **i** $\frac{7}{8}$ **j** $\frac{1}{2}$

2 Use the strips to write down the answer to each of the following sums. Each answer will be so many twentyfourths.

a $\frac{1}{3}+\frac{1}{8}$ **b** $\frac{1}{8}+\frac{1}{4}$ **c** $\frac{1}{6}+\frac{1}{8}$ **d** $\frac{2}{3}+\frac{1}{8}$ **e** $\frac{5}{8}+\frac{1}{3}$

f $\frac{1}{8}+\frac{5}{6}$ **g** $\frac{1}{2}+\frac{3}{8}$ **h** $\frac{1}{6}+\frac{3}{4}$ **i** $\frac{5}{8}+\frac{1}{6}$ **j** $\frac{1}{3}+\frac{5}{8}$

3 Draw three rectangles, each 5 cm by 4 cm. Cut one into fifths, another into quarters and the last into tenths.

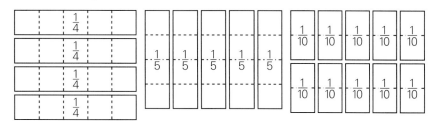

Use the strips to find the equivalent fraction in twentieths to each of the following.

a $\frac{1}{4}$ **b** $\frac{1}{5}$ **c** $\frac{3}{4}$ **d** $\frac{4}{5}$ **e** $\frac{1}{10}$

f $\frac{1}{2}$ **g** $\frac{3}{5}$ **h** $\frac{2}{5}$ **i** $\frac{7}{10}$ **j** $\frac{3}{10}$

4 Use the strips to write down the answer to each of the following.

a $\frac{1}{4}+\frac{1}{5}$ **b** $\frac{3}{5}+\frac{1}{10}$ **c** $\frac{3}{10}+\frac{1}{4}$ **d** $\frac{3}{4}+\frac{1}{5}$ **e** $\frac{7}{10}+\frac{1}{4}$

Equivalent fractions and cancelling down

Equivalent fractions are two or more fractions that represent the same part of a whole.

Example 1

Complete these statements

a $\frac{3}{4} \longrightarrow \frac{\times 4}{\times 4} = \frac{\ldots}{16}$ **b** $\frac{2}{5} = \frac{\ldots}{15}$

a Multiplying the top by 4 gives 12. This means $\frac{12}{16}$ is an equivalent fraction to $\frac{3}{4}$.

b To get from 5 to 15, you multiply by 3. Do the same thing to the top number, which gives $2 \times 3 = 6$. So, $\frac{2}{5} = \frac{6}{15}$.

Example 2

Cancel these fractions down to their lowest terms.

a $\dfrac{15}{35}$ **b** $\dfrac{24}{54}$

a Here is one reason why you need to know the times tables. What is the biggest times table that both 15 and 35 are in? You should know that this is the five times table. So, divide both top and bottom numbers by 5:

$$\frac{15}{35} = \frac{15 \div 5}{35 \div 5} = \frac{3}{7}$$

We say that we have 'cancelled by fives'.

b The biggest times table that both 24 and 54 are in is the six times table. So, divide both top and bottom numbers by 6:

$$\frac{24}{54} = \frac{24 \div 6}{54 \div 6} = \frac{4}{9}$$

Here, we have 'cancelled by sixes'.

Example 3

Put the following fractions in order with the smallest first.

$$\frac{5}{6}, \frac{2}{3}, \frac{3}{4}$$

First write each fraction with the same denominator by using equivalent fractions.

$$\frac{5}{6} = \frac{10}{\mathbf{12}}$$

$$\frac{2}{3} = \frac{4}{6} = \frac{6}{9} = \frac{8}{\mathbf{12}}$$

$$\frac{3}{4} = \frac{6}{8} = \frac{9}{\mathbf{12}}$$

This shows that $\dfrac{5}{6} = \dfrac{10}{12}$, $\dfrac{2}{3} = \dfrac{8}{12}$ and $\dfrac{3}{4} = \dfrac{9}{12}$.

In order, the fractions are

$$\frac{2}{3}, \frac{3}{4}, \frac{5}{6}$$

EXERCISE 2D

WHOLE EXERCISE

1 Copy and complete each of these statements.

a $\dfrac{2}{5} \longrightarrow \dfrac{\times 4}{\times 4} = \dfrac{\dots}{20}$ **b** $\dfrac{1}{4} \longrightarrow \dfrac{\times 3}{\times 3} = \dfrac{\dots}{12}$ **c** $\dfrac{3}{8} \longrightarrow \dfrac{\times 5}{\times 5} = \dfrac{\dots}{40}$

d $\dfrac{4}{5} \longrightarrow \dfrac{\times 3}{\times 3} = \dfrac{\dots}{15}$ **e** $\dfrac{5}{6} \longrightarrow \dfrac{\times 3}{\times 3} = \dfrac{\dots}{18}$ **f** $\dfrac{3}{7} \longrightarrow \dfrac{\times 4}{\times 4} = \dfrac{\dots}{28}$

g $\dfrac{3}{10} \longrightarrow \dfrac{\times \dots}{\times 2} = \dfrac{\dots}{20}$ **h** $\dfrac{1}{3} \longrightarrow \dfrac{\times \dots}{\times \dots} = \dfrac{\dots}{9}$ **i** $\dfrac{3}{5} \longrightarrow \dfrac{\times \dots}{\times \dots} = \dfrac{\dots}{20}$

j $\dfrac{2}{3} \longrightarrow \dfrac{\times \dots}{\times \dots} = \dfrac{\dots}{18}$ **k** $\dfrac{3}{4} \longrightarrow \dfrac{\times \dots}{\times \dots} = \dfrac{\dots}{12}$ **l** $\dfrac{5}{8} \longrightarrow \dfrac{\times \dots}{\times \dots} = \dfrac{\dots}{40}$

m $\dfrac{7}{10} \longrightarrow \dfrac{\times \dots}{\times \dots} = \dfrac{\dots}{20}$ **n** $\dfrac{1}{6} \longrightarrow \dfrac{\times \dots}{\times \dots} = \dfrac{4}{\dots}$ **o** $\dfrac{3}{8} \longrightarrow \dfrac{\times \dots}{\times \dots} = \dfrac{15}{\dots}$

2 Copy and complete each of these statements.

a $\dfrac{1}{2} = \dfrac{2}{\dots} = \dfrac{3}{\dots} = \dfrac{\dots}{8} = \dfrac{\dots}{10} = \dfrac{6}{\dots}$

b $\dfrac{1}{3} = \dfrac{2}{\dots} = \dfrac{3}{\dots} = \dfrac{\dots}{12} = \dfrac{\dots}{15} = \dfrac{6}{\dots}$

c $\dfrac{3}{4} = \dfrac{6}{\dots} = \dfrac{9}{\dots} = \dfrac{\dots}{16} = \dfrac{\dots}{20} = \dfrac{18}{\dots}$

d $\dfrac{2}{5} = \dfrac{4}{\dots} = \dfrac{6}{\dots} = \dfrac{\dots}{20} = \dfrac{\dots}{25} = \dfrac{12}{\dots}$

e $\dfrac{3}{7} = \dfrac{6}{\dots} = \dfrac{9}{\dots} = \dfrac{\dots}{28} = \dfrac{\dots}{35} = \dfrac{18}{\dots}$

3 Copy and complete each of these statements.

a $\dfrac{10}{15} = \dfrac{10 \div 5}{15 \div 5} = \dfrac{\dots}{\dots}$ **b** $\dfrac{12}{15} = \dfrac{12 \div 3}{15 \div 3} = \dfrac{\dots}{\dots}$

c $\dfrac{20}{28} = \dfrac{20 \div 4}{28 \div 4} = \dfrac{\dots}{\dots}$ **d** $\dfrac{12}{18} = \dfrac{12 \div \dots}{\dots \div \dots} = \dfrac{\dots}{\dots}$

e $\dfrac{15}{25} = \dfrac{15 \div 5}{\dots \div \dots} = \dfrac{\dots}{\dots}$ **f** $\dfrac{21}{30} = \dfrac{21 \div \dots}{\dots \div \dots} = \dfrac{\dots}{\dots}$

4 Cancel down each of these fractions.

a $\dfrac{4}{6}$ b $\dfrac{5}{15}$ c $\dfrac{12}{18}$ d $\dfrac{6}{8}$ e $\dfrac{3}{9}$

f $\dfrac{5}{10}$ g $\dfrac{14}{16}$ h $\dfrac{28}{35}$ i $\dfrac{10}{20}$ j $\dfrac{4}{16}$

k $\dfrac{12}{15}$ l $\dfrac{15}{21}$ m $\dfrac{25}{35}$ n $\dfrac{14}{21}$ o $\dfrac{8}{20}$

p $\dfrac{10}{25}$ q $\dfrac{7}{21}$ r $\dfrac{42}{60}$ s $\dfrac{50}{200}$ t $\dfrac{18}{12}$

u $\dfrac{6}{9}$ v $\dfrac{18}{27}$ w $\dfrac{36}{48}$ x $\dfrac{21}{14}$ y $\dfrac{42}{12}$

5 Put the following fractions in order with the smallest first.

a $\dfrac{1}{2}, \dfrac{5}{6}, \dfrac{2}{3}$ b $\dfrac{3}{4}, \dfrac{1}{2}, \dfrac{5}{8}$ c $\dfrac{7}{10}, \dfrac{2}{5}, \dfrac{1}{2}$ d $\dfrac{2}{3}, \dfrac{3}{4}, \dfrac{7}{12}$

e $\dfrac{1}{6}, \dfrac{1}{3}, \dfrac{1}{4}$ f $\dfrac{9}{10}, \dfrac{3}{4}, \dfrac{4}{5}$ g $\dfrac{4}{5}, \dfrac{7}{10}, \dfrac{5}{6}$ h $\dfrac{1}{3}, \dfrac{2}{5}, \dfrac{3}{10}$

Top-heavy fractions and mixed numbers

A fraction such as $\frac{9}{5}$ is called **top-heavy** because the numerator (top number) is bigger than the denominator (bottom number).

A fraction which is not top-heavy, such as $\frac{4}{5}$, is sometimes called a **proper fraction**. In other words, the numerator of a proper fraction is smaller than its denominator.

Activity

Converting top-heavy fractions

You need a calculator with a fraction key, which will look like this: a b/c

Your calculator probably shows fractions like this: $2\lrcorner 3$ or $2\ulcorner 3$

This means $\frac{2}{3}$ or two-thirds.

Key the top-heavy fraction $\frac{9}{5}$ into your calculator: 9 a b/c 5

The display will look like this: $9\lrcorner 5$

Now press the equals key =. The display will change to: $1\lrcorner 4\lrcorner 5$

➤

This is the **mixed number** $1\frac{4}{5}$.

(It is called a mixed number because it is a mixture of a whole number and a proper fraction.)

Write down the result: $\frac{9}{5} = 1\frac{4}{5}$

Key the top-heavy fraction $\frac{8}{4}$ into your calculator: **8** **a b/c** **4**

The display will look like this: $8\lrcorner 4$

Now press the equals key **=**. The display will change to: 2

This represents the whole number 2. Whole numbers are special fractions with a denominator of 1. So, 2 is the fraction $\frac{2}{1}$.

Write down the result: $\frac{8}{4} = \frac{2}{1}$

- Now key at least ten top-heavy fractions and convert them to mixed numbers. Keep the numbers sensible. For example, don't use 37 or 17.
- Write down your results.
- Look at your results. Can you see a way of converting a top-heavy fraction to a mixed number without using a calculator?
- Test your idea. Then check it using your calculator.

Converting mixed numbers

Key the mixed number $2\frac{3}{4}$ into your calculator: **2** **a b/c** **3** **a b/c** **4**

The display will look like this: $2\lrcorner 3\lrcorner 4$

Now press the shift (or **INV**) key and then press the fraction key **a b/c**

The display will change to: $11\lrcorner 4$

This represents the top-heavy fraction $\frac{11}{4}$.

Write down the result: $2\frac{3}{4} = \frac{11}{4}$

- Now key at least ten more mixed numbers and convert them to top-heavy fractions. Keep your numbers sensible. For example, don't use $8\frac{16}{19}$ or $17\frac{11}{32}$.
- Write down your results.
- Look at your results. Can you see a way of converting a mixed number to a top-heavy fraction without using a calculator?
- Test your idea. Then check it using your calculator.

EXERCISE 2E

WHOLE EXERCISE

Change each of these top-heavy fractions into a mixed number.

1 $\frac{7}{3}$	**2** $\frac{8}{3}$	**3** $\frac{9}{4}$	**4** $\frac{10}{7}$	**5** $\frac{12}{5}$	**6** $\frac{7}{5}$
7 $\frac{13}{5}$	**8** $\frac{15}{4}$	**9** $\frac{10}{3}$	**10** $\frac{15}{7}$	**11** $\frac{17}{6}$	**12** $\frac{18}{5}$
13 $\frac{19}{4}$	**14** $\frac{22}{7}$	**15** $\frac{14}{11}$	**16** $\frac{12}{11}$	**17** $\frac{28}{5}$	**18** $\frac{19}{7}$
19 $\frac{40}{7}$	**20** $\frac{42}{5}$	**21** $\frac{21}{10}$	**22** $\frac{5}{2}$	**23** $\frac{5}{3}$	**24** $\frac{25}{8}$
25 $\frac{23}{10}$	**26** $\frac{23}{11}$	**27** $\frac{38}{5}$	**28** $\frac{38}{7}$	**29** $\frac{40}{8}$	**30** $\frac{12}{6}$

Change each of these mixed numbers into a top-heavy fraction.

31 $3\frac{1}{3}$	**32** $5\frac{5}{6}$	**33** $1\frac{4}{5}$	**34** $5\frac{2}{7}$	**35** $4\frac{1}{10}$	**36** $5\frac{2}{3}$
37 $2\frac{1}{2}$	**38** $3\frac{1}{4}$	**39** $7\frac{1}{6}$	**40** $3\frac{5}{8}$	**41** $6\frac{1}{3}$	**42** $9\frac{8}{9}$
43 $11\frac{4}{5}$	**44** $3\frac{1}{5}$	**45** $4\frac{3}{8}$	**46** $3\frac{1}{9}$	**47** $5\frac{1}{5}$	**48** $2\frac{3}{4}$
49 $4\frac{2}{7}$	**50** $8\frac{1}{6}$	**51** $2\frac{8}{9}$	**52** $6\frac{1}{6}$	**53** $12\frac{1}{5}$	**54** $1\frac{5}{8}$
55 $7\frac{1}{10}$	**56** $8\frac{1}{9}$	**57** $7\frac{5}{8}$	**58** $10\frac{1}{2}$	**59** $1\frac{1}{16}$	**60** $4\frac{3}{4}$

Adding fractions with the same denominator

When we add two fractions with the same denominator, we get one of the following:

- a proper fraction which cannot be cancelled down: for example,
  $$\frac{1}{5} + \frac{2}{5} = \frac{3}{5}$$
- a proper fraction which can be cancelled down: for example,
  $$\frac{1}{8} + \frac{3}{8} = \frac{4}{8} = \frac{1}{2}$$
- a top-heavy fraction which cannot be cancelled down and so it is written at once as a mixed number: for example,
  $$\frac{7}{8} + \frac{1}{4} = \frac{7}{8} + \frac{2}{8} = \frac{9}{8} = 1\frac{1}{8}$$
- a top-heavy fraction which can be cancelled down before it is written as a mixed number: for example,
  $$\frac{5}{8} + \frac{7}{8} = \frac{12}{8} = \frac{3}{2} = 1\frac{1}{2}$$

Note The fractions in answers are **always** cancelled down to their **lowest terms**.

EXERCISE 2F

WHOLE EXERCISE

1 Calculate each of these additions.

   a $\frac{5}{8} + \frac{1}{8}$ **b** $\frac{3}{10} + \frac{1}{10}$ **c** $\frac{2}{9} + \frac{4}{9}$ **d** $\frac{1}{4} + \frac{1}{2}$

   e $\frac{3}{10} + \frac{3}{10}$ **f** $\frac{5}{12} + \frac{1}{12}$ **g** $\frac{3}{16} + \frac{5}{16}$ **h** $\frac{7}{16} + \frac{3}{16}$

2 Calculate each of these additions. Use equivalent fractions to make the denominators the same.

a $\frac{1}{2} + \frac{7}{10}$ **b** $\frac{1}{2} + \frac{5}{8}$ **c** $\frac{3}{4} + \frac{3}{8}$ **d** $\frac{3}{4} + \frac{7}{8}$

e $\frac{1}{2} + \frac{7}{8}$ **f** $\frac{1}{3} + \frac{5}{6}$ **g** $\frac{5}{6} + \frac{2}{3}$ **h** $\frac{3}{4} + \frac{1}{2}$

3 Calculate each of these additions.

a $\frac{3}{8} + \frac{7}{8}$ **b** $\frac{3}{4} + \frac{3}{4}$ **c** $\frac{2}{5} + \frac{3}{5}$ **d** $\frac{7}{10} + \frac{9}{10}$

e $\frac{5}{8} + \frac{5}{8}$ **f** $\frac{7}{16} + \frac{15}{16}$ **g** $\frac{5}{12} + \frac{11}{12}$ **h** $\frac{11}{16} + \frac{7}{16}$

i $1\frac{1}{2} + \frac{1}{4}$ **j** $2\frac{3}{4} + \frac{1}{2}$ **k** $3\frac{1}{2} + 2\frac{3}{4}$ **l** $2\frac{1}{3} + 1\frac{1}{2}$

4 Calculate each of these subtractions.

a $\frac{7}{8} - \frac{3}{8}$ **b** $\frac{7}{10} - \frac{1}{10}$ **c** $\frac{3}{4} - \frac{1}{2}$ **d** $\frac{5}{8} - \frac{1}{4}$

e $\frac{1}{2} - \frac{1}{4}$ **f** $\frac{7}{8} - \frac{1}{2}$ **g** $\frac{9}{10} - \frac{1}{2}$ **h** $\frac{11}{16} - \frac{3}{8}$

i $1 - \frac{3}{4}$ **j** $2 - \frac{1}{3}$ **k** $3\frac{3}{4} - 1\frac{1}{2}$ **l** $4\frac{5}{8} - 2\frac{1}{2}$

Problems put in words

Some of the GCSE questions you are going to meet will involve the use of fractions in real situations, which are described. You will have to decide what to do with the fractions given. Then write down the sum and work it out.

Example 4

In a box of chocolates, $\frac{1}{4}$ are truffles, $\frac{1}{2}$ are orange creams and the rest are mints. What fraction are mints?

Truffles and orange creams together are $\frac{1}{4} + \frac{1}{2} = \frac{3}{4}$ of the box.

Take the whole box as 1. So, mints are $1 - \frac{3}{4} = \frac{1}{4}$ of the box.

EXERCISE 2G

1 At a recent Third Division football match, $\frac{7}{8}$ of the crowd were home supporters. What fraction of the crowd were not home supporters?

2 After Mary had taken a slice of cake, $\frac{3}{4}$ of the cake was left. Brenda then had $\frac{1}{2}$ of what was left.
   a What fraction of the cake did Mary eat?
   b What fraction of the cake did Brenda get?
   c Who got more cake?

3 Three friends share two pizzas. Each pizza is cut into six equal slices. What fraction of a pizza did each friend get?

4 In a box of old records from a jumble sale, $\frac{1}{4}$ of them were singles, $\frac{3}{8}$ of them were extended play and the rest were long playing. What fraction of the records were long playing?

5 In a car park, $\frac{1}{5}$ of the cars were British makes. Half of the rest were Japanese makes. What fraction of the cars were Japanese makes?

6 A fruit drink consists of $\frac{1}{2}$ orange juice, $\frac{1}{8}$ lemon juice and the rest is pineapple juice. What fraction of the drink is pineapple juice.

7 In a hockey team, $\frac{2}{11}$ of the team are French, $\frac{2}{11}$ are Italian, $\frac{3}{11}$ are Scottish and the rest are English. What fraction of the team is English?

8 In a packet of biscuits, $\frac{1}{6}$ are digestives, $\frac{2}{3}$ are chocolate covered and the rest are jammy dodgers. What fraction are jammy dodgers?

9 John pays $\frac{1}{4}$ of his wages in tax and $\frac{1}{8}$ of his wages in National Insurance. What fraction of his wages does he take home?

To find a fraction of a quantity

To do this, you simply multiply the quantity by the fraction.

Example 5

Find $\frac{3}{4}$ of £196.

First, find $\frac{1}{4}$ by dividing by 4. Then find $\frac{3}{4}$ by multiplying your answer by 3:

$196 \div 4 = 49$ then $49 \times 3 = 147$

The answer is £147

Of course, you can do this problem using your calculator by either

- pressing the sequence   **1** **9** **6** **÷** **4** **×** **3** **=**
- or using the **a b/c** key   **3** **a b/c** **4** **×** **1** **9** **6** **=**

EXERCISE 2H

1 Calculate each of these.

     a $\frac{3}{5} \times 30$ **b** $\frac{2}{7} \times 35$ **c** $\frac{3}{8} \times 48$ **d** $\frac{7}{10} \times 40$

     e $\frac{5}{6} \times 18$ **f** $24 \times \frac{3}{4}$ **g** $60 \times \frac{4}{5}$ **h** $72 \times \frac{5}{8}$

2   Calculate each of these quantities.

    a $\frac{3}{4}$ of £2400   **b** $\frac{2}{5}$ of 320 grams   **c** $\frac{5}{8}$ of 256 kilograms

    d $\frac{2}{3}$ of £174   **e** $\frac{5}{6}$ of 78 litres   **f** $\frac{3}{4}$ of 120 minutes

    g $\frac{4}{5}$ of 365 days   **h** $\frac{7}{8}$ of 24 hours   **i** $\frac{3}{4}$ of 1 day

    j $\frac{5}{9}$ of 4266 miles

3   In each case, find out which is the larger number.

    a $\frac{2}{5}$ of 60 or $\frac{5}{8}$ of 40   **b** $\frac{3}{4}$ of 280 or $\frac{7}{10}$ of 290

    c $\frac{2}{3}$ of 78 or $\frac{4}{5}$ of 70   **d** $\frac{5}{6}$ of 72 or $\frac{11}{12}$ of 60

    e $\frac{4}{9}$ of 126 or $\frac{3}{5}$ of 95   **f** $\frac{3}{4}$ of 340 or $\frac{2}{3}$ of 381

4   A director was entitled to $\frac{2}{15}$ of his firm's profits. The firm made a profit of £45 600 in one year. What was the director's income from this profit?

5   A woman left $\frac{3}{8}$ of her estate to the local Methodist Church. What amount is this if her estate totalled £8400?

6   There were 36 800 people at Hillsborough to see Sheffield Wednesday play Manchester United. We know that $\frac{3}{8}$ of this crowd were female. How many males were at the ground?

7   Two thirds of a person's weight is water. Paul weighed 78 kg. How much of his body weight was water?

8   **a**   Information from the first census in Singapore suggests that $\frac{2}{25}$ of the population were then Indian. The total population was 10 700. How many people were Indian?

    b   By 1990 the population of Singapore had grown to 3 002 800. Only $\frac{1}{16}$ of this population were Indian. How many Indians were living in Singapore in 1990?

9   Mark earns £500 a week and one week is given a bonus of $\frac{1}{10}$ of his wage.

    a   Find $\frac{1}{10}$ of £500.

    b   How much does he earn altogether for this week?

10   A box of cereals normally weighs 720 g. A new sized box has $\frac{1}{4}$ extra.

    a   Find $\frac{1}{4}$ of 720 g.

    b   How much does the new box of cereals weigh?

11   A new TV costing £360 is reduced by $\frac{1}{3}$ in a sale.

    a   Find $\frac{1}{3}$ of £360.

    b   How much does the TV cost in the sale?

12   The price of a car in a showroom is given as £8000. Find the price of the car if a discount of $\frac{1}{8}$ of the price is given.

One quantity as a fraction of another

An amount often needs to be given as a fraction of another amount.

Example 6

Write £5 as a fraction of £20.

As a fraction this is written $\frac{5}{20}$. This cancels down to $\frac{1}{4}$.

EXERCISE 2 I

1 Write the first quantity as a fraction of the second.

   a 2 cm, 6 cm   **b** 4 kg, 20 kg

   c £8, £20   **d** 5 hours, 24 hours

   e 12 days, 30 days   **f** 50p, £3

   g 4 days, 2 weeks   **h** 40 minutes, 2 hours

2 In a form of 30 pupils, 18 are boys. What fraction of the form consists of boys?

3 During March, it rained on 12 days. What fraction of the month did it rain?

4 Linda wins £120 in a competition and puts £50 into her bank account. What fraction of her winnings does she keep?

Multiplying fractions

What is $\frac{1}{2}$ of $\frac{1}{4}$?

The diagram shows the answer is $\frac{1}{8}$.

In mathematics, we always write $\frac{1}{2}$ of $\frac{1}{4}$ as $\frac{1}{2} \times \frac{1}{4}$.

So we know that $\frac{1}{2} \times \frac{1}{4} = \frac{1}{8}$.

To multiply fractions, we multiply the numerators together and the denominators together.

Example 7

Work out $\frac{1}{4}$ of $\frac{2}{5}$.

This is $\dfrac{1}{4} \times \dfrac{2}{5} = \dfrac{1 \times 2}{4 \times 5} = \dfrac{2}{20} = \dfrac{1}{10}$

EXERCISE 2J

Work out each of these multiplications.

1 $\frac{1}{2} \times \frac{1}{3}$ **2** $\frac{1}{4} \times \frac{1}{5}$ **3** $\frac{1}{3} \times \frac{2}{3}$ **4** $\frac{1}{4} \times \frac{2}{3}$

5 $\frac{1}{3} \times \frac{3}{4}$ **6** $\frac{2}{3} \times \frac{3}{5}$ **7** $\frac{3}{4} \times \frac{2}{3}$ **8** $\frac{5}{6} \times \frac{3}{5}$

9 $\frac{2}{7} \times \frac{3}{4}$ **10** $\frac{5}{6} \times \frac{7}{8}$

Investigation

Cutting the Cake

A cake can be cut into three equal pieces by using two straight cuts:

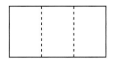

Find the maximum number of pieces into which the cake can be cut using two straight cuts if the pieces have to be the same size.

Investigate what happens as you use more straight cuts.

Here are some examples.

For 2 cuts:

 Not all pieces equal    4 equal pieces

For 3 cuts:

 4 equal pieces    6 equal pieces

➤

For 4 cuts:

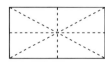 8 equal pieces

 9 equal pieces

For 5 cuts:

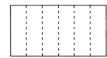 6 equal pieces

 12 equal pieces

Now continue for six cuts. Draw a table of results and try to find a rule.

Halves

In each pattern, the shaded parts add up to half of the area of the square.

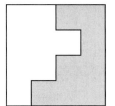 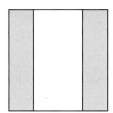 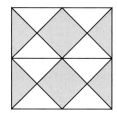 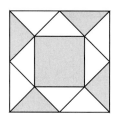

■ Draw your own patterns in which half of the area of a square is shaded.

■ Now draw your own patterns in which a third or a quarter is shaded.

■ Try drawing fraction patterns for other shapes: for example, rectangles or circles.

Examination questions

1 I planted $\frac{1}{4}$ of my garden with vegetables, $\frac{3}{8}$ of my garden with roses and the rest as lawn. What fraction of the garden have I left for lawn?

NEAB, Question 7, Specimen Paper 1F, 2000

2 Calculate $2\frac{3}{8} + 1\frac{1}{2}$.

MEG, Question 18, Specimen Paper 1, 1998

3 When a pendant is carved from a block of wood, $\frac{4}{9}$ of the wood is cut away. The original block weighs 225 grams. What weight of wood is cut away?

MEG, Question 7, Specimen Paper 2, 1998

4 $\frac{3}{5}$ of the cost of a music tape goes to the supplier. A music tape cost £6. How much goes to the supplier?

EDEXCEL, Question 12, Specimen Paper 1, 1998

5 a Shade $\frac{2}{3}$ of the shape below.

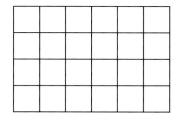

   b i What fraction of the shape below is shaded?

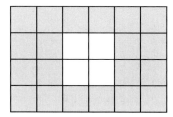

   ii What fraction of this shape is not shaded?

MEG (SMP), Question 5, Specimen Paper 1, 1998

6 Find $\frac{4}{5}$ of 35 kg.

WJEC, Question 3, Specimen Paper F1, 1998

7

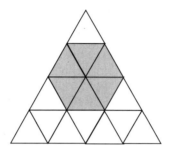

a What fraction of this shape is shaded? Give your answer in its simplest form.

b Fill in the missing number

$$\frac{1}{3} = \frac{\square}{12}$$

AQA, Question 2, Paper 2, June 2000

8 Boxes of Bobs Biscuits used to contain 650 grams of biscuits. New boxes contain one fifth more.
How much does a new box contain?

MEG(SMP), Question 6, Paper 2, June 1998

9 This is a drawing of a bolt. It is not drawn to scale.

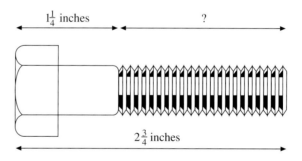

Calculate the length marked '?'.

MEG(SMP), Question 4, Paper 2, June 1998

What you should know after you have worked through Chapter 2

✔ How to recognise and draw fractions of shapes.
✔ How to add, subtract, multiply and cancel down simple fractions without a calculator.
✔ How to work out equivalent fractions.
✔ How to convert a top-heavy fraction to a mixed number (and the other way).
✔ How to calculate a fraction of a quantity.
✔ How to solve simple practical problems using fractions.

3 Negative numbers

This chapter is going to ...

introduce you to negative numbers and show you how they are used in everyday situations. It is also going to show you how to do simple arithmetic with negative numbers.

What you should already know

✔ What a negative number means
✔ How to put numbers in order

Activity

Caves and mountains

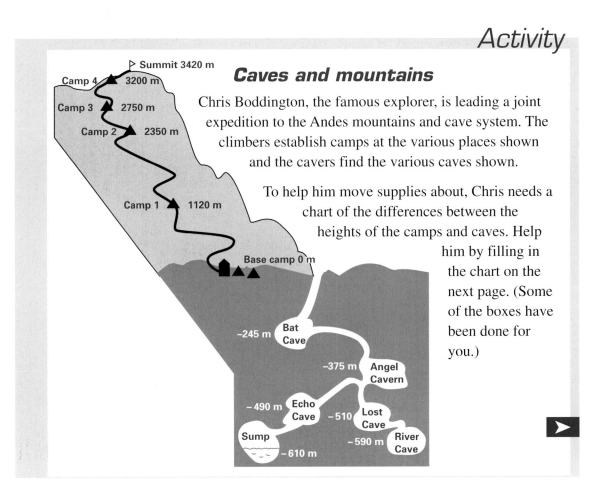

Chris Boddington, the famous explorer, is leading a joint expedition to the Andes mountains and cave system. The climbers establish camps at the various places shown and the cavers find the various caves shown.

To help him move supplies about, Chris needs a chart of the differences between the heights of the camps and caves. Help him by filling in the chart on the next page. (Some of the boxes have been done for you.)

Copy the chart into your book and complete it.

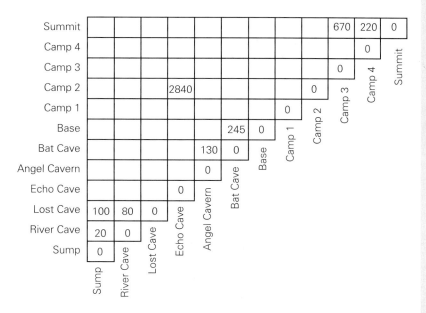

	Sump	River Cave	Lost Cave	Echo Cave	Angel Cavern	Bat Cave	Base	Camp 1	Camp 2	Camp 3	Camp 4	Summit
Summit										670	220	0
Camp 4											0	
Camp 3										0		
Camp 2				2840					0			
Camp 1								0				
Base						245	0					
Bat Cave					130	0						
Angel Cavern					0							
Echo Cave				0								
Lost Cave	100	80	0									
River Cave	20	0										
Sump	0											

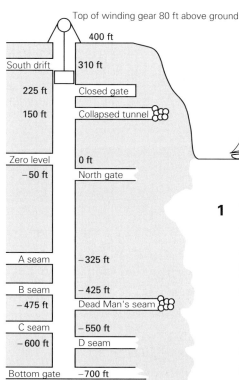

Top of winding gear 80 ft above ground

400 ft

South drift — 310 ft

225 ft — Closed gate

150 ft — Collapsed tunnel

Zero level — 0 ft

−50 ft — North gate

A seam — −325 ft

B seam — −425 ft

−475 ft — Dead Man's seam

C seam — −550 ft

−600 ft — D seam

Bottom gate — −700 ft

Sea level

Seaport Colliery

This is a section through Seaport Colliery.

The height above sea (zero) level for each tunnel is shown.

The ground is 400 ft above sea level.

1 What is the difference in height between the following levels?

a South drift and C seam

b The ground and A seam

c The closed gate and the collapsed tunnel

d Zero level and Dead Man's seam

e Ground level and the bottom gate

f Collapsed tunnel and B seam

g North gate and Dead Man's seam

h Zero level and the south drift

i Zero level and the bottom gate

j South drift and the bottom gate

2 How high above sea level is the top of the winding gear?

3 How high above the bottom gate is the top of the winding gear?

4 There are two pairs of tunnels that are 75 ft apart. Which two pairs are they?

5 How much cable does the engineman let out to get the cage from the south drift to D seam?

6 There are two pairs of tunnels that are 125 ft apart. Which two pairs are they?

7 Which two tunnels are 200 ft apart?

Everyday use of negative numbers

You meet negative numbers often in winter when the temperature falls below freezing (0 °C). Negative numbers are those less than 0.

You also meet negative numbers on graphs, and you may already have plotted co-ordinates with negative numbers.

There are many other situations where negative numbers are used. Here are three examples:
- When +15 m means 15 metres above sea level, then –15 m means 15 metres **below** sea level.
- When +2 h means 2 hours after midday, then –2 h means 2 hours **before** midday.
- When +£60 means a profit of £60, then –£60 means a **loss** of £60.

EXERCISE 3A

Copy and complete each of the following.

1 If +£5 means a profit of five pounds, then …… means a loss of five pounds.

2 If +£9 means a profit of £9, then a loss of £9 is …… .

3 If –£4 means a loss of four pounds, then +£4 means a …… of four pounds.

4 If +200 m means 200 metres above sea level, then …… means 200 metres below sea level.

5 If +50 m means fifty metres above sea level, then fifty metres below sea level is …… .

6 If –100 m means one hundred metres below sea level, then +100 m means one hundred metres …… sea level.

7 If +3 h means three hours after midday, then …… means three hours before midday.

8 If +5 h means 5 hours after midday, then …… means 5 hours before midday.

9 If –6 h means six hours before midday, then +6 h means six hours …… midday.

10 If +2 °C means two degrees above freezing point, then …… means two degrees below freezing point.

11 If +8 °C means 8 °C above freezing point, then …… means 8 °C below freezing point.

12 If –5 °C means five degrees below freezing point, then +5 °C means five degrees …… freezing point.

13 If +70 km means 70 kilometres north of the equator, then …… means 70 kilometres south of the equator.

14 If +200 km means 200 kilometres north of the equator, then 200 kilometres south of the equator is …… .

15 If –50 km means fifty kilometres south of the equator, then +50 km means fifty kilometres …… of the equator.

16 If 10 minutes before midnight is represented by –10 minutes, then five minutes after midnight is represented by …… .

17 If a car moving forwards at 10 mph is represented by +10 mph, then a car moving backwards at 5 mph is represented by …… .

18 In an office building, the third floor above ground level is represented by +3. So, the second floor below ground level is represented by …… .

The number line

Look at the number line.

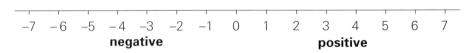

Notice how the negative numbers are to the left of 0, and the positive numbers are to the right of 0.

Numbers to the right of any number on the number line are always bigger than that number.

Numbers to the left of any number on the number line are always smaller than that number.

So, for example, we see that:
  2 is **smaller** than 5 because 2 is to the **left** of 5.
We can write this as 2 < 5.
  –3 is **smaller** than 2 because –3 is to the **left** of 2.
We can write this as –3 < 2.
  7 is **bigger** than 3 because 7 is to the **right** of 3.
We can write this as 7 > 3.
  –1 is **bigger** than –4 because –1 is to the **right** of –4.
We can write this as –1 > –4.

Reminder   The inequality signs:
  < means 'is less than'
  > means 'is greater than'

EXERCISE 3B

1   Complete each of the following by putting a suitable number in the box.

a   ☐ is smaller than 3   b   ☐ is smaller than 1

c   ☐ is smaller than –3   d   ☐ is smaller than –7

e   –5 is smaller than ☐   f   –1 is smaller than ☐

g   3 is smaller than ☐   h   –2 is smaller than ☐

i   ☐ is smaller than 0   j   –4 is smaller than ☐

k   ☐ is smaller than –8   l   –7 is smaller than ☐

2 Complete each of the following by putting a suitable number in the box.

a ☐ is bigger than –3   **b** ☐ is bigger than 1

c ☐ is bigger than –2   **d** ☐ is bigger than –1

e –1 is bigger than ☐   **f** –8 is bigger than ☐

g 1 is bigger than ☐   **h** –5 is bigger than ☐

i ☐ is bigger than –5   **j** 2 is bigger than ☐

k ☐ is bigger than –4   **l** –2 is bigger than ☐

3 Put the correct phrase in each of the following.

a –1 3   **b** 3 2   **c** –4 ...... –1

d –5 ...... –4   **e** 1 ...... –6   **f** –3 0

g –2 ...... –1   **h** 2 ...... –3   **i** 5 ...... –6

j 3 4   **k** –7 ...... –5   **l** –2 ...... –4

4

$$-1 \quad -\tfrac{3}{4} \quad -\tfrac{1}{2} \quad -\tfrac{1}{4} \quad 0 \quad \tfrac{1}{4} \quad \tfrac{1}{2} \quad \tfrac{3}{4} \quad 1$$

Put the correct phrase in each of the following.

a $\tfrac{1}{4}$ ...... $\tfrac{3}{4}$ **b** $-\tfrac{1}{2}$ 0   **c** $-\tfrac{3}{4}$ ...... $\tfrac{3}{4}$

d $\tfrac{1}{4}$ ...... $-\tfrac{1}{2}$ **e** -1 ...... $\tfrac{3}{4}$ **f** $\tfrac{1}{2}$ 1

5 In each case below, put the correct symbol, either < or >, in the box.

a 3 ☐ 5   **b** –2 ☐ –5   **c** –4 ☐ 3   **d** 5 ☐ 9

e –3 ☐ 2   **f** 4 ☐ –3   **g** –1 ☐ 0   **h** 6 ☐ –4

i 2 ☐ –3   **j** 0 ☐ –2   **k** –5 ☐ –4   **l** 1 ☐ 3

m –6 ☐ –7   **n** 2 ☐ –3   **o** –1 ☐ 1   **p** 4 ☐ 0

6 Copy these number lines and fill in the missing numbers on each line.

a –5   –2   0   1   3   5

b –20   –10   0   5   15

c –8   –4   0   2   6

d –30   –10   0   10   20

e –9   –6   0   3   6   12

f –8   0   8   16

g –2   –1   0   1   2

h –100   –40   0   20   60

i –100   0   50   200

Arithmetic with negative numbers

Adding and subtracting positive numbers

These two operations can be illustrated on a thermometer scale.

- **Adding** on a positive number moves us **up** the thermometer scale.
  For example,
  $$-2° + 6° = 4°$$

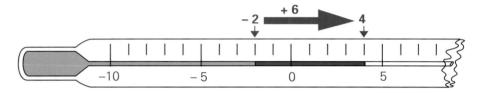

- **Subtracting** a positive number moves us **down** the thermometer scale.
  For example,
  $$3° - 5° = -2°$$

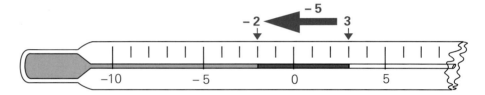

Example 1

The temperature at midnight was 2 °C but then it fell by 5°. What was the new temperature?

We have the problem of 2° – 5°, which is equal to –3°.

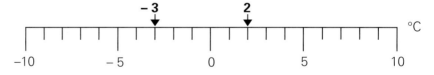

Example 2

The temperature drops 5° from –4 °C. What does it drop to?

We have the problem of –4° – 5°, which is equal to –9°. So, the new temperature is –9 °C.

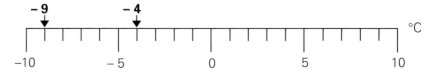

EXERCISE 3C

WHOLE EXERCISE

1 Use a thermometer scale to find the answer to each of the following.

a $2° - 4° =$ **b** $4° - 7° =$ **c** $3° - 5° =$ **d** $1° - 4° =$

e $6° - 8° =$ **f** $5° - 8° =$ **g** $-2 + 5 =$ **h** $-1 + 4 =$

i $-4 + 3 =$ **j** $-6 + 5 =$ **k** $-3 + 5 =$ **l** $-5 + 2 =$

m $-1 - 3 =$ **n** $-2 - 4 =$ **o** $-5 - 1 =$ **p** $3 - 4 =$

q $2 - 7 =$ **r** $1 - 5 =$ **s** $-3 + 7 =$ **t** $5 - 6 =$

u $-2 - 3 =$ **v** $2 - 6 =$ **w** $-8 + 3 =$ **x** $4 - 9 =$

2 Answer each of the following **without** the help of the thermometer scale.

a $5 - 9 =$ **b** $3 - 7 =$ **c** $-2 - 8 =$

d $-5 + 7 =$ **e** $-1 + 9 =$ **f** $4 - 9 =$

g $-10 + 12 =$ **h** $-15 + 20 =$ **i** $23 - 30 =$

j $30 - 42 =$ **k** $-12 + 25 =$ **l** $-30 + 55 =$

m $-10 - 22 =$ **n** $-13 - 17 =$ **o** $45 - 50 =$

p $17 - 25 =$ **q** $18 - 30 =$ **r** $-25 + 35 =$

s $-23 - 13 =$ **t** $31 - 45 =$ **u** $-24 + 65 =$

v $-19 + 31 =$ **w** $25 - 65 =$ **x** $199 - 300 =$

3 Work out each of the following.

a $8 + 3 - 5 =$ **b** $-2 + 3 - 6 =$ **c** $-1 + 3 + 4 =$

d $-2 - 3 + 4 =$ **e** $-1 + 1 - 2 =$ **f** $-4 + 5 - 7 =$

g $-3 + 4 - 7 =$ **h** $1 + 3 - 6 =$ **i** $8 - 7 + 2 =$

j $-5 - 7 + 12 =$ **k** $-4 + 5 - 7 =$ **l** $-4 + 6 - 8 =$

m $103 - 102 + 7 =$ **n** $-1 + 4 - 2 =$ **o** $-6 + 9 - 12 =$

p $-3 - 3 - 3 =$ **q** $-3 + 4 - 6 =$ **r** $-102 + 45 - 23 =$

s $8 - 10 - 5 =$ **t** $9 - 12 + 2 =$ **u** $99 - 100 - 46 =$

Adding and subtracting negative numbers

To **subtract a negative number** …

  … treat the $- -$ as a $+$.

For example: $4 - (-2) = 4 + 2 = 6$

To **add a negative number** …

  … treat the $+ -$ as a $-$.

For example: $3 + (-5) = 3 - 5 = -2$

Using your calculator

Calculations involving negative numbers can be done on a calculator using the ± ( ) keys.

Example 3

Work out –3 + 7

Press **3** **±** **+** **7** **=**

The answer should be 4.

Example 4

Work out –6 –(–2)

Press **6** **±** **–** **(** **2** **±** **)** **=**

The answer should be –4.

EXERCISE 3D

1   Answer each of the following. Check your answers on a calculator.

a	$2 - (-4) =$	**b**	$4 - (-3) =$	**c**	$3 - (-5) =$
d	$5 - (-1) =$	**e**	$6 - (-2) =$	**f**	$8 - (-2) =$
g	$-1 - (-3) =$	**h**	$-4 - (-1) =$	**i**	$-2 - (-3) =$
j	$-5 - (-7) =$	**k**	$-3 - (-2) =$	**l**	$-8 - (-1) =$
m	$4 + (-2) =$	**n**	$2 + (-5) =$	**o**	$3 + (-2) =$
p	$1 + (-6) =$	**q**	$5 + (-2) =$	**r**	$4 + (-8) =$
s	$-2 + (-1) =$	**t**	$-6 + (-2) =$	**u**	$-7 + (-3) =$
v	$-2 + (-7) =$	**w**	$-1 + (-3) =$	**x**	$-7 + (-2) =$

2   Write down the answer to each of the following, then check your answers on a calculator.

a	$-3 - 5 =$	**b**	$-2 - 8 =$	**c**	$-5 - 6 =$	**d**	$6 - 9 =$
e	$5 - 3 =$	**f**	$3 - 8 =$	**g**	$-4 + 5 =$	**h**	$-3 + 7 =$
i	$-2 + 9 =$	**j**	$-6 + -2 =$	**k**	$-1 + -4 =$	**l**	$-8 + -3 =$
m	$5 - -6 =$	**n**	$3 - -3 =$	**o**	$6 - -2 =$	**p**	$3 - -5 =$
q	$-5 - -3 =$	**r**	$-2 - -1 =$	**s**	$-4 - 5 =$	**t**	$2 - 7 =$
u	$-3 + 8 =$	**v**	$-4 + - 5 =$	**w**	$1 - -7 =$	**x**	$-5 - -5 =$

3   The temperature at midnight was 4 °C. Find the temperature if it **fell** by:

    a 1 °C   **b** 4 °C   **c** 7 °C   **d** 9 °C   **e** 15 °C

4   What is the **difference** between the following temperatures?

    a 4 °C and –6 °C   **b** –2 °C and –9 °C   **c** –3 °C and 6 °C

5 Rewrite the following list, putting the numbers in order of size, lowest first.

1 –5 3 –6 –9 8 –1 2

6 Write down the answers to each of the following, then check your answers on a calculator.

a $2 - 5 =$ **b** $7 - 11 =$ **c** $4 - 6 =$ **d** $8 - 15 =$

e $9 - 23 =$ **f** $-2 - 4 =$ **g** $-5 - 7 =$ **h** $-1 - 9 =$

i $-4 + 8 =$ **j** $-9 + 5 =$ **k** $9 - -5 =$ **l** $8 - -3 =$

m $-8 - -4 =$ **n** $-3 - -2 =$ **o** $-7 + -3 =$ **p** $-9 + 4 =$

q $-6 + 3 =$ **r** $-1 + 6 =$ **s** $-9 - -5 =$ **t** $9 - 17 =$

7 Find what you have to **add to** 5 to get:

a 7   **b** 2   **c** 0   **d** –2   **e** –5   **f** –15

8 Find what you have to **subtract from** 4 to get:

a 2   **b** 0   **c** 5   **d** 9   **e** 15   **f** –4

9 Find what you have to **add to** –5 to get:

a 8   **b** –3   **c** 0   **d** –1   **e** 6   **f** –7

10 Find what you have to **subtract from** –3 to get:

a 7   **b** 2   **c** –1   **d** –7   **e** –10   **f** 1

11 Write down ten different addition sums that give the answer 1.

12 Write down ten different subtraction problems that give the answer 1. There must be **one negative number** in each sum.

13 Work out each of these using a calculator.

a $-7 + - 3 - -5 =$ **b** $6 + 7 - 7 =$ **c** $-3 + -4 - -7 =$

d $-1 - 3 - -6 =$ **e** $8 - -7 + -2 =$ **f** $-5 - 7 - -12 =$

g $-4 + 5 - 7 =$ **h** $-4 + -6 - -8 =$ **i** $103 - -102 - -7 =$

j $-1 + 4 - -2 =$ **k** $6 - -9 - 12 =$ **l** $-3 - -3 - -3 =$

m $-45 + -56 - -34 =$ **n** $-3 + 4 - -6 =$ **o** $102 + -45 - 32 =$

14 Give the outputs of each of these function machines.

a $\xrightarrow{-4, -3, -2, -1, 0} \boxed{+ 3} \xrightarrow{?, ?, ?, ?, ?}$

b $\xrightarrow{-4, -3, -2, -1, 0} \boxed{- 2} \xrightarrow{?, ?, ?, ?, ?}$

c $\xrightarrow{-4, -3, -2, -1, 0} \boxed{+ 1} \xrightarrow{?, ?, ?, ?, ?}$

d $\xrightarrow{-4, -3, -2, -1, 0} \boxed{- 4} \xrightarrow{?, ?, ?, ?, ?}$

e $\xrightarrow{-4, -3, -2, -1, 0} \boxed{- 5} \xrightarrow{?, ?, ?, ?, ?}$

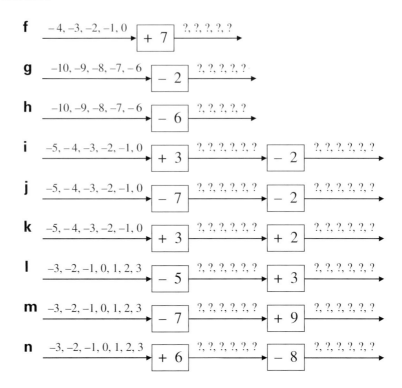

f $-4, -3, -2, -1, 0$ → $[+7]$ → $?, ?, ?, ?, ?$

g $-10, -9, -8, -7, -6$ → $[-2]$ → $?, ?, ?, ?, ?$

h $-10, -9, -8, -7, -6$ → $[-6]$ → $?, ?, ?, ?, ?$

i $-5, -4, -3, -2, -1, 0$ → $[+3]$ → $?, ?, ?, ?, ?, ?$ → $[-2]$ → $?, ?, ?, ?, ?, ?$

j $-5, -4, -3, -2, -1, 0$ → $[-7]$ → $?, ?, ?, ?, ?, ?$ → $[-2]$ → $?, ?, ?, ?, ?, ?$

k $-5, -4, -3, -2, -1, 0$ → $[+3]$ → $?, ?, ?, ?, ?, ?$ → $[+2]$ → $?, ?, ?, ?, ?, ?$

l $-3, -2, -1, 0, 1, 2, 3$ → $[-5]$ → $?, ?, ?, ?, ?, ?$ → $[+3]$ → $?, ?, ?, ?, ?, ?$

m $-3, -2, -1, 0, 1, 2, 3$ → $[-7]$ → $?, ?, ?, ?, ?, ?$ → $[+9]$ → $?, ?, ?, ?, ?, ?$

n $-3, -2, -1, 0, 1, 2, 3$ → $[+6]$ → $?, ?, ?, ?, ?, ?$ → $[-8]$ → $?, ?, ?, ?, ?, ?$

15 You have the following cards.

$$\boxed{+5}\ \boxed{+3}\ \boxed{+1}\ \boxed{0}\ \boxed{-4}\ \boxed{-8}\ \boxed{-9}$$

a What card should you choose to make the answer to the following sum as large as possible? What is the answer?

$$\boxed{+5}\ +\ \boxed{}\ =\ \ \dots\dots$$

b What card should you choose to make the answer to part **a** as small as possible? What is the answer?

c What card should you choose to make the answer to the following sum as large as possible? What is the answer?

$$\boxed{+5}\ -\ \boxed{}\ =\ \ \dots\dots$$

d What card should you choose to make the answer to part **c** as small as possible? What is the answer?

16 You have the following cards.

$$\boxed{+7}\ \boxed{+4}\ \boxed{+2}\ \boxed{+1}\ \boxed{0}\ \boxed{-4}\ \boxed{-5}\ \boxed{-7}\ \boxed{-9}$$

a What cards should you choose to make the answer to the following sum as large as possible? What is the answer?

b What cards should you choose to make the answer to part **a** as small as possible? What is the answer?

c What cards should you choose to make the answer to the following sum zero? Give all possible answers.

$$\boxed{} + \boxed{} = 0$$

17 What numbers are missing from the boxes to make the sums true?

a $2 + {-6} = \square$	**b** $4 + \square = 7$	**c** $-4 + \square = 0$
d $5 + \square = -1$	**e** $3 + 4 = \square$	**f** $\square - {-5} = 7$
g $\square - 5 = 2$	**h** $6 + \square = 0$	**i** $\square - {-5} = -2$
j $2 + {-2} = \square$	**k** $\square - 2 = -2$	**l** $-2 + {-4} = \square$
m $2 + 3 + \square = -2$	**n** $-2 + {-3} + {-4} = \square$	**o** $\square - 5 = -1$
p $\square - 8 = -8$	**q** $-4 + 2 + \square = 3$	**r** $-5 + 5 = \square$
s $7 - {-3} = \square$	**t** $\square - {-5} = 0$	**u** $3 - \square = 0$
v $-3 - \square = 0$	**w** $-6 + {-3} = \square$	**x** $\square - 3 - {-2} = -1$
y $\square - 1 = -4$	**z** $7 - \square = 10$	

Activity

Negative magic squares

Make your own magic square with negative numbers. You need nine small square cards and two pens or pencils of different colours.

This is perhaps the best known magic square.

8	3	4
1	5	9
6	7	2

But magic squares can be made from many different sets of numbers, as shown by this second square.

This square is now used to show you how to make a magic square with negative numbers. But the method works with any magic square. So, if you can find one of your own, use it!

8	13	6
7	9	11
12	5	10

- Arrange the nine cards in a square and write on them the numbers of the magic square. Picture **a**.
- Rearrange the cards in order, lowest number first, to form another square. Picture **b**.
- Now use a different coloured pen to avoid confusion.
- Keeping the cards in order, turn them over so that the blank side of each card is face up. Picture **c**.
- Choose any number (say 4) for the top left-hand corner of the square. Picture **d**.
- Choose another number (say 3) and subtract it from each number in the first row to get the next number. Picture **e**.
- Now choose a third number (say 2) and subtract it from each number in the top row to make the second row, and then again from each number in the second row. Picture **f**.
- Turn the cards over. Picture **g**.
- Rearrange the cards into the original magic square. Picture **h**.
- Turn them over again. Picture **i**.

You should have a **magic square of negative numbers.**

a

8	13	6
7	9	11
12	5	10

b

5	6	7
8	9	10
11	12	13

c

d

4		

e

4	1	−2

f

4	1	−2
2	−1	−4
0	−3	−6

g

5	6	7
8	9	10
11	12	13

h

8	13	6
7	9	11
12	5	10

i

2	−6	1
−2	−1	0
−3	4	−4

Try it on any square. It works even with squares bigger than 3×3. Try it on this 4×4 square.

2	13	9	14
16	7	11	4
15	8	12	3
5	10	6	17

EXERCISE 3E

WHOLE EXERCISE

Copy and complete each of these magic squares. In each case, write down the 'magic number'.

1

−1		
−5	−4	−3
		−7

2

	−4	3
		−2
	4	−1

3

−6	−5	−4
		−10

4

2		
−4		
−7	6	−8

5

		−9
−3	−6	−9

6

		−1
	−7	
−13		−12

7

−4		
−8		−6
−9		

8

2	1	−3
	0	

9

−2		
		−5
−7		−8

10

−8			−14
−8	−9		
		−4	−5
1	−10	−12	−5

11

−7		2	−16
		−8	
−11	−3	0	−2
		−13	−1

Investigation

Number Pyramids

■ Choose any three numbers and place them in any order in the boxes in the bottom row of the pyramid. For example, take 2, 4 and 5.

▶

■ The number in each box in the row above is found by adding together the numbers in the two boxes below. This gives

$2 + 4 = 6$
$4 + 5 = 9$

complete →

$6 + 9 = 15$

■ On the right is another example, starting with 4, 7 and 5.

■ What do you notice about the number in the box at the top of the pyramid? Can you predict the top number in the pyramid for any three numbers that you choose?

■ Does your rule work if you use negative numbers?

Race Track

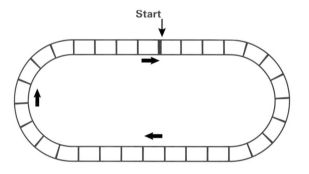

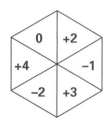

■ The game is for two players, using the six-sided spinner and two counters.

■ A score of +2, for example, means move a counter 2 spaces forward, while a score of −2 means move a counter 2 spaces back. The winner is the first person to go completely round the track.

■ Do you think that the spinner is a good one to use for the game?

■ Make different spinners to make the game more exciting. Explain the reasons for your choice of numbers on each spinner.

Examination questions

1 As a gas cools it eventually turns to liquid. Radon gas turns to liquid at −62 °C. Argon gas turns to liquid at −186 °C.
   a What is the difference between the two temperatures?
   b In each of the statements below, write a possible temperature. (Temperatures below −273 °C are not possible.)
      i At ...... °C radon is a gas.
      ii At ...... °C argon is a liquid.

MEG(SMP), Question 7, Specimen Paper 2, 1998

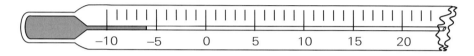

2 **a** What temperature is shown on the thermometer?
   One autumn morning, the temperature went up from −4 °C to 5 °C.
   b By how many degrees did the temperature rise?

   During the afternoon, the temperature then fell by seven degrees from 5 °C.
   c What was the temperature at the end of the afternoon?

EDEXCEL, Question 5, Specimen Paper 2, 1998

3 These maps show the temperatures at midday and at midnight on a certain day in five different places.

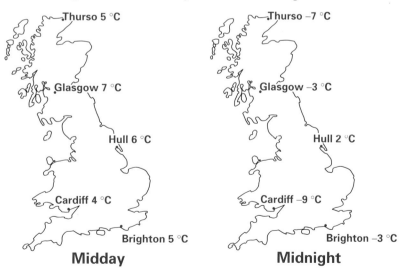

Thurso 5 °C

Glasgow 7 °C

Hull 6 °C

Cardiff 4 °C

Brighton 5 °C

Midday

Thurso −7 °C

Glasgow −3 °C

Hull 2 °C

Cardiff −9 °C

Brighton −3 °C

Midnight

   a Which place was the warmest at midday?

b How much colder was Cardiff than Glasgow at midnight?

c Which place had the greatest drop in temperature from midday to midnight?

d Which place had the least difference in temperature from midday to midnight?

NEAB, Question 1, Speciment Paper 1F, 1998

4 The point $1\frac{1}{2}$ has been marked on the number line below. Copy the line and mark the following numbers in the same way.

i $-1\frac{1}{4}$ **ii** $2\frac{1}{2}$ **iii** $\frac{2}{3}$ **iv** $-2\frac{3}{4}$

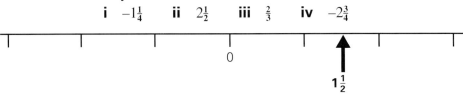

NEAB, Question 11, Specimen Paper 2F, 1998

5 The temperatures of three food cabinets in a shop are $2\,°C$, $-5\,°C$ and $-1\,°C$.

a Write down these temperatures, in order, with the coldest first.

b What is the difference in temperature between the coldest and the hottest cabinet?

WJEC, Question 5, Paper B1, June 1994

6 At 1 pm the temperature in Birmingham was $5\,°C$. According to the weather forecast, the temperature at midnight was expected to be $-4\,°C$.

a By how many degrees was the temperature expected to fall?

b In fact, the temperature at midnight was $2\,°C$ lower than expected. What was the temperature that night?

MEG, Question 16, Specimen Paper 1, 1998

What you should know after you have worked through Chapter 3

✔ How to order positive and negative numbers.
✔ How to add and subtract positive and negative numbers.
✔ How to use negative numbers in practical situations.
✔ How to use a calculator when dealing with negative numbers.

PUZZLE PAGE

Franklin's square

On the right is a 3×3 magic square. Its magic number is 15 because that is the total across each row, down each column, and along each diagonal.

2	9	4
7	5	3
6	1	8

This 8×8 magic square is believed to have been discovered by Benjamin Franklin (1706–90), the eminent US scientist and philosopher, who invented the lightning conductor, the rocking chair and the iron stove.

What is the magic number of Franklin's square?

52	61	4	13	20	29	36	45
14	3	62	51	46	35	30	19
53	60	5	12	21	28	37	44
11	6	59	54	43	38	27	22
55	58	7	10	23	26	39	42
9	8	57	56	41	40	25	24
50	63	2	15	18	31	34	47
16	1	64	49	48	33	32	17

■ Using Franklin's square, work out the total of the eight numbers in each of these blocks:

a

18	31	34	47
48	33	32	17

b

52	61	4	13
14	3	62	51

c

29	36
35	30
28	37
38	27

d

6	59	54	43
58	7	10	23

■ How many more blocks of eight numbers like those above can you find, which add up to the magic number?

■ Locate the following sets of eight numbers on Franklin's square. You should find that each set makes a pattern on the square.

a 61 36 / 14 19 / 50 47 / 1 32

b 52 61 36 45 / 16 1 32 17

c 13 20 / 11 22 / 55 42 / 49 48

What is the total of each set of eight numbers?

4 More about number

This chapter is going to ...

explain the meaning of multiples, factors and prime numbers. It is also going to show you how to work out squares, square roots and powers.

What you should already know

✔ Times tables up to 10×10

Multiples of whole numbers

When we multiply any whole number by another whole number, the answer is called a **multiple** of either of those numbers.

For example, $5 \times 7 = 35$, which means that 35 is a multiple of 5 and it is also a multiple of 7. Here are some other multiples of 5 and 7:

multiples of 5 are   5   10   15   20   25   30   35   ...
multiples of 7 are   7   14   21   28   35   42   ...

Multiples are also called **times tables**.

Recognising multiples

You can recognise the multiples of 2, 3, 5 and 9 in the following ways:

- Multiples of 2 always end in an even number or 0. For example,
  12   34   96   1938   370
- Multiples of 3 are always made up of digits that add up to a multiple of 3. For example,

15	because	$1 + 5 = 6$	which is $2 \times \mathbf{3}$
72	because	$7 + 2 = 9$	which is $3 \times \mathbf{3}$
201	because	$2 + 0 + 1 = 3$	which is $1 \times \mathbf{3}$

- Multiples of 5 always end in 5 or 0. For example,

  35   60   155   300

- Multiples of 9 are always made up of digits that add up to a multiple of 9. For example,

  63   because $6 + 3 = 9$ which is 1×9

  738   because $7 + 3 + 8 = 18$ which is 2×9

You can find out whether numbers are multiples of 4, 6, 7 and 8 by using your calculator. For example, to find out whether 341 is a multiple of 7, you have to see whether 341 gives a whole number when it is divided by 7. You therefore key

The answer is 48.714286, which is a decimal number not a whole number. So, 341 is **not** a multiple of 7.

EXERCISE 4A

1 Write out the first five multiples of

    a 3   **b** 7   **c** 9   **d** 11   **e** 16

    Remember: the first multiple is the number itself.

2 From the list of numbers below, write down those that are

    a multiples of 2   **b** multiples of 3   **c** multiples of 5

    d multiples of 9

        111   254   255   108   73

         68   162   711   615   98

         37   812   102   75   270

3 Use your calculator to see which of the numbers below are

    a multiples of 4   **b** multiples of 7   **c** multiples of 6

         72   135   102   161   197

        132   78   91   216   514

        312   168   75   144   294

4 Find the biggest number smaller than 100 that is

    a a multiple of 2   **b** a multiple of 3   **c** a multiple of 4

    d a multiple of 5   **e** a multiple of 7

5 Find the smallest number that is bigger than 1000 which is

    a a multiple of 6   **b** a multiple of 8   **c** a multiple of 9

Activity

Grid locked

You need eight copies of this 10×10 grid.

1	2	3	4	5	6	7	8	9	10
11	12	13	14	15	16	17	18	19	20
21	22	23	24	25	26	27	28	29	30
31	32	33	34	35	36	37	38	39	40
41	42	43	44	45	46	47	48	49	50
51	52	53	54	55	56	57	58	59	60
61	62	63	64	65	66	67	68	69	70
71	72	73	74	75	76	77	78	79	80
81	82	83	84	85	86	87	88	89	90
91	92	93	94	95	96	97	98	99	100

Take one of the grids and shade in all the multiples of 2. You should find that they make a neat pattern.

Do the same thing for the multiples of 3, 4, … up to 9, using a fresh 10×10 grid for each digit.

Next, draw a grid which is 9 squares wide and write the numbers from 1 to 100 in the grid, like this:

1	2	3	4	5	6	7	8	9
10	11	12	13	14	15	16	17	18
19	20	21	22	23	24			27

Make seven more copies of this grid. Then shade in the multiples of 2, 3, … up to 9, using a fresh grid for each digit.

Write out the numbers from 1 to 100 on grids of different widths and shade in the multiples of 2, 3, … up to 9, as before.

Describe the patterns that you get.

Factors of whole numbers

A factor of a whole number is any whole number that divides into it exactly. So,

factors of 20 are   1   2   4   5   10   20

factors of 12 are   1   2   3   4   6   12

This is where it helps to know your times tables!

Factor facts

Remember these facts:

- 1 is always a factor and so is the number itself.
- When you have found one factor, there is always another factor that goes with it – unless the factor is multiplied by itself to give the number. For example, look at the number 20:

$1 \times 20 = 20$ so 1 and 20 are both factors of 20

$2 \times 10 = 20$ so 2 and 10 are both factors of 20

$4 \times 5 = 20$ so 4 and 5 are both factors of 20

You may need to use your calculator to find the factors of large numbers. (You can, of course, use your calculator to find the factors of small numbers, if necessary.)

Example 1

Find the factors of 32

Look for the pairs of numbers which make 32 when multiplied together. These are

$1 \times 32 = 32$ $2 \times 16 = 32$ $4 \times 8 = 32$

So, the factors of 32 are 1, 2, 4, 8, 16, 32

Example 2

Find the factors of 36

Look for the pairs of numbers which make 36 when multiplied together. These are

$1 \times 36 = 36$ $2 \times 18 = 36$ $3 \times 12 = 36$ $4 \times 9 = 36$ $6 \times 6 = 36$

6 is a repeated factor which is counted only once.

So, the factors of 36 are 1, 2, 3, 4, 6, 9, 12, 18, 36

EXERCISE 4B

1 What are the factors of each of these?
  a 10 **b** 28 **c** 18 **d** 17 **e** 25
  f 40 **g** 30 **h** 45 **i** 24 **j** 16

2 Use your calculator to find the factors of each of these.
  a 120 **b** 150 **c** 144 **d** 180 **e** 169
  f 108 **g** 196 **h** 153 **i** 198 **j** 199

3 What is the biggest factor which is less than 100 in each of these?
  a 110 **b** 201 **c** 145 **d** 117 **e** 130
  f 240 **g** 160 **h** 210 **i** 162 **j** 250

4 Find the common factor for each of the following pairs of numbers. (Do not include 1.)
  a 2 and 4 **b** 6 and 10 **c** 9 and 12
  d 15 and 25 **e** 9 and 15 **f** 12 and 21
  g 14 and 21 **h** 25 and 30 **i** 30 and 50
  j 55 and 77

Activity

Prime search

You need a 10 × 10 grid.

Cross out 1.

Leave 2 and cross out the rest of the multiples of 2.

Leave 3 and cross out the rest of the multiples of 3. Some of them will already have been crossed out.

Leave 5 and cross out the rest of the multiples of 5. Some of them will already have been crossed out.

1	2	3	4	5	6	7	8	9	10
11	12	13	14	15	16	17	18	19	20
21	22	23	24	25	26	27	28	29	30
31	32	33	34	35	36	37	38	39	40
41	42	43	44	45	46	47	48	49	50
51	52	53	54	55	56	57	58	59	60
61	62	63	64	65	66	67	68	69	70
71	72	73	74	75	76	77	78	79	80
81	82	83	84	85	86	87	88	89	90
91	92	93	94	95	96	97	98	99	100

Leave 7 and cross out the rest of the multiples of 7. All but three of them will already have been crossed out.

The numbers left are **prime numbers**.

The activity is known as the Sieve of Eratosthenes. (Eratosthenes, a Greek scholar, lived from about 275 BC to 194 BC.)

Prime numbers

What are the factors of 2, 3, 5, 7, 11 and 13?

Notice that each number has only two factors: itself and 1. They are all examples of **prime numbers**.

So, a prime number is a whole number which has only two factors: itself and 1.

Note 1 is **not** a prime number, since it has only one factor – itself.

The prime numbers up to 50 are
2, 3, 5, 7, 11, 13, 17, 19, 23, 29, 31, 37, 41, 43, 47

You will need to know these for your GCSE examination.

Square numbers

What is the next number in this sequence?
1, 4, 9, 16, 25, …

Writing each number in terms of its factors gives
$1 \times 1, 2 \times 2, 3 \times 3, 4 \times 4, 5 \times 5, …$

These factors can be represented by square patterns of dots:

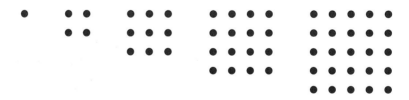

From these patterns, we can see that the next pair of factors must be $6 \times 6 = 36$, which is therefore the next number in the sequence.

Because they form square patterns, the numbers 1, 4, 9, 16, 25, 36, … are called **square numbers**.

So, when we multiply any number by itself, the answer is called the **square of the number** or the **number squared**. This is because the answer is a square number. For example,
the square of 5 (or 5 squared) is $5 \times 5 = 25$
the square of 6 (or 6 squared) is $6 \times 6 = 36$

There is a short way to write the square of any number. For example,

5 squared (5×5) can be written as $\mathbf{5^2}$

13 squared (13×13) can be written as $\mathbf{13^2}$

So, the sequence of square numbers, 1, 4, 9, 16, 25, 36, …, can be written as

1^2, 2^2, 3^2, 4^2, 5^2, 6^2,   …

EXERCISE 4C

1 The square number pattern starts

1   4   9   16   25   …

Continue the pattern above until you have written down the first 20 square numbers. You may use your calculator for this.

2 Work out the answer to each of these sums:

$1 + 3 =$

$1 + 3 + 5 =$

$1 + 3 + 5 + 7 =$

Look carefully at the pattern of the three sums. Then write down the next three sums in the pattern and work them out.

3 **a** Draw one counter.

b Now add more counters to your picture to make the next square number.

c How many extra counters did you add?

d Now add more counters to your picture to make the next square number.

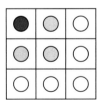

e How many extra counters did you add?

f Without drawing, how many more counters will you need to make the next square number?

g Describe the pattern of counters you are adding.

4 Find the next three numbers in each of these number patterns. (They are all based on square numbers.) You may use your calculator.

	1	4	9	16	25	36	49	64	81
a	2	5	10	17	26	37	...	...	...
b	2	8	18	32	50	72	...	...	...
c	3	6	11	18	27	38	...	...	...
d	0	3	8	15	24	35	...	...	...
e	101	104	109	116	125	136	...	...	...

5 Write down the answer to each of the following. You will need to use your calculator. Look for the x^2 key.

   a 23^2 **b** 57^2 **c** 77^2 **d** 123^2 **e** 152^2

   f 3.2^2 **g** 9.5^2 **h** 23.8^2 **i** $(-4)^2$ **j** $(-12)^2$

6 a Work out each of the following. You may use your calculator.

$$3^2 + 4^2 \quad \text{and} \quad 5^2$$
$$5^2 + 12^2 \quad \text{and} \quad 13^2$$
$$7^2 + 24^2 \quad \text{and} \quad 25^2$$
$$9^2 + 40^2 \quad \text{and} \quad 41^2$$
$$11^2 + 60^2 \quad \text{and} \quad 61^2$$

  b Describe what you notice about your answers.

Square roots

The square root of a given number is a number which, when multiplied by itself, produces the given number.

For example, the square root of 9 is 3, since $3 \times 3 = 9$

A square root is represented by the symbol $\sqrt{}$. For example, $\sqrt{16} = 4$

EXERCISE 4D

1 Write down the square root of each of these.

   a 4   **b** 25   **c** 49   **d** 1   **e** 81

   f 100   **g** 64   **h** 9   **i** 36   **j** 16

   k 121   **l** 144   **m** 400   **n** 900   **o** 169

2 Write down the value of each of these.

   a $\sqrt{25}$ **b** $\sqrt{36}$ **c** $\sqrt{100}$ **d** $\sqrt{49}$ **e** $\sqrt{64}$

   f $\sqrt{16}$ **g** $\sqrt{9}$ **h** $\sqrt{81}$ **i** $\sqrt{1}$ **j** $\sqrt{144}$

3 Write down the value of each of these. You will need to use your calculator for some of them. Look for the $\boxed{\sqrt{x}}$ key.

    a 9^2 **b** $\sqrt{1600}$ **c** 10^2 **d** $\sqrt{196}$ **e** 6^2

    f $\sqrt{225}$ **g** 7^2 **h** $\sqrt{144}$ **i** 5^2 **j** $\sqrt{441}$

    k 11^2 **l** $\sqrt{256}$ **m** 8^2 **n** $\sqrt{289}$ **o** 21^2

4 Write down the answer to each of the following. You will need to use your calculator.

    a $\sqrt{567}$ **b** $\sqrt{961}$ **c** $\sqrt{2025}$ **d** $\sqrt{1600}$ **e** $\sqrt{4489}$

    f $\sqrt{10\,201}$ **g** $\sqrt{12.96}$ **h** $\sqrt{42.25}$ **i** $\sqrt{193.21}$ **j** $\sqrt{492.84}$

Powers

4^2 is a short way of writing 4×4 to give the answer 16.

In the same way, 4^3 means $4 \times 4 \times 4$, so that $4^3 = 64$. We call this **four cubed**.

A power tells us how many times to multiply a number by itself.

So, $7^4 = 7 \times 7 \times 7 \times 7 = 2401$. We call this **seven to the power of four**.

Example 3

Work out 3^5

$3^5 = 3 \times 3 \times 3 \times 3 \times 3 = 243$

EXERCISE 4E

1 Use your calculator to work out the value of each of the following.

    a 3^3 **b** 5^3 **c** 6^3 **d** 12^3 **e** 2^4

    f 4^4 **g** 5^4 **h** 2^5 **i** 3^7 **j** 2^{10}

2 Work out the answers to the following powers of 10.

    a 10^2 **b** 10^3 **c** 10^4 **d** 10^5 **e** 10^6

    f Describe what you notice about your answers.

    g Now write down the answer to each of these

        i 10^8 **ii** 10^{10} **iii** 10^{15}

Investigation

The T Problem

1	2	3	4	5	6
7	8	9	10	11	12
13	14	15	16	17	18
19	20	21	22	23	24
25	26	27	28	29	30
31	32	33	34	35	36

The numbers in the T shape add up to 33.

The bottom number in the T is 15. So, call this T shape T15.
Therefore, T26 will be

- What do the numbers in T26 add up to?
- Find the totals for different T shapes.
- Put all your results in a table. Can you find a connection between the T number and the total?
- Investigate what happens if you use a bigger-sized square grid.

Triangle Numbers

  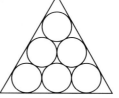

Pattern 1   **Pattern 2**   **Pattern 3**

Each of these patterns of circles forms a triangle:
- How many circles are there in each pattern?
- Draw Patterns 4 and 5. Count the number of circles in each pattern.

Pattern number	1	2	3	4	5	6	7	8
Number of circles	1	3						

Note The numbers in the bottom row of the table are called **triangle numbers**.
- Find the connection between the pattern numbers and the triangle numbers.
- Invent some of your own circle patterns.

Examination questions

1 Look at these numbers: 7, 10, 13, 16, 19, 22, 25
From this list write down
a the multiples of 5
b the square numbers
c the prime numbers.

OCR(SMP), Question 8, Terminal Paper, 1999

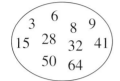

2 From the numbers in the ring on the left, write down all the
a square numbers
b cube numbers
c prime numbers
d factors of 56.

EDEXCEL, Question 8, Paper 1, June 1998

3 a From the number grid below,

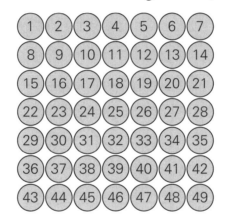

write down
i a square number
ii a factor of 100, other than 1
iii a multiple of 5
iv a prime number.
b Three brothers each choose a number from the grid above.
i Paul chooses a square number bigger than 45. What is Paul's number?
ii Michael chooses an even prime number. What is Michael's number?
iii Geoffrey chooses a number which is a multiple of 6 and also a multiple of 7. What is Geoffrey's number?

NEAB, Question 15, Paper 1F, June 1998

4 Here are the first five multiples of 3:

3   6   9   12   15

a Write down the first five multiples of 5.

b The number 15 is a multiple of both 3 and 5. Write down two more numbers that are multiples of both 3 and 5.

c Find a number that is a multiple of both 3 and 5 and is also bigger than 100.

NEAB, Question 1, Paper 1, June 1996

5 a Belinda is thinking of a number.

What is Belinda's number?

b Which of the numbers greater than one but less than six, are prime numbers?

SEG, Question 3, Specimen Paper 11, 1998

6 Helen makes a three-figure number using each of the numbers 8, 4 and 3. She notices that it is a multiple of 8. What is her number?

SEG, Question 1, Specimen Paper 12, 1998

7

1	2	3	4	5	6	7	8	9	10
11	12	13	14	15	16	17	18	19	20
21	22	23	24	25	26	27	28	29	30
31	32	33	34	35	36	37	38	39	40

From the numbers above, write down

i all of the multiples of 8

ii the square of 6

iii the prime factors of 70

iv the values of

a 3^2 **b** $\sqrt{25}$

WJEC, Question 16, Specimen Paper 1F, 1998

8 Consider only these numbers: 2, 3, 6, 8, 9.

		4
1	5	
	7	

   i   Which of these numbers is a multiple of 4?

   ii Which of these numbers are factors of 9?

  iii Which of these numbers are prime numbers?

  iv By using each of these numbers once, complete the number square on the left so that every row, column and diagonal adds to 15.

SEG, Question 8, Specimen Paper 11, 1998

9 **a** Add together the cube of four and the square of three.

   b Work out $7^2 + 24^2 - 25^2$.

   c Work out 6×2^4.

OCR, Question 13, Paper 2, June 1999

10 **a** Complete the following number pattern.

$$1^3 \quad = \quad 1 \times 1 \times 1 \quad = 1$$
$$2^3 \quad = \quad 2 \times 2 \times 2 \quad = 8$$
$$3^3 \quad = \quad \text{...............} \quad = 27$$
$$4^3 \quad = \quad \text{...............} \quad = \ldots$$

   b Use your answers to part **a** to complete this number pattern.

$$1^3 \qquad\qquad = \quad 1 \quad = \quad 1^2$$
$$1^3 + 2^3 \qquad = \quad 9 \quad = \quad 3^2$$
$$1^3 + 2^3 + 3^3 \qquad = \quad 36 \quad = \quad 6^2$$
$$1^3 + 2^3 + 3^3 + 4^3 \quad = \quad ..... \quad = \quad ....$$

   c A line of the pattern in part **b** is shown below. Fill in the missing parts of this line.

$$\text{.........................} \quad = \quad 441 \quad = \text{........}$$

NEAB, Question 16, Paper 2, June 1998

What you should know after you have worked through Chapter 4

✔   What multiples are.
✔   How to find the factors of any whole number.
✔   What a prime number is.
✔   What square numbers are.
✔   What square roots are.
✔   How to find powers of numbers.

Revision for Chapters 1 to 4

WHOLE EXERCISE

- Answer all the questions
- Show your working

1 Write down the answers to each of the following. Look carefully at the signs, because they are a mixture of ×, +, – and ÷.

a	$6 + 8$	**b**	$20 - 6$	**c**	4×7	**d**	$7 + 9$	**e**	$28 \div 4$
f	$17 - 8$	**g**	$5 + 8$	**h**	$36 \div 9$	**i**	6×7	**j**	$30 \div 6$
k	8×5	**l**	$15 \div 5$	**m**	$23 - 8$	**n**	$24 \div 4$	**o**	$8 + 9$
p	$9 + 5$	**q**	$46 - 9$	**r**	$40 \div 5$	**s**	$18 + 7$	**t**	9×6
u	7×5	**v**	$49 \div 7$	**w**	$8 + 19$	**x**	8×9	**y**	$54 - 18$

2 Write each of these numbers using just words.

    a 3 085 200   **b** 12 007 806

3 Write down in order of size, smallest first, all the two-digit numbers that can be made using the digits 2, 5 and 7. (The digits can be repeated.)

4 Put a bracket in each of these to make the answer correct.

    a $3 + 5 \times 6 = 48$ **b** $30 - 2 \times 3 + 1 = 22$

5 By doing a suitable multiplication, answer each of these questions.

    a How many days are there in 15 weeks?

    b How many hours are there in nine days?

    c Bottles are packed in boxes of eight. How many bottles are in 36 boxes?

6 By doing a suitable division, answer each of these questions.

    a How many weeks are there in 238 days?

    b How long will it take me to save £138, if I save £6 a week?

    c A rope, 115 metres long, is cut into five equal pieces. How long is each piece?

    d Mary has a bottle of 96 tablets. How many days will they last if she takes four each day?

7 Calculate each of these.

a	$\frac{3}{4} + \frac{1}{4}$	**b**	$\frac{4}{5} - \frac{1}{5}$	**c**	$\frac{7}{8} + \frac{4}{8}$	**d**	$\frac{8}{10} + \frac{5}{10}$
e	$\frac{2}{3} - \frac{1}{3}$	**f**	$\frac{5}{6} - \frac{1}{6}$	**g**	$\frac{5}{7} + \frac{2}{7}$	**h**	$\frac{5}{9} - \frac{2}{9}$
i	$\frac{3}{5} - \frac{2}{5}$	**j**	$\frac{4}{7} + \frac{1}{7}$	**k**	$\frac{8}{9} - \frac{5}{9}$	**l**	$\frac{7}{10} - \frac{3}{10}$
m	$\frac{4}{6} + \frac{1}{6}$	**n**	$\frac{5}{8} - \frac{3}{8}$	**o**	$\frac{7}{11} + \frac{5}{11}$	**p**	$\frac{9}{10} + \frac{3}{10}$

Revision section

8 Calculate each of these.

a $\frac{7}{8} + \frac{3}{4}$ **b** $\frac{7}{10} - \frac{1}{5}$ **c** $\frac{3}{4} + \frac{1}{2}$ **d** $\frac{5}{8} - \frac{1}{4}$

e $\frac{1}{2} + \frac{1}{4}$ **f** $\frac{5}{8} - \frac{1}{2}$ **g** $\frac{9}{10} + \frac{1}{2}$ **h** $\frac{9}{16} - \frac{3}{8}$

9 Calculate each of these.

a $\frac{2}{3}$ of £12   **b** $\frac{3}{4}$ of 56 kg   **c** $\frac{4}{5}$ of 60 minutes

d $\frac{7}{8}$ of 64 cm

10 Calculate each of these.

a $2\frac{3}{8} + 1\frac{1}{2}$ **b** $5\frac{1}{2} + 3\frac{3}{4}$ **c** $4\frac{7}{8} - 1\frac{1}{2}$ **d** $8\frac{3}{4} - 3\frac{5}{8}$

11 Write down the answers to each of these.

a $2 - 6$ **b** $7 - 12$ **c** $4 - 7$ **d** $8 - 13$

e $9 - 13$ **f** $-3 - 4$ **g** $-4 - 7$ **h** $-2 - 9$

i $-4 + 7$ **j** $-19 + 5$ **k** $9 - -5$ **l** $7 - -3$

m $-9 - -4$ **n** $-5 - -2$ **o** $-8 + -3$ **p** $-8 + 4$

q $-5 + 3$ **r** $-2 + 6$ **s** $-8 - -5$ **t** $9 - 27$

12 At midday, the temperature in Sheffield was 3 °C. The temperature at midnight was forecast to be –2 °C.

a By how many degrees was the temperature expected to fall?

b The temperature at midnight was actually 5 °C lower than the forecast. What was the temperature at midnight?

13 From the list of numbers below, write down those that are

a multiples of 3   **b** multiples of 5   **c** multiples of 9

222   294   145   207   75

78   261   117   305   89

37   815   402   65   720

14 What are the factors of each of these numbers?

a 12   **b** 28   **c** 16   **d** 19   **e** 35

f 30   **g** 36   **h** 45   **i** 24   **j** 18

15 Work out the value of each of the following.

a 5^2 **b** $\sqrt{2500}$ **c** 8^2 **d** $\sqrt{196}$ **e** 7^2

f $\sqrt{225}$ **g** 9^2 **h** $\sqrt{121}$ **i** 1^2 **j** $\sqrt{441}$

k 12^2 **l** $\sqrt{256}$ **m** 3^2 **n** $\sqrt{289}$ **o** 22^2

16 Write down all the prime numbers bigger than 20 and less than 50.

17 Here are some numbers:

4   7   10   13   16   19   21

Which of them are

a prime numbers   **b** factors of 80

c square numbers   **d** multiples of 3?

Revision section

5 Some plane shapes

This chapter is going to ...

remind you how to work out the perimeters and the areas of some common shapes. It will introduce you to the types of problem you will be able to solve with knowledge of area.

What you should already know

✔ Perimeter is the distance all the way round a 2-D shape
✔ Area is measured in square units such as the square centimetre (cm^2) or the square metre (m^2)

Activity

Round about

On a piece of 1-cm squared paper draw this rectangle.

Measure its perimeter. You should get $3 + 2 + 3 + 2 = 10\,cm$.

Draw a different rectangle which also has a perimeter of 10 cm.

See how many different rectangles you can draw which each have a perimeter of 10 cm.

Using $\frac{1}{2}$ cm squares, draw some more rectangles which each have a perimeter of 10 cm.

There are only four different rectangles which each have a perimeter of 12 cm and whole numbers for their length and breadth. Can you draw all four?

Can you draw a rectangle which has a perimeter of 7 cm?

If not, why not? If you can, what is so strange about it?

Try drawing a rectangle which has a perimeter of 13 cm.

EXERCISE 5A

Calculate the perimeter of each of the following shapes. Draw them first on squared paper if it helps you.

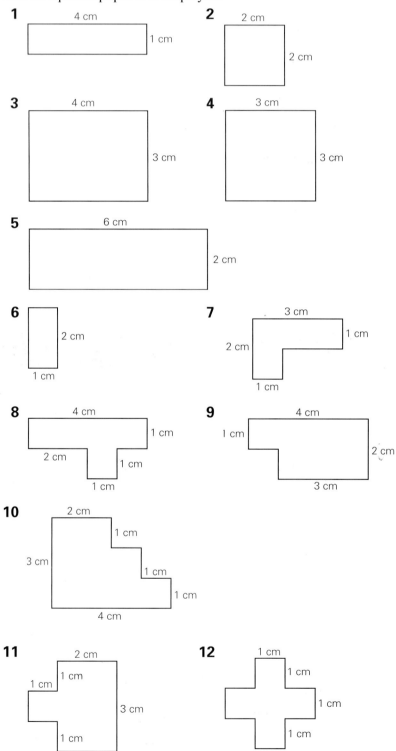

1
4 cm
1 cm

2
2 cm
2 cm

3
4 cm
3 cm

4
3 cm
3 cm

5
6 cm
2 cm

6
2 cm
1 cm

7
3 cm
1 cm
2 cm
1 cm

8
4 cm
1 cm
2 cm
1 cm
1 cm

9
4 cm
1 cm
2 cm
3 cm

10
2 cm
1 cm
3 cm
1 cm
1 cm
4 cm

11
2 cm
1 cm
1 cm
3 cm
1 cm

12
1 cm
1 cm
1 cm
1 cm

Activity

A different area

Take a piece of 1-cm squared paper. Draw on it a rectangle of 2 cm by 6 cm.

Check that it has a perimeter of 16 cm.

Count the number of squares inside the rectangle. This should come to 12. We say that the area of this shape is 12 square centimetres.

Draw a different rectangle which has an area of 12 square centimetres, but a perimeter which is smaller than 16 cm.

Draw another different rectangle which also has an area of 12 square centimetres, but a perimeter which is larger than 16 cm.

Using whole squares only, how many rectangles can you draw which have **different** perimeters but the **same** area of 16 square centimetres?

Area of irregular shapes

To find the area of an irregular shape, we can put a grid over the shape and estimate the number of complete squares which are covered.

The most efficient way to do this is:
- First, count all the whole squares.
- Second, put together parts of squares to make whole and almost whole squares.
- Finally, add together the two results.

Example 1

Below is a map of a lake. Each square represents 1 km². Estimate the surface area of the lake.

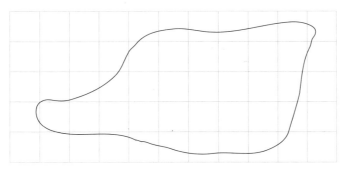

First, count all the whole squares. You should count 16.

Next, put together the parts of squares around the edge of the lake.

You should make up about ten squares. Let's say there are ten.

Finally, add together the 16 and the 10 to get an area of 26 km².

Note This is only an **estimate**. Someone else may get a slightly different answer. But provided the answer is close to 26, it is acceptable.

EXERCISE 5B

1 By counting squares, estimate the area of each of these shapes.

a
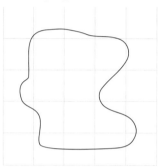

b
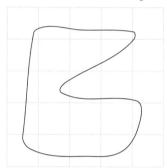

c
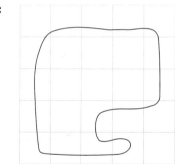

d
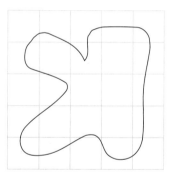

2 On a piece of squared paper, draw round each of your hands to find its area. Are they the same?

3 Find some leaves, draw round them, and estimate their areas.

4 Draw some shapes of your own on squared paper. First, guess the area of each shape. Then count up the squares and see how close you were.

Area of a rectangle

Look at these rectangles and their areas.

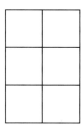

Area 6 cm²

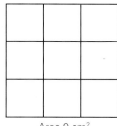

Area 9 cm²

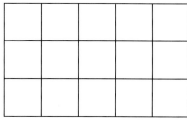

Area 15 cm²

Notice that the area of each rectangle is given by its length multiplied by its width.

Example 2

Calculate the area of this rectangle.

Area of rectangle = Length × Width
$$= 11\,\text{cm} \times 4\,\text{cm}$$
$$= 44\,\text{cm}^2$$

EXERCISE 5C

Calculate the area and the perimeter of each rectangle below.

1

7 cm

5 cm

2

11 cm

3 cm

3

15 cm

3 cm

4

10 cm

7 cm

5

8 cm

7 cm

6

5 cm

2 cm

7 8 cm / 6 cm

8 11 cm / 7 cm

9   Copy and complete the following table for rectangles **a** to **h**.

	Length	Width	Perimeter	Area
a	7 cm	3 cm		
b	5 cm	4 cm		
c	4 cm		12 cm	
d	5 cm		16 cm	
e	6 cm			18 cm²
f	7 cm			28 cm²
g		2 cm	14 cm	
h		5 cm		35 cm²

10   The two squares below have the same area.

1 m A 1 m   100 cm B 100 cm

Calculate the area of square A and of square B.
Copy and complete: $1\,\text{m}^2 = \ldots\ldots\text{cm}^2$

Areas of composite shapes

Some plane shapes can be split into two or more rectangles, which makes it
easy to calculate the areas of these shapes. See Example 3 below.

Other plane shapes can be split into a rectangle and a triangle, or into two
or more triangles, when calculating their areas. See Example 6 on page 88.

Example 3

Find the area of the
shape on the right

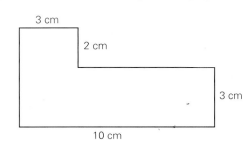

3 cm
2 cm
3 cm
10 cm

First, split the shape into two rectangles, A and B.

Then calculate the area of each one.

Area of A = $2 \times 3 = 6\,cm^2$
Area of B = $10 \times 3 = 30\,cm^2$

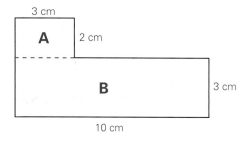

The area of the shape is given by
Area of A + Area of B = $6 + 30 = 36\,cm^2$

EXERCISE 5D

Calculate the area of each shape below as follows.
- First, split it into rectangles.
- Then, calculate the area of each rectangle.
- Finally, add together the areas of the rectangles.

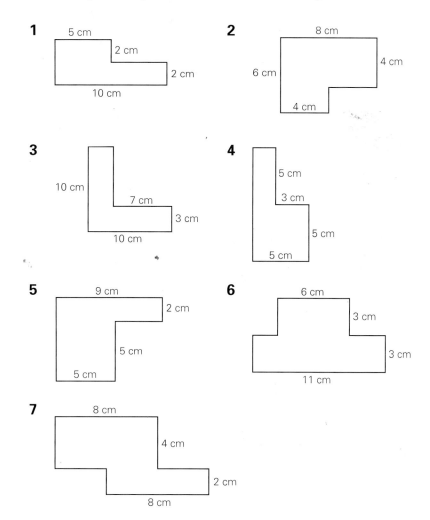

8

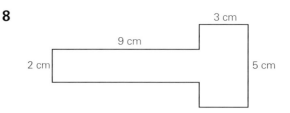

Areas of triangles

Area of a right triangle

The area of a right triangle (one containing a right angle) is easily seen to be half the area of the rectangle it comes from. Hence the area is

$\frac{1}{2} \times$ Base length $\times$ Height

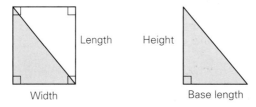

Example 4

Find the area of this triangle.

$\text{Area} = \frac{1}{2} \times 7\,\text{cm} \times 4\,\text{cm}$
$\qquad = \frac{1}{2} \times 28\,\text{cm}^2 = 14\,\text{cm}^2$

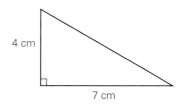

EXERCISE 5E

1 Write down the area and the perimeter of each triangle.

a

b

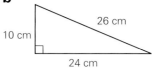

c

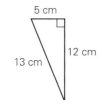

2 Find the area of the shaded part of each triangle.

a

10 cm

4 cm

3 cm   2 cm

b

3 cm

6 cm

5 cm

16 cm

c

22 cm

20 cm

11 cm

10 cm

3 A tree is in the middle of a garden. Around the tree there is a square region where nothing will be planted. The dimensions of the garden are shown in the diagram.

How much area can be planted?

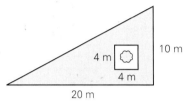

4 m   10 m

4 m

20 m

4 Find the area of the shaded triangle RST.

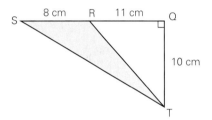

8 cm   R   11 cm   Q

S

10 cm

T

5 Which of these three triangles has the largest area?

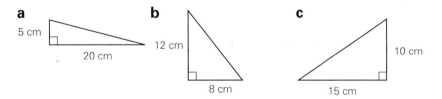

a

5 cm

20 cm

b

12 cm

8 cm

c

10 cm

15 cm

Area of any triangle

The area of any triangle is given by
$\frac{1}{2} \times$ Base length $\times$ Vertical height

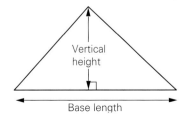

Vertical height

Base length

Example 5

Calculate the area of this triangle.

$$\text{Area} = \tfrac{1}{2} \times 9\,\text{cm} \times 4\,\text{cm}$$
$$= \tfrac{1}{2} \times 36\,\text{cm}^2 = 18\,\text{cm}^2$$

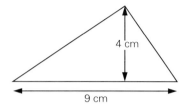

Example 6

Calculate the area of the shape shown below.

This is a composite shape which can be split into a rectangle (R) and a triangle (T):

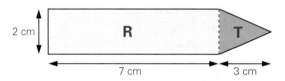

$$\text{Area of the shape} = \text{Area of R} + \text{Area of T}$$
$$= 7\,\text{cm} \times 2\,\text{cm} + \tfrac{1}{2} \times 2\,\text{cm} \times 3\,\text{cm}$$
$$= 14\,\text{cm}^2 + 3\,\text{cm}^2$$
$$= 17\,\text{cm}^2$$

EXERCISE 5F

1 Calculate the area of each of these triangles.

a

b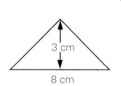

c

d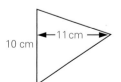

e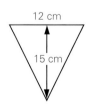

f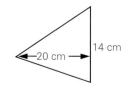

2 Copy and complete the following table for triangles **a** to **f**.

	Base	Vertical height	Area
a	8 cm	7 cm	
b		9 cm	36 cm²
c		5 cm	10 cm²
d	4 cm		6 cm²
e	6 cm		21 cm²
f	8 cm	11 cm	

3 Find the area of each of these shapes.

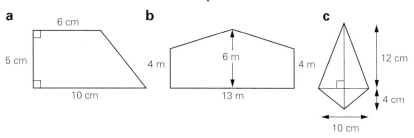

4 Find the area of each shaded shape.

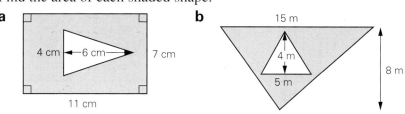

5 Write down the dimensions of two different-sized triangles that have the same area of 50 cm².

Areas of parallelograms

A parallelogram can be changed into a rectangle by moving a triangle.

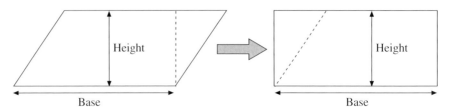

This shows that the area of the parallelogram is the area of a rectangle with the same base length and height.

Area of a parallelogram = Base length × Height

Example 7

Find the area of this parallelogram.

Area = 8 cm × 6 cm
= 48 cm²

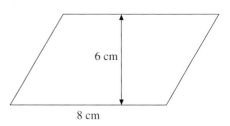

EXERCISE 5G

Calculate the area of each parallelogram below.

1

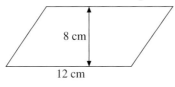

8 cm

12 cm

2

10 cm

7 cm

3

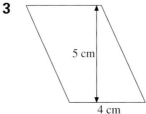

5 cm

4 cm

4

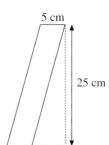

5 cm

25 cm

5

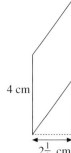

4 cm

$2\frac{1}{2}$ cm

6

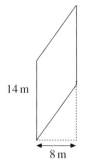

14 m

8 m

Investigation

A farmer's problem

A farmer uses 60 metres of fencing to build an enclosure against a wall.

Find the largest area that can be made for the enclosure.

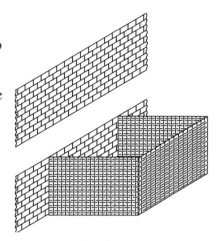

Pick's theorem

This quadrilateral has an area of $16\frac{1}{2}$ square units.

The perimeter of the quadrilateral passes through nine dots. Thirteen dots are contained within the perimeter of the quadrilateral.

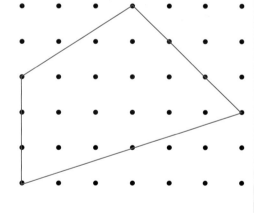

Investigate for quadrilaterals of different shapes and sizes. Then, from your findings, write down Pick's theorem.

Examination questions

1 A map of a treasure island is shown. Each square on the map represents $1\,km^2$. Estimate the area of the island.

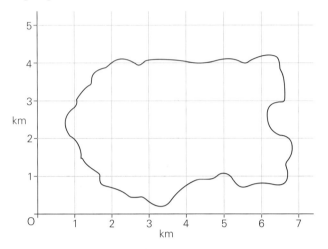

SEG, Question 3, Second Specimen Paper 11, 1998

2 a Work out the perimeter of the shape.

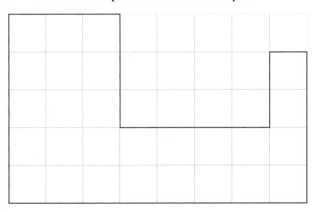

b Work out the area of the shape.

EDEXCEL, Question 7, Specimen Paper 2, 1998

3 Leah has six rods. Their lengths are

8 cm   6 cm   5 cm   3 cm   2 cm   2 cm

They can be joined together as shown below.

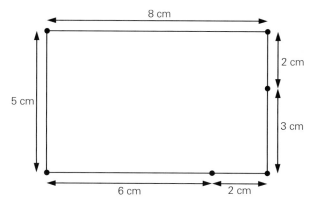

a What is the perimeter of this rectangle?

b A right-angled triangle can be formed using four of her rods. What is the area of this triangle?

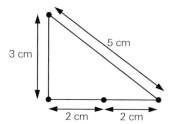

NEAB, Question 12, Paper 2F, June 1997

4

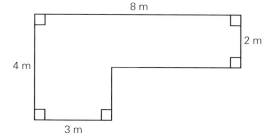

The diagram represents an L-shaped room all of whose corners are right angles.

a Work out the perimeter of the room.

b Work out the area of the room.

EDEXCEL, Question 7, Specimen Paper 2, 1998

5 Find the area of these shapes.
Give the units for your answers.

a

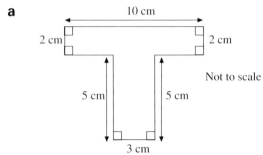

10 cm

2 cm

2 cm

Not to scale

5 cm

5 cm

3 cm

b

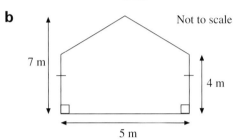

Not to scale

7 m

4 m

5 m

OCR, Question 12, Paper 1, June 1999

6 This is a scale drawing of an island off the coast of Scotland.
Each square on the map represents an area of 50 square kilometres. Estimate the area of the island.

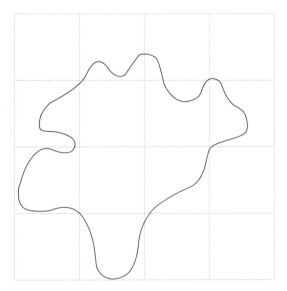

NEAB, Question 11, Paper 1F, June 1997

7 Find the area of this shape.

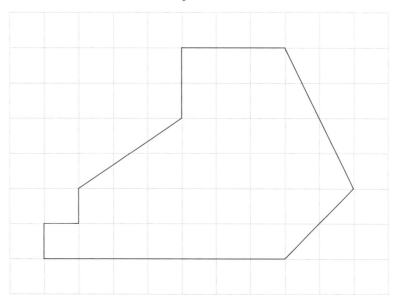

NEAB, Question 12, Specimen Paper 1F 1998

8 A letter V is cut from a rectangle, 9 cm by 8 cm, as shown.
The area of the triangle marked A is 12 cm².
What is the area of the V shape?

Not to scale

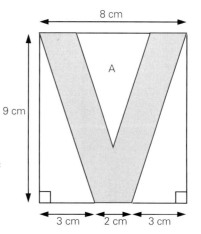

SEG, Question 17, Second Specimen Paper 11, 1998

9 James and Helen are fitting a new carpet in their living room to cover the whole floor. The diagram shows the measurements of the room.

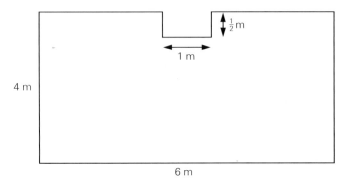

Not to scale

a Tape is put round the edge of the carpet. Calculate the total length of tape needed.

b What is the area of the floor?

NEAB, Question 4, Paper 1F, June 1994

10 Tiles measure 10 cm by 10 cm. Chantal is tiling her kitchen. She tiles the surface, shown below.

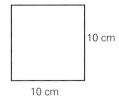

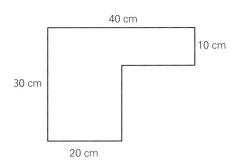

a How many tiles does she need for this surface?

b Calculate the area of this surface.

c Chantal wants to put a plastic strip around the perimeter of this surface. How many metres of plastic strip will she need?

SEG, Question 8, Specimen Paper 12, 1998

What you should know after you have worked through Chapter 5

✔ How to calculate the perimeter of a shape.
✔ How to calculate the area of an irregular shape by counting squares.
✔ How to calculate the areas of rectangles, triangles and parallelograms.
✔ How to calculate the areas of composite shapes made up of rectangles and/or triangles.

6 Some statistics

This chapter is going to ...

show you how to collect and organise data and how to represent data on various types of diagram.

What you should already know

✔   How to use a tally for recording data
✔   How to read information from charts and tables

Frequency tables

Statistics is concerned with the collection and organisation of data, the representation of data on diagrams, and the interpretation of data.

When data is being collected for simple surveys, it is usual to use a **data collection sheet**, also called a **tally chart**. For example, data collection sheets are used to gather information on how people travel to work, how students spend their free time, and the amount of time people spend watching TV.

The data is easily recorded using tally marks, as shown in Example 1. Counting up the tally marks in each row of the chart gives the **frequency** of each category. By listing the frequencies in a column on the right-hand side of the chart, you can make a **frequency table** (see Example 1). Frequency tables are an important part of making statistical calculations, as you will see on pages 205–6.

Three methods are used to collect data:
- **Taking a sample**   For example, to find out which 'soaps' students watch, you would need to take a sample from the whole school population by asking at random an equal number of boys and girls from each year group. A good sample size is usually more than 50.
- **Observation**   For example, to find how many vehicles a day use a certain road, you would need to count and record the number of vehicles passing a point at different times of the day.

- **Experiment** For example, to find out how often a six occurs when you throw a dice, you would need to throw the dice 50 times or more and record each score.

Example 1

Sandra carried out a survey to find how students travelled to school. Her frequency table looked like this:

Method of travel	Tally	Frequency
Walk	JHT JHT JHT JHT JHT III	28
Car	JHT JHT II	12
Bus	JHT JHT JHT JHT III	23
Bicycle	JHT	5
Taxi	II	2

By adding together all the frequencies, you can see that 70 students took part in the survey. The frequencies also show you that most students walked to school.

Example 2

Andrew wanted to know how many heads you are likely to get when you toss two coins. To do this, he carried out an experiment by tossing two coins 50 times. His frequency table looked like this:

Number of heads	Tally	Frequency
0	JHT JHT II	12
1	JHT JHT JHT JHT JHT II	27
2	JHT JHT I	11

From Andrew's table, you can see that a single head appeared the most number of times.

Grouped data

Many surveys produce a lot of data which covers a wide range of values. In these cases, it is sensible to put the data into groups before attempting to compile a frequency table. These groups of data are called **classes.**

Once the data has been grouped into classes, a **grouped frequency table** can be completed. The method is shown in Example 3.

Example 3

These marks are for 36 students in a Year 10 mathematics examination.
Construct a grouped frequency table.

31	49	52	79	40	29	66	71	73	19	51	47
81	67	40	52	20	84	65	73	60	54	60	59
25	89	21	91	84	77	18	37	55	41	72	38

The students' marks range from 18 to 91. So, divide the range of marks into the following classes of equal size:

1–20   21–40   41–60   61–80   81–100

Then draw the grid of the table shown below and put in the headings.

Next, list the classes, in order, in the column headed **Marks**.

Using tally marks, indicate each student's score against the class to which it belongs. For example, 81, 84, 89 and 91 belong to the class 81–100, giving five tally marks, as shown below.

Finally, count the tally marks for each class and enter the result in the column headed **Frequency**. The table is now complete.

Marks	Tally	Frequency
1–20	|||	3
21–40	ЖHT |||	8
41–60	ЖHT ЖHT |	11
61–80	ЖHT ||||	9
81–100	ЖHT	5

From the grouped frequency table, you can see that most students obtained a mark in the 41–60 interval.

EXERCISE 6A

1 For the following surveys, decide whether the data should be collected by:

i sampling   **ii** observation   **iii** experiment

a The number of people using a new superstore.

b How people will vote in a forthcoming election.

c The number of times a person scores double top in a game of darts.

d Where people go for their summer holidays.

e The frequency of a bus service on a particular route.

f The number of times a drawing pin lands point up.

2 Philip kept a record of the number of goals scored by Burnley Rangers in the last 20 matches. These are his results:

0 1 1 0 2 0 1 3 2 1 0 1
0 3 2 1 0 2 1 1

a Draw a frequency table for his data.

b Which score had the highest frequency?

c How many goals were scored in total for the 20 matches?

3 In a game of Hextulple, Mark used a six-sided dice. He decided to keep a record of his scores to see whether the dice was fair. His scores were:

2 4 2 6 1 5 4 3 3 2 3 6 2 1 3
5 4 3 4 2 1 6 5 1 6 4 1 2 3 4

a Draw a frequency table for his data.

b How many throws did Mark have during the game?

c Do you think the dice was a fair one? Explain why.

4 Monica was doing a geography project on the weather. As part of her work, she kept a record of the daily midday temperatures in June.

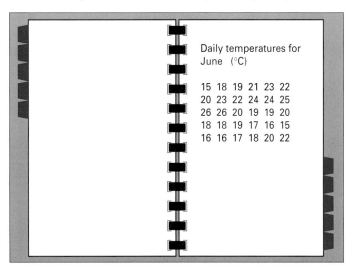

Daily temperatures for June (°C)

15 18 19 21 23 22
20 23 22 24 24 25
26 26 20 19 19 20
18 18 19 17 16 15
16 16 17 18 20 22

a Copy and complete the grouped frequency table for her data.

Temperature (°C)	Tally	Frequency
14–16		
17–19		
20–22		
23–25		
26–28		

b In which interval do the most temperatures lie?

c Describe what the weather was probably like throughout the month.

5 The data shows the heights, in centimetres, of a sample of 32 Year 10 students.

172	158	160	175	180	167	159	180
167	166	178	184	179	156	165	166
184	175	170	165	164	172	154	186
167	172	170	181	157	165	152	164

a Draw a grouped frequency table for the data using class intervals 151–155, 156–160, …

b In which interval do the most heights lie?

c Does this agree with the students in your class?

6 Conduct some surveys of your own choice and draw frequency tables for your data.

Activity

Double dice

This is an activity for two or more players. Each player needs two six-sided dice.

Each player throws his/her two dice together 100 times. For each throw, add together the two scores to get a total score.

What is the lowest total score anyone can get? What is the highest total score?

Everyone keeps a record of their 100 throws in a frequency table.

Compare your frequency table with someone else's, and comment on what you notice. For example: Which scores appear the most? What about 'doubles'?

How might this information be useful in games which use two dice?

Repeat the activity in one or more of the following ways:

- For each throw, multiply the score on one dice by the score on the other.
- Use two four-sided dice (tetrahedral dice), adding and/or multiplying the scores.
- Use two different sided dice, adding and/or multiplying the scores.
- Use three or more dice, adding and/or multiplying the scores.

Statistical diagrams

Data collected from a survey can be presented in pictorial or diagrammatic form to help people to understand it more quickly. You see plenty of examples of this in newspapers and magazines and on TV, where every type of visual aid is used to communicate statistical information.

Pictograms

A pictogram is a frequency table in which frequency is represented by a repeating symbol. The symbol itself usually represents a number of items, as Example 5 shows. But sometimes it is more sensible to let a symbol represent just a single unit, as in Example 4.

Example 4

The pictogram shows the number of telephone calls made by Mandy during a week.

From the pictogram, you can see that Mandy made a total of 27 telephone calls.

Sunday	☎ ☎ ☎ ☎ ☎
Monday	☎ ☎ ☎
Tuesday	☎ ☎
Wednesday	☎ ☎ ☎ ☎
Thursday	☎ ☎ ☎
Friday	☎ ☎ ☎ ☎
Saturday	☎ ☎ ☎ ☎ ☎ ☎

Key ☎ represents 1 call

Example 5

The pictogram shows the number of Year 10 students who were late for school during a week.

Monday	☗ ☗ ☗ ☗
Tuesday	☗ ☗
Wednesday	☗ ☗ ☗
Thursday	☗ ☗ ☗
Friday	☗ ☗ ☗ ☗ ☗

Key ☗ represents 5 pupils

Although pictograms can have great visual impact – particularly as used in advertising – and are easy to understand, they have a serious drawback. Apart from a half, fractions of a symbol cannot usually be drawn accurately and so frequencies often can be represented only approximately by symbols.

Example 5 highlights this difficulty. Precisely how many students were late on Monday and Thursday respectively? If we can assume that each 'limb' of the symbol represents one student and its 'body' also represents one student, then the answer is 19 students were late on Monday and 13 on Thursday.

EXERCISE 6B

1 The pictogram, taken from a Suntours brochure, shows the average daily hours of sunshine for five months in Tenerife.

May	✹✹✹✹✤
June	✹✹✹✹✹✤
July	✹✹✹✹✹✹
August	✹✹✹✹✹✤
September	✹✹✹✹✹

Key ✹ represents 2 hours

a Write down the average daily hours of sunshine for each month.

b Which month had the most sunshine?

c Give a reason why pictograms are useful in holiday brochures.

2 The pictogram shows the amount of money collected by six students after they had completed a sponsored walk for charity.

Anthony	£ £ £ £
Ben	£ £ £ £ £
Emma	£ £ £ £
Leanne	£ £ £
Reena	£ £ £ £ £
Simon	£ £ £ £ £ £

Key £ represents £5

a Who raised the most money?

b How much money was raised altogether by the six pupils?

c Robert also took part in the walk and raised £32. Why would it be difficult to include him on the pictogram?

3 The frequency table shows the number of cars parked in a supermarket's car park at various times of the day. Draw a pictogram to illustrate the data.

Time	9am	11am	1pm	3pm	5pm
Frequency	40	50	70	65	45

4 Mr Weeks, a milkman, kept a record of how many pints of milk he delivered to ten flats on a particular morning. Draw a pictogram for the data.

Flat 1	Flat 2	Flat 3	Flat 4	Flat 5	Flat 6	Flat 7	Flat 8	Flat 9	Flat 10
2	3	1	2	4	3	2	1	5	1

5 Draw pictograms of your own to show the following data.
    a The number of hours you watched TV for every evening last week.
    b The magazines which students in your class read.
    c The favourite colour of students in your class.
    d People's hobbies.

Bar charts

A bar chart consists of a series of bars or blocks of the **same width,** drawn either vertically or horizontally from an axis.

The heights or lengths of the bars **always represent frequencies.**

Sometimes, the bars are separated by narrow gaps of equal width, which make the chart easier to read.

Lines can be used instead of bars, as on page 115.

Example 6

The grouped frequency table below shows the marks of 24 students after a test. Draw a bar chart for the data.

Marks	1–10	11–20	21–30	31–40	41–50
Frequency	2	3	5	8	6

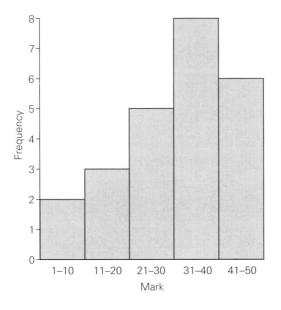

Note
- Both axes are labelled.
- The class intervals are put under the middle of each bar.

By using a **dual bar chart,** it is easy to compare two sets of related data, as Example 7 shows.

Example 7

This dual bar chart shows the average daily maximum temperature for England and Turkey over a five-month period.

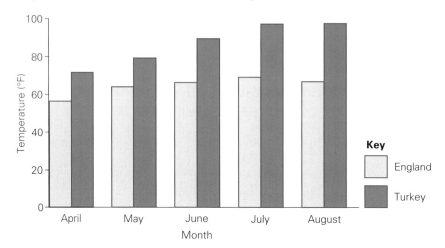

Note You must always include a **key** to identify the two different sets of data.

EXERCISE 6C

1 For her survey on fitness, Maureen asked a sample of people, as they left a sports centre, which activity they had taken part in. She then drew a bar chart to show her data.

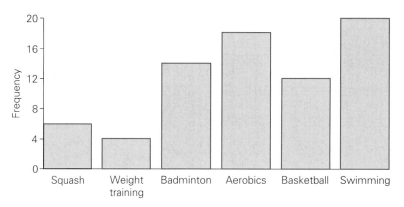

a Which was the most popular activity?

b How many people took part in Maureen's survey?

c Give a probable reason why fewer people took part in weight training.

d Is a sports centre a good place in which to do a survey on fitness? Explain why.

2 The frequency table below shows the levels achieved by 100 Year 9 students in their KS 3 mathematics tests.

Level	3	4	5	6	7	8
Frequency	12	22	24	25	15	2

   a Draw a suitable bar chart to illustrate the data.

   b What fraction of the students achieved Level 6 or Level 7?

   c State an advantage of drawing a bar chart rather than a pictogram for this data.

3 This table shows the number of points Richard and Derek were each awarded in eight rounds of a general knowledge quiz.

Round	1	2	3	4	5	6	7	8
Richard	7	8	7	6	8	6	9	4
Derek	6	7	6	9	6	8	5	6

   a Draw a dual bar chart to illustrate the data.

   b Comment on how well each of them did in the quiz.

4 Kay did a survey on the time it took students in her form to get to school on a particular morning. She wrote down their times to the nearest minute.

     15   23   36   45   8   20   34   15   27   49

     10   60   5   48   30   18   21   2   12   56

     49   33   17   44   50   35   46   24   11   34

   a Draw a grouped frequency table for Kay's data, using class intervals 1–10, 11–20, …

   b Draw a bar chart to illustrate the data.

   c Comment on how far from school the students live.

5 This table shows the number of accidents at a dangerous crossroads over a six-year period.

Year	1990	1991	1992	1993	1994	1995
No. of accidents	6	8	7	9	6	4

   a Draw a pictogram for the data.

   b Draw a bar chart for the data.

   c Which diagram would you use if you were going to write to your local council to suggest that traffic lights should be installed at the crossroads? Explain why.

6 Conduct a survey to find the colour of cars that pass your school or your home.

    a Draw pictograms and bar charts to illustrate your data.

    b Compare your results with someone else's in your class and comment on anything you find about the colour of cars in your area.

7 Choose two daily newspapers (for example, *Sun* and *The Times*), and take a fairly long article from each paper. Count the number of words in the first 50 sentences of each article.

    a For each article, draw a grouped frequency table for the number of words in each of the first 50 sentences.

    b Draw a dual bar chart for your data.

    c Comment on your results.

Line graphs

Line graphs are usually used in statistics to show how data changes over a period of time. One such use is to indicate **trends**: for example, whether the Earth's temperature is increasing as the concentration of carbon dioxide builds up in the atmosphere, or whether a firm's profit margin is falling year on year.

Line graphs are best drawn on graph paper.

Example 8

This line graph shows the outside temperature at a weather station, taken at hourly intervals.

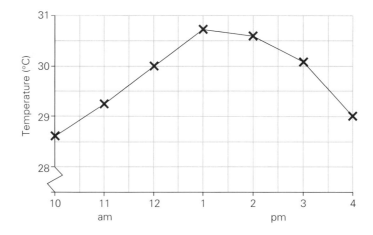

Notice that the temperature axis starts at 28 °C rather than 0 °C. The points are joined with lines so that the intermediate temperatures can be estimated for other times of the day. This allows the use of a scale which makes it easy to plot the points and then to read the graph.

Example 9

This line graph shows the profit made each year by a company over a six-year period.

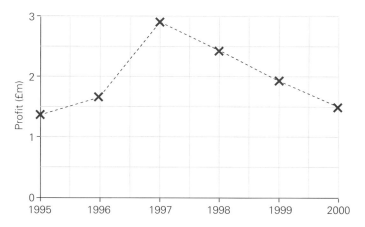

For this graph, the values between the plotted points have no meaning because the profit of the company would have been calculated at the end of every year. In cases like this, the lines are often dashed. Although the trend appears to be that profits have fallen after 1997, it would not have been sensible to predict what would have happened after 2000.

EXERCISE 6D

1 This line graph shows the value of Spevadon shares on seven consecutive trading days.

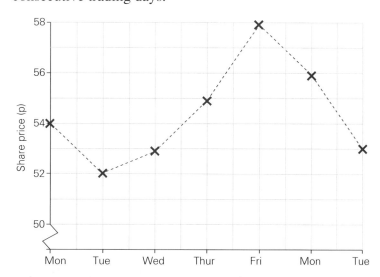

a On which day did the share price have its lowest value and what was that value?

    b   By how much did the share price rise from Wednesday to Thursday?

    c   Which day had the greatest rise in the share price from the previous day?

    d   Mr Hardy sold 500 shares on Friday. How much profit did he make if he originally bought the shares at 40p each?

2   The table shows the population of a town, rounded to the nearest thousand, after each census.

Year	1931	1941	1951	1961	1971	1981	1991
Population (1000s)	12	14	15	18	21	25	23

    a   Draw a line graph for the data.

    b   From your graph estimate the population in 1956.

    c   Between which two consecutive censuses did the population increase the most?

    d   Can you predict the population for 2001? Give a reason for your answer.

3   The table shows the estimated number of tourists world wide.

Year	1960	1965	1970	1975	1980	1985	1990	1995
No. of tourists (millions)	60	100	150	220	280	290	320	340

    a   Draw a line graph for the data.

    b   From your graph estimate the number of tourists in 1972.

    c   Between which two consecutive years did world tourism increase the most?

    d   Explain the trend in world tourism. What reasons can you give to explain this trend?

4   The table shows the maximum and minimum daily temperatures for London over a week.

Day	Sunday	Monday	Tuesday	Wednesday	Thursday	Friday	Saturday
Maximum (°C)	12	14	16	15	16	14	10
Minimum (°C)	4	5	7	8	7	4	3

    a   Draw line graphs on the **same axes** to show the maximum and minimum temperatures.

    b   Find the smallest and greatest difference between the maximum and minimum temperatures.

Activity

Diagrams from the press

This is an activity for a group of two or more people. You will need a large selection of recent newspapers and magazines.

In a group, look through the newspapers and magazines.

Cut out any statistical diagrams and stick them on large sheets of coloured paper. Underneath each diagram, explain what the diagram shows and how useful the diagram is in showing that information.

If any of the diagrams appear to be misleading, explain why.

You now have a lot of up-to-date statistics to display in your classroom.

Investigation

Countdown

Choose a novel by a popular author.

Pick a page at random and count each of the five vowels and each of the consonants.

List separately, in order, the two sets of totals, putting the commonest vowel first and the commonest consonant first.

Compare these with books in other languages.

Databases

If you have access to a computer database, get your class to enter data for different fields. For example, name, form, height, weight, age, shoe size, arm span, family size, number of pets, ….

Find out how to put the fields in alphabetical or numerical order, how to use subsets and how to draw bar charts and line graphs.

Print out copies of any diagrams so that you can display your results. You may even be able to use colour.

Examination questions

1 Zara measured the heights of the students in her class. She measured the heights in centimetres. Here are her results.

155 147 158 172 152 159 165 154 163 171
166 144 172 168 159 162 182 164 167 173
164 168 154 163 173 149 157 153 162 168

a What was the height of the shortest student in the class?

b Copy and complete this frequency table for these measurements.

Height (centimetres)	Tally	Frequency
140 → 149		
150 → 159		
160 → 169		
170 → 179		
180 → 189		

c **i** How many students were in the class?

   ii How many students were 170 cm or taller?

MEG(SMP), Question 8, Specimen Paper 1F, 1998

2 **'What is your favourite group?'**

The bar chart shows what some people said.

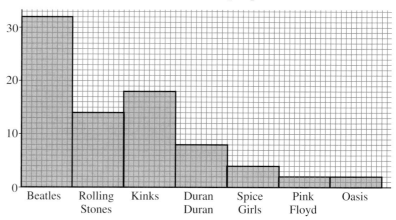

a Which group got 14 votes?

b How many people voted altogether?

c The information was collected between 10 o'clock and 11 o'clock on a Wednesday morning in Chesterfield market square. Give reasons why this was not a good way to collect the information?

OCR, Question 5, Paper 1, June 2000

3 The table below shows the number of records sold by a small record shop in Megtown.

MEGTOWN RECORD SHOP	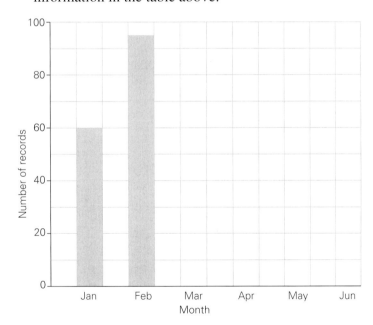 represents 20 records	
January	🔘 🔘 🔘	60
February	🔘 🔘 🔘 🔘 ◖	95
March	🔘 🔘 🔘 🔘	
April	🔘 🔘 ◖	
May		100
June		45

a How many records were sold in
  i March **ii** April?

b Draw the symbols that should be entered into the table to represent
  i May **ii** June

c Copy and complete the bar chart below to illustrate the information in the table above.

MEG, Question 12, Specimen Paper 2F, 1998

4 A class of 30 students were asked to choose their favourite children's television programme. The results are given in the table below.

Television programme	Tally	Number of students
Grange Hill	ЖЖ II	7
Blue Peter	ЖЖ	5
Newsround	ЖЖ I	6
Jackanory		0
Disney Club	ЖЖ I	6
Live and Kicking	II	2
Children's Hospital	IIII	4
	Total	**30**

a Draw a bar chart to show this information.

b Which programme was not chosen by anyone?

NEAB, Question 2, Specimen Paper 2F, 1998

5 Thirty students took a mathematics test. Here are their marks.

23 32 40 51 60 70 32 18 26 42
27 34 39 48 47 62 35 18 19 17
43 46 47 36 32 53 29 33 28 26

a Copy and complete the frequency table.

Mark	Tally	Frequency
11–20		
21–30		
31–40		
41–50		
51–60		
61–70		

b Draw a bar chart for the frequency table above.

The same students took a second mathematics test. A frequency table was completed for their marks in the second test and a bar chart was drawn. The table and the bar chart for the second test are shown on the next page.

Mark	Frequency
11–20	2
21–30	3
31–40	8
41–50	11
51–60	6
61–70	0

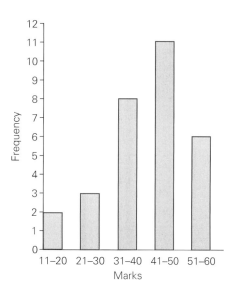

c **i** Did the students find the first or the second test the easier?

   ii Write down a reason for your answer to part **i**.

EDEXCEL, Question 11, Specimen Paper 2F, 1998

6 The chart below shows the temperature at noon on a certain day in 11 countries.

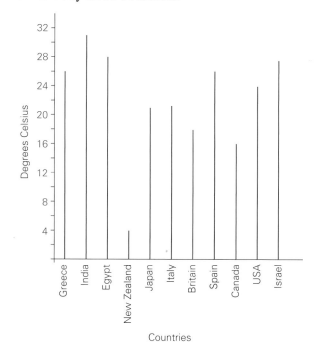

a   Which country was the hottest?

b   Which country was the coldest?

c   Which countries had a temperature of less than 20 degrees Celsius?

d   Which countries had the same temperature?

NEAB, Question 1, Specimen Paper 2F, 1998

7   The bar chart shows which day of the week shoppers went to a supermarket in 1998 and 2000.

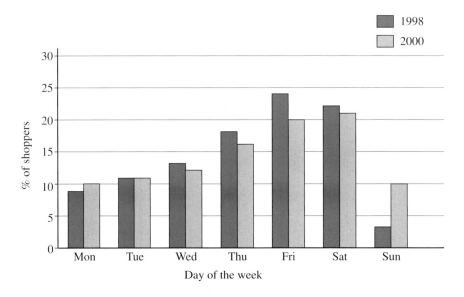

a   Which day of the week was the most popular day for shopping in 1998?

b   Did the shoppers choose different days to shop in 1998 compared with 2000?

c   'In 2000, about half the shoppers did their shopping at the end of the week (Friday, Saturday and Sunday).'
Is this statement true or false?
Show all your working.

NEAB, Question 2, Paper 1, June 1998

8 The graph shows the percentage of homes in the United Kingdom with a computer.

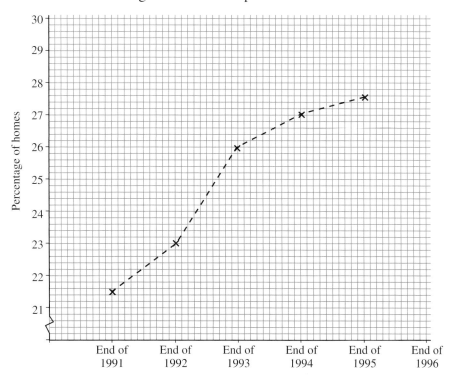

a What percentage of homes had a computer by the end of 1995?

b 28.9% of homes had a computer by the end of 1996. Mark this point of the graph.

c The graph shows that the percentage of homes with a computer increased every year.
Which year had the greatest increase?
Explain how the graph tells you this.

NEAB, Question 10, Paper 1, June 2000

What you should know after you have worked through Chapter 6

✔ **How to draw frequency tables for grouped and ungrouped data.**

✔ **How to draw and interpret pictograms, bar charts and line graphs.**

PUZZLE PAGE

Map colouring

What is the least number of colours needed to colour this map so that areas of the same colour do not touch?

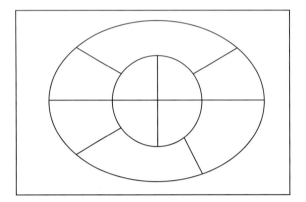

Missing £1

A father wants to share £17 between his three children so that one has $\frac{1}{2}$, one has $\frac{1}{3}$ and the other has $\frac{1}{9}$, but decides that this is not possible.

The youngest son, who is good at maths, had a clever idea. He borrowed £1 and added it to the £17 to get £18. He then split up the £18 as follows:

$\frac{1}{2}$ of £18 = £9
$\frac{1}{3}$ of £18 = £6
$\frac{1}{9}$ of £18 = £2

which add up to £17.

So, the son was able to give back the £1 he had borrowed. Can you explain this?

Going round in circles

Arrange all the other numbers from 1 to 9 so that each line of three numbers adds up to the same number.

Does the puzzle work if you put a different number in the middle circle?

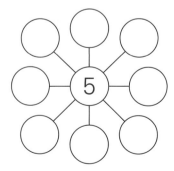

7 Some algebra

This chapter is going to ...

introduce you to the use of letters to represent numbers, showing you how to form simple algebraic expressions, how to simplify such expressions by collecting like terms, and how to factorise expressions. It will also show you how to express simple rules in algebraic form, and how to substitute numbers into expressions and formulae.

What you should already know

✔ The BODMAS rule, which gives the order in which you must do the operations of arithmetic when they occur together

The language of algebra

Algebra is based on the idea that if something works with numbers, it will work with letters. The main difference is that when you work with only numbers, you get a number as the answer. When you work with letters, you get an **expression** as the answer.

Algebra follows the same rules as arithmetic, and uses the same symbols ($+$, $-$, $\times$ and $\div$). Here are examples of six important algebraic rules:

- We write 4 more than x as $4 + x$ or $x + 4$.
- We write 6 less than p as $p - 6$.
- We write 4 times y as $4 \times y$ or $y \times 4$ or $4y$. The last one of these is the neatest way to write it.
- We write b divided by 2 as $b \div 2$ or $\dfrac{b}{2}$.
- When a number and a letter or a letter and a letter appear together, there is a hidden times sign between them. So,

  $7x$ means $7 \times x$ and ab means $a \times b$
- We always write $1 \times x$ as x.
- We write t times t as $t \times t$ or t^2.

Example 1

What is the area of each of these rectangles?
a 4 cm by 6 cm   **b** 4 cm by w cm   **c** l cm by w cm

You will already have met the rule for working out the area of a rectangle:
Area = Length × Width

So, the area of rectangle **a** is 4 cm × 6 cm = 24 cm^2

The area of rectangle **b** is 4 cm × w cm = $4w$ cm^2

And the area of rectangle **c** is l cm × w cm = lw cm^2

Now, if we let A represent the area of rectangle **c**, we get
$A = lw$

This is an example of a rule expressed algebraically.

Example 2

What is the perimeter of each of these rectangles?
a 6 cm by 4 cm   **b** 4 cm by w cm   **c** l cm by w cm

Again, you will already have met the rule for working out the perimeter of a rectangle:
Perimeter = Twice the longer side + Twice the shorter side

So, the perimeter of rectangle **a** is $2 \times 6 + 2 \times 4 = 20$ cm

The perimeter of rectangle **b** is $2 \times 4 + 2 \times w = 8 + 2w$ cm

And the perimeter of rectangle **c** is $2 \times l + 2 \times w = 2l + 2w$ cm

Now, if we let P represent the perimeter of rectangle **c**, we get
$P = 2l + 2w$

which is another example of a rule expressed algebraically.

Expressions like $A = lw$ and $P = 2l + 2w$ are called **formulae** (the plural of formula).

As these two examples show, a formula states the connection between two or more quantities, each of which is represented by a different letter.

In a formula, the letters are replaced by numbers when a calculation has to be made. This is called **substitution** and is explained on page 129.

EXERCISE 7A

1 Write down the algebraic expression that says
a 2 more than x **b** 6 less than x
c k more than x **d** t less than x
e x added to 3   **f** d added to m
g y taken away from b **h** p added to t added to w
i 8 multiplied by x **j** h multiplied by j
k x divided by 4   **l** 2 divided by x
m y divided by t **n** w multiplied by t
o a multiplied by a **p** g multiplied by itself

2 Here are four squares.

i   **ii**   **iii**   **iv**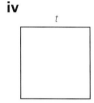

a Work out the area and perimeter of each square.
b Copy and complete these rules:
   i The perimeter, P, of a square of side s centimetres is $P = \ldots\ldots$
   ii The area, A, of a square of side s centimetres is $A = \ldots\ldots$

3 Asha, Bernice and Charu are three sisters. Bernice is x years old. Asha is three years older than Bernice. Charu is four years younger than Bernice.
a How old is Asha?
b How old is Charu?

4 An approximation method of converting from degrees Celsius to degrees Fahrenheit is given by this rule:

Multiply by 2 and add 30

Using C to stand for degrees Celsius and F to stand for degrees Fahrenheit, complete this formula:
   $F = \ldots\ldots$

5 Cows have four legs. Which of these rules connects the number of legs (L) and the number of cows (C)?
a $C = 4L$ **b** $L = C + 4$ **c** $L = 4C$ **d** $L + C = 4$

6 There are 3 feet in a yard. The rule $F = 3Y$ connects the number of feet (F) and the number of yards (Y). Write down rules, using the letters shown, to connect

   a the number of centimetres (C) in metres (M)

   b the number of inches (N) in feet (F)

   c the number of wheels (W) on cars (C)

   d the number of heads (H) on people (P).

7 **a** Anne has three bags of marbles. Each bag contains n marbles. How many marbles does she have altogether?

   b Beryl gives her another three marbles. How many does she have now?

   c Anne puts one of her new marbles in each bag? How many marbles are now in each bag?

   d Anne takes two marbles out of each bag. How many marbles are now in each bag?

8 Simon holds n cubes.

- Rob has twice as many as Simon.
- Tom has 2 more than Simon.
- Vic has 3 less than Simon.
- Wes has 3 more than Rob.

How many cubes does each person have?

9 **a** John has been drawing squares and writing down the area and the perimeter of each. He has drawn three squares. Finish off his work by writing down the missing areas and perimeters.

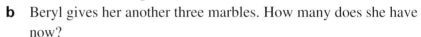

   b Write down the area and the perimeter of this partly covered square.

10 **a** I go shopping with £10 and spend £6. How much do I have left?

  b I go shopping with £10 and spend £x. How much do I have left?

  c I go shopping with £y and spend £x. How much do I have left?

  d I go shopping with £3x and spend £x. How much do I have left?

11 Give the total cost of

  a 5 pens at 15p each   **b** x pens at 15p each

  c 4 pens at Ap each   **d** y pens at Ap each

12 A boy went shopping with £A. He spent £B. How much has he got left?

13 Five ties cost £A. What is the cost of one tie?

14 My dad is 72 and I am T years old. How old will we each be in x years time?

15 I am twice as old as my son. I am T years old.

  a How old is my son?

  b How old will my son be in 4 years time?

  c How old was I x years ago?

16 What is the total perimeter of each of these figures?

a

Square

b

Equilateral triangle

c

Regular hexagon

17 Write down the number of marbles each pupil ends up with.

Pupil	Action	Marbles
Andrea	Start with 3 bags each containing n marbles and take 1 marble from each bag	
Bert	Start with 3 bags each containing n marbles and take 1 marble from one bag	
Colin	Start with 3 bags each containing n marbles and take 2 marbles from each bag	
Davina	Start with 3 bags each containing n marbles and take n marbles from each bag	
Ethel	Start with 3 bags each containing n marbles and take n marbles from one bag	
Florinda	Start with 3 bags each containing n marbles and take m marbles from each bag	

Simplifying expressions

Simplifying an algebraic expression means making it neater and, usually, shorter by combining its terms where possible.

This generally involves two steps:
- Collect **like terms** into groups.
- Then combine the like terms in each group.

Like terms are those which are multiples of the same letter or of the same combination of letters. For example, a, $3a$, $9a$, $\frac{1}{4}a$ and $-5a$ are all like terms. So are $2xy$, $7xy$ and $-5xy$, and so are $6x^2$, x^2 and $-3x^2$.

Only like terms can be added or subtracted to simplify an expression. For example,

$a + 3a + 9a - 5a$ simplifies to $8a$

$2xy + 7xy - 5xy$ simplifies to $4xy$

and

$6x^2 + x^2 - 3x^2$ simplifies to $4x^2$

But an expression such as $4p + 8t + 5x - 9$ cannot be made into anything simpler, because $4p$, $8t$, $5x$ and -9 are **unlike terms**, which **cannot** be combined.

Example 3

Simplify $7x^2 + 3y - 6z + 2x^2 + 3z - y + w + 9$

Write out the expression $7x^2 + 3y - 6z + 2x^2 + 3z - y + w + 9$

Then collect like terms $\boxed{7x^2 + 2x^2}$ $\boxed{+3y - y}$ $\boxed{-6z + 3z}$ $+ w + 9$

Then combine them $9x^2 \quad + \quad 2y \quad - \quad 3z \quad + w + 9$

So, the expression in its simplest form is

$9x^2 + 2y - 3z + w + 9$

Brackets

A number or letter next to a bracket means that everything in the bracket can be multiplied by that number or letter.

This operation is called **multiplying out** or **expanding** a bracket.

Example 4

$3(2t - 5) = 3 \times 2t - 3 \times 5$

$3(2t - 5) = 6t - 15$

Note that the bracket is removed.

Example 5

Expand the bracket $x(x + 2)$.

$$x(x + 2) = x \times x + x \times 2 = x^2 + 2x$$

Simple factorisation

Factorisation is the reverse process of expanding a bracket. It puts an expression back into the bracket it came from. When factorising, we have to look for the common factors in every term of the expression.

For example, if we expand $3(x + 2)$, we get $3x + 6$. So, if we factorise $3x + 6$, we go back to $3(x + 2)$.

Follow through the examples below to see how this works.

$$10t + 15 = 5(2t + 3)$$
$$4y + 2 = 2(2y + 1)$$
$$x^2 + 3x = x(x + 3)$$

EXERCISE 7B

1 Joseph is given £t, John has £3 more than Joseph, Joy has £$2t$.
  a How much more has Joy than Joseph?
  b How much have all three of them got?

2 Write down the perimeter of each of these shapes.

a

b

c
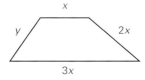

3 Write each of these expressions in a shorter form.
  a $a + a + a + a + a$
  b $b + b + b + b$
  c $c + c + c + c + c + c$
  d $2d + 3d$
  e $4e + 5e$
  f $f + 2f + 3f$
  g $g + g + g + g - g$
  h $h + h + h - h - h$
  i $3i + 2i - i$
  j $5j + j - 2j$
  k $4k + 5k - 2k$
  l $3l - 2l + 4l$
  m $4m - 5m + 3m$
  n $n + 5n - 6n$
  o $20x + 14x$
  p $16p + 4p - 2p$

q $9q - 3q - 3q$ **r** $3r - 3r$

s $6s + s + s - 5s$ **t** $5t + 5t + 5t$

u $5u - 4u + u + u$ **v** $2v - 3v$

w $2w + 4w - 7w$ **x** $5x^2 + 6x^2 - 7x^2 + 2x^2$

y $8y^2 + 5y^2 - 7y^2 - y^2$ **z** $2z^2 - 2z^2 + 3z^2 - 3z^2$

4 Simplify each of the following expressions.

   a $3x + 4x$ **b** $4y + 2y$ **c** $5t - 2t$

   d $3m - m$ **e** $k + 7k$ **f** $3x - 5x$

   g $t - 4t$ **h** $-2x - 3x$ **i** $-k - 4k$

   j $-3x + 7x$ **k** $2a + a + 6a$ **l** $4t + 2t - t$

   m $m^2 + 2m^2 - m^2$ **n** $2y^2 + 3y^2 - 5y^2$ **o** $-f^2 + 4f^2 - 2f^2$

5 Simplify each of the following expressions.

   a $4y + 2x + 5y + 3x$ **b** $3m + p - m + 4p$

   c $5x + 8 + 2x - 3$ **d** $7 - 2x - 1 + 7x$

   e $4p + 2t + p - 2t$ **f** $8 + x + 4x - 2$

   g $5p - 4 - p - 2$ **h** $x + 4y + 3x + y + 2x - 3y$

   i $3 + 2t + p - t + 2 + 4p$ **j** $5w - 2k - 2w - 3k + 5w$

   k $7 + 4x - 8 - 6x + 4$ **l** $5x + 2y + 5 - y - 5x - y$

   m $a + b + c + d - a - b - d$ **n** $9k - y - 5y - k + 10$

6 Write each of these in a shorter form. (Be careful – three of them will not simplify.)

   a $a + b + a + b + a$ **b** $b + c + b + c + c$

   c $c + d + d + d + c$ **d** $2d + 2e + 3d$

   e $4e + 5f + 2f + e$ **f** $f + 3g + 4h$

   g $g + h + g + h - g$ **h** $h + j + h - j + j - h$

   i $3i + 2k - i + k$ **j** $5j + 3k - 2j + 4k$

   k $4k + 5p - 2k + 4p$ **l** $3k + 2m + 5p$

   m $4m - 5n + 3m - 2n$ **n** $n + 3p - 6p + 5n$

   o $20x + 14y$ **p** $19p + 4q - 2p + 5q$

   q $9q - 3r - 3r + 7q$ **r** $3r - 3s + 3s - 3r$

   s $6s + t + s - 5t$ **t** $5t + 5s + 5t$

   u $5u - 4v + u + v$ **v** $2v - 5w + 5w$

   w $2w + 4y - 7y$ **x** $5x^2 + 6x^2 - 7y + 2y$

   y $8y^2 + 5z - 7z - 9y^2$ **z** $2z^2 - 2x^2 + 3x^2 - 3z^2$

7 Find the perimeter of each of these shapes in its simplest form.

a

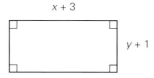

b

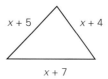

c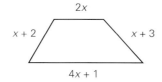

8 Multiply out each of the following brackets.

a	$2(f + 3)$	**b**	$3(k - 4)$	**c**	$4(t + 1)$
d	$3(2d + 3)$	**e**	$4(3t - 2)$	**f**	$2(5m + 3)$
g	$4(5 + 2w)$	**h**	$2(3 - 4x)$	**i**	$3(4 + 5p)$
j	$5(2t + 3w)$	**k**	$4(3m - 2d)$	**l**	$3(2x + 5y)$
m	$2(4f + 3)$	**n**	$5(8 - 2t)$	**o**	$3(4g + 2t)$
p	$x(x + 5)$	**q**	$t(t + 8)$	**r**	$s(4 - s)$

9 Factorise each of these.

a	$3x + 6$	**b**	$5x + 15$	**c**	$6x + 9$
d	$4x - 6$	**e**	$16y - 12$	**f**	$25t - 5$
g	$8z - 20$	**h**	$15 + 10t$	**i**	$21 - 28m$
j	$x^2 + 8x$	**k**	$t^2 + 5t$	**l**	$y^2 - 7y$

Algebra dominoes

This is an activity for two people.

You need some card to make a set of fraction dominoes like those below.

$4 \times n$	t^2	$2b$	$2 - t$	$\dfrac{12n}{2}$	$0.5n$	$5w$	$b + b$

$3t - 2$	$3 \times 2y$	$5 + y$	$n + 2 + n + 3$	$\dfrac{4t + 2n}{2}$	$t \times t$	$5b - 3b$	$6n$

$6y$	$t - 2$	$2a + 2$	$2t + 2 - 3t$	$y + 5$	$7n - n$	$3n + 3n$	$4t - 2 - t$

b^2	$\dfrac{1}{2}n$	$t + 3 - 2$	$2n - 1$	$t + 5$	$b \times 2$	$10w \div 2$	$n + n + n + n$

$2t + n$	$4n$	$n + 2 + n - 3$	$2n + 5$	$\dfrac{n}{2}$	$2(a + 1)$	$n \div 2$	$n \times 4$

Turn the dominoes over and shuffle them.

Deal five dominoes to each player.

One player starts by putting down a domino.

If the other player has a domino that matches either end of the domino on the table, he/she puts down that domino. If the second player cannot go, he/she picks up a domino from the spares.

The first player follows and so on, in turn.

The winner is the first player with no dominoes in his/her hand.

Make up your own set of dominoes.

Substitution

One of the most important features of algebra is the use of expressions and formulae, and the substitution of real numbers into them.

The value of an expression, such as $3x + 2$, will change with the different values of x substituted into it. For example, the expression $3x + 2$ has the value

    5 when $x = 1$ 14 when $x = 4$

and so on. A formula, too, is used to express the value of one variable as the others in the formula change. For example, the formula for the area of a triangle is

$$A = \frac{b \times h}{2}$$

When $b = 4$ and $h = 8$,

$$A = \frac{4 \times 8}{2} = 16$$

Example 6

The formula for the area of a trapezium is

$$A = \frac{(a + b)h}{2}$$

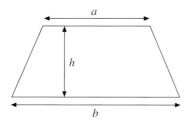

Find the area of the trapezium when $a = 5$, $b = 9$ and $h = 3$.

$$A = \frac{(5 + 9) \times 3}{2} = \frac{14 \times 3}{2} = 21$$

EXERCISE 7C

WHOLE EXERCISE

1 Find the value of $3x + 2$ when
  i $x = 2$ **ii** $x = 5$ **iii** $x = 10$

2 Find the value of $4k - 1$ when
  i $k = 1$ **ii** $k = 3$ **iii** $k = 11$

3 Find the value of 5 + 2t when

   i $t = 2$ **ii** $t = 5$ **iii** $t = 12$

4 Evaluate $15 - 2f$ when **i** $f = 3$ **ii** $f = 5$ **iii** $f = 8$

5 Evaluate $5m + 3$ when **i** $m = 2$ **ii** $m = 6$ **iii** $m = 15$

6 Evaluate $3d - 2$ when **i** $d = 4$ **ii** $d = 5$ **iii** $d = 20$

7 Find the value of $\dfrac{8 \times 4h}{5}$ when

   i $h = 5$ **ii** $h = 10$ **iii** $h = 35$

8 Find the value of $\dfrac{25 - 3p}{2}$ when

   i $p = 4$ **ii** $p = 8$ **iii** $p = 10$

9 Evaluate $\dfrac{x}{3}$ when **i** $x = 6$ **ii** $x = 24$ **iii** $x = -30$

10 Evaluate $\dfrac{A}{4}$ when **i** $A = 12$ **ii** $A = 10$ **iii** $A = -20$

11 Find the value of $\dfrac{12}{y}$ when **i** $y = 2$ **ii** $y = 4$ **iii** $y = 6$

12 Find the value of $\dfrac{24}{x}$ when **i** $x = 2$ **ii** $x = 3$ **iii** $x = 16$

Using your calculator

You could try working out a solution on your calculator, remembering to put in the brackets as required.

Take the expression

$$t = 5\left(\frac{w + 2d}{4}\right)$$

To find t when, for example, $w = 6$ and $d = 3$, you put this into your calculator as

You should get the answer 15.

When you have to work out the bottom part of a fraction, you will also need to use brackets to do this part separately. For example, take

$$k = \frac{8}{b - d}$$

To evaluate k when $b = 7$ and $d = 3$, you put this into your calculator as

8 ÷ (7 − 3) =

You should get the answer 2.

Notice that the expression does **not** include brackets, but you need to use them on your calculator.

EXERCISE 7D

1 Where $A = 4t + h$, find A when
   a $t = 2$ and $h = 3$ **b** $t = 3$ and $h = 5$ **c** $t = 1$ and $h = 9$

2 Where $P = 5w - 4y$, find P when
   a $w = 3$ and $y = 2$ **b** $w = 6$ and $y = 4$ **c** $w = 2$ and $y = 3$

3 Where $A = b^2 + c$, find A when
   a $b = 2$ and $c = 3$ **b** $b = 5$ and $c = 7$ **c** $b = 1$ and $c = -4$

4 Where $L = f^2 - g^2$, find L when
   a $f = 6$ and $g = 3$ **b** $f = 3$ and $g = 2$ **c** $f = 5$ and $g = 5$

5 Where $T = P - n^2$, find T when
   a $P = 100$ and $n = 5$ **b** $P = 17$ and $n = 3$
   c $P = 10$ and $n = 4$

6 Where $A = 180(n - 2)$, find A when
   a $n = 7$ **b** $n = 3$ **c** $n = 2$

7 Where $t = 10 - \sqrt{P}$, find t when
   a $P = 25$ **b** $P = 4$ **c** $P = 81$

8 Where $W = v + \dfrac{m}{5}$, find W when
   a $v = 3$ and $m = 7$ **b** $v = 2$ and $m = 3$ **c** $v = -3$ and $m = 8$

Investigation

Picture Frames

You need some squared paper.

Three pupils are doing coursework on picture frames.

They have to find a rule for the number of 1-cm cubes needed to put a 1-cm wide frame around a square picture whose side is n cm.

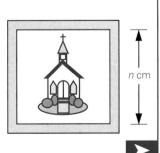

For each pupil:

■ First draw the frames shown and then draw the next two frames, following the same method of dividing up the frame.
■ Write the number of cubes as a sum, in the same way that each pupil has.
■ Make sure that you understand why each pupil has given the rule in that way.

These are Fred's first four frames:

4 × 1 + 4   4 × 2 + 4   4 × 3 + 4   4 × 4 + 4

Fred says the rule is
Around a square of side n cm there are **4 × n + 4** cubes

These are Sarah's first four frames:

4 × (1 + 1)   4 × (2 + 1)   4 × (3 + 1)   4 × (4 + 1)

Sarah says the rule is
Around a square of side n cm there are **4 × (n + 1)** cubes

These are Derek's first four frames:

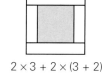
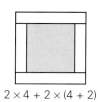

2 × 1 + 2 × (1 + 2)   2 × 2 + 2 × (2 + 2)   2 × 3 + 2 × (3 + 2)   2 × 4 + 2 × (4 + 2)

What is Derek's rule?
Around a square of side n cm there are ......

Show that they are all the same rule.

Can you think of other ways of dividing up the frame?

Examination questions

1

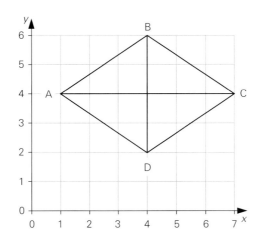

A rhombus ABCD is drawn on the grid shown above.

A formula to find the area of a rhombus is

$$A = pq \div 2$$

where p and q are the lengths of the diagonals.

Use this formula to calculate the area of the rhombus shown here.

NEAB, Question 10, Paper 1F, June 1997

2 Use the formula

$$v = u + at$$

to calculate v when $u = 2$, $a = 3$ and $t = 6$.

MEG, Question 8, Paper 2, June 1998

3 This is an approximate rule to change a temperature in degrees Celsius (C), into one in degrees Fahrenheit (F):

Double the Celsius temperature then add 30

    a Write this approximate rule as a formula for F in terms of C.

    b Use your formula, or otherwise, to find

        i F when $C = 54$ **ii** C when $F = 54$

NEAB, Question 20, Specimen Paper 1F, 1998

4 **a** If 2 metres is cut off a rope 8 metres long, how much rope is left?

    b If x metres of rope is cut off a rope 10 metres long, how much is left?

    c If z metres of rope is cut off a rope y metres long, how much is left?

NEAB, Question 9, Specimen Paper 2F, 1998

5 The diagram shows a square and a rectangle. The square has sides of length 2*y* metres. The rectangle has length 3*y* metres and breadth 3 metres.

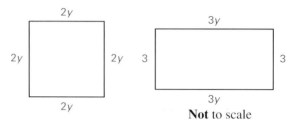

Not to scale

a The perimeter of the square is $2y + 2y + 2y + 2y$.
Simplify this expression.

b The perimeter of the rectangle is $3y + 3 + 3y + 3$.
Simplify this expression.

c The perimeter of the square is equal to the perimeter of the rectangle. Work out the value of *y*.

SEG, Question 19, Specimen Paper 12, 1998

6 Simplify

a $4q + 9q + 3q$

b $6n + 5p + 2n - p$

OCR, Question 16, Paper 1, June 2000

7 a The cost of one banana is *b* pence.
The cost of one grapefruit is *g* pence.
Write down an expression for the total cost of 3 bananas and 5 grapefruit.

b Multiply out the brackets $4(3a - 2)$.

OCR, Question 15, Paper 2, June 1999

8 The following formula can be used to find the cost, in pounds, of servicing a washing machine:

Cost = 45 + 30 × Number of hours

a Calculate the cost of servicing a machine when the work took half an hour.

b How many hours did it take to service a washing machine when the cost was £90?

WJEC, Question 10, Specimen Paper 1F, 1998

9 a Write each of the following expressions in its simplest form.

  i $f + g + f + f + g$

  ii $y \times t \times 3$

  iii $r \times r$

  b Multiply out the following expression by removing the brackets.

  $3(2t + 5)$

MEG, Question 17, Paper 1, June 1998

10 The cost, C pence, of an advertisement in the newspaper is worked out using the formula

  $C = 25n + 40$

where n is the number of words in the advertisement.

  a Joy puts in an advertisement of 16 words. Work out the cost.

  b The cost of Debbie's advertisement is 540 pence. How many words were in Debbie's advertisement?

MEG, Question 6, Specimen Paper 2F, 1998

11 A formula to estimate the number of rolls of wallpaper, R, for a room is

  $R = \dfrac{ph}{5}$

where p is the perimeter of the room in metres and h is the height of the room in metres.

The perimeter of Carol's bedroom is 15.5 m and it is 2.25 m high. How many rolls of wallpaper will she have to buy?

AQA, Question 17, Paper 2, June 1999

12 In this 'algebraic' magic square, every row, column and diagonal should add up and simplify to $15a + 12b + 6c$.

$8a + 5b + 5c$	$a + 6b - 2c$	$6a + b + 3c$
	$5a + 4b + 2c$	$7a + 8b + 4c$
$4a + 7b + c$		$2a + 3b - c$

a Complete the magic square.

b Calculate the value of $15a + 12b + 6c$ if $a = 1$, $b = 2$ and $c = 3$.

AQA, Question 12, Paper 1, June 2000

What you should know after you have worked through Chapter 7

✔ How to read and write simple algebraic expressions.
✔ How to simplify algebraic expressions by collecting terms, how to multiply out brackets, and how to factorise expressions.
✔ How to substitute positive and negative whole numbers, into simple expressions and formulae and then evaluate them.

PUZZLE PAGE

A$_1$ B$_2$ C$_3$ D$_4$ E$_5$ F$_6$ G$_7$ H$_8$ I$_9$ J$_{10}$

K$_{11}$
L$_{12}$
M$_{13}$
N$_{14}$
O$_{15}$
P$_{16}$
Q$_{17}$

Z$_{26}$ Y$_{25}$ X$_{24}$ W$_{23}$ V$_{22}$ U$_{21}$ T$_{20}$ S$_{19}$ R$_{18}$

Letter-numbers

Here are two examples of this code in action.

Forming a **proper even number**:

Two is a proper even number because
$$T_{20} + W_{23} + O_{15} = Two_{58} \quad \text{Word and number } \textbf{even}$$

Forming a **proper odd number**:

Seven is a proper odd number because
$$S_{19} + E_5 + V_{22} + E_5 + N_{14} = Seven_{65} \quad \text{Word and number } \textbf{odd}$$

■ How many *proper even numbers* can you find?

■ How many *proper odd numbers* can you find?

■ Can you find the name of a fruit whose total value is 47?

■ What is the *biggest value word* you can make?

■ What is the *lowest value word* you can make which has *more than two letters*?

■ Can you find the *longest word* with the *lowest total value*?

■ Can you find the *shortest word* with the *highest total value*?

■ Whose first name in your family has

　□ the lowest total value?

　□ the highest total value?

8 Further number skills

This chapter is going to ...

remind you how to do long multiplication and long division. It will then show you how to calculate with decimal numbers and how to interchange decimals and fractions. For this chapter, you will be making calculations without the help of your calculator.

What you should already know

✔ Times tables up to 10×10
✔ How to cancel down fractions

It is **imperative** that you **know all the times tables** up to 10×10. If you don't yet know them, make every effort to learn them – starting **now**.

Activity

Napier's bones

John Napier was born in Edinburgh in 1550 and died there in 1617. He was a mathematician. One of his achievements was to invent a calculator that consisted of a set of ten rods made from bones. A different times table was marked on each rod, as shown in the diagram below.

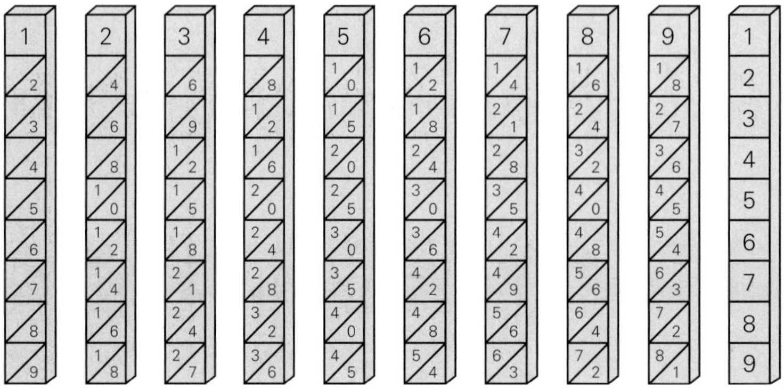

Using squared paper, make your own simple set of Napier's 'bones' by following the diagram. Notice how a times table is marked on each bone.

Carefully cut out the 'bones' so that you can use them.

Look at the diagram below to see how these 'bones' are used to calculate 247×36.

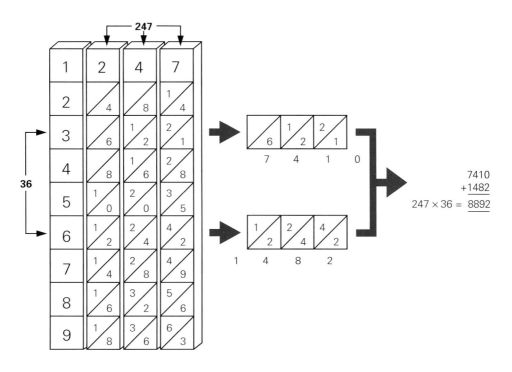

In a similar way, use your 'bones' to calculate each of these.

348×43 719×76 834×27 576×49

623×52 475×32 957×38 168×57

Check your answers with a calculator.

Long multiplication

When you are asked to do long multiplication on the GCSE non-calculator paper, you will be expected to use an appropriate method, such as that given in Example 1.

Example 1

Work out 357×24 without using a calculator.

There are several different ways to do long multiplication, but the following is perhaps the most commonly used method.

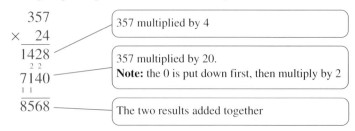

$$\begin{array}{r} 357 \\ \times\ \ 24 \\ \hline 1428 \\ 7140 \\ \hline 8568 \end{array}$$

357 multiplied by 4

357 multiplied by 20.
Note: the 0 is put down first, then multiply by 2

The two results added together

Note the use of **carry marks** to help you with the sums. But try to keep carry marks much smaller than the other numbers, so that you don't confuse them with the main calculation.

EXERCISE 8A

WHOLE EXERCISE

1 357×34	**2** 724×63	**3** 714×42	**4** 898×23
5 958×54	**6** 676×37	**7** 239×81	**8** 437×29
9 539×37	**10** 477×55	**11** 371×85	**12** 843×93
13 507×34	**14** 810×54	**15** 905×73	**16** 1435×72
17 2504×56	**18** 4037×23	**19** 8009×65	**20** 2070×38

Long division

There are several different ways of doing long division. It is acceptable to use any of them provided it gets the correct answer and you can clearly show all your working. The method used in this book is called the *Italian Method*. It is the most commonly used way of doing long division.

For example, to work out $840 \div 24$, you do a sum like the one below.

It is a good idea to jot down the appropriate times table before you start the long division. In this case, it will be the 24 times table.

1	2	3	4	5	6	7	8	9
24	48	72	96	120	144	168	192	216

Sometimes, as here, you will not need a whole times table, and so you could jot down only those parts of the table that you will need. But, don't forget, you are going to have to work **without** a calculator, so you do need all the help you can get.

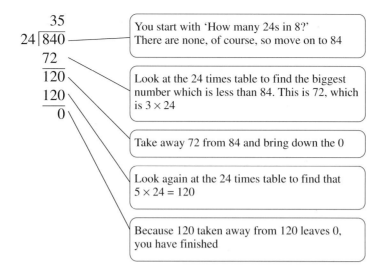

So, the answer to 840 ÷ 24 is 35.

You may do a long division without writing down all the numbers. It will look like this:

$$
\begin{array}{r}
3\ 5 \\
24\,\overline{|8\ 4^{12}0}
\end{array}
$$

Notice how the remainder from 84 is placed in front of the 0 to make it 120.

Let's take another example: 1655 ÷ 35.

Here, jot down the 35 times table before starting the long division.

1	2	3	4	5	6	7	8	9
35	70	105	140	175	210	245	280	315

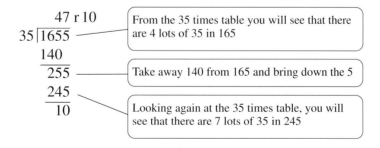

This is the end of the line. There is 10 left over.

So, the answer to 1655 ÷ 35 is 47, remainder 10.

EXERCISE 8B

WHOLE EXERCISE

1 $525 \div 21$	**2** $480 \div 32$	**3** $925 \div 25$	**4** $645 \div 15$
5 $621 \div 23$	**6** $576 \div 12$	**7** $1643 \div 31$	**8** $728 \div 14$
9 $832 \div 26$	**10** $2394 \div 42$	**11** $829 \div 22$	**12** $780 \div 31$
13 $895 \div 26$	**14** $873 \div 16$	**15** $875 \div 24$	**16** $225 \div 13$
17 $759 \div 33$	**18** $1478 \div 24$	**19** $756 \div 18$	**20** $1163 \div 43$

Solving real problems

In your GCSE examination, you will not always be given simple, straightforward problems like Exercises 8A and 8B but **real** problems that you have to **read carefully, think about** and then **sort out** without using a calculator.

Example 2

How many coaches, each holding 53 people, will be needed to take a party of 672 children on a day out?

We read the problem and realise that we have to do a division sum: the number of seats on a coach into the number of children. This is $672 \div 53$:

```
      12
53 ) 672
     530
     ‾‾‾‾
     142
     106
     ‾‾‾‾
      36
```

The answer is 12 remainder 36. So, there will be 12 full coaches and one coach with 36 children on. So, we would have to book 13 coaches.

EXERCISE 8C

WHOLE EXERCISE

1 There are 48 cans of soup in a crate. A supermarket had a delivery of 125 crates of soup. How many cans of soup were received?

2 Greystones Primary School has 12 classes, each of which has 26 pupils. How many pupils are there at Greystones Primary School?

3 3600 supporters of Barnsley Football Club want to go to an away game by coach. Each coach can hold 53 passengers. How many coaches will they need altogether?

4 How many stamps costing 26p each can I buy for £10?

5 Joseph walks to school each day, there and back. The distance to school is 450 metres. How far will he walk in a school term consisting of 64 days?

6 On one page of a newspaper there are seven columns. In each column there are 172 lines, and in each line there are 50 letters. How many letters on the page?

7 A tank of water was being emptied into casks. Each cask held 81 litres. 71 casks were filled with 68 litres left over. How much water was in the tank to start with?

8 Joy was going to do a sponsored walk for the Macmillan Nurses. She managed to get 18 people to sponsor her, each for 35p per kilometre. She walked a total of 48 kilometres. How much sponsor money should she expect to collect?

9 Kirsty collects small models of animals. Each one costs 45p. Her pocket money is £15 a month. How many model animals could Kirsty buy with one month's pocket money?

10 Eunice wanted to save up to see a concert. The cost of a ticket was £25. She was paid 75p per hour to mind her little sister. For how many hours would Eunice have to mind her sister to be able to afford the ticket?

11 The magazine *Teen Dance* comes out every month. The annual (yearly) subscription for the magazine is £21. How much does each magazine cost per month?

12 Paula buys a music centre for her club at a cost of 95p for 144 weeks. How much will she actually pay for this music centre?

Decimal numbers

We extend our number system by using decimal numbers to represent fractions.

We use the decimal point to separate the fraction part of a quantity from its whole-number part.

For example, the number 25.374 means

Tens	Units		Tenths	Hundredths	Thousandths
10	1		$\frac{1}{10}$	$\frac{1}{100}$	$\frac{1}{1000}$
2	**5**	**.**	**3**	**7**	**4**

You are already familiar with the use of decimal notation to express amounts of money. For example,

£32.67   means $3 \times £10$
$2 \times £1$
$6 \times £0.1$ (10 pence)
$7 \times £0.01$ (1 penny)

Decimal places

When a number is written in decimal form, the digits on the right-hand side of the decimal point are called **decimal places**. For example,

79.4 is written to one decimal place
6.83 is written to two decimal places
0.526 is written to three decimal places

To round off a decimal number to a particular number of places, take these steps.

- Count down the decimal places from the decimal point and look at the first digit to be removed.
- When this digit is less than 5, just remove the unwanted places.
- When this digit is 5 or more, add 1 onto the digit in the last decimal place while removing the unwanted places.

Here are some examples.

5.852 will round off to 5.85 to two decimal places
7.156 will round off to 7.16 to two decimal places
0.274 will round off to 0.3 to one decimal place
15.3518 will round off to 15.4 to one decimal place

EXERCISE 8D

WHOLE EXERCISE

1 Round off each of the following numbers to one decimal place.

a 4.83	**b** 3.79	**c** 2.16	**d** 8.25
e 3.673	**f** 46.935	**g** 23.883	**h** 9.549
i 11.08	**j** 33.509	**k** 7.054	**l** 46.807
m 0.057	**n** 0.109	**o** 0.599	**p** 64.99
q 213.86	**r** 76.07	**s** 455.177	**t** 50.999

2 Round off each of the following numbers to two decimal places.

a 5.783	**b** 2.358	**c** 0.977	**d** 33.085
e 6.007	**f** 23.5652	**g** 91.7895	**h** 7.995
i 2.3076	**j** 23.9158	**k** 5.9999	**l** 1.0075
m 3.5137	**n** 96.508	**o** 0.009	**p** 0.065
q 7.8091	**r** 569.897	**s** 300.004	**t** 0.0099

3 Round off each of the following to the number of decimal places (dp) indicated.

a	4.568 (1 dp)	**b**	0.0832 (2 dp)	**c**	45.715 93 (3 dp)		
d	94.8531 (2 dp)	**e**	602.099 (1 dp)	**f**	671.7629 (2 dp)		
g	7.1124 (1 dp)	**h**	6.903 54 (3 dp)	**i**	13.7809 (2 dp)		
j	0.075 11 (1 dp)	**k**	4.001 84 (3 dp)	**l**	59.983 (1 dp)		
m	11.9854 (2 dp)	**n**	899.995 85 (3 dp)	**o**	0.0699 (1 dp)		
p	0.009 87 (2 dp)	**q**	6.070 8 (1 dp)	**r**	78.3925 (3 dp)		
s	199.9999 (2 dp)	**t**	5.0907 (1 dp)				

4 Round off each of the following to the nearest whole number.

a	8.7	**b**	9.2	**c**	2.7	**d**	6.5
e	3.28	**f**	7.82	**g**	3.19	**h**	7.55
i	6.172	**j**	3.961	**k**	7.388	**l**	1.514
m	46.78	**n**	23.19	**o**	96.45	**p**	32.77
q	153.9	**r**	342.5	**s**	704.19	**t**	909.5

Adding and subtracting with decimals

Every sum **must** be properly set out.

Make sure that the decimal points are in line underneath the first point so that each digit is in its correct place or column.

Then you can add or subtract just as you have done before. The decimal point of the answer is placed directly underneath the other decimal points.

Example 3
Work out 4.72 + 13.53

```
    4.72
+ 13.53
  18.25
     ₁
```

Notice how to deal with 7 + 5 = 12, with the 1 being carried forward into the next column.

Example 4
Work out 7.3 – 1.5

```
  ⁶7.¹3
– 1. 5
  5. 8
```

Notice how to deal with the fact that we cannot take 5 from 3. We have to take one of the tens from 7, replace the 7 with a 6 and make the 3 into 13.

Hidden decimal point

Whole numbers are commonly written without decimal points.

But sometimes we need to show the decimal point in a whole number (see Example 5), in which case it is placed at the right-hand side of the number, followed by a zero. (You may remember this by 'Put it RIGHT at the end'.)

Example 5

Work out $4.2 + 8 + 12.9$

$$
\begin{array}{r}
4.2 \\
8.0 \\
+ \; 12.9 \\
\hline
25.1 \\
\hline
{\scriptstyle 1\;1}
\end{array}
$$

EXERCISE 8E

WHOLE EXERCISE

1 Work out each of these.

a	$47.3 + 2.5$	**b**	$16.7 + 4.6$	**c**	$43.5 + 4.8$
d	$28.5 + 4.8$	**e**	$1.26 + 4.73$	**f**	$2.25 + 5.83$
g	$83.5 + 6.7$	**h**	$8.3 + 12.9$	**i**	$3.65 + 8.5$
j	$7.38 + 5.7$	**k**	$7.3 + 5.96$	**l**	$6.5 + 17.86$

2 Work out each of these.

a	$3.8 - 2.4$	**b**	$4.3 - 2.5$	**c**	$7.6 - 2.8$
d	$8.7 - 4.9$	**e**	$8.25 - 4.5$	**f**	$19.7 - 13.8$
g	$9.4 - 5.7$	**h**	$8.62 - 4.85$	**i**	$8 - 4.3$
j	$9 - 7.6$	**k**	$15 - 3.2$	**l**	$24 - 8.7$

3 Evaluate each of the following. (Take care – they are a mixture.)

a	$23.8 + 6.9$	**b**	$8.3 - 1.7$	**c**	$9 - 5.2$
d	$12.9 + 3.8$	**e**	$17.4 - 5.6$	**f**	$23.4 + 6.8$
g	$35 + 8.3$	**h**	$9.54 - 2.81$	**i**	$34.8 + 3.15$
j	$8.1 - 3.4$	**k**	$12.5 - 8.7$	**l**	$198.5 + 12$

Multiplying and dividing decimals by single-digit numbers

These operations are done in exactly the same way as they are with whole numbers, with each digit put in its correct column.

Again, the decimal point is kept in the **same** column.

Example 6

Work out 4.5×3

$$
\begin{array}{r}
4.5 \\
\times \quad 3 \\
\hline
13.5 \\
\scriptstyle 1
\end{array}
$$

Example 7

Work out $8.25 \div 5$

$$
\begin{array}{r}
1.\,6\,5 \\
5\,\overline{)8.^3 2^2 5}
\end{array}
$$

Example 8

Work out $5.7 \div 2$

$$
\begin{array}{r}
2.\,8\,5 \\
2\,\overline{)5.^1 7^1 0}
\end{array}
$$

Notice how we need to add a zero to be able to complete the division.

EXERCISE 8F

WHOLE EXERCISE

1 Evaluate each of these.

a 2.4×3	**b** 3.8×2	**c** 4.7×4	**d** 5.3×7
e 6.5×5	**f** 3.6×8	**g** 2.5×4	**h** 9.2×6
i 12.3×5	**j** 24.4×7	**k** 13.6×6	**l** 19.3×5

2 Evaluate each of these.

a 2.34×4	**b** 3.45×3	**c** 5.17×5	**d** 4.26×3
e 0.26×7	**f** 0.82×4	**g** 0.56×5	**h** 0.92×6
i 6.03×7	**j** 7.02×8	**k** 2.55×3	**l** 8.16×6

3 Evaluate each of these.

a $3.6 \div 2$	**b** $5.6 \div 4$	**c** $4.2 \div 3$	**d** $8.4 \div 7$
e $4.26 \div 2$	**f** $3.45 \div 5$	**g** $8.37 \div 3$	**h** $9.68 \div 8$
i $7.56 \div 4$	**j** $5.43 \div 3$	**k** $1.32 \div 4$	**l** $7.6 \div 4$

4 Evaluate each of these.

a	$3.5 \div 2$	**b**	$6.4 \div 5$	**c**	$7.4 \div 4$	**d**	$7.3 \div 2$
e	$8.3 \div 5$	**f**	$5.8 \div 4$	**g**	$7.1 \div 5$	**h**	$9.2 \div 8$
i	$6.7 \div 2$	**j**	$4.9 \div 5$	**k**	$9.2 \div 4$	**l**	$7.3 \div 5$

5 Evaluate each of these.

a	$7.56 \div 4$	**b**	$4.53 \div 3$	**c**	$1.32 \div 5$	**d**	$8.53 \div 2$
e	$2.448 \div 2$	**f**	$1.274 \div 7$	**g**	$0.837 \div 9$	**h**	$16.336 \div 8$
i	$9.54 \div 5$	**j**	$14 \div 5$	**k**	$17 \div 4$	**l**	$37 \div 2$

6 Soup is sold in packs of five for £3.25 and packs of eight for £5. Which is the cheaper soup?

7 Mike took his wife and four children to the theatre. The tickets were £13.25 for each adult and £5.85 for each child. How much did all the tickets cost Mike?

8 Mary was putting a path through her garden. She bought nine paving stones, each 1.35 m long. She wanted the path to run straight down the garden, which is 10 m long. Has Mary bought too many paving stones? Show all your working.

Long multiplication with decimals

As before, each digit is put in its correct column and the decimal point is kept in the **same** column.

Example 9

Evaluate 4.27×34

$$
\begin{array}{r}
4.27 \\
\times \quad 34 \\
\hline
17.08 \\
128.10 \\
\hline
145.18 \\
\end{array}
$$

EXERCISE 8G

WHOLE EXERCISE

1 Evaluate each of these.

a	3.72×24	**b**	5.63×53	**c**	1.27×52	**d**	4.54×37
e	67.2×35	**f**	12.4×26	**g**	62.1×18	**h**	81.3×55
i	5.67×82	**j**	0.73×35	**k**	23.8×44	**l**	99.5×19

2 Find the total cost of each of the following purchases.
   a Eighteen ties at £12.45 each.
   b Twenty-five shirts at £8.95 each.
   c Thirteen pairs of tights at £2.30 a pair.

3 A party of 24 scouts and their leader went into a zoo. The cost of a ticket for each scout was £2.15, and the cost of a ticket for the leader was £2.60. What was the total cost of entering the zoo?

4 A market gardener bought 35 trays of seedlings. Each tray cost £3.45. What was the total cost of the trays?

Multiplying two decimal numbers together

To multiply one decimal number by another decimal number:
- First, do the whole calculation as if the decimal points were not there.
- Then, count the total number of decimal places in the two decimal numbers. This gives the number of decimal places in the answer.

Example 10

Evaluate 3.42×2.7

Ignoring the decimal points gives the following calculation:

$$
\begin{array}{r}
342 \\
\times \quad 27 \\
\hline
2394 \\
{\scriptstyle 2\,1} \\
6840 \\
\hline
9234 \\
\hline
{\scriptstyle 1\,1}
\end{array}
$$

Now, 3.42 has two decimal places (.42) and 2.7 has one decimal place (.7). So, the total number of decimal places in the answer is three, which gives
   $3.42 \times 2.7 = 9.234$

EXERCISE **8H**

WHOLE EXERCISE

1 Evaluate each of these.
   a 2.4×0.2 **b** 7.3×0.4 **c** 5.6×0.2 **d** 0.3×0.4
   e 0.14×0.2 **f** 0.3×0.3 **g** 0.24×0.8 **h** 5.82×0.52
   i 5.8×1.23 **j** 5.6×9.1 **k** 0.875×3.5 **l** 9.12×5.1

2 For each of the following:

   i Estimate the answer by first rounding off each number to the nearest whole number.

   ii Calculate the exact answer, and then calculate how much out your answer to part **i** is.

   a 4.8×7.3 **b** 2.4×7.6 **c** 15.3×3.9 **d** 20.1×8.6

   e 4.35×2.8 **f** 8.13×3.2 **g** 7.82×5.2 **h** 19.8×7.1

Interchanging decimals and fractions

Changing a decimal into a fraction

A decimal can be changed into a fraction by using the place-value table on page 143.

Example 11

Express 0.32 as a fraction.

$$0.32 = \frac{32}{100}$$

This will cancel down to $\frac{8}{25}$.

Changing a fraction into a decimal

A fraction can be changed into a decimal by dividing the numerator by the denominator. Example 12 shows how this can be done without a calculator.

Example 12

Express $\frac{3}{8}$ as a decimal.

$\frac{3}{8}$ means $3 \div 8$. This is done as a division calculation.

$$\begin{array}{r} 0.\,3\,7\,5 \\ 8\,\overline{)\,3.^30^60^40} \end{array}$$

Notice how the extra zeros have been added.

EXERCISE 8I

WHOLE EXERCISE

1 Change each of these decimals to fractions, cancelling down where possible.

   a 0.7 **b** 0.4 **c** 0.5 **d** 0.03 **e** 0.06

   f 0.13 **g** 0.25 **h** 0.38 **i** 0.55 **j** 0.64

2 Change each of these fractions to decimals. Where necessary give your answer to three decimal places.

a $\frac{1}{2}$ **b** $\frac{3}{4}$ **c** $\frac{3}{5}$ **d** $\frac{9}{10}$ **e** $\frac{1}{3}$

f $\frac{5}{8}$ **g** $\frac{2}{3}$ **h** $\frac{7}{20}$ **i** $\frac{7}{11}$ **j** $\frac{4}{9}$

3 Put each of the following sets of numbers in order with the smallest first. It is easier first to change the fractions into decimals.

a $0.6, 0.3, \frac{1}{2}$ **b** $\frac{2}{5}, 0.8, 0.3$ **c** $0.35, \frac{1}{4}, 0.15$

d $\frac{7}{10}, 0.72, 0.71$ **e** $0.8, \frac{3}{4}, 0.7$ **f** $0.08, 0.1, \frac{1}{20}$

g $0.55, \frac{1}{2}, 0.4$ **h** $1\frac{1}{4}, 1.2, 1.23$

Investigation

A Number Trick

Pick any three-digit number, for example 741

Repeat it to make a six-digit number: 741 741

Divide this six-digit number by 7: $741\,741 \div 7 = 105\,963$

Divide the answer by 11: $105\,963 \div 11 = 9633$

Divide again by 13: $9633 \div 13 = \ldots\ldots$

■ What do you notice? Will this always happen? Why does this happen?

Invent a number trick of your own.

Russian Multiplication

Look at this popular Russian way to do long multiplication.

36×17 or 27×19

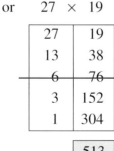

36	17
18	34
9	68
4	136
2	272
1	544

612

27	19
13	38
6	76
3	152
1	304

513

Investigate and see whether you can find out

■ how it works

■ why it works

■ how to work it yourself

Examination questions

All of these questions are typical of those in the non-calculator paper.

1 A mathematics teacher buys 92 textbooks, costing £3.95 each. What is the exact total cost?

MEG, Question 2, Specimen Paper 2, 1998

2 In a shop, Alan spends

      £1.33 on milk

      £3.14 on coffee

      £0.74 on sugar

i Calculate the total amount that Alan spends.

ii Alan pays with a £10 note. How much change should be given?

iii Barbara is organising a coach trip for 260 people. Each coach will hold 48 people.

How many coaches will be needed?

MEG, Question 4, Specimen Paper 2, 1998

3 How many pupils are there in Year 7?

There are 13 classes in Year 7. Each class has 28 pupils.

Headmaster

NEAB, Question 5, Specimen Paper IF, 2000

4 A theatre has 48 rows of seats. Each row has 31 seats.

a Work out the exact number of seats in the theatre.

b Show what **approximate** calculation you would do in order to check your answer.

MEG, Question 7, Paper 1, June 1998

5 a Work out $75.6 \div 27$.

b What approximate calculation could you do to check the answer to part **a**?

OCR(SMP), Question 17, Paper 1, June 2000

6 Alun has a part-time job. He is paid £18 each day he works. In 1998 he worked 148 days.

   a **Estimate** Alun's total pay for 1998. Write down your calculation and answer.

   b Work out exactly how much Alun was paid in 1998.

AQA, Question 16, Paper 2, June 1999

7 Tony bought these four items.

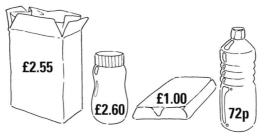

   a What was the total cost of these items?

   b Tony paid with a £10 note. How much change did he get?

SEG, Question 2, Specimen Paper 5, 2000

8 A school party of 500 people is going on a coach trip. Each coach can seat 44 passengers. Each coach costs £85 to hire.

   a Work out how many coaches are needed.

   b Work out the total cost of all the coaches that are needed.

SEG, Question 12, Specimen Paper 5, 2000

9 A gardener buys 375 trays of plants. There are 54 plants in a tray. How many plants is this altogether?

NEAB, Question 2, Paper 2F, June 1998

10 Korky cat food costs 44p a tin.
Alec buys 18 cans of Korky cat food.
He pays with a £10 note.
How much change should he receive?

NEAB, Question 17, Paper 2F, June 1998

11 Members of the Swallow Club are going on a coach outing. The coach costs £448 to hire. There are 32 people going on the outing. They share the cost equally between them. How much do they each pay?

MEG(SMP), Question 4, Terminal Paper, 1998

12 **a** Write $\frac{3}{8}$ as a decimal.
   b Write 0.8 as a fraction. Give your answer in its lowest terms.

AQA, Question 11, Paper 2, June 2000

13 A shopkeeper wishes to store 500 marbles into boxes. Each box can store 36 marbles. How many boxes can he fill and how many marbles will be left over?

WJEC, Question 5, Specimen Paper 1F, 1998

14 Three friends, Ali, Brenda and Chris, go to the cinema together. The total cost of their three tickets is £11.55. Each ticket costs the same. Work out the cost of one ticket.

NEAB, Question 5, Paper 1F, June 1995

What you should know after you have worked through Chapter 8

✔ How to work out, without the help of your calculator, both long multiplication and long division.
✔ How to calculate with decimal numbers.
✔ How to interchange decimals and fractions.

PUZZLE PAGE

Big, bigger, biggest!

■ Look at these two sums. They both have the same digits in opposite rows, but one row is the reverse of the other. Which sum is the bigger?
Guess first then work it out.

```
    1 2 3 4 5 6 7 8 9        9 8 7 6 5 4 3 2 1
    1 2 3 4 5 6 7 8 0        0 8 7 6 5 4 3 2 1
    1 2 3 4 5 6 7 0 0        0 0 7 6 5 4 3 2 1
    1 2 3 4 5 6 0 0 0        0 0 0 6 5 4 3 2 1
    1 2 3 4 5 0 0 0 0        0 0 0 0 5 4 3 2 1
    1 2 3 4 0 0 0 0 0        0 0 0 0 0 4 3 2 1
    1 2 3 0 0 0 0 0 0        0 0 0 0 0 0 3 2 1
    1 2 0 0 0 0 0 0 0        0 0 0 0 0 0 0 2 1
+   1 0 0 0 0 0 0 0 0      + 0 0 0 0 0 0 0 0 1
    ─────────────────        ─────────────────

    ─────────────────        ─────────────────
```

■ Which of the following two sums is the bigger?
    123.45×6.75 or 1.2345×675
Guess first, then work it out.

■ Take these digits: **5   6   3   1**
   □ Make the biggest possible number from them, using each digit once only.
   □ Putting the multiplication sign, $\times$, where you want, what is the biggest total you can make using each digit only once in your sum?

■ Using all the digits 0, 1, 2, 3, 4, 5, 6, 7, 8 and 9 once only, together with all the signs $\times$, $\div$, – and + once only, make
   □ the biggest possible answer
   □ the smallest possible answer.
For example, you might try
    $712 - 560 \times 48 + 9 \div 3$

Revision for Chapters 1 to 8

- Answer all the questions
- Show your working

1 Write down the answers to each of these.

   a $19 - 5$ **b** $17 + 8$ **c** 7×4 **d** $36 \div 4$ **e** $23 + 8$

   f $21 - 8$ **g** 8×3 **h** $32 \div 4$ **i** 9×6 **j** $32 - 15$

2 Put a bracket in each of these to make the answer correct.

   a $16 - 2 + 3 = 11$ **b** $5 + 4 \times 3 - 1 = 16$

3 **a** How many days are there in 28 weeks?

   b How long will it take me to save £296, if I save £8 a week?

   c There are six stickers in every pack.

      i How many stickers will I get if I buy 13 packs?

      ii Joe has just bought 138 stickers. How many packs did he buy?

4 Calculate each of the following.

   a $\frac{1}{2} + \frac{1}{2}$ **b** $\frac{7}{8} - \frac{5}{8}$ **c** $\frac{3}{8} + \frac{6}{8}$ **d** $\frac{4}{5} - \frac{1}{5}$ **e** $\frac{2}{7} + \frac{3}{7}$

   f $\frac{7}{10} + \frac{4}{10}$ **g** $\frac{7}{8} - \frac{3}{8}$ **h** $\frac{3}{5} + \frac{4}{5}$ **i** $\frac{5}{6} - \frac{1}{6}$ **j** $\frac{5}{9} + \frac{7}{9}$

5 Calculate

   a $\frac{2}{7}$ of 14 days   **b** $\frac{3}{4}$ of £20   **c** $\frac{4}{5}$ of 15 weeks

   d $\frac{2}{3}$ of 30 cm   **e** $\frac{3}{8}$ of 40 minutes   **f** $\frac{5}{6}$ of 1 hour

   g $\frac{1}{10}$ of 1 metre   **h** $\frac{7}{10}$ of £50

6 Write down the answer to each of the following.

   a $3 - 7$ **b** $6 - 11$ **c** $-2 - 5$ **d** $-3 - 4$ **e** $3 - -5$

   f $2 - -7$ **g** $-2 - -3$ **h** $-5 + 7$ **i** $-8 + 3$ **j** $-2 + -3$

7 **a** Write down the first five multiples of 7.

   b Write down all the factors of 24.

   c Write down all the prime numbers smaller than 30.

   d Write down the first ten square numbers.

8 Which is bigger, the square of 9 or the square root of 25?

9 Calculate the perimeter of each of these shapes.

   a
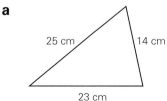
25 cm   14 cm   23 cm

   b

18 cm   8 cm

10 Calculate the area of each of these shapes.

a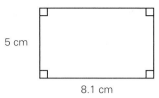

5 cm

8.1 cm

b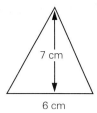

7 cm

6 cm

c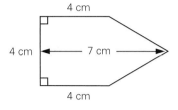

4 cm

4 cm ← 7 cm →

4 cm

11 Pat did a survey on the cost of a jar of coffee in different shops. Here are her results.

£1.76	£1.75	£1.72	£1.78	£1.55	£1.65	£1.80	£1.75
£1.74	£1.69	£1.50	£1.67	£1.83	£1.57	£1.59	£1.53

a What was the most expensive jar of coffee?

b Copy and complete this frequency table for these jars of coffee.

Cost (£)	Tally	Frequency
1.50–1.59		
1.60–1.69		
1.70–1.79		
1.80–1.89		

c Show this information as a pictogram.

12 John spent £90 in one week. The table shows what he spent it on.

Items	Amount spent (£)
Newspapers	6
Food	30
Football	28
Drink	16
Other	10

Draw and fully label a bar chart to illustrate this information.

13 **a** If 3 metres is cut off a rope 7 metres long, how much rope is left?
    b If x metres of rope is cut off a rope 9 metres long, how much is left?
    c If z metres of rope is cut off a rope y metres long, how much is left?

14 Use the formula $W = 2q + 24$ to work out each of the following.
    a Find W, when $q = 8$ **b** Find W, when $q = -4$
    c Find q, when $W = 11$

15 **a** When a number is multiplied by 3 and then 5 is added to the result, the answer is 23. What is the number?
    b Simplify
        i $4a + 3b - 2a$ **ii** $12x + 3(3x + 5y)$

16 For each of the following:
    i Estimate the answer by first rounding off each number to the nearest whole number.
    ii Calculate the exact answer.
    a 3.8×5.3 **b** 2.5×7.3 **c** 35.4×3.8 **d** 25.2×8.7

17 Jane buys a computer. If she pays a deposit of £115 and 18 monthly instalments of £38.45, work out the total amount that Jane pays.

18 A gardener wishes to put 400 rose plants into boxes. He plans to put 24 rose plants into each box. How many boxes can he fill and how many rose plants will be left over?

9 Ratios, fractions, speed and proportion

> ### This chapter is going to ...
>
> show you how to divide an amount by a given ratio and how to calculate speed. It also shows you how to solve problems involving direct proportion and how to compare prices of products.
>
> ### What you should already know
>
> ✔ What a fraction is
> ✔ How to cancel down fractions
> ✔ How to find a fraction of a quantity
> ✔ How to multiply and divide, with and without a calculator

Activity

Golden Rectangles

Look at the four rectangles below. Show them to your friends to see which one they would choose to put a picture in.

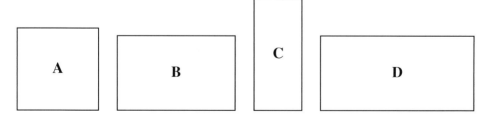

You will find that most people choose shape B. It is called a Golden Rectangle.

The length and breadth of a Golden Rectangle are in a special ratio, which we are now going to look at.

Follow through these six steps to draw a Golden Rectangle.

- Draw a square ABCD of any size.

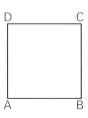

- Find the middle of the line AB, and mark it with an X.

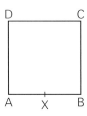

- Extend the line AXB with a feint line.

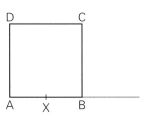

- Take a pair of compasses and open them to match the length XC.

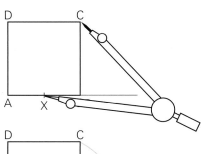

- With X as centre, draw a feint arc from C to cut the extended line AXB. Mark this point of intersection as Y.

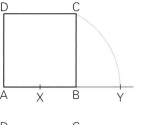

- Starting from Y, complete the rectangle. This is a Golden Rectangle.

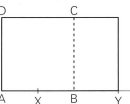

Draw **four** more Golden Rectangles, following the same rules as above. But each time choose a different sized square to start with.

Now measure the length and breadth of each Golden Rectangle you have drawn. For each rectangle calculate its length ÷ its width, giving your answer to one decimal place.

What do you notice?

Measure the length and breadth of pictures and posters that are hung around your school and home. See just how many of them are true Golden Rectangles.

Ratio

A ratio is a way of comparing the sizes of two or more quantities.

A ratio can be expressed in a number of ways. For example, Joy is 5 years old and James is 20 years old. The ratio of their ages is

> Joy's age : James's age
>
> which is $\qquad$ 5 : 20
> which simplifies to $\qquad$ 1 : 4 (Dividing both sides by 5)

A ratio is usually given in one of these three ways:

> Joy's age : James's age   or   5 : 20   or   1 : 4
> Joy's age to James's age   or   5 to 20   or   1 to 4

> $\dfrac{\text{Joy's age}}{\text{James's age}}$ or $\dfrac{5}{20}$ or $\dfrac{1}{4}$

Common units

When working with a ratio involving different units, **always change them to a common unit.** A ratio can be simplified only when the units of each quantity are the **same**, because the ratio itself doesn't have any units.

For example, the ratio of 125 g to 2 kg must be changed to 125 g to 2000 g, so that we can simplify it to

> $\qquad\qquad$ 125 : 2000
> Divide both sides by 25 $\quad$ 5 : 80
> Divide both sides by 5 $\quad$ 1 : 16

Ratios as fractions

A ratio in its simplest form can be expressed as portions by changing the whole numbers in the ratio into fractions with the same denominator (bottom number).

161

For example, in a garden which is divided into lawn and shrubs in the ratio 3 : 2,

the lawn covers $\frac{3}{5}$ of the garden

and the shrubs cover $\frac{2}{5}$ of the garden

The common denominator (bottom number) 5 comes from **adding the numbers in the ratio**.

EXERCISE 9A

1   Express each of the following ratios in their simplest form.
 a 6 : 18 **b** 15 : 20 **c** 16 : 24 **d** 24 : 36
 e 20 to 50 **f** 12 to 30 **g** 25 to 40 **h** 125 to 30
 i 15 : 10 **j** 32 : 12 **k** 28 to 12 **l** 100 to 40
 m 0.5 to 3 **n** 1.5 to 4 **o** 2.5 to 1.5 **p** 3.2 to 4

2   Express each of the following ratios of quantities in their simplest form. (Remember always to get a common unit.)
 a £5 to £15   **b** £24 to £16
 c 125 g to 300 g **d** 40 minutes : 5 minutes
 e 34 kg to 30 kg **f** £2.50 to 70p
 g 3 kg to 750 g **h** 50 minutes to 1 hour
 i 1 hour to 1 day **j** 12 cm to 2.5 mm
 k 1.25 kg : 500 g **l** 75p : £3.50
 m 4 weeks : 14 days **n** 600 m : 2 km
 o 465 mm : 3 m **p** 15 hours : 1 day

3   A length of wood is cut into two pieces in the ratio 3 : 7. What fraction of the original length is the longer piece?

4   Jack and Thomas find a bag of marbles which they divide between them in the ratio of their ages. Jack is 10 years old and Thomas is 15. What fraction of the marbles did Jack get?

5   One morning a farmer notices that her hens, Gladys and Henrietta, have laid eggs in the ratio 2 : 3
 a What fraction of the eggs did Henrietta lay?
 b What fraction of the eggs did Gladys lay?

6   In a circus at feeding time, the lions and the chimpanzees are given food in the ratio 7 to 3. What fraction of the total food is given to
 a the lions   **b** the chimpanzees?

7   Two brothers, John and Joseph, share a huge block of chocolate in the ratio of their ages. John's age is 20 and Joseph's is 10. What fraction of the bar of chocolate does each brother get?

8 The recipe for jam is 125 g of sugar and 175 g of fruit. What fraction of the jam is each ingredient?

Dividing amounts by ratios

To divide an amount into portions according to a given ratio, you first change the whole numbers in the ratio into fractions with the same common denominator. Then you multiply the amount by each fraction.

Example 1

Divide £40 between Peter and Hitan in the ratio 2:3

Changing the ratio to fractions gives

$$\text{Peter's share} = \frac{2}{(2+3)} = \frac{2}{5}$$

$$\text{Hitan's share} = \frac{3}{(2+3)} = \frac{3}{5}$$

So, Peter receives £40 × $\frac{2}{5}$ = £16 and Hitan receives £40 × $\frac{3}{5}$ = £24

EXERCISE 9B

1 Divide each of the following amounts in the given ratios.
  a 400 g in the ratio 2:3   **b** 280 kg in the ratio 2:5
  c 500 in the ratio 3:7   **d** 1 km in the ratio 19:1
  e 5 hours in the ratio 7:5   **f** £100 in the ratio 2:3
  g £240 in the ratio 3:5   **h** 600 g in the ratio 1:5
  i £5 in the ratio 17:8   **j** 200 kg in the ratio 9:1

2 The ratio of female to male members of Banner Cross Church is about 5:3. The total number of members of the church is 256.
  a How many members are female?
  b How many members are male?

3 A supermarket tries to have in stock branded goods and their own goods in the ratio 2:5. They stock 350 kg of breakfast cereal. How much of the breakfast cereal stock is their own?

4 The Illinois Department of Health reported that, for the years 1981 to 1992 when they tested a total of 357 horses for rabies, the ratio of horses with rabies to those without was 1:16. How many of these horses had rabies?

5 Being overweight increases the chances of an adult suffering from heart disease. The table headings below show a way to test whether an adult has an increased risk.

Waist *W* and hip *H* measurements

For women, increased risk when $W/H > 0.8$

For men, increased risk when $W/H > 1.0$

a Find whether the following people have an increased risk of heart disease or not.

Miss Mott	waist 26 inches	hips 35 inches
Mrs Wright	waist 32 inches	hips 37 inches
Mr Brennan	waist 32 inches	hips 34 inches
Ms Smith	waist 31 inches	hips 40 inches
Mr Kaye	waist 34 inches	hips 33 inches

b Give three examples of waist and hip measurements which would suggest no risk of heart disease for a man, but would suggest a risk for a woman.

6 Rewrite, as simply as possible, each of the following scales as ratios.

a 1 cm to 4 km   **b** 4 cm to 5 km   **c** 2 cm to 5 km

d 4 cm to 1 km   **e** 5 cm to 1 km   **f** 2.5 cm to 1 km

g 8 cm to 5 km   **h** 10 cm to 1 km   **i** 5 cm to 3 km

7 A map has a scale of 1 cm to 10 km.

a Rewrite the scale as a ratio in its simplest form.

b How long is a lake that is 4.7 cm on the map?

c How long will an 8 km road be on the map?

8 A map has a scale of 2 cm to 5 km.

a Rewrite the scale as a ratio in its simplest form.

b How long is a path that measures 0.8 cm on the map?

c How long should a 12 km road be on the map?

9 The scale of a map is 5 cm to 1 km.

a Rewrite the scale as a ratio in its simplest form.

b How long is a wall that is shown as 2.7 cm on the map?

c The distance between two points is 8 km, how far will this be on the map?

10 You can simplify a ratio by changing it into the form 1: *n*.

For example, 5 : 7 can be rewritten as

$$\frac{5}{5} : \frac{7}{5} = 1 : 1.4$$

Rewrite each of the following ratios in the form $1:n$.

a $5:8$ **b** $4:13$ **c** $8:9$

d $25:36$ **e** $5:27$ **f** $12:18$

g 5 hours : 1 day   **h** 4 hours : 1 week   **i** £4 : £5

Calculating in a ratio when only part of the information is known

For example, two business partners, John and Ben, divided their total profit in the ratio $3:5$. John received £2100. How much did Ben get?

John's £2100 was $\frac{3}{8}$ of the total profit. (Check you know why.)
So, $\frac{1}{8}$ of the total profit $= £2100 \div 3 = £700$

Therefore, Ben's share, which was $\frac{5}{8}$, amounted to $£700 \times 5 = £3500$

EXERCISE 9C

1 Derek, aged 15, and Ricki, aged 10, shared, in the same ratio as their ages, all the conkers they found in the woods. Derek had 48 conkers.

   a Simplify the ratio of their ages.

   b How many conkers did Ricki have?

   c How many conkers did they find altogether?

2 The soft drinks Coko and Orango were bought for the school disco in the ratio $5:3$. They bought 60 cans of Orango.

   a How much Coko did they buy?

   b How many drinks altogether did they buy?

3 Gwen is making a drink from lemonade and ginger essence in the ratio $9:1$. If Gwen has only 4.5 litres of lemonade, how much ginger essence does she need to make the drink?

4 When I harvested my apples, I found some eaten by wasps. The rest were good ones. These were in the ratio $3:17$. Eighteen of my apples had been eaten by wasps. How many good apples did I get?

5 A blend of tea is made by mixing Lapsang with Assam in the ratio $3:5$. I have a lot of Assam tea but only 600 g of Lapsang. How much Assam do I need to make the blend with all the Lapsang?

6 The ratio of male to female spectators at ice hockey games is $4:5$. At the Steelers' last match, 4500 men watched the match. What was the total attendance at the game?

7 A 'good' children's book is supposed to have pictures and text in the ratio 4 : 1. In a book I have just looked at, the pictures occupy 20 pages. Approximately how many pages of text should this book have to be deemed a 'good' children's book?

8 Two business partners, Kevin and Margaret, put money into a venture in the ratio 3 : 5. They shared any profits in the same ratio. Last year Margaret made £3400 out of the profits. How much did Kevin make last year?

9 'Proper tea' is made by putting milk and tea together in the ratio 2 : 9. How much 'proper tea' can be made by using 1 litre of milk?

10 A teacher always arranged each of his lessons to Y10 as 'teaching' and 'practising learnt skills' in the ratio 2 : 3.
  a If a lesson lasted 35 minutes, how much teaching would he do?
  b If he decided to teach for 30 minutes, how long would the lesson be?

Speed, time and distance

The relationship between speed, time and distance can be expressed in three ways:

$$\text{Speed} = \frac{\text{Distance}}{\text{Time}} \qquad \text{Distance} = \text{Speed} \times \text{Time} \qquad \text{Time} = \frac{\text{Distance}}{\text{Speed}}$$

When we refer to speed, we usually mean **average** speed, as it is unusual to maintain one exact speed for the whole of a journey.

The relationships between distance D, time T and speed S can be recalled using this diagram.

$$D = S \times T \qquad S = \frac{D}{T} \qquad T = \frac{D}{S}$$

Example 2

Paula drove a distance of 270 miles in 5 hours. What was her average speed?

$$\text{Paula's average speed} = \frac{\text{Distance she drove}}{\text{Time she took}} = \frac{270}{5} = 54 \text{ miles/h}$$

Example 3

Edith drove from Sheffield to Peebles for $3\frac{1}{2}$ hours at an average speed of 60 miles/h. How far is it from Sheffield to Peebles?

Distance = Speed × Time

So, distance from Sheffield to Peebles is given by
$60 \times 3.5 = 210$ miles

Note We changed the time to a decimal number and used 3.5, **not** 3.30.

Example 4

Sean is going to drive from Newcastle upon Tyne to Nottingham, a distance of 190 miles. He estimates that he will drive at an average speed of 50 miles/h. How long will it take him?

$$\text{Sean's time} = \frac{\text{Distance he covers}}{\text{His average speed}} = \frac{190}{50} = 3.8 \text{ hours}$$

Change the 0.8 hour to minutes by multiplying by 60, to give 48 minutes.

So, the time for Sean's journey will be 3 hours 48 minutes.
(A sensible rounding off would give 4 hours.)

Remember When you calculate a time and get a decimal answer, as in Example 4, **do not mistake** the decimal part for minutes. You must either
- leave the time as a decimal number and give the unit as hours, or
- change the decimal part to minutes by multiplying it by 60
  (1 hour = 60 minutes) and give the answer in hours and minutes.

EXERCISE 9D

1 A cyclist travels a distance of 90 miles in 5 hours. What was her average speed?

2 How far along a motorway will you travel if you drive at 70 mph for 4 hours?

3 I drive to Bude in Cornwall from Sheffield in about 6 hours. The distance from Sheffield to Bude is 315 miles. What is my average speed?

4 The distance from Leeds to London is 210 miles. The train travels at an average speed of 90 mph. If I catch the 9.30 am train in London, at what time would you expect me to get into Leeds?

5 How long will an athlete take to run a 2000 metres race at an average speed of 8 metres per second?

6 Complete the following table.

	Distance travelled	Time taken	Average speed
a	150 miles	2 hours	
b	260 miles		40 mph
c		5 hours	35 mph
d		3 hours	80 km/h
e	544 km	8 hours 30 minutes	
f		3 hours 15 minutes	100 km/h
g	215 km		50 km/h

7 A train travels at 50 km/h for 2 hours, then slows down to do the last 30 minutes of its journey at 40 km/h.
   a What is the total distance of this journey?
   b What is the average speed of the train over the whole journey?

8 Jane runs and walks to work each day. She runs the first 2 miles at a speed of 8 mph and then walks the next mile at a steady 4 mph.
   a How long does it take Jane to get to work?
   b What is her average speed?

9 I drove from Sheffield to Inverness, a distance of 410 miles, in 7 hours 45 minutes.
   a Change the time 7 hours 45 minutes to decimal time.
   b What was the average speed of the journey? Round off your answer to 1 decimal place.

10 Colin drives home from work in 2 hours 15 minutes. He says that he drives home at an average speed of 44 mph.
   a Change the 2 hours 15 minutes to decimal time.
   b How far is it from Colin's home to his work?

11 The distance between Paris and Le Mans is 200 km. The express train between Paris and Le Mans travels at an average speed of 160 km/h.
   a Calculate the time taken for the journey from Paris to Le Mans, giving your answer in decimal hour notation.
   b Change your answer to part **a** to hours and minutes.

12 The distance between Sheffield and Land's End is 420 miles.
   a What is the average speed of a journey from Sheffield to Land's End that takes 8 hours 45 minutes?
   b If I covered the distance at an average speed of 63 mph, how long would it take me?

Direct proportion problems

Suppose you buy 12 items which each cost the **same**. The total amount you spend is 12 times the cost of one item.

That is, the total cost is said to be in **direct proportion** to the number of items bought. The cost of a single item (the unit cost) is the constant factor that links the two quantities.

Direct proportion is concerned not only with costs. Any two related quantities can be in direct proportion to each other.

First finding the single unit value is the best way to solve all problems involving direct proportion. Work through Examples 5 and 6 to see how it is done.

This method is called the **unitary method**, because it involves referring to a single unit value.

Remember Before solving a direct proportion problem, think carefully about it to make sure that you know how to find the required single unit value.

Example 5

If eight pens cost £2.64, what is the cost of five pens?

First, we need to find the cost of **one** pen. This is £2.64 ÷ 8 = £0.33

So, the cost of five pens is £0.33 × 5 = £1.65

Example 6

Eight loaves of bread will make packed lunches for 18 people. How many packed lunches can be made from 20 loaves?

First, we need to find how many lunches **one** loaf will make.

One loaf will make 18 ÷ 8 = 2.25 lunches

So, 20 loaves will make 2.25 × 20 = 45 lunches

 EXERCISE 9E

1 If 30 matches weigh 45 g, what would 40 matches weigh?

2 Five bars of chocolate cost £2.90. Find the cost of 9 bars.

3 Eight men can chop down 18 trees in a day. How many trees can 20 men chop down in a day?

4 Find the cost of 48 eggs when 15 can be bought for £2.10

5 Seventy maths textbooks cost £875
   a How much will 25 maths textbooks cost?
   b How many maths textbooks can you buy for £100?

6 A lorry uses 80 litres of diesel fuel on a trip of 280 miles.
   a How much would be used on a trip of 196 miles?
   b How far would the lorry get on a full tank of 100 litres?

7 During the winter, I find that 200 kg of coal keeps my open fire burning for 12 weeks.
   a If I want an open fire all through the winter (18 weeks), how much coal will I need to get?
   b Last year I bought 150 kg of coal. For how many weeks did I have an open fire?

8 It takes a photocopier 16 seconds to produce 12 copies. How long will it take to produce 30 copies?

9 A recipe for 12 biscuits uses:
200 g margarine   400 g sugar   500 g flour   300 g ground rice
   a What is the recipe for
     i 6 biscuits   **ii** 9 biscuits   **iii** 15 biscuits?
   b What is the maximum number of biscuits I can make from having just 1 kg of each ingredient?

Best buys

When you wander around a supermarket and see all the different prices for the many different-sized packets, it is rarely obvious which are the 'best buys'. However, with a calculator you can easily compare value for money by finding either:

   the cost per unit weight **or** the weight per unit cost

To find:
- **cost per unit weight**, divide **cost by weight**
- **weight per unit cost**, divide **weight by cost**.

The next two examples show you how to do this.

Example 7

A 300 g tin of cocoa costs £1.20.

First change £1.20 to 120p. Then divide, using a calculator, to get:
Cost per unit weight $120 \div 300 = 0.4$p per gram
Weight per unit cost $300 \div 120 = 2.5$g per penny

Example 8

There are two different-sized packets of Whito soap powder at a supermarket. The medium size contains 800 g and costs £1.60 and the large size contains 2.5 kg and costs £4.75. Which is the better buy?

Find the weight per unit cost for both packets.
Medium: $800 \div 160 = 5$ g per penny
Large: $2500 \div 475 = 5.26$ g per penny

From these we see that there is more weight per pence with the large size, which means that the large size is the better buy.

EXERCISE 9F

1 Compare the following pairs of product and state which is the better buy and why.
   a Coffee: a medium jar which is 140 g for £1.10 or a large jar which is 300 g for £2.18.
   b Beans: a 125 g tin at 16p or a 600g tin at 59p.
   c Flour: a 3 kg bag at 75 p or a 5k g bag at £1.20.
   d Toothpaste: a large tube which is 110 ml for £1.79 or a medium tube which is 75 ml for £1.15.
   e Frosties: a large box which is 750 g for £1.64 or a medium box which is 500 g for £1.10.
   f Rice Crispies: a medium box which is 440 g for £1.64 or a large box which is 600 g for £2.13.
   g Hair shampoo: a bottle containing 400 ml for £1.15 or a bottle containing 550 ml for £1.60.

2 Julie wants to respray her car with yellow paint. In the local automart, she sees the following tins:
   Small tin   350 ml at a cost of £1.79
   Medium tin   500 ml at a cost of £2.40
   Large tin   1.5 litres at a cost of £6.70
   Which tin is offered at the cheapest cost per litre?

Investigation

Half-time Scores

The final score in a football match was 3 – 2. Some possible half-time scores were 0 – 0, 0 – 1, 0 – 2, 1 – 0, 1 – 1, …
- Find all the possible half-time scores for this match.
- Investigate the total number of half-time scores possible if you know the final score.

Paper Sizes

Obtain a sheet of paper in each of these sizes: A3, A4 and A5.
- How are the sheets related to each other?
- Investigate the ratio of the length to the width for each size.

Grandmother's Last Will and Testament

In her will, a grandmother has left £120 every year to be divided among her two grandchildren in the ratio of their ages in that year. At the moment, the two grandchildren are aged 4 and 8 years.

Investigate how the amounts for each grandchild change each year.

On the Billiard-table

On a billiard-table of size 1 : 2, the ball starts at pocket A, rebounds from the cushion once and ends up in pocket D.
- What happens if the ball rebounds at other points on the cushion?
- Investigate for a billiard-table of size $a : b$.

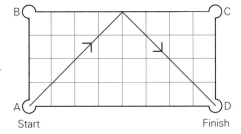

Examination questions

1 Share £250 in the ratio 1 : 9.

WJEC, Question 23, Paper 2, June 1999

2 Some cars and vans are parked in a car park. The ratio of vans to cars is 1 : 6. There are 30 vans. How many cars are there?

OCR, Question 3, Paper 1, June 2000

3 Ann and Bill share £400 in the ratio 5 : 3. How much does each of them receive?

MEG, Question 21, Specimen Paper 1, 1998

4 Gunpowder was invented by Chinese scientists over one thousand years ago.
Gunpowder was made from these three chemicals,
  • saltpetre
  • sulphur
  • charcoal
One recipe was: 5 shu of saltpetre, 1 shu of sulphur and 2 shu of charcoal mixed together. (The shu is an Ancient Chinese weight.)
Tara wants to investigate this recipe. She has 20 g of saltpetre. How much will she need of
  a sulphur?
  b charcoal?

OCR(SMP), Question 22, Paper 2, June 1999

5 Each year, Beeches School holds a sponsored swim. The money raised is shared between two charities, A and B, in the ratio 5 to 3.
  a In 1997, a total of £1600 was raised. How much was given to charity A?
  b In 1998, charity A was given £1500. How much was given to charity B?

OCR(SMP), Question 24, Terminal Paper, 1999

6 A coach has 32 pupils on. The ratio of boys to girls on this coach is 3 to 5. How many boys are on the coach?

SEG, Question 12, Specimen Paper 5, 2000

7 Simone drove a van along a motorway at a steady speed of 50 miles per hour. How far did she travel in $3\frac{1}{2}$ hours?

OCR(SMP), Question 5, Paper 1, June 1999

8 In November 1998 a load, 100 metres long, travelled from Tilbury to Enfield along the M25.
The distance from Tibury to Enfield is 30 miles. The load travelled at 4 miles per hour.
How long did the journey take? Write your answer in hours and minutes.

OCR(SMP), Question 7, Terminal Paper, 2000

9 A sponge cake for eight people needs 120 g of sugar. John makes a sponge cake for five people. Calculate the weight of sugar he needs.

SEG, Question 15, Specimen Paper 6, 2000

10 a Brian travels 225 miles by train. His journey takes $2\frac{1}{2}$ hours. What is the average speed of the train?
   b Val drives 225 miles at an average speed of 50 mph. How long does her journey take?

AQA, Question 19, Paper 2, June 2000

11 Recipe for bread and butter pudding.
   6 slices of bread
   2 eggs
   1 pint of milk
   150 g raisins
   10 g margarine
This recipe is enough for 4 people.
Work out the amounts needed so that there will be enough for 6 people.
   ...... slices of bread
   ...... eggs
   ...... pints of milk
   ...... g raisins
   ...... g margarine

EDEXCEL, Question 25, Paper 2, June 1999

12 Fred has a recipe for 30 biscuits. Here is a list of ingredients for 30 biscuits

Self-raising flour	230 g
Butter	150 g
Caster sugar	100 g
Eggs	2

Fred wants to make 45 biscuits. Complete his new list of ingredients for 45 biscuits.

Self-raising flour	....
Butter	....
Caster sugar	....
Eggs	....

EDEXCEL, Question 19, Paper 2, June 1998

13 A 500 g packet of *Healthy Flakes* costs £1.60.
A 750 g packet of *Healthy Flakes* costs £2.30.
Which size packet is the better buy?
Show all your calculations and explain your answer clearly.

OCR(SMP), Question 17, Terminal Paper, 1999

14 Three sizes of cola are sold in a garage shop.
The volume in millilitres and the cost in pence are shown under each one.

A   B   C

250 ml	330 ml	500 ml
40 p	50 p	78 p

a Work out how many millilitres of cola you get for 1 p in bottle A.

b Which size gives you best value?

Show your working clearly.

MEG(SMP), Question 14, Terminal Paper, 1998

15 £80 million of lottery funds was given to the sports of swimming and athletics. This money was shared between these two sports in the ratio

Swimming : Athletics

3 : 1

Calculate the amount that was given to swimming.

NEAB, Question 6, Paper 1F, June 1998

16 a The train from London to Manchester takes 2 hours 30 minutes. This train travels at an average speed of 80 miles per hour. What is the distance from London to Manchester?

b The railway company is going to buy some faster trains. These new trains will have an average speed of 100 miles per hour. How much time will be saved on the journey from London to Manchester?

NEAB, Question 8, Paper 1F, June 1998

What you should know after you have worked through Chapter 9

✔ How to divide any amount into a given ratio.
✔ The relationships between speed, time and distance.
✔ How to do problems involving direct proportion.
✔ How to compare the prices of products.

PUZZLE PAGE

What a family!

Think about your parents, their parents, your grandparents' parents and so on. These people are called ancestors.

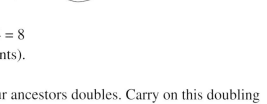

On average, first babies are born to their parents when the parents are about 25 years old.

So, let's do some research into **your** family.

- Twenty-five years ago you had two ancestors (your parents).
- So, 50 years ago you had $2 \times 2 = 4$ ancestors (your grandparents).
- And 75 years ago you had $2 \times 4 = 8$ ancestors (your great grandparents).

Every 25 years, the number of your ancestors doubles. Carry on this doubling and find out how many ancestors you had 2000 years ago, which is about the time of the birth of Christ.

The population of the UK in the year 2000 is approximately 60 million. How many ancestors do the people in the UK have altogether?

All these figures are absurdly high. What is wrong with the assumptions we have made in our calculations?

Think the other way, and estimate how many descendants you may have in

- 25 years time
- 50 years time
- 200 years time
- the year 3000

10 Symmetry

This chapter is going to ...

remind you about lines of symmetry and rotational symmetry. It will then show you the symmetrical properties of some 2-D and 3-D shapes.

What you should already know

✔ The names of these 2-D shapes: isosceles triangle, equilateral triangle, right-angled triangle, square, rectangle, parallelogram, rhombus, trapezium, kite
✔ The names of these 3-D shapes: cube, cuboid, square-based pyramid, triangular prism, cylinder, cone and sphere (see diagrams below)

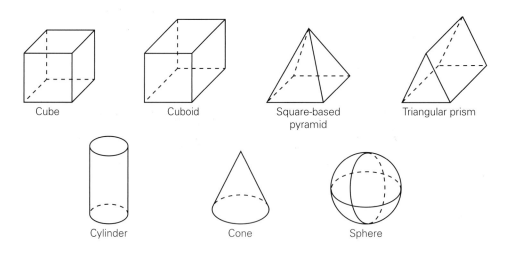

Cube   Cuboid   Square-based pyramid   Triangular prism

Cylinder   Cone   Sphere

Activity

Mirror writing

You need a plane mirror and some plain or squared paper.

You probably know that certain styles of some upright capital letters have one or more lines of symmetry. For example, the upright A given below has one line of symmetry (shown here as a dashed line).

Draw a large A on your paper and put the mirror along the line of symmetry.

What do you notice when you look in the mirror?

Upright capital letters such as A, O and M have a vertical line of symmetry. Can you find any others?

Other upright capital letters (E, for example) have a horizontal line of symmetry. Can you find any others?

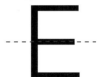

Now try to form words which have a vertical or a horizontal line of symmetry.

Here are two examples:

Make a display of all the different words you have found.

Lines of symmetry

Many 2-D shapes (flat shapes) have one or more lines of symmetry.

A line of symmetry is a line that can be drawn through a shape so that one side of the line is the mirror image of the other side. This is why a line of symmetry is sometimes called a **mirror line.**

It is also the line along which a shape can be folded exactly onto itself.

Finding lines of symmetry

In an examination, you may not be allowed to use a mirror to find lines of symmetry but it is just as easy to use tracing paper, which is always available in any mathematics examination.

For example, to find the lines of symmetry for a rectangle follow these steps:

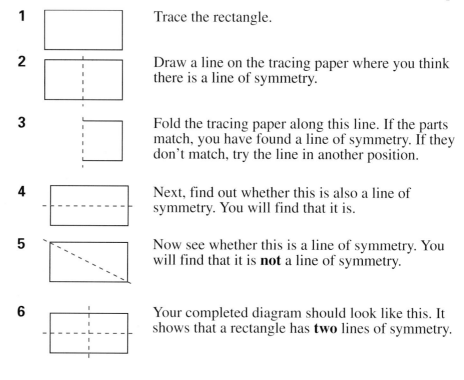

1   Trace the rectangle.

2   Draw a line on the tracing paper where you think there is a line of symmetry.

3   Fold the tracing paper along this line. If the parts match, you have found a line of symmetry. If they don't match, try the line in another position.

4   Next, find out whether this is also a line of symmetry. You will find that it is.

5   Now see whether this is a line of symmetry. You will find that it is **not** a line of symmetry.

6   Your completed diagram should look like this. It shows that a rectangle has **two** lines of symmetry.

Example 1

Find the number of lines of symmetry for this cross.

First, follow steps 1 to 4, which give the vertical and horizontal lines of symmetry.

Then search for any other lines of symmetry in the same way.

Two more will be found, as the diagram shows.

So, this cross has a total of four lines of symmetry.

EXERCISE 10A

1 Copy these shapes and draw on the lines of symmetry for each one. If it will help you, use tracing paper or a mirror to check your results.

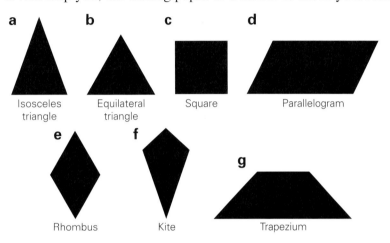

a Isosceles triangle **b** Equilateral triangle **c** Square **d** Parallelogram

e Rhombus **f** Kite **g** Trapezium

2 a Find the number of lines of symmetry for each of these regular polygons.

i Regular pentagon **ii** Regular hexagon **iii** Regular octagon

b How many lines of symmetry do you think a regular decagon has? (A decagon is a ten-sided polygon.)

3 Copy these star shapes and draw in all the lines of symmetry for each one.

a   **b**   **c**

4 Copy these patterns and draw in all the lines of symmetry for each one.

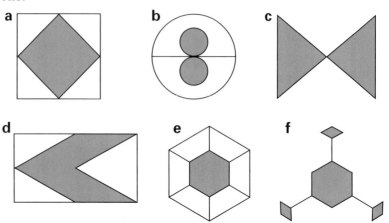

5 Write down the number of lines of symmetry for each of these flags.

Austria   Canada   Iceland   Switzerland   Greece

6 a These road signs all have lines of symmetry. Copy them and draw on the lines of symmetry for each one.

b Draw sketches of other common signs that also have lines of symmetry. State the number of lines of symmetry in each case.

7 The animal and plant kingdoms are full of symmetry. Four examples are given below. Sketch them and state the number of lines of symmetry for each one. Can you find other examples? Find suitable pictures, copy them and state the number of lines of symmetry each one has.

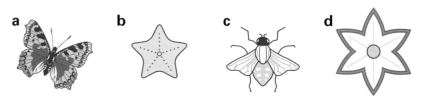

8 **a** Draw a circle with a radius of 3 cm.

   b Draw on any lines of symmetry. What do you notice?

   c How many lines of symmetry does a circle have?

9

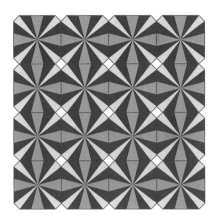

This decorative pattern is made by repeating shapes that have lines of symmetry. By using squared or isometric paper, try to make a similar pattern of your own.

Rotational symmetry

A 2-D shape has rotational symmetry if it can be rotated about a point to look exactly the same in a new position.

The **order of rotational symmetry** is the number of different positions in which the shape looks the same when it is rotated about the point.

The easiest way to find the order of rotational symmetry for any shape is to trace it and count the number of times that the shape stays the same as you turn the tracing paper through one complete turn.

Example 2

Find the order of rotational symmetry for this shape.

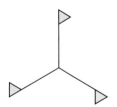

First, hold the tracing paper on top of the shape and trace it. Then rotate the tracing paper and count the number of times the tracing matches the original shape in one complete turn.

Three different positions will be found. So, the order of rotational symmetry for the shape is 3.

EXERCISE 10B

1 Copy these shapes and write below each one the order of rotational symmetry. If it will help you, use tracing paper.

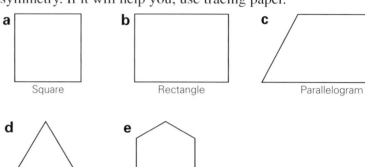

a Square   b Rectangle   c Parallelogram

d Equilateral triangle   e Regular hexagon

2 Find the order of rotational symmetry for each of these shapes.

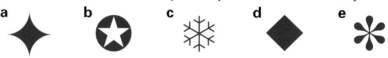

a   b   c   d   e

3 The following are Greek capital letters. Write down the order of rotational symmetry for each one.

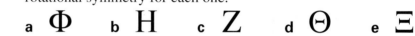

a Φ   b H   c Z   d Θ   e Ξ

4 Copy these shapes on tracing paper and find the order of rotational symmetry for each one.

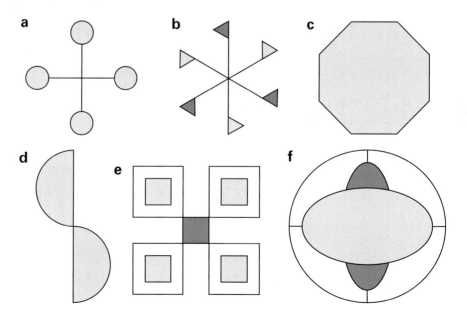

a   b   c

d   e   f

5   The upright capital letter A fits exactly onto itself only **once**. So, its order of rotational symmetry is 1. This means that it has **no** rotational symmetry. Write down all the upright capital letters of the alphabet which have rotational symmetry of order 1.

6   Find the order of rotational symmetry for a circle.

7   Obtain a pack of playing cards or a set of dominoes. Which cards or dominoes have rotational symmetry? Can you find any patterns? Write down everything you discover about the symmetry of the cards or dominoes.

Planes of symmetry

Because of their 'depth', 3-D shapes have **planes of symmetry**, instead of the lines of symmetry found in 2-D shapes.

A plane of symmetry divides a 3-D shape into two identical parts or halves. That is, one half of the shape is the reflection of the other half in the plane of symmetry.

Example 3

A cuboid has three planes of symmetry because it can be sliced into halves in three different ways.

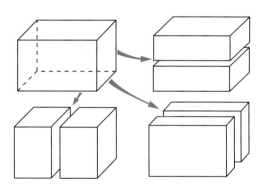

EXERCISE 10C

1   Find the number of planes of symmetry in each of these.

a

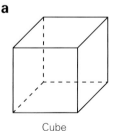

Cube

b

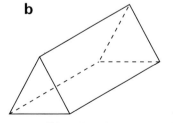

Triangular prism

c

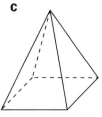

Square-based pyramid

2 This 3-D shape has five planes of symmetry. Draw diagrams to show where they are.

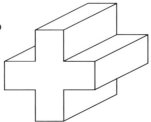

3 a The diagram shows half of a 3-D shape. Draw the complete shape so that the shaded part forms a plane of symmetry. What name do we give to this 3-D shape?

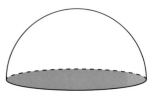

   b Draw similar diagrams to show a plane of symmetry for a cylinder and for a cone.

4 How many planes of symmetry do each of the following have?

a brick	**b** shovel	**c** chair
d spoon	**e** milk bottle	**f** kettle

Investigation

Symmetrical Tiles

On this 3×3 tile, three squares are shaded so that the tile has one line of symmetry.

Investigate the symmetry of the tile by shading different numbers of squares.

Pentomino Patterns

Pentominoes are shapes made with five squares that touch edge to edge.

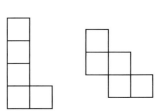

Investigate line symmetry and rotational symmetry for different pentominoes.

Four Cubed

How many symmetrical shapes can be made from four cubes placed face to face?

Examination questions

1 State which of the following designs have line symmetry.

a

Taj Mahal floor tile

b

Asian carpet design

c

Contemporary art

d
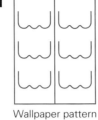
Wallpaper pattern

e
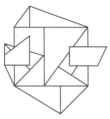
Tile design

EDEXCEL, Question 3, Specimen Paper 2 1998

2 State the order of rotational symmetry for each tile below.

a
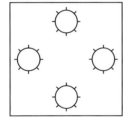

b
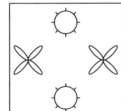

c
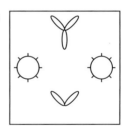

NEAB, Question 4, Paper 1F, June 1994

3 a What is the order of rotational symmetry for each of these shapes?

i

ii
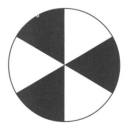

b Janice is making a blank crossword. The lines marked x and y are to be its two lines of symmetry. Copy and complete the crossword blank by shading in the correct squares.

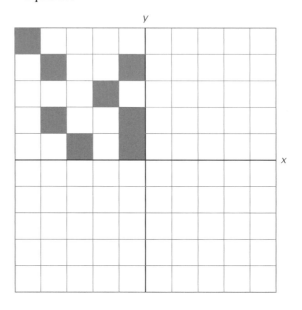

NEAB, Question 6, Specimen Paper 2F, 2000

4 Write down the order of rotational symmetry for each of these designs.

a   **b**   **c**

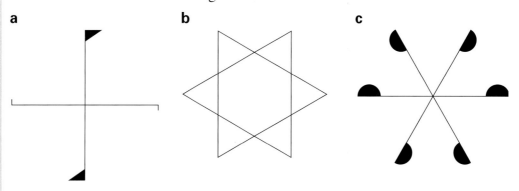

OCR(SMP), Question 20, Terminal Paper, 2000

5 Write down the order of rotational symmetry for each of
these shapes.

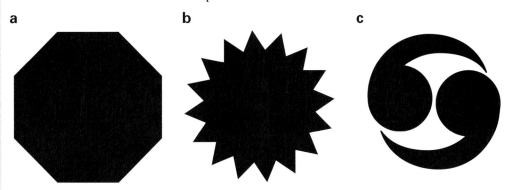

EDEXCEL, Question 2, Paper 1, June 1999

6 Patchwork cushion-cover designs are made using
the shapes below.

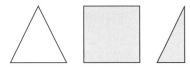

Copy and complete this design so that it has
rotational symmetry.

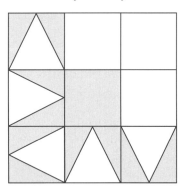

SEG, Question 20, Second Specimen Paper 12, 1998

⁷ M A T H S

Which of the letters above have

a line symmetry?

b rotational symmetry of order 2?

AQA, Question 14, Paper 2, June 2000

8 a This diagram shows a six-sided shape.

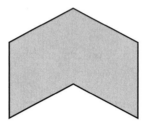

    i Draw the line of symmetry on the diagram.

    ii What is the name for a shape with six sides?

b Three of these shapes are used in a design for a badge.

    i How many lines of symmetry does this badge have?

    ii What is the order of rotational symmetry?

NEAB, Question 6 Paper 1, June 1998

What you should know after you have worked through Chapter 10

✔ How to find the number of lines of symmetry of a 2-D shape.

✔ How to find the order of rotational symmetry of a 2-D shape.

✔ How to find the number of planes of symmetry of a 3-D shape.

PUZZLE PAGE

Strike a light!

You need a collection of **used** matches.

In squares

Arrange 12 matches to form this large square.

Take away four matches to leave two squares.

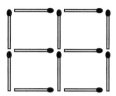

In triangles

Arrange nine matches to form this large triangle.

Take away two matches to leave two triangles.

In a diamond

Arrange 16 matches to form this large diamond.

Take away four matches to leave four triangles that are the same size.

Inside out

Move two matches so that the circle is outside the glass shape.

Two be or not two be

Arrange ten matches to spell the word 'two'.

Rearrange the matches to spell another number by leaving one letter the same.

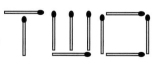

11 Averages

This chapter is going to ...

show you how to find three different types of average. It will also introduce you to the idea of range and show you how to use it to compare two sets of data.

What you should already know

✔ How to collect and organise data
✔ How to draw frequency tables
✔ How to extract information from tables and diagrams

'Average' is a term we often use when describing or comparing sets of data. For example, we refer to the average rainfall in Britain, the average score of a batsman, an average weekly wage, the average mark in an examination.

In each of the above examples, we are representing the whole set of **many values** by just a **single, 'typical' value**, which we call the average.

The idea of an average is extremely useful, because it enables us to compare one set of data with another set by comparing just two values – their averages.

There are several ways of expressing an average, but the most commonly used averages are the **mode,** the **median** and the **mean**.

The mode

The mode is the value that occurs the most in a set of data. That is, it is the value with the **highest frequency**.

The mode is a useful average because it is very easy to find and it can be applied to non-numerical data (qualitative data). For example, we could find the modal style of skirts sold in a particular month.

Example 1

Terry scored the following number of goals in 12 school football matches:
1 2 1 0 1 0 0 1 2 1 0 2

The number which occurs most often in this list is 1. So, the mode is 1.
We can also say that the **modal score** is 1.

Example 2

Barbara asked her friends how many books they each had taken out of the school library during the previous month. Their responses were
2 1 3 4 6 4 1 3 0 2 6 0

Here, there is **no** mode, because no number occurs more than the others.

EXERCISE 11A

1 Find the mode for each set of data.
   a 3, 4, 7, 3, 2, 4, 5, 3, 4, 6, 8, 4, 2, 7
   b 47, 49, 45, 50, 47, 48, 51, 48, 51, 48, 52, 48
   c −1, 1, 0, −1, 2, −2, −2, −1, 0, 1, −1, 1, 0, −1, 2, −1, 2
   d $\frac{1}{2}, \frac{1}{4}, 1, \frac{1}{2}, \frac{3}{4}, \frac{1}{4}, 0, \frac{1}{4}, 0, 1, \frac{3}{4}, \frac{1}{4}, 1, \frac{1}{4}, \frac{3}{4}, \frac{1}{4}, \frac{1}{2}$
   e 100, 10, 1000, 10, 100, 1000, 10, 1000, 100, 1000, 100, 10
   f 1.23, 3.21, 2.31, 3.21, 1.23, 3.12, 2.31, 1.32, 3.21, 2.31, 3.21

2 Find the modal category for each set of data.
   a Red, green, red, amber, green, red, amber, green, red, amber
   b Rain, sun, cloud, sun, rain, fog, snow, rain, fog, sun, snow, sun
   c α, γ, α, β, γ, α, α, γ, β, α, β, γ, β, β, α, β, γ, β
   d ✳, ☆, ★, ★, ☆, ✳, ★, ☆, ★, ☆, ★, ✳, ✪, ☆, ★, ★, ☆

3 The frequency table shows the marks that Form 10MP obtained in a spelling test.

Mark	3	4	5	6	7	8	9	10
Frequency	1	2	6	5	5	4	3	4

   a Write down the mode for their marks.
   b Do you think this is a typical mark for the form? Explain your answer.

4 Joan did a survey to find the shoe sizes of pupils in her class. The bar chart illustrates her data.

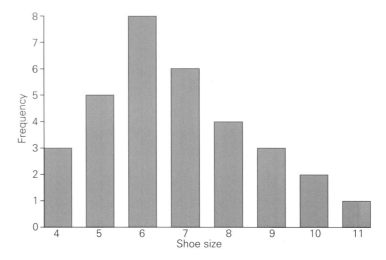

a How many pupils are in Joan's class?

b What is the modal shoe size?

c Can you tell from the bar chart which are the boys or which are the girls in her class?

d Joan then decided to draw a bar chart to show the shoe sizes of the boys and the girls separately. Do you think that the mode for the boys and the mode for the girls will be the same as the mode for the whole class? Explain your answer.

5 The grouped frequency table shows the number of letters each household in Corporation Street received during one week.

No. of letters	0–4	5–9	10–14	15–19	20–24	25–29	30–34	35–39
Frequency	9	12	14	11	10	8	4	2

a Draw a bar chart to illustrate the data.

b How many households are there in Corporation Street?

c How many households received 20 or more letters?

d How many households did not receive any mail during the week? Explain your answer.

The mode of the data in a grouped frequency table cannot be found. So, instead, we find the **modal class**. This is the class interval which has the highest frequency.

e Write down the modal class for the data in the table.

6 Explain why the mode is often referred to as the 'shopkeeper's average'.

The median

The median is the value at the **middle** of a list of values after they have been put in **order** of size, from lowest to highest.

The advantage of using the median as an average is that half the data is below the median value and half is above it. Therefore, the average is only slightly affected by the presence of any particularly high or low values which are not typical of the data as a whole.

Example 3

Find the median for the following list of numbers:
   2, 3, 5, 6, 1, 2, 3, 4, 5, 4, 6

Putting the list in numerical order gives
   1, 2, 2, 3, 3, **4**, 4, 5, 5, 6, 6

There are 11 numbers in the list, so the middle of the list is the 6th number. Therefore, the median is 4.

For a set of data which has a lot of values, it is sometimes more convenient and quicker to draw a **stem-and-leaf** diagram. Example 4 shows you how to do this.

Example 4

The ages of 20 people attending a conference were as follows:
   28, 32, 46, 23, 28, 34, 52, 61, 45, 34, 39, 50, 26, 44, 60, 53, 31, 25, 37, 48

Find the median age of the group.

Taking the tens to be the 'stem' and the units to be the 'leaves', you draw the stem-and-leaf diagram as shown below.

```
20 | 3 5 6 8 8
30 | 1 2 4 4 7 9
40 | 4 5 6 8
50 | 0 2 3
60 | 0 1
```

There is an **even** number of values in this list, so the middle of the list is **between the two central values,** 37 and 39. Therefore, the median is the value which is **exactly midway** between 37 and 39.

Hence, the median is 38.

EXERCISE 11B

1   Find the median for each set of data.

   a   7, 6, 2, 3, 1, 9, 5, 4, 8

   b   26, 34, 45, 28, 27, 38, 40, 24, 27, 33, 32, 41, 38

   c   4, 12, 7, 6, 10, 5, 11, 8, 14, 3, 2, 9

   d   12, 16, 12, 32, 28, 24, 20, 28, 24, 32, 36, 16

   e   10, 6, 0, 5, 7, 13, 11, 14, 6, 13, 15, 1, 4, 15

   f   −1, −8, 5, −3, 0, 1, −2, 4, 0, 2, −4, −3, 2

   g   5.5, 5.05, 5.15, 5.2, 5.3, 5.35, 5.08, 5.9, 5.25

2   **a**   Find the median of 7, 4, 3, 8, 2, 6, 5, 2, 9, 8, 3

   b   Without putting them in numerical order, write down the median for each of these sets.

   i   17, 14, 13, 18, 12, 16, 15, 12, 19, 18, 13

   ii   217, 214, 213, 218, 212, 216, 215, 212, 219, 218, 213

   iii   12, 9, 8, 13, 7, 11, 10, 7, 14, 13, 8

   iv   14, 8, 6, 16, 4, 12, 10, 4, 18, 16, 6

3   A group of 15 sixth-formers had lunch in the school's cafeteria. Given below is the amount that each of them spent.

   £2.30, £2.20, £2, £2.50, £2.20, £3.50, £2.20, £2.25, £2.20, £2.30, £2.40, £2.20, £2.30, £2, £2.35

   a   Find the mode for the data.

   b   Find the median for the data.

   c   Which is the better average to use? Explain your answer.

4   Given below are the age, height and weight of each of the seven players in a netball team.

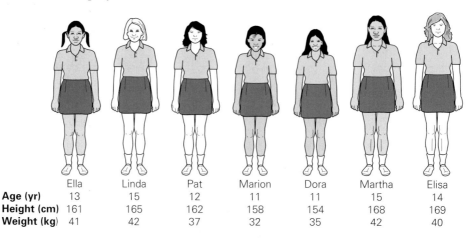

	Ella	Linda	Pat	Marion	Dora	Martha	Elisa
Age (yr)	13	15	12	11	11	15	14
Height (cm)	161	165	162	158	154	168	169
Weight (kg)	41	42	37	32	35	42	40

a Find the median age of the team. Which player has the median age?

b Find the median height of the team. Which player has the median height?

c Find the median weight of the team. Which player has the median weight?

d Who would you choose as the average player in the team? Give a reason for your answer.

5 **a** Write down a list of nine numbers which has a median of 12.

b Write down a list of ten numbers which has a median of 12.

c Write down a list of nine numbers which has a median of 12 and a mode of 8.

d Write down a list of ten numbers which has a median of 12 and a mode of 8.

6 A list contains seven even numbers. The largest number is 24. The smallest number is half the largest. The mode is 14 and the median is 16. Two of the numbers add up to 42. What are the seven numbers?

7 The bar chart shows the marks that Mrs Woodhead gave her students for their first mathematics coursework task.

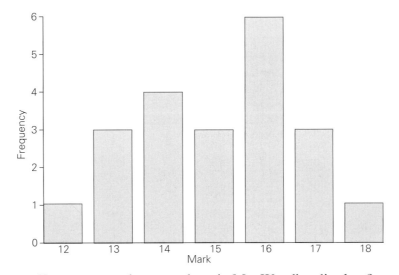

a How many students are there in Mrs Woodhead's class?

b What is the modal mark?

c What is the median mark? Remember that you must list everyone's mark.

8 The marks of 25 students in an English examination were as follows:

55, 63, 24, 47, 60, 45, 50, 89, 39, 47, 38, 42, 69, 73, 38, 47, 53, 64, 58, 71, 41, 48, 68, 64, 75

Draw a stem-and-leaf diagram to find the median.

The mean

The mean of a set of data is the sum of all the values in the set divided by the total number of values in the set. That is:

$$\text{Mean} = \frac{\text{Sum of all the values}}{\text{Total number of values}}$$

This is what most people mean when they use the term 'average'.

The advantage of using the mean as an average is that it takes into account all the values in the set of data.

Example 5

Find the mean of 4, 8, 7, 5, 9, 4, 8, 3

Sum of all the values = 4 + 8 + 7 + 5 + 9 + 4 + 8 + 3 = 48

Total number of values = 8

Therefore, mean = $\frac{48}{8} = 6$

Example 6

The ages of 11 players in a football squad are:
    21, 23, 20, 27, 25, 24, 25, 30, 21, 22, 28

What is the mean age of the squad?

Sum of all the ages = 266

Total number in squad = 11

Therefore, mean age = $\frac{266}{11} = 24.1818\ldots = 24.2$ (1 dp)

When the answer is not exact, it is usual to round the mean to one decimal place (1 dp).

EXERCISE 11C

1 Find, without the help of a calculator, the mean for each set of data.
   a 7, 8, 3, 6, 7, 3, 8, 5, 4, 9
   b 47, 3, 23, 19, 30, 22
   c 42, 53, 47, 41, 37, 55, 40, 39, 44, 52
   d 1.53, 1.51, 1.64, 1.55, 1.48, 1.62, 1.58, 1.65
   e 1, 2, 0, 2, 5, 3, 1, 0, 1, 2, 3, 4

2 Calculate the mean for each set of data, giving your answer correct to one decimal place. You may use your calculator.
  a 34, 56, 89, 34, 37, 56, 72, 60, 35, 66, 67
  b 235, 256, 345, 267, 398, 456, 376, 307, 282
  c 50, 70, 60, 50, 40, 80, 70, 60, 80, 40, 50, 40, 70
  d 43.2, 56.5, 40.5, 37.9, 44.8, 49.7, 38.1, 41.6, 51.4
  e 2, 3, 1, 0, 2, 5, 4, 3, 2, 0, 1, 3, 4, 5, 0, 3, 1, 2

3 The table shows the marks which ten students obtained in mathematics, English and science in their Year 10 examinations.

Student	Abigail	Brian	Chloe	David	Eric	Frances	Graham	Howard	Ingrid	Jane
Maths	45	56	47	77	82	39	78	32	92	62
English	54	55	59	69	66	49	60	56	88	44
Science	62	58	48	41	80	56	72	40	81	52

  a Calculate the mean mark for mathematics.
  b Calculate the mean mark for English.
  c Calculate the mean mark for science.
  d Which student obtained marks closest to the mean in all three subjects?
  e How many students were above the average mark in all three subjects?

4 Heather kept a record of the amount of time she spent on her homework over 10 days:
  $\frac{1}{2}$ h, 20 min, 35 min, $\frac{1}{4}$ h, 1 h, $\frac{1}{2}$ h, $1\frac{1}{2}$ h, 40 min, $\frac{3}{4}$ h, 55 min
  Calculate the mean time, in minutes, that Heather spent on her homework.

5 David caught eight fish in an angling competition. Their weights were:
  8 oz, 11 oz, 1 lb, 15 oz, 12 oz, 1 lb 3 oz, 14 oz, 1 lb 1 oz
  Calculate the mean weight of the fish he caught. (1 lb = 16 oz)

6 The weekly wages of ten people working in an office are:
  £350   £200   £180   £200   £350   £200   £240   £480
  £300   £280
  a Find the modal wage.
  b Find the median wage.
  c Calculate the mean wage.
  d Which of the three averages best represents the office staff's wages? Give a reason for your answer.

7   The ages of five people in a group of walkers are 38, 28, 30, 42, 37
    a   Calculate the mean age of the group.
    b   Steve, who is 41, joins the group. Calculate the new mean age of the group.

8   The mean age of another group of eight walkers is 42. Joanne joins the group and the mean age changes to 40. How old is Joanne?

9   a   Calculate the mean of 3, 7, 5, 8, 4, 6, 7, 8, 9, 3
    b   Calculate the mean of 13, 17, 15, 18, 14, 16, 17, 18, 19, 13
        What do you notice?
    c   **Write down** the mean for each of the following.
        i   53, 57, 55, 58, 54, 56, 57, 58, 59, 53
        ii   103, 107, 105, 108, 104, 106, 107, 108, 109, 103
        iii 4, 8, 6, 9, 5, 7, 8, 9, 10, 4

The range

The range for a set of data is the highest value of the set minus the lowest value.

The range is **not** an average. It shows the **spread** of the data. It is therefore used when comparing two or more sets of similar data.

Example 7

Rachel's marks in ten mental arithmetic tests were 4, 4, 7, 6, 6, 5, 7, 6, 9, 6

Therefore, her mean mark is 60 ÷ 10 = 6, and the range is 9 – 4 = 5

Robert's marks in the same tests were 6, 7, 6, 8, 5, 6, 5, 6, 5, 6

Therefore, his mean mark is 60 ÷ 10 = 6, and the range is 8 – 5 = 3

Although the means are the same, Robert has a smaller range. This shows that Robert's results are **more consistent.**

EXERCISE 11D

1   Find the range for each set of data.
    a   3, 8, 7, 4, 5, 9, 10, 6, 7, 4
    b   62, 59, 81, 56, 70, 66, 82, 78, 62, 75
    c   1, 0, 4, 5, 3, 2, 5, 4, 2, 1, 0, 1, 4, 4
    d   3.5, 4.2, 5.5, 3.7, 3.2, 4.8, 5.6, 3.9, 5.5, 3.8
    e   2, –1, 0, 3, –1, –2, 1, –4, 2, 3, 0, 2, –2, 0, –3

2 The table shows the maximum and minimum temperatures at midday for five cities in England during a week in August.

	Birmingham	Leeds	London	Newcastle	Sheffield
Maximum temperature (°F)	81	77	78	80	75
Minimum temperature (°F)	73	72	76	68	70

    a Write down the range of the temperatures for each city.

    b What do the ranges tell you about the weather for England during the week?

3 In a ladies' golf tournament, the club chairperson had to choose either Sheila or Margaret to play in the first round. In the previous eight rounds, their scores were as follows:

    Sheila's scores: 75, 92, 80, 73, 72, 88, 86, 90

    Margaret's scores: 80, 87, 85, 76, 85, 79, 84, 88

    a Calculate the mean score for each golfer.

    b Find the range for each golfer.

    c Which golfer would you choose to play in the tournament? Explain why.

4 Over a three-week period, the school tuck shop took the following amounts.

	Monday	Tuesday	Wednesday	Thursday	Friday
Week 1	£32	£29	£36	£30	£28
Week 2	£34	£33	£25	£28	£20
Week 3	£35	£34	£31	£33	£32

    a Calculate the mean amount taken each week.

    b Find the range for each week.

    c What can you say about the total amounts taken for each of the three weeks?

5 Stan has a choice of two buses to get to school: Number 50 or Number 63. Over a month, he kept a record of the number of minutes each bus was late when it set off from his home bus stop.

    No. 50: 4, 2, 0, 6, 4, 8, 8, 6, 3, 9

    No. 63: 3, 4, 0, 10, 3, 5, 13, 1, 0, 1

    a For each bus, calculate the mean number of minutes late.

    b Find the range for each bus.

    c Which bus would you advise Stan to catch? Give a reason for your answer.

Activity

Your time is up

You are going to find out how good you are at estimating 1 minute.

You need a stop-watch and a calculator.

This is a group activity. One person in the group acts as a timekeeper, says 'Start' and starts the stop-watch.

When someone thinks 1 minute has passed, he/she says 'Stop', and the timekeeper writes down the actual time, in seconds, that has passed. The timekeeper should try to record everyone's estimate.

Repeat the activity, with every member of the group taking a turn as the timekeeper.

Collate all the times and from the data find the mean (to the nearest second) and the range.

* How close is the mean to 1 minute?
* Why is the range useful?
* What strategies did people use to estimate 1 minute?

Repeat the activity for estimating different times: for example, 30 seconds or 2 minutes.

Write a brief report on what you find out about people's ability to estimate time.

Which average do I use?

An average must be truly representative of a set of data. So, when you have to find an average, it is crucial to choose the **correct type of average** for this particular set of data.

If you use the wrong average, your results will be distorted and give misleading information.

The table at the top of the next page, which compares the advantages and disadvantages of each type of average, will help you to make the correct decision.

	Mode	Median	Mean
Advantages	Very easy to find Not affected by extreme values Can be used for non-numerical data	Easy to find for ungrouped data Not affected by extreme values	Easy to find Uses all the values The total for a given number of values can be calculated from it
Disadvantages	Doesn't use all the values May not exist	Doesn't use all the values Often not understood	Extreme values can distort it Has to be calculated
Used for	Non-numerical data For finding the most likely value	Data with extreme values	Data whose values are spread in a balanced way

EXERCISE 11E

1 a For each set of data find the mode, the median and the mean.
  i 6, 10, 3, 4, 3, 6, 2, 9, 3, 4
  ii 6, 8, 6, 10, 6, 9, 6, 10, 6, 8
  iii 7, 4, 5, 3, 28, 8, 2, 4, 10, 9
 b For each set of data decide which average is the best one to use and give a reason.

2 A newsagent sold the following number of copies of *The Evening Star* on 12 consecutive evenings during a promotion exercise organised by the newspaper's publisher:
  65   73   75   86   90   112   92   87   77   73   68   62
 a Find the mode, the median and the mean for the sales.
 b The newsagent had to report the average sale to the publisher after the promotion. Which of the three averages would you advise the newsagent to use? Explain why.

3 Decide which average you would use for each of the following. Give a reason for your answer.
 a The average mark in an examination.
 b The average pocket money for a group of 16-year-old students.
 c The average shoe size for all the girls in Year 10.
 d The average height for all the artistes on tour with a circus.
 e The average hair colour for pupils in your school.
 f The average weight of all newborn babies in a hospital's maternity ward.

4 A pack of matches consisted of 12 boxes. The contents of each box were counted as

34 31 29 35 33 30 31 28 29 35 32 31

On the box it stated 'Average contents 32 matches'. Is this correct?

5 The ages of the members of a hockey team were

29 26 21 24 26 28 35 23 29 28 29

What is

a the modal age   **b** the median age

c the mean age?   **d** What is the range of the ages?

6 The mean age of a group of 10 young people was 15.

a What do all their ages add up to?

b What will be their mean age in 5 years time?

7 A firm showed the annual salaries for its employees as:

Chairman	£43 000
Managing director	£37 000
Floor manager	£25 000
Skilled worker 1	£24 000
Skilled worker 2	£24 000
Machinist	£18 000
Computer engineer	£18 000
Secretary	£18 000
Office junior	£7 000

a What is

i the modal salary   **ii** the median salary

iii the mean salary?

b The management suggested a pay rise for all of 6%. The skilled workers suggested a pay rise for all of £1500. One of the suggestions would cause problems for the firm. Which one is that and why?

8 Mr Brennan, a caring maths teacher, told each pupil their test mark and only gave the test statistics to the whole class. He gave the class the modal mark, the median mark and the mean mark.

a Which average would tell a pupil whether he/she were in the top half or the bottom half of the class?

b Which average tells the pupils nothing really?

c Which average allows a pupil really to gauge how well he/she has done compared with everyone else?

Frequency tables

When a lot of information has been gathered, it is often convenient to put it together in a frequency table. From this table you can then find the values of the three averages.

Example 8

A survey was done on the number of people in each car leaving the Meadowhall Shopping Centre, in Sheffield. The results are summarised in the table below.

Number of people in each car	1	2	3	4	5	6
Frequency	45	198	121	76	52	13

Find the mode, the median and the mean of the number of people in a car.

The **modal number** of people in a car is easy to spot. It is the number with the largest frequency of 198. Hence, the modal number is 2

The **median number** of people in a car is found by working out where the middle of the set of numbers is located. First, we add up frequencies to get the total number of cars surveyed, which comes to 505. Next, we calculate the middle position:

$(505 + 1) \div 2 = 253$

Because 505 is odd, we add 1 to the total before dividing by 2. This tells us how many cars to count off before we get to the middle one.

We now need to count the frequencies across the table to find which group contains the 253rd item. The 243rd item is the end of the group with 2 in a car. Therefore, the 253rd item must be in the group with 3 in a car. Hence, the median number in a car is 3

The **mean number** of people in a car is found by adding together all the people and then dividing this total by the number of cars surveyed. This is best done by completing the following table.

Number in a car	Frequency	Number × Frequency
1	45	$1 \times 45 = 45$
2	198	$2 \times 198 = 396$
3	121	$3 \times 121 = 363$
4	76	$4 \times 76 = 304$
5	52	$5 \times 52 = 260$
6	13	$6 \times 13 = 78$
Totals	505	1446

Hence, the mean number of people in a car is $1446 \div 505 = 2.9$ (1 dp).

EXERCISE 11F

1 Find **i** the mode, **ii** the median and **iii** the mean from each frequency table below.

a A survey of the shoe sizes of all the Y10 boys in a school gave these results.

Shoe size	4	5	6	7	8	9	10
Number of pupils	12	30	34	35	23	8	3

b A survey of the number of eggs laid by hens over a period of one week gave these results.

Number of eggs	0	1	2	3	4	5	6
Frequency	6	8	15	35	48	37	12

c This is a record of the number of babies born each week over one year in a small maternity unit.

Number of babies	0	1	2	3	4	5	6	7	8	9	10	11	12	13	14
Frequency	1	1	1	2	2	2	3	5	9	8	6	4	5	2	1

d A school did a survey on how many times in a week pupils arrived late at school. These are the findings.

Number of times late	0	1	2	3	4	5
Frequency	481	34	23	15	3	4

2 A survey of the number of children in each family of a school's intake gave these results.

Number of children	1	2	3	4	5
Frequency	214	328	97	26	3

a Assuming each child at the school is shown in the data, how many children are at the school?

b Calculate the mean number of children in a family?

c How many families have this mean number of children?

d How many families would consider themselves average from this survey?

3 A dentist kept records of how many teeth he extracted from his patients.

In 1980 he extracted 598 teeth from 271 patients.

In 1990 he extracted 332 teeth from 196 patients.

In 2000 he extracted 374 teeth from 288 patients.

a Calculate the average number of teeth taken from each patient in each year.

b Explain why you think the average number of teeth extracted falls each year.

4 100 cases of apples delivered to a supermarket were inspected and the number of bad apples counted.

Bad apples	0	1	2	3	4	5	6	7	8	9
Frequency	52	29	9	3	2	1	3	0	0	1

What is

a the modal number of bad apples per case

b the mean number of bad apples per case?

5 Two dice are thrown together 60 times. The sum of the scores is shown below.

Score	2	3	4	5	6	7	8	9	10	11	12
Frequency	1	2	6	9	12	15	6	5	2	1	1

Find **a** the modal score, **b** the median score and **c** the mean score.

6 During a 1 month period, the number of days off by 100 workers in a factory were noted as follows.

Number of days off	0	1	2	3	4
Number of workers	35	42	16	4	3

Calculate

a the modal number of days off

b the median number of days off

c the mean number of days off.

7 Two friends often played golf together. They recorded their scores for each hole over the last five games to discover who was more consistent and who was the better player. Their results are summarised in the following table.

Number of shots to hole ball	1	2	3	4	5	6	7	8	9
Roger	0	0	0	14	37	27	12	0	0
Brian	5	12	15	18	14	8	8	8	2

a What is the modal score for each player?
b What is the range of scores for each player?
c What is the median score for each player?
d What is the mean score for each player?
e Which player is the more consistent and explain why?
f Who would you say is the better player and state why?

Investigation

Win the Lottery

Find the mean and the range for the numbers of the main six balls drawn in last week's National Lottery.

From a newspaper, or from TV's teletext, obtain the previous 20 weeks' draws and again find the mean and the range for each week's draw. What do you notice?

Averages Rule OK

In statistics there is a rule which states that
Mean – Mode = 3(Mean – Median)

Throw a dice 50 times and record the scores in a frequency table.

Calculate the mode, the median and the mean of the scores to test the accuracy of this rule.

Carry out other experiments and surveys of your own to test the rule.

Top of the Pops

Carry out a survey to investigate teenagers' views on, and interest in, pop music.

Your account should include tables, graphs, averages and have a conclusion.

Examination questions

1 William is a member of a quiz team.
Here are William's scores in the last nine quizzes.
   67, 52, 59, 43, 49, 65, 68, 48, 53
   a Calculate his mean score.
   b Find his median score.
   c Find the range of his scores

MEG(SMP), Question 20, Paper 1, June 1998

2 Nicky recorded the numbers of people getting off her bus at 10 stops. Here are her results.
   2, 4, 3, 6, 3, 6, 3, 7, 11, 8
For these ten numbers, work out
   a the mean
   b the median
   c the range.

EDEXCEL, Question 5, Paper 1, June 1999

3 Some teachers were asked how many National Lottery tickets they bought last week. The results are shown in the table.

Number of tickets	Number of teachers
0	2
1	7
2	5
3	2
4	0
5	3
6	1

   a Which number of tickets is the mode?
   b Work out the mean number of tickets.
   c Find the median number of tickets.

EDEXCEL, Question 20, Specimen Paper 1, 1998

4 Mrs Chowdery gives her class a maths test. Here are the test marks for the girls.

7, 5, 8, 5, 2, 8, 7, 4, 7, 10, 3, 7, 4, 3, 6

a Work out the mode.

b Work out the median.

The median mark for the boys was 7 and the range of marks for the boys was 4. The range of the girls' marks was 8.

c By comparing the results, explain whether the boys or the girls did better in the test.

EDEXCEL, Question 16, Paper 2, June 1998

5 The weights, in kilograms, of a boat crew are:

96, 86, 94, 96, 91, 95, 90, 96, 43

a Calculate

   i their median weight

   ii the range of their weights

   ii their mean weight.

b Which of the two averages, mean or median, best describes the data above? Give a reason for your answer.

AQA, Question 6, Paper 2, June 2000

6 One day the postman recorded how many letters he delivered to each house in Orchard Road. The bar chart shows his results.

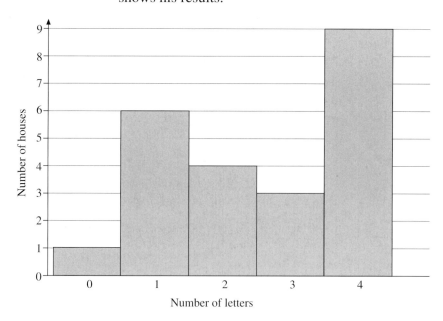

a How many houses had one letter delivered?

b What was the modal number of letters delivered?

c Find the median number of letters he delivered in Orchard Road that day. Show clearly how you found it.

OCR(SMP), Question 21, Paper 2, June 2000

7 The results of a mathematics test for 25 pupils are shown below.

Mark	Number of pupils	
4	1	
5	3	
6	2	
7	2	
8	7	
9	8	
10	2	

a Which mark is the mode?

b Find the median mark.

c Calculate the mean mark.

MEG, Question 19, Paper 1, June 1998

8 Eunice measures the lengths of runner beans in a gardening competition. The lengths, in centimetres, of the longest ten runner beans are given below.

27, 35, 28, 25, 28, 37, 31, 28, 27, 34

a What is the range in the lengths of these runner beans?

b Calculate the mean length of these runner beans.

c In last year's competition, the mean length of the longest ten runner beans was 30 cm and the range was 8 cm. Explain how the lengths of the runner beans differ this year from last year.

SEG, Question 9, Specimen Paper 12, 1998

9 Twelve boys ran a 100 metres race. Their times, in seconds, are shown.

11.0 11.5 11.5 12.3 12.9 13.1
13.6 14.2 14.8 15.6 16.4 17.1

a **i** What is the range in the running times of these boys?

ii Calculate the mean running time.

b Twelve girls run a 100 metres race and their times are recorded. The range in the running times for the girls is 5.6 seconds and the mean is 14.3 seconds. Comment on the differences in running times for boys and girls.

SEG, Question 12, Second Specimen Paper 11, 1998

10 Arthur caught the Thompson bus each morning. For 20 days he kept a record of how many minutes late it was. His results, to the nearest minute, are shown below.

Minutes late	Frequency
6	5
7	10
8	3
9	2

a For these results:
   i What is the mode?
   ii What is the range?
b The Jones bus travels on the same route. For the same days, Kay did a similar survey on how many minutes late this bus was. Her results were:

   Mode: 2 minutes late   Range: 15 minutes

   Use the mode and the range to decide which is the better bus to use.

NEAB, Question 5, Paper 2F, June 1998

11 A teacher asks all his class: 'How many children are there in your family?' Their replies are given below

Number of children in a family	Number of replies
1	7
2	12
3	5
4	2
5	0

a How many children are in the class?

    b What is the most common number of children in a family for this class?

    c Calculate the mean number of children per family in this class. Give your answer to one decimal place.

NEAB, Question 8, Paper 1F, June 1998

12 Julia plays in her school netball team. She will be selected to play for the county team next season if her mean score of goals for the school team after the first seven games is at least 12.

After six games, her mean score of goals is 11.5.

    a What is the total number of goals that Julia has scored in these six games?

    b What is the least number of goals she must score in the next game in order to be chosen for the county team?

    c In the seventh game, she scores 13 goals. Does her mean score of goals increase or decrease?

You must show all your working.

NEAB, Question 23, Paper 2F, June 1998

13 Twenty five people took part in a competition. The points scored are grouped in the frequency table below.

Points scored	Number of people
1 to 5	1
6 to 10	2
11 to 15	5
16 to 20	7
21 to 35	8
26 to 30	2

Write down the modal class of points scored.

EDEXCEL, Question 19, Paper 1, June 1998

14 A set of 25 times in seconds is recorded.

12.9	10.0	4.2	16.0	5.6	18.1	8.3
14.0	11.5	21.7	22.2	6.0	13.6	3.1
11.5	10.8	15.7	3.7	9.4	8.0	6.4
17.0	7.3	12.8	13.5			

a Complete the frequency table below, using intervals of 5 seconds.

Time, t (seconds)	Tally	Frequency
$0 \leqslant t < 5$		

b Write down the modal class interval.

EDEXCEL, Question 17, Paper 2, June 1998

What you should know after you have worked through Chapter 11

✔ How to find the mode, the median and the mean for a set of data.

✔ How to find the range for a set of data.

✔ Advantages and disadvantages of each of the three types of average.

✔ How to choose the most appropriate average.

Percentage

This chapter is going to ...

explain what is meant by percentage and then show you how to do calculations involving percentage. It will also show you how to use your calculator to work out percentages.

What you should already know

✔ How to cancel down fractions
✔ How to calculate with fractions
✔ How to multiply decimals by 100 (move the digits two places to the left)
✔ How to divide decimals by 100 (move the digits two places to the right)

Percentages as fractions and decimals

Per cent means 'out of 100'. So, any percentage can be expressed as a **fraction** whose denominator is 100. For example,

$$32\% = \frac{32}{100} \text{ which can be cancelled down to } \frac{8}{25}$$

Also, any percentage can be expressed as a **decimal** by dividing by 100. That is, by moving the digits two places to the right. For example,

$$65\% = 65 \div 100 = 0.65$$

Knowing the percentage equivalents of the following fractions is extremely useful. So, do try to learn them.

$\frac{1}{2} = 50\%$ $\frac{1}{4} = 25\%$ $\frac{3}{4} = 75\%$

$\frac{1}{10} = 10\%$ $\frac{1}{5} = 20\%$ $\frac{1}{3} = 33\frac{1}{3}\%$

100% means the **whole** of something. So, if we want to, we can express **part** of the whole as a **percentage.**

For example:

When 5% of the pupils are absent, then 95% of the pupils are present.

When 35% of the audience at a rock concert are women, then 65% of the audience are men.

EXERCISE 12A

1 Write each percentage as a fraction in its lowest terms.

    a 8%   **b** 50%   **c** 20%   **d** 5%   **e** 10%   **f** 75%

    g 25%   **h** 45%   **i** 60%   **j** 40%   **k** 35%   **l** 90%

    m 4%   **n** 30%   **o** 100%   **p** 70%   **q** 15%   **r** 65%

2 Write each percentage as a decimal.

    a 27%   **b** 85%   **c** 13%   **d** 6%   **e** 8%   **f** 2%

    g 34.6%   **h** 12.5%   **i** 98.4%   **j** 200%   **k** 125%   **l** 175%

    m 34%   **n** 26.8%   **o** 112%   **p** 72%   **q** 17.5%   **r** 90%

3 Of the 300 members of a social club 50% are men. How many members are women?

4 Gillian came home and told her dad that she got 100% of her spellings correct. She told her mum that there were 25 spellings to learn. How many spellings did Gillian get wrong?

5 Every year a school library likes to get rid of 1% of its books. One year the library had 2000 books. How many did it get rid of?

6 **a** If 23% of pupils go home for lunch, how many do not go home for lunch?

    b If 61% of the population take part in the National Lottery, how many do not take part?

    c If 37% of members of a church are males, how many members are females?

7 28% of my time is spent sleeping, 45% is spent working. How much time is left to spend doing something else?

8 24.7% of the population is below the age of 16, and 13.8% of the population is aged over 65. How much of the population is aged between 16 and 65 inclusive?

9 Approximately what percentage of each bottle is filled with water?

    a   **b**   **c**

10 Helen made a cake for James. The amount of cake left each day is shown in the diagram.

   a What percentage is left each day?

   b What percentage has been eaten each day?

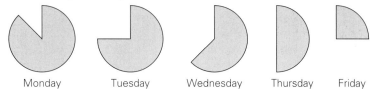

    Monday   Tuesday   Wednesday   Thursday   Friday

Activity

Percentage dominoes

You need a piece of card about 30 cm by 30 cm.

On the card, draw a grid of 49 rectangles, as shown below. Each rectangle measures 4 cm by 2 cm, and is divided in half by a dashed line.

In each rectangle, write the appropriate percentage and fraction as given in the diagram.

The fractions in the top row of rectangles are the correct equivalents of the percentages. Using a light blue pencil or crayon, colour in the top row, so that the rectangles can be easily spotted during the game.

50%	$\frac{1}{2}$	25%	$\frac{1}{4}$	10%	$\frac{1}{10}$	75%	$\frac{3}{4}$	20%	$\frac{1}{5}$	40%	$\frac{2}{5}$	80%	$\frac{4}{5}$
50%	$\frac{1}{4}$	25%	$\frac{1}{10}$	10%	$\frac{3}{4}$	75%	$\frac{1}{5}$	20%	$\frac{2}{5}$	40%	$\frac{4}{5}$	80%	$\frac{1}{2}$
50%	$\frac{1}{10}$	25%	$\frac{3}{4}$	10%	$\frac{1}{5}$	75%	$\frac{2}{5}$	20%	$\frac{4}{5}$	40%	$\frac{1}{2}$	80%	$\frac{1}{4}$
50%	$\frac{3}{4}$	25%	$\frac{1}{5}$	10%	$\frac{2}{5}$	75%	$\frac{4}{5}$	20%	$\frac{1}{2}$	40%	$\frac{1}{4}$	80%	$\frac{1}{10}$
50%	$\frac{1}{5}$	25%	$\frac{2}{5}$	10%	$\frac{4}{5}$	75%	$\frac{1}{2}$	20%	$\frac{1}{4}$	40%	$\frac{1}{10}$	80%	$\frac{3}{4}$
50%	$\frac{2}{5}$	25%	$\frac{4}{5}$	10%	$\frac{1}{2}$	75%	$\frac{1}{4}$	20%	$\frac{1}{10}$	40%	$\frac{3}{4}$	80%	$\frac{1}{5}$
50%	$\frac{4}{5}$	25%	$\frac{1}{2}$	10%	$\frac{1}{4}$	75%	$\frac{1}{10}$	20%	$\frac{3}{4}$	40%	$\frac{1}{5}$	80%	$\frac{2}{5}$

Carefully cut out all the rectangles to form a set of 'dominoes' that you can play with.

Now play a game of dominoes, putting **equivalents** next to each other. For example,

| 50% | $\frac{1}{10}$ | 10% | $\frac{1}{10}$ | 10% | $\frac{4}{5}$ |

Do **not** put identical percentages next to each other or identical fractions.

Calculating a percentage of a quantity

To calculate a percentage of a quantity, we multiply the quantity by the percentage. The percentage may be expressed as either a fraction or a decimal.

Example 1

Calculate 12% of 54 kg.

$$\frac{12}{100} \times 54 = (12 \div 100) \times 54 = 6.48 \text{ kg}$$

Example 2

Calculate 25% of £80.

We recognise 25% as a decimal is 0.25. Hence, the problem is
$$0.25 \times £80 = £20$$

Using your calculator

All calculators have a percentage key $\boxed{\%}$. The problem is that the way to use the percentage key varies according to the type of calculator.

So, you need to investigate how to use the percentage key on **your** calculator. For example, to calculate 15% of 120

you could try $\boxed{1}$ $\boxed{5}$ $\boxed{\%}$ $\boxed{\times}$ $\boxed{1}$ $\boxed{2}$ $\boxed{0}$ $\boxed{=}$

or $\boxed{1}$ $\boxed{2}$ $\boxed{0}$ $\boxed{\times}$ $\boxed{1}$ $\boxed{5}$ $\boxed{\%}$

Maybe both of these ways work for your calculator, or only one of them. The correct answer is 18.

On some calculators you will need to press the $\boxed{=}$ key, while on others you won't.

It is important for you to be familiar with your calculator and to use it whenever it is sensible to do so. With percentages, it is preferable to use a calculator, particularly when solving problems.

EXERCISE 12B

1 Calculate the following.
  a 15% of £300   **b** 6% of £105   **c** 23% of 560 kg
  d 45% of 2.5 kg   **e** 12% of 9 hours   **f** 21% of 180 cm
  g 4% of £3   **h** 35% of 8.4 m   **i** 95% of £8
  j 11% of 308 min   **k** 20% of 680 kg   **l** 45% of £360

2 15% of the pupils in a school bring sandwiches with them. If there are 640 pupils in the school, how many bring sandwiches?

3 An estate agent charges 2% commission on every house he sells. How much commission will he earn on a house that he sells for £60 250?

4 A department store had 250 employees. During one week of a flu epidemic, the shop had 14% of its employees absent.
  a What percentage of the employees got into work?
  b How many of the employees got into work?

5 It is thought that about 20% of fans at a rugby match are women. For a match at Twickenham there were 42 600 fans. How many of these do you think would be women?

6 At St Pancras Railway Station, in one week 350 trains arrived. 5% of these trains arrived early, 13% of them arrived late. How many arrived on time?

7 For the FA Cup Final at Wembley each year the 75 000 tickets are split up as follows.
    Each of the teams playing gets 30% of the tickets.
    The referees association get 1% of the tickets.
    The other 90 teams get 10% of the tickets between them.
    The FA associates get 20% of the tickets between them.
    The rest are for the special celebrities.
  How many tickets go to each set of people?

8 A school estimates that for a parents' evening it will see the parents of 60% of all the students. Year 10 consists of 190 students. How many of them expected to be represented by their parents?

9 A school had 850 pupils, and the attendance record in the week before Christmas was

      Monday 96%   Tuesday 98%   Wednesday 100%
      Thursday 94%   Friday 88%

How many pupils were present each day?

10 Soft solder consists of 60% lead, 35% tin and 5% bismuth (by weight). How much of each metal is in 250 grams of solder?

11 Calculate the following.

   a 12.5% of £26   **b** 6.5% of 34 kg   **c** 26.8% of £2100
   d 7.75% of £84   **e** 16.2% of 265 m   **f** 0.8% of £3000

12 Air consists of 80% nitrogen and 20% oxygen (by volume). A man's lungs have a capacity of 600 cm^3. How much of each gas will he have in his lungs when he has just taken a deep breath?

13 A factory estimates that 1.5% of all the garments they produce will have a fault in them. One week they make 850 garments. How many are likely to have a fault?

14 An insurance firm sells house insurance and the annual premiums are usually at a cost of 0.3% of the value of the house. What will be the annual premium for a house valued at £90 000?

Percentage increase and decrease

Increase

There are two methods for increasing by a percentage.

Method 1

Find the increase and add it to the original amount. For example, to increase £6 by 5%:

    Find 5% of £6: $(5 \div 100) \times 6 = £0.30$
    Add the £0.30 to the original amount: $£6 + £0.30 = £6.30$

Method 2

Using the calculator **%** key.

As you saw earlier, each type of calculator can operate percentage quite differently. So you have to find out how your calculator deals with percentage increase (if it does at all – since some don't).

For example, to increase £6 by 5%

you could try `6` `+` `5` `%` `=`

Check that you get the answer £6.30

EXERCISE 12C

1 Increase each of the following by the given percentage. (Use any method you like.)

a	£60 by 4%	**b**	12 kg by 8%	**c**	450 g by 5%
d	545 m by 10%	**e**	£34 by 12%	**f**	£75 by 20%
g	340 kg by 15%	**h**	670 cm by 23%	**i**	130 g by 95%
j	£82 by 75%	**k**	640 m by 15%	**l**	£28 by 8%

2 Kevin, who was on a salary of £27 500, was given a pay rise of 7%. What was his new salary?

3 In 1995 the population of Melchester was 1 565 000. By 2000 that had increased by 8%. What was the population of Melchester in 2000?

4 A small firm made the same pay increase for all its employees: 5%.
 a Calculate the new pay of each employee listed below. Each of their salaries before the increase is given.
  Bob, caretaker, £16 500   Jean, supervisor, £19 500
  Anne, tea lady, £17 300   Brian, manager, £25 300
 b Is the actual pay increase the same for each worker?

5 A bank pays 7% interest on the money that each saver keeps in the bank for a year. Allison keeps £385 in this bank for a year. How much will she have in the bank after the year?

6 In 1980 the number of cars on the roads of Sheffield was about 4200. Since then it has increased by 80%. Approximately how many cars are on the roads of Sheffield now?

7 An advertisement for a breakfast cereal states that a special offer packet contains 15% more cereal for the same price than a normal 500 g packet. How much breakfast cereal is in a special offer packet?

8 A headteacher was proud to point out that, since he had arrived at the school, its population then of 680 students had increased by 35%. How many students are now in the school?

9 At a school disco there are always about 20% more girls than boys. If at one disco there were 50 boys, how many girls were there?

10 VAT is a tax that the Government adds to the price of most goods in shops. At the moment, it is 17.5% on all electrical equipment. Calculate the price of the following electrical equipment after VAT of 17.5% has been added.

Equipment	Pre-VAT price
TV set	£245
Microwave oven	£72
CD player	£115
Personal stereo	£29.50

Decrease

There are two methods for decreasing by a percentage.

Method 1

Find the decrease and take it away from the original amount. For example, to decrease £8 by 4%:

Find 4% of £8: $(4 \div 100) \times 8 = £0.32$

Take the £0.32 away from the original amount: $£8 - £0.32 = £7.68$

Method 2

Using the calculator **%** key.

You tried the percentage increase with your calculator, now try percentage decrease by, perhaps, using subtraction instead of addition. For example, to decrease £8 by 5%

you could try **8** **−** **5** **%** **=**

Check that you get the answer £7.60

EXERCISE 12D

1 Decrease each of the following by the given percentage. (Use any method you like.)

a £10 by 6%	**b** 25 kg by 8%	**c** 236 g by 10%
d 350 m by 3%	**e** £5 by 2%	**f** 45 m by 12%
g 860 m by 15%	**h** 96 g by 13%	**i** 480 cm by 25%
j 180 min by 35%	**k** 86 kg by 5%	**l** £65 by 42%

2 A car valued at £6 500 last year is now worth 15% less. What is its value now?

3 A new P-plan diet guarantees that you will lose 12% of your weight in the first month. How much should the following people weigh after one month on the diet?
   a Gillian, who started at 60 kg
   b Peter, who started at 75 kg
   c Margaret, who started at 52 kg

4 A motor insurance firm offers no-claims discounts off the given premium, as follows:

   1 year no claim   15% discount
   2 years no claim   25% discount
   3 years no claim   45% discount
   4 years no claim   60% discount

   Mr Speed and his family are all offered motor insurance from this firm:

   Mr Speed, who has 4 years no-claim discount, is quoted a premium of £140.

   Mrs Speed, who has 1 year no-claim discount, is quoted a premium of £350.

   James, who has 3 years no-claim discount, is quoted a premium of £230.

   John, who has 2 years no-claim discount, is quoted a premium of £450.

   Calculate the actual amount each member of the family has to pay for the motor insurance.

5 A large factory employed 640 people. It had to streamline its workforce and lose 30% of the workers. How big is the workforce now?

6 On the last day of the Christmas term, a school expects to have an absence rate of 6%. If the school population is 750 pupils, how many pupils will the school expect to see on the last day of the Christmas term?

7 Since the start of the National Lottery a particular charity called Young Ones said they now have a decrease of 45% in the money raised by scratch cards. If before the Lottery the charity had an annual income of £34 500 from their scratch cards, how much do they collect now?

8 Most speedometers in cars have an error of about 5% from the true reading. When my speedometer says I am driving at 70 mph,
   a what is the slowest speed I could be doing
   b what is the fastest speed I could be doing?

9 You are a member of a club which allows you to claim a 12% discount off any marked price in shops. What will you pay in total for the following goods?

Sweatshirt   £19

Track suit   £26

10 I read an advertisement in my local newspaper last week which stated: 'By lagging your roof and hot water system you will use 18% less fuel.' Since I was using an average of 640 units of gas a year, I thought I would lag my roof and my hot water system. How much gas would I expect to use now?

Changing fractions and decimals to percentages

Fractions and decimals can be expressed as percentages.

To change a fraction to a percentage, simply multiply it by 100.

Example 3

Express $\frac{4}{5}$ as a percentage.

$$\frac{4}{5} \times 100 = (4 \div 5) \times 100 = 80\%$$

To change a decimal to a percentage, simply multiply it by 100. That is, move the digits two places to the left.

Example 4

Express 0.68 as a percentage.

$$0.68 \times 100 = 68\%$$

EXERCISE 12E

1 Change each of these fractions into a percentage.

a $\frac{1}{5}$ **b** $\frac{1}{4}$ **c** $\frac{3}{4}$ **d** $\frac{9}{20}$ **e** $\frac{7}{8}$

f $\frac{1}{2}$ **g** $\frac{3}{5}$ **h** $\frac{7}{40}$ **i** $\frac{11}{20}$ **j** $\frac{3}{10}$

2 Change each of these fractions into a percentage. Give your answers to one decimal place.

a $\frac{1}{3}$ **b** $\frac{1}{6}$ **c** $\frac{2}{3}$ **d** $\frac{5}{6}$ **e** $\frac{2}{7}$

f $\frac{47}{60}$ **g** $\frac{31}{45}$ **h** $\frac{8}{9}$ **i** $\frac{73}{90}$ **j** $\frac{23}{110}$

3 Change each of these decimals into a percentage.

a 0.07   **b** 0.8   **c** 0.66   **d** 0.25   **e** 0.545

f 0.82   **g** 0.3   **h** 0.891   **i** 1.2   **j** 2.78

4 Chris scored 24 marks out of a possible 40 in a maths test.

    a Write this score as a fraction.

    b Write this score as a decimal.

    c Write this score as a percentage.

5 Convert each of the following test scores into a percentage. Give each answer to the nearest whole number.

Subject	Result	Percentage
Mathematics	38 out of 60	
English	29 out of 35	
Science	26 out of 70	
History	56 out of 90	
Technology	58 out of 75	

6 The air we breathe consists of about $\frac{4}{5}$ nitrogen and $\frac{1}{5}$ oxygen. What percentage of the air is **a** nitrogen, **b** oxygen?

7 There were two students missing from my class of 30. What percentage of my class were away?

8 In one season, Paulo Di Canio had 110 shots on goal. He scored with 28 of these shots. What percentage of his shots resulted in goals?

Expressing one quantity as a percentage of another

We express one quantity as a percentage of another by setting up the first quantity as a fraction of the second, making sure that the **units of each are the same**. Then, we convert that fraction to a percentage by simply multiplying it by 100.

Example 5

Express £6 as a percentage of £40.

Set up the fraction $\frac{6}{40}$ and multiply it by 100. This gives

$\qquad (6 \div 40) \times 100 = 15\%$

Example 6

Express 75 cm as a percentage of 2.5 m.

First, change 2.5 m to 250 cm to get a common unit.

Hence, the problem becomes 75 cm as a percentage of 250 cm.

Set up the fraction $\frac{75}{250}$ and multiply it by 100. This gives

$(75 \div 250) \times 100 = 30\%$

We can use this method to calculate percentage gain or loss in a financial transaction, as Example 7 shows.

Example 7

Bert buys a car for £1500 and sells it for £1800. What is Bert's percentage gain?

Bert's gain is £300, so his percentage gain is

$$\frac{300}{1500} \times 100 = 20\%$$

Notice how the percentage gain is found by

$$\frac{\text{Difference}}{\text{Original}} \times 100$$

Using your calculator

Here is another place you can use the **%** key on your calculator.

For example, to express 5 as a percentage of 40

try **5** **÷** **4** **0** **%** **=**

You should get the answer 12.5%.

You may not have to press the **=** key, depending on how your calculator works this out.

EXERCISE 12F

1 Express each of the following as a percentage. Give suitably rounded-off figures where necessary.

a	£5 of £20	**b**	£4 of £6.60
c	241 kg of 520 kg	**d**	3 hours of 1 day
e	25 minutes of 1 hour	**f**	12 m of 20 m
g	125 g of 600 g	**h**	12 minutes of 2 hours
i	1 week of a year	**j**	1 month of 1 year
k	25 cm of 55 cm	**l**	105 g of 1 kg
m	5 oz of 16 oz	**n**	2.4 litres of 6 litres
o	8 days of 1 year	**p**	25p of £3
q	18p of £2.50	**r**	40 seconds of 1 day
s	8 hours of 1 year	**t**	5 mm of 4 cm

2 Find, to one decimal place, the percentage profit on the following.

Item	Retail price (selling price)	Wholesale price (price the shop paid)
a CD player	£89	£60
b TV set	£345	£210
c Computer	£829	£750
d Video player	£199.99	£110
e Microwave oven	£98.50	£78

3 John went to school with his pocket money of £2.50. He spent 80p at the tuck shop. What percentage of his pocket money had he spent?

4 Before Anton started to diet, he weighed 95 kg. He now weighs 78 kg. What percentage of his original weight has he lost?

5 In 1999 the Melchester County Council raised £14 870 000 in council tax. In 2000 it raised £15 597 000 in council tax. What was the percentage increase?

6 In Greece, there are 3 654 000 acres of agricultural land. Olives are grown on 237 000 acres of this land. What percentage of the agricultural land is used for olives?

7 Martin had an annual salary of £22 600 in 1999, which was increased to £23 100 in 2000. What percentage increase does this represent?

8 During the wet year of 1981, it rained in Manchester on 123 days of the year. What percentage of days were wet?

9 When Blackburn Rovers won the championship in 1995, they lost only four of their 42 league games. What percentage of games did they not lose?

10 In the year 1900 Britain's imports were as follows:

British Commonwealth	£109 530 635
USA	£138 789 261
France	£53 618 656
Other countries	£221 136 611

What percentage of the total imports came from each source?

Investigation

Double Your Money

You put £100 in a building society deposit account that pays 8% interest every year and leave it there for a number of years.

How long will it take to double your money?

Snails in the Well

A snail tries to climb out of a well 10 m deep.

It climbs 60 cm in 1 hour, but for every 1 m that it climbs it falls back 5% of the total height climbed.

Approximately how long will the snail take to climb out of the well?

Which Percentage Is Bigger?

■ I make something 10% bigger, then make it 10% smaller.
What happens to the original? Is it bigger, smaller or what?

■ I make something 10% smaller, then make it 10% bigger.
Is it the same as in the first case? If not, why not?

Examination questions

1 Copy and complete the table below.

Fraction	Decimal	Percentage
$\frac{1}{2}$	is the same as 0.5 is the same as	50%
$\frac{1}{4}$	is the same as ......is the same as	......
......	is the same as 0.3 is the same as	......

NEAB, Question 10, Specimen Paper 1F, 2000

2 Brenda looked at a door that was 90 cm wide, and said:
'The door needs to be 30% bigger.' Calculate the width that Brenda thinks the door should be.

NEAB, Question 26, Specimen Paper 1F, 2000

3 **a** Write 48% as a fraction in its simplest form.

b Write $\frac{7}{20}$ as a percentage.

OCR, Question 12, Paper 1, June 2000

4 Class 11A has 30 pupils. 18 of these pupils are girls. What percentage of the class is girls?

EDEXCEL, Question 11, Paper 1, June, 1999

5 The land area of a farm is 385 acres.

a $\frac{1}{5}$ of the land is used to grow barley. How many acres in this?

b 15% of the land is not used. How many acres is this?

c 96 acres is pasture. What percentage of the total land is pasture? Give your answer to the nearest 1%.

AQA, Question 10, Paper 2, June 2000

6 John makes a sponge cake, and cuts it into five equal pieces. He gives three slices to his mother. What percentage of the cake does John have left?

SEG, Question 15, Specimen Paper 6, 2000

7

SALE
25% off all marked prices

The marked price of a pullover is £15.99. What is the sale price, to the nearest penny?

MEG, Question 7, Specimen Paper 2, 1998

8

London – Paris by plane
Normal price: £91
Special offer: 15% discount

An airline company has flights from London to Paris for £91. They offer a 15% discount. Calculate the cost of the flight after the discount.

AQA, Question 11, Paper 1, June 1999

9

£850 + VAT

This computer was sold in 1996. The rate of VAT was 17.5%.
How much did the computer cost altogether?

MEG, Question 25, Paper 2, June 1998

10 David's salary in 1998 was £17 550. He was promoted in
January 1999 and given an 18% increase in his salary.
What is his new salary?

WJEC, Question 23, Paper 2, June 1999

11 In a maternity hospital, 200 babies were born during May.
110 of them were girls.
 a What percentage of the babies were girls?
 b In June the number of babies born in the hospital
 increased by 5%. Calculate the number of babies born in
 June.

MEG, Question 5, Paper 2, June 1998

12 A pupil carries out a survey in her school. She chooses 200
pupils at random. 90 of these pupils said they used the
library in their town. What percentage is 90 out of 200?

NEAB, Question 8, Paper 1F, June 1998

13 Fill in the boxes.

	Fraction		Decimal		Percentage
a	$\frac{1}{2}$	=	0.5	=	
b		=	0.75	=	75%
c	$\frac{7}{100}$	=		=	7%

NEAB, Question 1, Paper 2F, June 1998

14 In an election there were three condidates. They were Alan Archer, Priti Patel and Simon Smith. Alan Archer got 25% of the votes, Priti Patel got 35% of the votes and Simon Smith got the rest.

a What percentage of the votes did Simon Smith get?

b Who won the election?

Altogether 40 000 people voted in the election.

c How many people voted for Priti Patel?

OCR, Question 9, Paper 1, June 1999

15 Salid buys a new car for £12 000. He is told that his car will lose 23% of its value during the first year.

a How much will Salid's car be worth when it is one year old?

Peter bought a second-hand car for £4000. After a year it was worth £3200.

b **i** Express £3200 as a percentage of £4000.

ii What percentage of its value did the car lose during the year?

OCR, Question 17, Paper 1, June 1999

What you should know after you have worked through Chapter 12

✔ How to change a percentage to a fraction and to a decimal.

✔ How to change a fraction to a percentage, and a decimal to a percentage.

✔ How to calculate a percentage of a given amount.

✔ How to increase and decrease by a certain percentage.

✔ How to express one quantity as a percentage of another.

PUZZLE PAGE

Age old

Try this out on yourself first to make sure you know what is happening.

You will find it extremely helpful to use a calculator.

Then ask someone to:

- Add 1 to the number of the month in which he/she was born.
  For example, January = 1 + 1, February = 2 + 1, March = 3 + 1 and so on.
- Multiply the result by 100.
- To this add the day of the month in which he/she was born.
- Multiply by 2 and add 11.
- Multiply by 5 and add 50.
- Multiply by 10 and add his/her age.
- Finally, add 61.

Now, ask the person for the number he/she ended up with, and subtract 11 111.

Write down the number he/she gets as pairs of digits, like this:

3	15	16

The first box is the month in which he/she was born – March (the 3rd month) in this example.

The second box is the day on which the person was born – the 15th in this example.

The last box is his/her age.

If you managed to make this work, try it out on some of your friends, then maybe your teacher, then your parents and possibly even either of your grannies – or both!

Once you've done all this, you might like to think about why it works.

Revision for Chapters 1 to 12

- Answer all the questions
- Show your working

1 Put a bracket in each of these to make the answer correct.
  a $9 - 2 \times 3 = 21$ **b** $7 + 5 \times 4 - 2 = 17$

2 **a** How long will it take me to save £192, if I save £6 a week?
  b How many days are there in 32 weeks?

3 Calculate the following.
  a $\frac{3}{5} + \frac{1}{5}$ **b** $\frac{5}{8} - \frac{3}{8}$ **c** $\frac{7}{8} + \frac{5}{8}$
  d $\frac{4}{5} + \frac{1}{5}$ **e** $\frac{6}{7} + \frac{3}{7}$ **f** $\frac{3}{4}$ of £60
  g $\frac{2}{3}$ of 60 m   **h** $\frac{5}{8}$ of 40 minutes   **i** $\frac{5}{6}$ of 2 hours
  j $\frac{4}{5}$ of 35 weeks

4 Write down the answer to each of these.
  a $3 - 8$ **b** $-6 - 11$ **c** $-2 + 7$ **d** $-8 + 3$
  e $2 - -6$ **f** $3 - -17$ **g** $-12 - -8$ **h** $-5 + -7$
  i $-9 + 14$ **j** $-21 + -13$

5 **a** Write down the first nine multiples of 8.
  b Write down all the factors of 48.
  c Write down all the prime numbers larger than 10 and smaller than 40.
  d Write down the square number larger than 70 and smaller than 90.

6 For each of the following shapes:

i

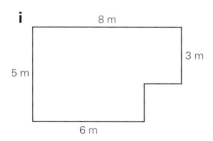

ii

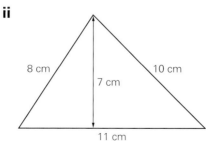

  a Calculate the perimeter.   **b** Calculate the area.

7 The pictogram below illustrates the numbers of different electronic games in Y11.

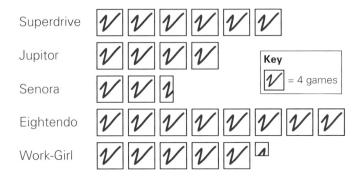

a How many games do Y11 have altogether?

b Draw a fully labelled bar chart to illustrate this information.

8 Express the perimeter of each of the following shapes as simply as possible.

a 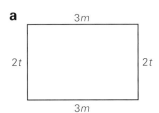   b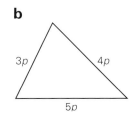

9 Use the formula $T = 3w + 8$ to work out the following.

a Find T when $w = 7$ b Find T when $w = \frac{1}{2}$

c Find w when $T = 20$

10 Calculate each of these without using your calculator.

a 237×43 b $544 \div 16$ c $18.4 \div 5$ d 5.3×4.8

11 George and Jo share £600 in the ratio $5 : 3$. How much does each of them receive?

12 My garden is $40\,\text{m}^2$. I want to cover $\frac{3}{8}$ of the garden with a lawn, plant vegetables in $\frac{1}{8}$, and have the rest for flowers.

a What will be the area of my lawn?

b What fraction of my garden will be for flowers. Give your answer as simply as possible.

13 Alia drives from her home to her mother's home in 1 hour 15 minutes. She drives at an average speed of 40 mph.

a Change the 1 hour 15 minutes to decimal time.

b How far is it from Alia's home to her mother's home?

Revision section

14 **a** If nine men can build three huts in a day, how many huts can six men build in a day?

b If four ladies take 6 hours to decorate a room, how long would it have taken three ladies?

15 Make a copy of each shape below.

i   **ii**   **iii**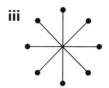

a Draw in all the lines of symmetry.

b State the order of rotational symmetry for each shape.

16 Take these numbers:

5 4 3 2 5 3 2 5 4 3 5

a State the mode. **b** State the median.

c Calculate the mean.

17 Farmer Brown noted how many eggs each of his hens had laid one morning.

Number of eggs laid	Frequency
0	3
1	5
2	6
3	9
4	2

a State the range of eggs laid per hen.

b Calculate the mean number of eggs per hen.

18 Fill in the empty boxes.

	Fraction		Decimal		Percentage
a	$\frac{1}{4}$		0.25		
b		$=$	0.5	$=$	
c	$\frac{13}{100}$	$=$		$=$	

19 **a** What fraction of this diagram is shaded?

b What percentage of this diagram is shaded?

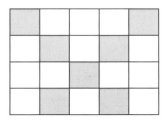

20 **a** On Friday, 4% of the 350 workers at a pottery were absent. How many were absent?

b Beth, who earned £86 a week, was given a 5% pay rise. Calculate Beth's new weekly pay.

Revision section

More algebra

This chapter is going to ...

show you how to solve simple linear equations in which the variable appears on only one side of the equals sign. It will then lead you through the solution of more complicated equations in which the variable appears on both sides of the equals sign.

What you should already know

✔ The basic language of algebra (see pages 119–20)
✔ Only like terms can be added or subtracted to simplify an expression
✔ A number next to a bracket means that *everything* in the bracket can be multiplied by that number
✔ The opposite (inverse) operation to addition is subtraction (and vice versa)
✔ The opposite (inverse) operation to multiplication is division (and vice versa)

Simple linear equations

A teacher gave these instructions to her class.

- Think of a number.
- Double it.
- Add 3.

What algebraic expression represents the teacher's statement? (See pages 119–20)

This is what two of her students said.

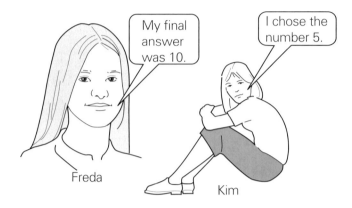

My final answer was 10.

I chose the number 5.

Freda

Kim

Can you work out Kim's answer and the number that Freda started with?

Freda's answer can be set up as an **equation**.

An equation is formed when an expression is put equal to a number or another expression. You are expected to deal with equations which have only **one variable** or letter.

The **solution** to an equation is the value of the variable that makes the equation true. For example, the equation for Freda's answer is

$$2x + 3 = 10$$

where x represents Freda's number.

The value of x that makes this true is $x = 3\frac{1}{2}$.

Solving equations

To solve an equation, we have to 'undo' it. That is, we have to reverse the processes that set up the equation in the first place.

Freda did two things. First she multiplied by 2 and then added 3. The reverse process is first to subtract 3 and then to divide by 2. So, to solve

$$2x + 3 = 10$$

Subtract 3 $\quad 2x + 3 - 3 = 10 - 3$

$$2x = 7$$

Divide by 2 $\quad \dfrac{2x}{2} = \dfrac{7}{2}$

$$x = 3\frac{1}{2}$$

The problem is knowing how an equation is set up in the first place, so that you can undo it in the right order.

There are three ways to solve equations: inverse flow diagrams, 'doing the same to both sides' and rearrangement. They are all essentially the same. You will have to decide which method you prefer, although you should know how to use all three.

There is one rule about equations that you should **always** follow:
    Check that your answer works in the original equation.

For example, to check our answer to Freda's equation, put $x = 3\frac{1}{2}$ into Freda's equation. This gives
    $2 \times 3\frac{1}{2} + 3 = 7 + 3 = 10$

which is correct.

Inverse flow diagrams

This flow diagram represents the instructions that their teacher gave to Kim and Freda:

```
──────▶│ × 2 │──────▶│ + 3 │──────▶
```

The **inverse flow diagram** is:

```
◀──────│ ÷ 2 │◀──────│ − 3 │◀──────
```

Running Freda's answer through this we get:

```
  3½            7            10
◀──────│ ÷ 2 │◀──────│ − 3 │◀──────
```

So, we started with $3\frac{1}{2}$ to get an answer of 10

Example 1

Solve the following equation using an inverse flow diagram:
    $3x - 4 = 11$

Flow diagram:

Inverse flow diagram:

Put through the value on the right-hand side of the equals sign:

$$\overset{5}{\longleftarrow} \boxed{\div 3} \overset{15}{\longleftarrow} \boxed{+ 4} \overset{11}{\longleftarrow}$$

So, the answer is $x = 5$

Checking the answer gives
$$3 \times 5 - 4 = 11$$

which is correct.

EXERCISE 13A

Solve each of the following equations using inverse flow diagrams. Do not forget to check that each answer works for its original equation.

1 $3x + 5 = 11$	**2** $3x - 13 = 26$	**3** $3x - 7 = 32$
4 $4y - 19 = 5$	**5** $3a + 8 = 11$	**6** $2x + 8 = 14$
7 $2y + 6 = 18$	**8** $8x + 4 = 12$	**9** $2x - 10 = 8$
10 $\dfrac{x}{5} + 2 = 3$	**11** $\dfrac{t}{3} - 4 = 2$	**12** $\dfrac{y}{4} + 1 = 7$
13 $\dfrac{k}{2} - 6 = 3$	**14** $\dfrac{h}{8} - 4 = 1$	**15** $\dfrac{w}{6} + 1 = 4$
16 $\dfrac{x}{4} + 5 = 7$	**17** $\dfrac{y}{2} - 3 = 5$	**18** $\dfrac{f}{5} + 2 = 8$

Doing the same to both sides

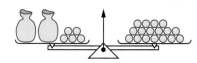

Mary had two bags of marbles, each of which contained the same number of marbles, and five spare marbles.

She put them on scales and balanced them with 17 single marbles.

How many marbles were in each bag?

If x is the number of marbles in each bag, then the equation representing Mary's balanced scales is:
$$2x + 5 = 17$$

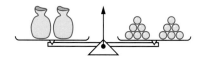

Take 5 marbles from each pan:
$$2x + 5 - 5 = 17 - 5$$
$$2x = 12$$

Now halve the number of marbles on each pan.

That is, divide both sides by 2:

$$\frac{2x}{2} = \frac{12}{2}$$

$$x = 6$$

Checking the answer gives $2 \times 6 + 5 = 17$, which is correct.

Example 2

Solve each of these equations by 'doing the same to both sides'.

a $3x - 5 = 16$ **b** $\frac{x}{2} + 2 = 10$

Add 5 to both sides: Subtract 2 from both sides:

$$3x - 5 + 5 = 16 + 5 \qquad \frac{x}{2} + 2 - 2 = 10 - 2$$

$$3x = 21 \qquad\qquad \frac{x}{2} = 8$$

Divide both sides by 3:   Multiply both sides by 2:

$$\frac{3x}{3} = \frac{21}{3} \qquad\qquad \frac{x}{2} \times 2 = 8 \times 2$$

$$x = 7 \qquad\qquad x = 16$$

Checking the answer gives   Checking the answer gives

$$3 \times 7 - 5 = 16 \qquad\qquad 16 \div 2 + 2 = 10$$

which is correct.   which is correct.

Dealing with negative numbers

The solution to an equation may be a negative number. You need to know that when a negative number is multiplied or divided by a whole number, then the answer is also a negative number. For example:

$$-3 \times 4 = -12 \quad \text{and} \quad -10 \div 5 = -2$$

Check these on your calculator.

EXERCISE 13B

Solve each of the following equations by 'doing the same to both sides'. Do not forget to check that each answer works for its original equation.

1 $x + 4 = 60$ 2 $3y - 2 = 4$ 3 $3x - 7 = 11$

4 $5y + 3 = 18$ 5 $7 + 3t = 19$ 6 $5 + 4f = 15$

7 $3 + 6k = 24$ 8 $4x + 7 = 17$ 9 $5m - 3 = 17$

10 $\dfrac{w}{3} - 5 = 2$ 11 $\dfrac{x}{8} + 3 = 12$ 12 $\dfrac{m}{7} - 3 = 5$

13 $\dfrac{x}{5} + 3 = 3$ 14 $\dfrac{h}{7} + 2 = 1$ 15 $\dfrac{w}{3} + 10 = 4$

16 $\dfrac{x}{3} - 5 = 7$ 17 $\dfrac{y}{2} - 13 = 5$ 18 $\dfrac{f}{6} - 2 = 8$

Activity

Balancing with unknowns

Suppose you want to solve an equation like

$$2x + 3 = x + 4$$

You can imagine it as a balancing problem using marbles.

2 bags + 3 marbles = 1 bag + 4 marbles

Take one bag from each side.

Take three marbles from each side.

There must be one marble in the bag.

This means that $x = 1$

Checking the answer gives $2 \times 1 + 3 = 1 + 4$, which is correct.

Set up each of the following problems as a 'balancing picture' and solve it by 'doing the same to both sides'. Remember to check that each answer works. The first two problems include the pictures to start you off.

1 $2x + 6 = 3x + 1$

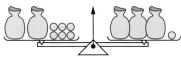

2 $4x + 2 = x + 8$

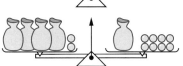

3 $5x + 1 = 3x + 11$ **4** $x + 9 = 2x + 7$
5 $3x + 8 = 2x + 10$ **6** $5x + 7 = 3x + 21$
7 $2x + 12 = 5x + 6$ **8** $3x + 6 = x + 9$

(Some of the marbles could be broken in half!)

9 Explain why there is no answer to this problem:
$$x + 3 = x + 4$$

10 One of the bags of marbles on the left-hand pan has had three marbles taken out.

Try to draw the pictures to solve this problem:
$$4x - 3 = 2x + 5.$$

Rearrangement

A third way of solving an equation is by rearranging its terms until eventually we get the variable on its own – usually on the left-hand side of the equals sign.

Example 3

Solve $4x + 3 = 23$

Move the 3 to give $4x = 23 - 3 = 20$

Now divide both sides by 4 to give $x = \dfrac{20}{4} = 5$

So, the solution is $x = 5$

Example 4

Solve $\dfrac{y-4}{5} = 3$

Move the 5 to give $\qquad y - 4 = 3 \times 5 = 15$

Now move the 4 to give $\qquad y = 15 + 4 = 19$

So, the solution is $y = 19$

EXERCISE 13C

Solve each of the following equations. Do not forget to check that each answer works for its original equation.

1 $2x + 4 = 6$ **2** $2t + 7 = 13$ **3** $3x + 10 = 16$

4 $4y + 15 = 23$ **5** $2x - 8 = 10$ **6** $4t - 3 = 17$

7 $5x - 6 = 24$ **8** $\dfrac{x}{3} + 7 = 15$ **9** $\dfrac{t}{5} + 3 = 5$

10 $\dfrac{w}{3} - 5 = 2$ **11** $\dfrac{x}{8} + 3 = 12$ **12** $\dfrac{m}{7} - 3 = 5$

13 $\dfrac{k+1}{2} = 3$ **14** $\dfrac{h-4}{8} = 3$ **15** $\dfrac{w+1}{6} = 1$

16 $\dfrac{x+5}{4} = 10$ **17** $\dfrac{y-3}{6} = 5$ **18** $\dfrac{f+2}{5} = 5$

19 $7 - x = 3$ **20** $12 - 3y = 6$ **21** $4 - 2k = 8$

Brackets

When we have an equation which contains brackets, we first must multiply out the brackets and then solve the equation by using one of the previous methods.

Example 5

Solve $3(2x - 7) = 15$

First multiply out the bracket to get
$\quad 6x - 21 = 15$

Add 21 to both sides $\qquad 6x = 36$

Divide both sides by 6 $\qquad x = 6$

EXERCISE 13D

Solve each of the following equations. Some of the answers may be decimals or negative numbers. Remember to check that each answer works for its original equation. Use your calculator if necessary.

1 $2(x + 5) = 16$ **2** $5(x - 3) = 20$ **3** $3(t + 1) = 18$

4 $4(2x + 5) = 44$ **5** $2(3y - 5) = 14$ **6** $5(4x + 3) = 135$

7 $4(3t - 2) = 88$ **8** $6(2t + 5) = 42$ **9** $2(3x + 1) = 11$

10 $4(5y - 2) = 42$ **11** $6(3k + 5) = 39$ **12** $5(2x + 3) = 27$

13 $5(3y - 2) = 26$ **14** $2(7t - 3) = 57$ **15** $4(5x - 4) = 54$

16 $9(3x - 5) = 9$ **17** $2(x + 5) = 6$ **18** $5(x - 4) = -25$

19 $3(t + 7) = 15$ **20** $2(3x + 11) = 10$ **21** $4(5t + 8) = 12$

22 $5(2x - 1) = -45$ **23** $7(3y + 5) = -7$ **24** $2(3x + 8) = 7$

Equations with the letter on both sides

When a letter appears on both sides of an equation, it is best to use the 'do the same to both sides' method of solution and collect all the terms containing the letter on the left-hand side of the equation. But when there are more of the letter on the right-hand side, it is easier to turn round the equation. When an equation contains brackets, they must be multiplied out first.

Example 6

Solve $5x + 4 = 3x + 10$

There are more x's on the left-hand side, so leave the equation as it is.

Subtract $3x$ from both sides $2x + 4 = 10$

Subtract 4 from both sides $2x = 6$

Divide both sides by 2 $x = 3$

Example 7

Solve $2x + 3 = 6x - 5$

There are more x's on the right-hand side, so turn round the equation.

$$6x - 5 = 2x + 3$$

Subtract $2x$ from both sides $4x - 5 = 3$

Add 5 to both sides $4x = 8$

Divide both sides by 4 $x = 2$

Example 8

Solve 3 $\qquad$ $(2x + 5) + x = 2(2 - x) + 2$

Multiply out both brackets $\qquad$ $6x + 15 + x = 4 - 2x + 2$

Simplify both sides $\qquad$ $7x + 15 = 6 - 2x$

There are more x's on the left-hand side, so leave the equation as it is.

Add $2x$ to both sides $\qquad$ $9x + 15 = 6$

Subtract 15 from both sides $\qquad$ $9x = -9$

Divide both sides by 9 $\qquad$ $x = -1$

EXERCISE 13E

Solve each of the following equations.

1 $2x + 3 = x + 5$ $\qquad$ **2** $5y + 4 = 3y + 6$

3 $4a - 3 = 3a + 4$ $\qquad$ **4** $5t + 3 = 2t + 15$

5 $7p - 5 = 3p + 3$ $\qquad$ **6** $6k + 5 = 2k + 1$

7 $4m + 1 = m + 10$ $\qquad$ **8** $8s - 1 = 6s - 5$

9 $9w - 12 = 4w + 13$ $\qquad$ **10** $2x + 5 = 3x + 1$

11 $2t - 7 = 4t - 3$ $\qquad$ **12** $2p - 1 = 9 - 3p$

13 $2(d + 3) = d + 12$ $\qquad$ **14** $5(x - 2) = 3(x + 4)$

15 $3(2y + 3) = 5(2y + 1)$ $\qquad$ **16** $3(h - 6) = 2(5 - 2h)$

17 $4(3b - 1) + 6 = 5(2b + 4)$ $\qquad$ **18** $2(5c + 2) - 2c = 3(2c + 3) + 7$

Setting up equations

Equations are used to represent situations, so that we can solve real-life problems.

Example 9

A milkman sets off from the dairy with eight crates of milk each containing b bottles. He delivers 92 bottles to a large factory and finds that he has exactly 100 bottles left on his milk float. How many bottles were in each crate?

The equation is
$$8b - 92 = 100$$
$$8b = 192 \qquad \text{(Add 92 to both sides)}$$
$$b = 24 \qquad \text{(Divide both sides by 8)}$$

Checking the answer gives
$$8 \times 24 - 92 = 192 - 92 = 100$$

which is correct.

EXERCISE 13F

Set up an equation to represent each situation described below. Then solve the equation. Do not forget to check each answer.

1 A boy is Y years old. His father is 25 years older than he is. The sum of their ages is 31. How old is the boy?

2 Another boy is X years old. His sister is twice as old as he is. The sum of their ages is 27. How old is the boy?

3 The diagram shows a square. Find x if the perimeter is 44 cm.

$(4x - 1)$

4 A man buys a daily paper from Monday to Saturday for d pence. On Sunday he buys the *Observer* for £1. His weekly paper bill is £4.30. How much is his daily paper?

5 The diagram shows a rectangle.
  a What is the value of x?
  b What is the value of y?

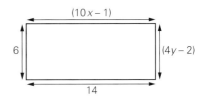

$(10x - 1)$

6

$(4y - 2)$

14

6 In this rectangle, the length is 3 more than the width. The perimeter is 12 cm.
  a What is the value of x?
  b What is the area of the rectangle?

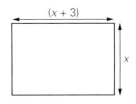

$(x + 3)$

x

7 Mary has two bags of sweets, each of which contains the same number of sweets. She eats four sweets. She then finds that she has 30 sweets left. How many sweets were in each bag to start with?

8 Max thought of a number. He then multiplied his number by 3. He added 4 to the answer. He then doubled that answer to get a final value of 38. What number did he start with?

Amnesty

In an obscure South American state, the president decides to set free some political prisoners. One hundred prisoners are selected and given the numbers 1 to 100

Each prisoner in turn has to walk around this maze painted in the exercise yard of the prison.

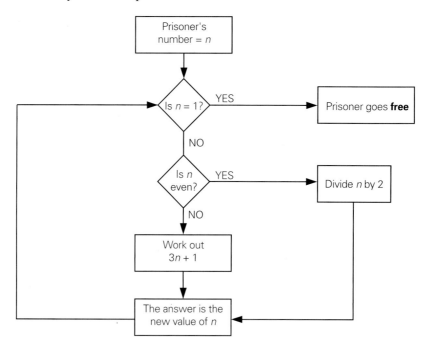

Which of the prisoners are set free?

Examination questions

1 Solve the following equations.

    a $4x - 5 = 7$ **b** $\dfrac{x}{2} = -10$

    c $3(z - 2) = 27$

WJEC, Question 21, Paper 2, June 1999

2 Solve the equations.

    a $5x + 4 = 39$ **b** $4(x + 4) = 26$

    c $\dfrac{x - 5}{4} = 2$

AQA, Question 15, Paper 2, June 2000

3 Solve these equations.

    a $4x = 12$ **b** $5x + 2 = 9$

    c $3 - x = 7$ **d** $4x - 3 = 2x + 11$

OCR, Question 23, Paper 2, June 2000

4 Solve the following equations.

    a $3x - 4 = 11$ **b** $5x + 17 = 3(x + 6)$

WJEC. Question 15, Paper 1, June 1998

5 Solve the equations.

    a $3w = -18$ **b** $3(x - 4) = 12$

    c $3y + 7 = 13 - y$

MEG, Question 14, Paper 1, June 1998

6

    a   What answer did Zeenat get?

    b   What was the number John thought of?

NEAB, Question 8, Specimen Paper 2F, June 2000

7 The lengths of the sides of a triangle are $(x + 1)$ cm, $(x + 3)$ cm and $(x - 2)$ cm.

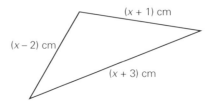

a Write an expression, in terms of x, for the perimeter of this triangle. Give your answer in its simplest form.
The perimeter is 23 cm.
b Write down an equation in x and use it to find the value of x.

SEG, Question 22, Specimen Paper 6, 2000

8

For their wedding reception Vicki and Stephen paid £380 to hire a small marquee. They also paid £17 per person for food.

a Write down an expression for the total cost, in pounds, of the reception if n people attended.
The reception cost £1196.
b Write down an equation in n, and solve it to find out how many people attended the reception.

OCR, Question 21, Paper 2, June 1999

9

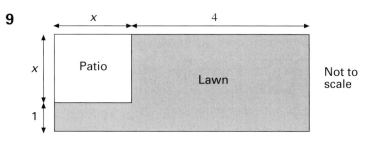

All lengths in this question are in metres.

A rectangular garden has a square patio of side x metres in one corner. The remainder of the garden is a lawn.

a   Write down an expression, in terms of x, for the longer side of the lawn.

b   Find an expression, in terms of x, for the perimeter of the lawn.

c   The perimeter of the lawn is 34 metres. Find the value of x.

MEG, Question 16, Paper 2, June 1998

10   An apple costs y pence. An orange costs 5 pence more than an apple.

a   Write down an expression, in terms of y, for the cost of one orange.

b   Write down an expression, in terms of y, for the total cost of three apples and one orange.

c   The total cost of three apples and one orange is 61 pence.
Form an equation in terms of y and solve it to find the cost of one apple.

OCR, Question 15, Paper 2, June 2000

What you should know after you have worked through Chapter 13

✔   How to form simple linear equations.
✔   How to solve simple linear equations.

14 Graphs

This chapter is going to ...

remind you about conversion graphs and travel graphs. It will then show you how to draw a straight-line graph from its equation.

What you should already know

✔ How to read information from conversion graphs
✔ How to read information from travel graphs
✔ How to read and plot co-ordinates in the first quadrant
✔ How to work out expressions using negative numbers
✔ How letters can be used to represent numbers
✔ How to substitute into simple algebraic formulae

Conversion graphs

Look at Examples 1 and 2, and make sure that you follow through the conversions.

Example 1

This is a conversion graph between litres and gallons.

From the graph we can see that:

5 gallons are approximately equivalent to 23 litres

15 litres are approximately equivalent to $3\frac{1}{4}$ gallons

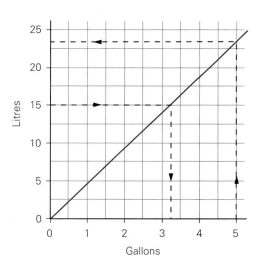

Example 2

This is a graph of the charges made in 1996 for units of electricity used in the home.

From the graph we can see that:

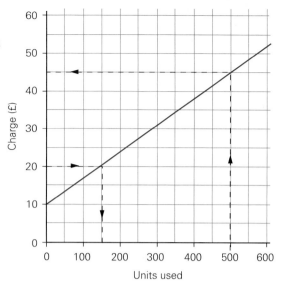

If a customer uses 500 units of electricity, the customer will be charged £45.

If a customer is charged £20, the customer will have used about 150 units.

You need to be able to read these types of graph by finding a value on one axis and following it through to the other axis.

EXERCISE 14A

1   The following is a conversion graph between kilograms (kg) and pounds (lb).

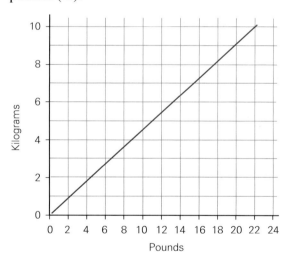

a   Use the graph to approximately convert:
   i   18 lb to kilograms   **ii**   5 lb to kilograms
   iii 4 kg to pounds   **iv** 10 kg to pounds
b   Approximately how many pounds are equivalent to 1 kg?

2 The following is a conversion graph between inches (in) and centimetres (cm).

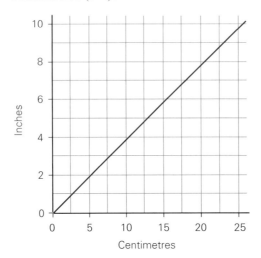

a Use the graph to approximately convert:

   i   4 inches to centimetres   **ii** 9 inches to centimetres

   iii 5 cm to inches   **iv** 22 cm to inches

b Approximately how many centimetres are equivalent to 1 inch?

3 The following graph was produced to show the approximate equivalence of the British £ to the Singapore $ during the summer of 1995.

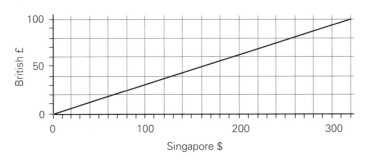

a Use the graph to approximately convert:

   i   £100 to Singapore $ **ii** £30 to Singapore $

   iii $150 to British £   **iv** $250 to British £

b Approximately how many Singapore $ are equivalent to £1?

4 A hire firm hired out industrial blow heaters. They used the following graph to approximate what the charges would be.

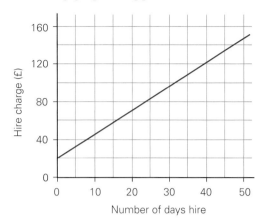

a Use the graph to find the approximate charge for hiring a heater for

   i 40 days   **ii** 25 days

b Use the graph to find out how many days hire you would get for a cost of

   i £100   **ii** £140

5 A conference centre had the following chart on the office wall so that the staff could see the approximate cost of a conference based on the number of people attending it.

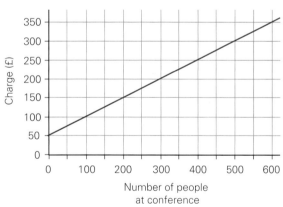

a Use the graph to find the approximate charge for

   i 100 people   **ii** 550 people

b Use the graph to estimate how many people can attend a conference at the centre for a cost of

   i £300   **ii** £175

6 At a small shop, the manager marked all goods at the pre-VAT prices and the sales assistant had to use the following chart to convert these marked prices to selling prices.

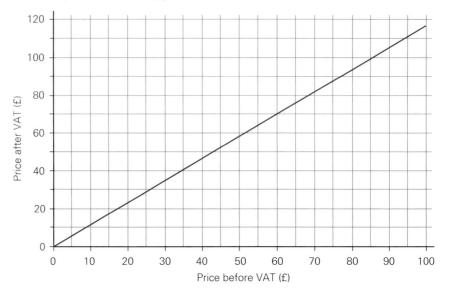

a Use the chart to find the selling price of goods marked
  i £60   **ii** £25
b What was the marked price if you bought something for
  i £100   **ii** £45?

7 When Leon travelled abroad in his car, he always took this conversion graph. It helped him to convert between miles and kilometres.

a Use the graph to approximately convert:
  i 25 miles to km
  ii 10 miles to km
  iii 40 km to miles
  iv 15 km to miles
b Approximately how many kilometres are equivalent to 5 miles?

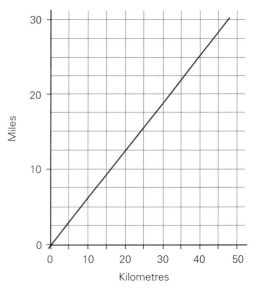

8 Granny McAllister still finds it hard to think in degrees Celsius. So she always uses the following conversion graph to help her to understand the weather forecast.

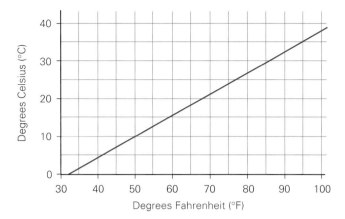

a Use the graph to approximately convert:

    i   35 °C to Fahrenheit   **ii** 20 °C to Fahrenheit

    iii 50 °F to Celsius   **iv** 90 °F to Celsius

b Water freezes at 0 °C, what temperature is this in Fahrenheit?

9 Tea is sold at a school fete between 1.00 pm and 2.30 pm. The numbers of cups of tea that had been sold were noted at half-hour intervals.

Time	1.00	1.30	2.00	2.30	3.00	3.30
No. of cups of tea sold	0	24	48	72	96	120

a Draw a graph to illustrate this information. Use a scale from 1 to 4 hours on the horizontal time axis, and from 1 to 120 on the vertical axis for cups of tea sold.

b Use your graph to estimate when the 60th cup of tea was sold.

10 I lost my fuel bill, but while talking to my friends I found out that:

    Bill who had used 850 units was charged £57.50

    Wendy who had used 320 units was charged £31

    Rhanni who had used 540 units was charged £42

a Plot the given information and draw a straight-line graph. Use a scale from 0 to 900 on the horizontal units axis, and from £0 to £60 on the vertical cost axis.

b Use your graph to find what I will be charged for 700 units.

11 Concrete was sold in cubic yards for many years.

In 1995 Mr Hutchinson was told that he now had to sell it in cubic metres (m^3). He made himself the following conversion graph to help him get to grips with the new measure.

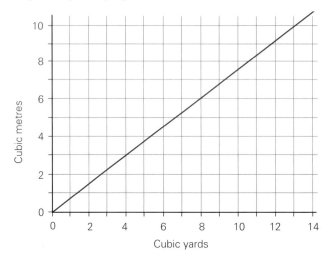

a Use the graph to approximately convert:

  i 4 cubic yards to m^3 **ii** 11 cubic yards to m^3
  iii 10 m^3 to cubic yards   **iv** 5 m^3 to cubic yards

b Approximately how big in cubic yards is 1 m^3?

12 The table below shows the height (h), in metres, of a golf ball above the ground after t seconds, once it has been hit from the tee.

Time, t	0	1	2	3	4	5	6
Height, h	0	5	8	9	8	5	0

a Draw a graph to illustrate this information. Your graph should be a smooth curve

b Use your graph to estimate the height of the ball after $1\frac{1}{2}$ seconds.

Travel graphs

As the name suggests, a travel graph gives information about how someone or something has travelled. It is also called a distance–time graph.

A travel graph is read in a similar way to the conversion graphs you have just done. But you can also find the average speed from a distance–time graph by using the formula

$$\text{Average speed} = \frac{\text{Total distance travelled}}{\text{Time taken}}$$

Example 3

The distance–time graph below represents a car journey from Barnsley to Nottingham, a distance of 50 km, and back again.

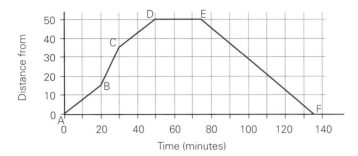

From the graph, we can read the following information.

After 10 minutes the car was 8 km away from Barnsley.

After 50 minutes the car was 50 km away from Barnsley, at Nottingham.

The car stayed at Nottingham for 25 minutes, and took 60 minutes for the return journey.

The **average speeds** over the five stages of the journey are worked out as follows.

A to B represents 16 km in 20 minutes.

Multiplying both numbers by 3 gives 48 km in 60 minutes, which is 48 km/h.

B to C represents 19 km in 10 minutes.

Multiplying both numbers by 6 gives 114 km in 60 minutes, which is 114 km/h.

C to D represents 15 km in 20 minutes.

Multiplying both numbers by 3 gives 45 km in 60 minutes, which is 45 km/h.

D to E represents a stop: no further distance travelled.

E to F represents the return journey of 50 km in 60 minutes, which is 50 km/h.

So, the return journey was at an average speed of 50 km/h.

You always work out the distance travelled in 1 hour to get the speed in kilometres per hour (km/h) or miles per hour (mph or miles/h).

EXERCISE 14B

1 Paul was travelling in his car to a meeting. He set off from home at 7.00 am, and stopped on the way for a break. This distance–time graph illustrates his journey.

a At what time did he
   i   stop for his break
   ii set off after his break
   iii get to his meeting place?
b At what average speed was he travelling
   i   over the first hour
   ii over the second hour
   iii for the last part of his journey?

2 James was travelling to Cornwall on his holidays. This distance–time graph illustrates his journey.

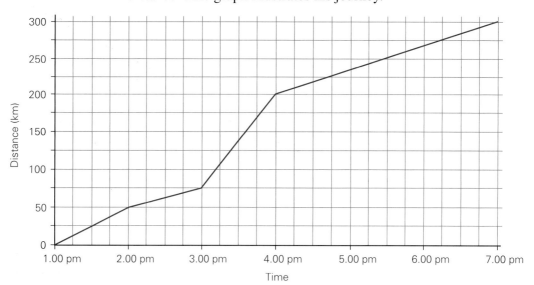

a His fastest speed was on the motorway.
   i   How much motorway did he use?
   ii What was his average speed on the motorway?
b **i** When did he travel the slowest?
   ii What was his slowest average speed?

3 A small bus set off from Leeds to pick up Mike and his family. It then went on to pick up Mike's parents and grandparents. It then travelled further, dropping them all off at a hotel. The bus then went on a further 10 km to pick up another party and took them back to Leeds. This distance–time graph illustrates the journey.

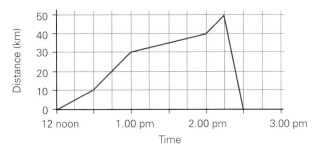

    a How far from Leeds did Mike's parents and grandparents live?

    b How far from Leeds is the hotel at which they all stayed?

    c What was the average speed of the bus back to Leeds?

4 Azam and Jafar were having a race. The distance–time graph below illustrates the distances covered.

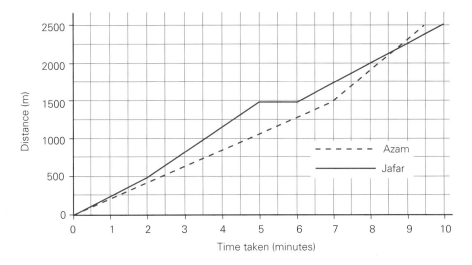

    a Jafar stopped during the race. Why might this have happened?

    b **i** When Jafar was running his fastest, he ran from 500 metres to 1500 metres in 3 minutes. What was his speed in m/min?

        ii How many seconds are there in 3 minutes?

        iii What is Jafar's speed in metres per second?

    c **i** At about what time into the race did Azam overtake Jafar?

        ii By how many seconds did Azam beat Jafar?

5 Three school friends all set off from school at the same time, 3.45 pm. They all lived 12 km away from the school. The distance–time graph below illustrates their journeys.

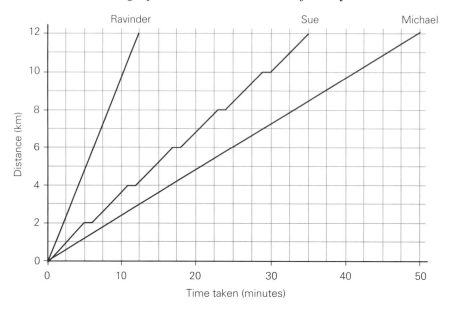

One of them went by bus, one cycled and one was taken by car.

a **i** Explain how you know that Sue used the bus.

    ii Who went by car?

b At what time did each friend get home?

c **i** When the bus was moving, it covered 2 kilometres in 5 minutes. What is this speed in kilometres per hour?

    ii Overall, the bus covered 12 kilometres in 36 minutes. What is this speed in kilometres per hour?

    iii How many stops did the bus make before Sue got home?

6 Three friends, Patrick, Araf and Sean, ran a 1000 metres race. The race is illustrated on the distance–time graph below.

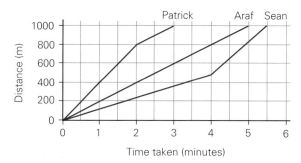

The school newspaper gave the following report of Patrick's race:
  'Patrick took an early lead, running the first 800 metres in 2 minutes. He then slowed down a lot and ran the last 200 metres in 1 minute, to finish first in a total time of 3 minutes.'

a Describe the races of Araf and Sean in a similar way.

b **i** What is the average speed of Patrick in kilometres per hour?

ii What is the average speed of Araf in kilometres per hour?

iii What is the average speed of Sean in kilometres per hour?

Activity

Four in a row

This needs two people.

First, draw and label a 5 by 5 grid, as shown on the right.

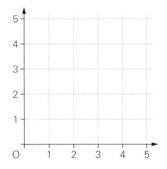

One player uses crosses X, and the other noughts O.

The players take it in turns to put a cross or a nought where the grid lines intersect.

The winner of this first part of the game is the player who first gets four crosses (or noughts) in a line, as in the example on the right.

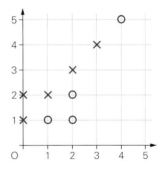

Write down the co-ordinates of the winning line. These are (0, 1), (1, 2), (2, 3), (3, 4).

Now see if you can write down a rule that connects the coordinates. In this case, you could say:

'For each pair of numbers, the second number is always bigger by 1 than the first.'

Co-ordinates are always written in the order (x, y).

The rule above could be written as $y = x + 1$.

You score a point if you get four crosses or noughts in a line, another point if you write the rule in words, and another point if you write the rule using x and y.

This means you can score up to three points in each go.

Repeat the game until one player gets ten points.

Here are three examples of winning lines and their rules:

■ (1, 0), (1, 1), (1, 2), (1, 3). The first number is always 1 **or** $x = 1$

■ (2, 3), (3, 2), (4, 1), (5, 0). The numbers add up to 5 **or** $x + y = 5$

■ (2, 2), (3, 2), (4, 2), (5, 2). The second number is always 2 **or** $y = 2$

Graphs from linear equations

Plotting negative coordinates

So far, all the points you have read or plotted on graphs have been co-ordinates in the first quadrant. The grid below reminds you how to read and plot co-ordinates in all four quadrants and how to find the equations of vertical and horizontal lines. This involves using **negative numbers**.

The co-ordinates of a point are given in the form (x, y), where x is the number along the x-axis and y is the number up the y-axis.

The co-ordinates of the four points on the grid are:

  A(2, 3)   B(−1, 2)   C(−3, −4)   D(1, −3)

The x-co-ordinates of all the points on line X are 3. So we say the equation of line X is $x = 3$.

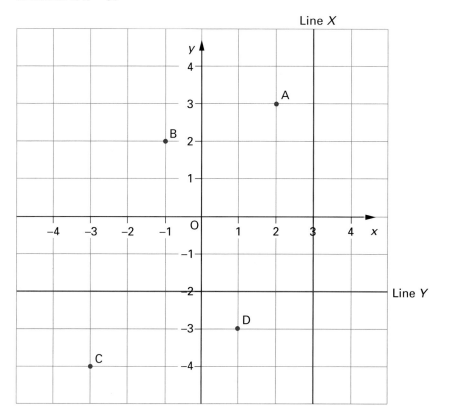

The y-co-ordinates of all the points on line Y are −2 . So we say the equation of line Y is $y = −2$.

Make sure you understand the above, before moving on to draw linear graphs.

Flow diagrams

One way of drawing the graph of an equation is to obtain a set of **co-ordinates** from the equation by means of a flow diagram. These co-ordinates are then plotted and the graph is drawn.

In its simplest form, a flow diagram consists of a single box which may be thought of as containing a mathematical operation, called a **function**. A set of numbers fed into one side of the box is changed by the operation into another set which comes out from the opposite side of the box. For example, the box shown below represents the operation of multiplying by 3.

Input   Output
0, 1, 2, 3, 4   │ × 3 │   0, 3, 6, 9, 12

The numbers that are fed into a box are called **input values,** and the numbers that come out are called **output values.**

We can match the input and output values and arrange them as a table,

x	0	1	2	3	4
y	0	3	6	9	12

in which the input values are called **x-values,** and the output values are called **y-values**. We thus obtain a set of **co-ordinates** that can be **plotted on a graph**. In this case, we have

(0, 0), (1, 3), (2, 6), (3, 9) and (4, 12)

Most functions consist of more than one operation, so most flow diagrams consist of more than one box. In such cases, we match the **first** input values to the **last** output values. The values produced in the middle operations are just working numbers and can be missed out.

0, 1, 2, 3, 4   │ × 2 │   0, 2, 4, 6, 8   │ + 3 │   3, 5, 7, 9, 11

So, for the two-box flow diagram the table is

x	0	1	2	3	4
y	3	5	7	9	11

This gives us the coordinates (0, 3), (1, 5), (2, 7), (3, 9) and (4, 11).

The two flow diagrams above represent respectively the equation $y = 3x$ and the equation $y = 2x + 3$, as shown on the next page.

265

It is now an easy step to plot the co-ordinate pairs for each equation on a set of axes, to produce the graphs of $y = 3x$ and $y = 2x + 3$, as shown below.

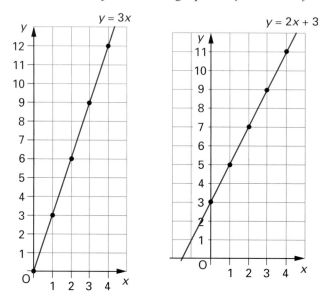

One of the practical problems in graph work is deciding the extent (range) of the axes. In examinations this is not usually a problem as either the axes are drawn for you or you are given a piece of graph paper and told how large to draw them. Throughout this chapter, we will use diagrams like the one below right to show you the range of your axes for each question. These diagrams are not necessarily drawn to scale.

This particular diagram means draw the x-axis (horizontal axis) from 0 to 10 and the y-axis (vertical axis) from 0 to 10. You can use any type of graph or squared paper to draw your axes.

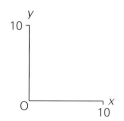

But do note that the **scale** on each axis need **not always be the same**.

Example 4

Use the flow diagram below to help you to draw the graph of
$y = 4x - 1$

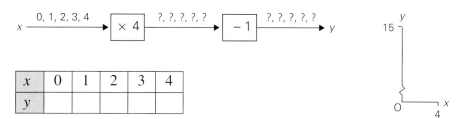

x	0	1	2	3	4
y					

The table becomes

x	0	1	2	3	4
y	−1	3	7	11	15

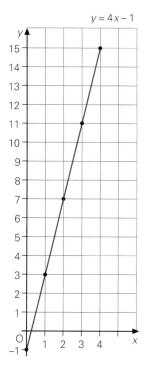

So, the co-ordinate pairs are:
  (0, −1), (1, 3), (2, 7), (3, 11), (4, 15)

Plot these points and join them up to
obtain the graph shown on the right.

This is the graph of $y = 4x - 1$

EXERCISE 14C

1

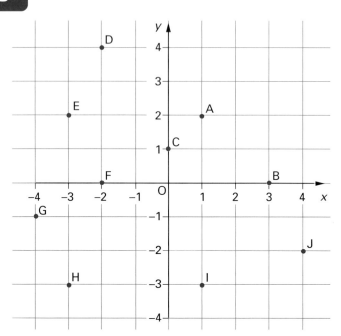

a Write down the co-ordinates of all the points A to J on the grid.
b Write down the co-ordinates of the mid-point of the line joining
  i A and B   **ii** H and I   **iii** D and J

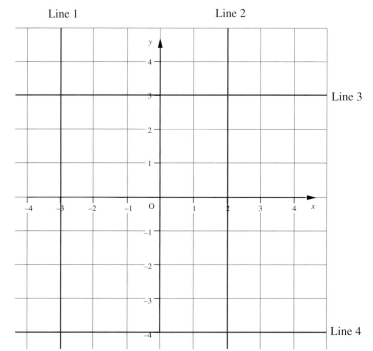

c Write down the equations of the lines 1 to 4 on the grid.
d Write down the equation of the line that is exactly half way
  between
  i line 1 and line 2   **ii** line 3 and line 4

2 Draw the graph of $y = x + 2$

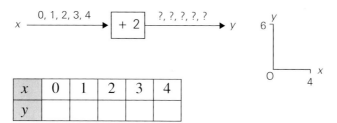

x	0	1	2	3	4
y					

3 Draw the graph of $y = 2x - 2$

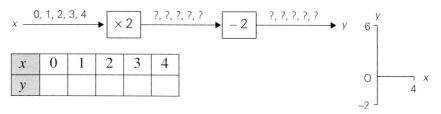

x	0	1	2	3	4
y					

4 Draw the graph of $y = \dfrac{x}{3} + 1$

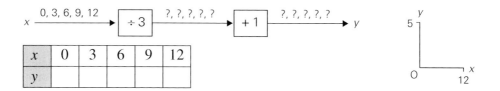

x	0	3	6	9	12
y					

5 Draw the graph of $y = \dfrac{x}{2} - 4$

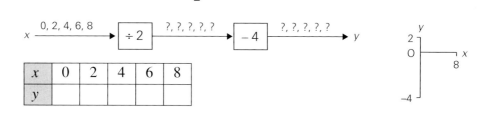

x	0	2	4	6	8
y					

6 **a** Draw the graphs of $y = x - 3$ and $y = 2x - 6$ on the same grid.

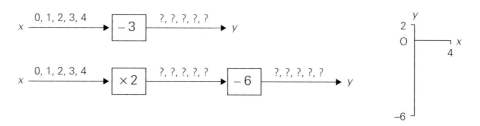

b Where do the graphs cross?

7 **a** Draw the graphs of $y = 2x$ and $y = x + 6$ on the same grid.

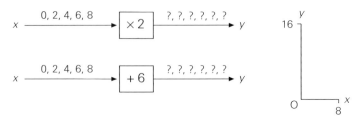

b Where do the graphs cross?

8 **a** Draw the graphs of $y = 3x - 1$ and $y = \dfrac{x}{2} + 4$ on the same grid.

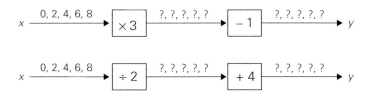

b Where do the graphs cross?

9 Draw the graph of $y = 5x - 1$. Choose your own inputs. Draw your own axes.

Plotting points

As you have now seen, this chapter is concerned with linear graphs. That is, graphs that give a straight line.

The minimum number of points needed to draw a straight line is two but three or more are better because that gives at least one point to act as a check. In the graphs you drew in Exercise 14C, you plotted five points. There is no rule about how many points to plot but here are some tips.

• Use a sharp pencil and mark each point with a fine dot or an accurate cross.

• When the points are far apart, it is easier to draw a line within the tolerance allowed – even if you have difficulty in drawing accurately.

• Get your eyes directly over the graph. If you look from the side, you will not be able to line up your ruler accurately.

Drawing graphs by finding points

This method is a bit quicker and does not need flow diagrams. However, if you prefer flow diagrams, use them.

Follow through Example 5 to see how this method works.

Example 5

Draw the graph of $y = 4x - 5$ for values of x from 0 to 5 ($0 \le x \le 5$).

Choose three values for x, not too close together, say 0, 3 and 5. Work out the y-values by substituting the x-values into the equation.

Keep a record of your calculations in a table, as shown below.

x	0	3	5
y			

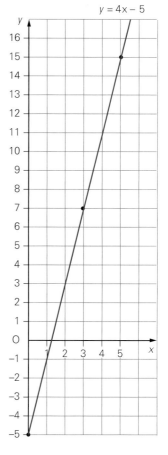

When $x = 0$, $y = 4(0) - 5 = -5$
This gives the point (0, –5).

When $x = 3$, $y = 4(3) - 5 = 7$
This gives the point (3, 7).

When $x = 5$, $y = 4(5) - 5 = 15$
This gives the point (5, 15).

Hence your table is

x	0	3	5
y	–5	7	15

You now have to decide the extent (range) of the axes. You can find this out by looking at the coordinates that we have so far.

The smallest x-value is 0, the largest is 5.
The smallest y-value is –5, the largest is 15.

Now draw the axes, plot the points and complete the graph.

It is nearly always a good idea to choose 0 as one of the x-values. In an examination, the limits of x will be given and the axes already drawn or their size stated, so you will not have to make too many decisions.

EXERCISE 14D

Draw the graph for each of the equations given.

Follow these hints and try to remember them.
- Don't pick silly numbers, such as 17 or $3\frac{1}{2}$, as x-values.
- Use the highest and smallest values of x given as your range.
- Don't pick x-values that are too close together, e.g. 1 and 2. Try to space them out so that you can draw a more accurate graph.
- When the first part of the function is a division, pick x-values that divide exactly to avoid fractions.
- Always label your graphs. This is particularly important when you are drawing two graphs on the same set of axes.
- If you want to use a flow diagram, use one.
- Create a table of values. You will often have to complete these in your examinations.

1   Draw the graph of $y = 3x + 4$ for x-values from 0 to 5 ($0 \leq x \leq 5$)

2   Draw the graph of $y = 2x - 5$ ($0 \leq x \leq 5$)

3   Draw the graph of $y = \frac{x}{2} - 3$ ($0 \leq x \leq 10$)

4   Draw the graph of $y = 3x + 5$ ($-3 \leq x \leq 3$)

5   Draw the graph of $y = \frac{x}{3} + 4$ ($-6 \leq x \leq 6$)

6   **a**   On the same set of axes, draw the graphs of $y = 3x - 2$ and $y = 2x + 1$, ($0 \leq x \leq 5$)
    b   Where do the two graphs cross?

7   **a**   On the same axes, draw the graphs of $y = 4x - 5$ and $y = 2x + 3$ ($0 \leq x \leq 5$)
    b   Where do the two graphs cross?

8   **a**   On the same axes, draw the graphs of $y = \frac{x}{3} - 1$ and $y = \frac{x}{2} - 2$ ($0 \leq x \leq 12$)
    b   Where do the two graphs cross?

9   **a**   On the same axes, draw the graphs of $y = 3x + 1$ and $y = 3x - 2$ ($0 \leq x \leq 4$)
    b   Do the graphs cross? If not, why not?

10 **a**   Copy and complete the table to draw the graph of $x + y = 5$ ($0 \leq x \leq 5$)

x	0	1	2	3	4	5
y	5		3		1	

    b   Now draw the graph of $x + y = 7$ ($0 \leq x \leq 7$)

Activity

A family of graphs

On the same grid (take x from -10 to 10 and y from -10 to 10) draw this **family** of lines:

a $y = 2x - 1$ **b** $y = 2x + 4$ **c** $y = 2x + 3$ **d** $y = 2x$

- What do you notice about the equations?
- What do you notice about the lines?

On another grid (take x from -10 to 10 and y from -10 to 10) draw this family of lines:

a $y = 3x + 1$ **b** $y = \dfrac{x}{2} + 1$ **c** $y = x + 1$ **d** $y = 4x + 1$

- What do you notice about the equations?
- What do you notice about the lines?

The number in front of x is called the **coefficient** of x and determines how steep the line is.

The number on its own is called the **constant term** and determines where the graph crosses the y-axis. It is often referred to as the **y-axis intercept.**

Examination questions

1 The diagram shows a rectangle PQRS.

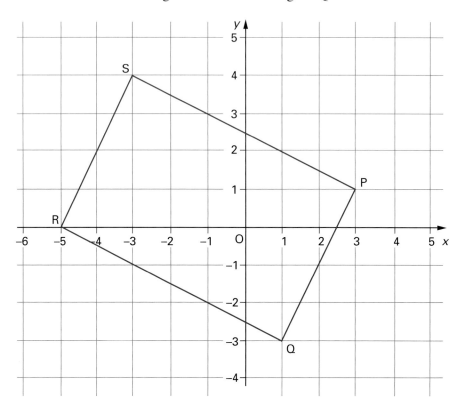

a Write down the coordinates of P, Q, R and S.

b The equation of one of the sides of the rectangle is
  $y = 2x + 10$
  State which side it is, showing working to support your answer.

OCR, Question 17, Paper 2, June 1999

2 Area of land is measured in either acres or hectares.
350 acres is 140 hectares. This is represented by the point P on the grid.

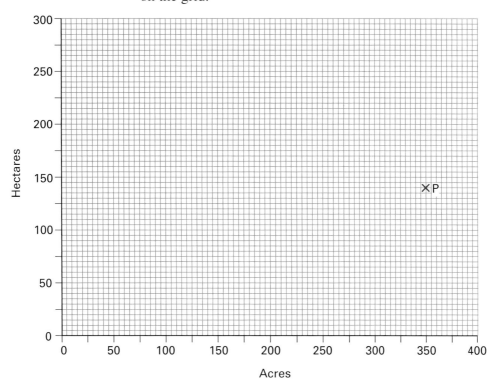

a 75 acres is 30 hectares. Plot a point to represent this.
Label this point Q.

b i Complete the conversion graph by drawing a
straight line through the points P and Q.

ii Use this graph to change 200 acres into hectares.
Show clearly how you use the graph.

AQA, Question 7, Paper 2, June 2000

3 This is a distance–time graph of Albert's journey from home (A) to school (E).

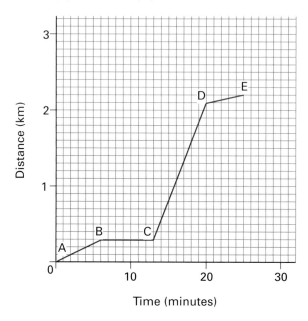

Time (minutes)

a What distance does Albert travel from home to school?

b How long does it take Albert to get from C to D?

c What does the part of the graph between B and C show about Albert's journey?

d For which part of the journey is Albert travelling fastest?

MEG, Question 17, Paper 2, June 1998

4 The temperature of the water in a kettle jug was recorded every 20 seconds from when it was switched on until it switched itself off. The figures are shown in the table.

Time (seconds)	0	20	40	60	80	100	120
Temperature (°C)	10	16	28	46	76	92	100

a Plot these points on a graph with axes as:
  horizontal axis showing 10 seconds to 1 cm
  vertical axis showing 10 °C to 1 cm.
  Join up the points with a curve.

Use the graph to answer the following questions.

b What was the water temperature
   i when the kettle was switched on
   ii after 50 seconds?
c How long did it take for the water to reach 85 °C?

MEG, Question 15, Specimen Paper 2F, 1998

5 The graph below shows the journey made by a cyclist from Gloucester to Bristol.

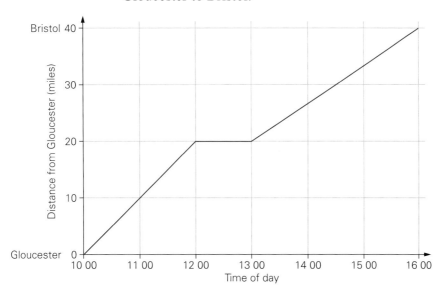

a **i** How far is Bristol from Gloucester?
   ii Describe what happens between 12 00 and 13 00 hours.
b The cyclist later cycled back to Gloucester at an average speed of 16 miles per hour. How long did it take the cyclist to get back to Gloucester?

SEG, Question 17, Specimen Paper 6, 2000

6 **a** Use the formula $y = 2x - 1$ to complete the table.

x	−1	0	1	2
$y = 2x - 1$		−1		

b Use your table of values to draw the graph of
$y = 2x - 1$.
Draw the x-axis from –1 to 3, with 2 cm to 1 unit and the
y-axis from –3 to 3, with 2 cm to 1 unit.

c Use your graph to find the value of x when $y = 2.5$

SEG, Question 14, Specimen Paper 6, 2000

7 **a** Complete this table of values for $y = 2x + 3$.

x	–3	–2	–1	0	1	2
y		–1				

b Draw the graph of $y = 2x + 3$ on the grid below.

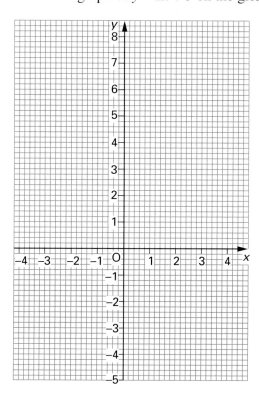

c Use your graph to find
  i   The value of y when $x = 1.5$
  ii The value of x when $y = -0.5$

EDEXCEL, Question 19, Paper 2, June 1999

8   **a**   Given that $y = x - 1$, complete the table of values below.

x	−2	0	2	0
y				

   b   Draw the graph of $y = x - 1$ on the grid below.

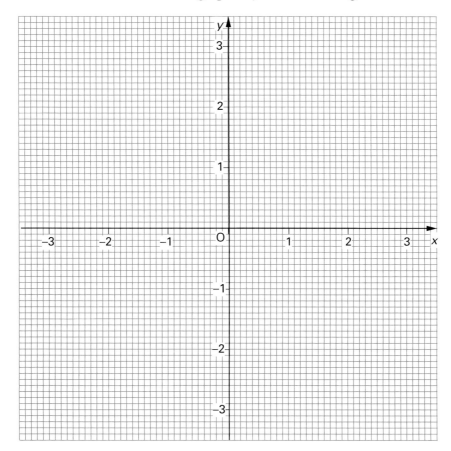

MEG, Question 10, Paper 2, June 1998

9 Jenny cycles to school each day. The graph shows her journey from home to school.

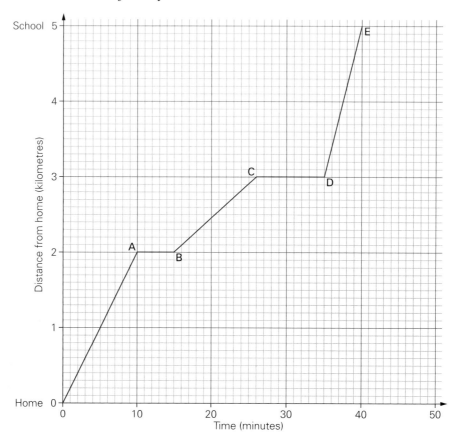

On the way she stops to talk to her friends.
a How many times does she stop to talk to her friends?
b i How far does she travel in the first stage from home to A?
ii What is her average speed over the first 10 minutes? Give your answer in kilometres per hour.
c On which stage of the journey is her average speed the fastest?

NEAB, Question 18, Paper 2F, June 1998

10 A spring stretches when objects are hung on it. The formula for its length is

$l = 2w + 16$

w is the weight of in kg.

l is the length of the spring in cm.

a Complete this table.

w	0	2	4	6	8	10
l	16			28		36

b Draw the graph on the grid below.

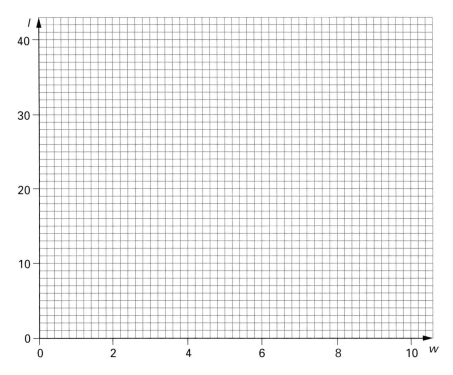

c Jane hangs an object on the spring. She measures the length of the spring. It is 29 cm.

Use your graph to find the weight of the object.

MEG(SMP), Question 10, June 1998

11 A rocket is fired out to sea from the top of a cliff. The graph shows the height of the rocket above sea level until it lands in the sea.

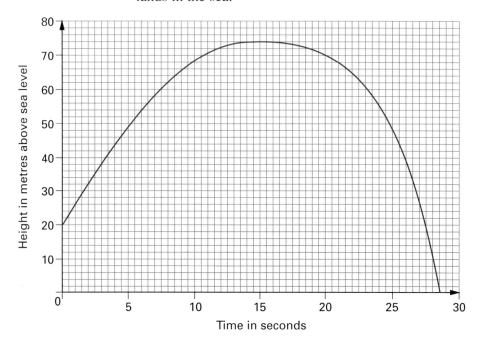

a How high is the rocket above the sea after 10 seconds?

d How long does it take before the rocket lands in the sea?

c Write down the time when the rocket is at the same height above the sea as when it started.

d Write down the times when the rocket is 10 metres above the cliff.

OCR, Question 9, Paper 1, June 1999

What you should know after you have worked through Chapter 14

✔ How to use a conversion graph.

✔ How to read simple distance–time graphs.

✔ How to find speed from a distance–time graph.

✔ How to find co-ordinates using a flow diagram or by substituting values.

✔ How to draw the graphs of linear equations.

15 Angles

This chapter is going to ...

remind you of some of the geometrical terms you have met before, as well as show you the rules of geometry you need to be familiar with. It will also revise some of the properties of polygons and show you how to find the sizes of their angles.

What you should already know

✔ How to use a protractor to find the size of any angle
✔ How to estimate the sizes of angles, and be able to draw an angle accurately
✔ The meaning of the terms 'acute', 'obtuse', 'reflex', 'right', and be able to describe angles using these terms
✔ A polygon is a 2-D shape with any number of straight sides
✔ A diagonal is a line joining two vertices (corners) of a polygon
✔ The meaning of the terms 'parallel lines' and 'perpendicular lines'

Measuring angles

When you are using a protractor, it is important that you

• place the centre of the protractor **exactly on** the corner (vertex) of the angle, and

• lay the base-line of the protractor **exactly along** one side of the angle.

You must follow these two steps to obtain an **accurate value** for the angle you are measuring.

You should already have discovered how easy it is to measure acute angles and obtuse angles using the common semicircular protractor.

Look at Example 1 on the next page if you are not too sure.

Example 1

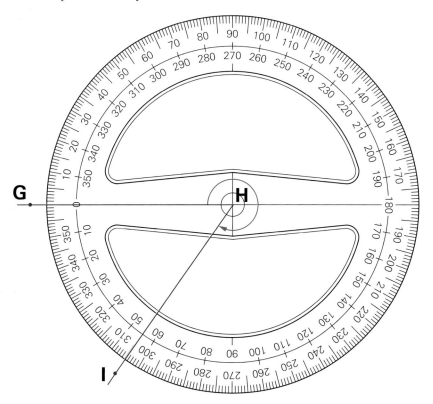

Acute angle ABC is 35° and obtuse angle DEF is 145°.

To measure reflex angles, such as GHI shown below, it is easier to use a circular protractor if you have one.

Reflex angle GHI is 305°.

EXERCISE 15A

1 Use a protractor to find the size of each marked angle.

a

b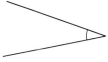

c

d

e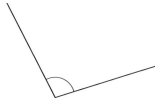

f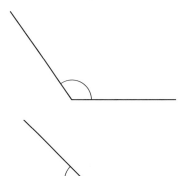

g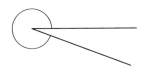

h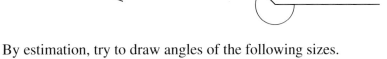

2 **a** By estimation, try to draw angles of the following sizes.
  i 30° **ii** 60° **iii** 90° **iv** 100° **v** 20° **vi** 45° **vii** 75°
  b Now accurately measure your angles to see how much out you were.
  c **i** What error did you have for each angle?
  ii Which angles were your most accurate?
  d Try drawing these again to see whether you can improve your accuracy.

3 **a** **i** Draw any three acute angles.
  ii Estimate their sizes. Record your results.
  iii Measure the angles. Record your results.
  iv Work out the difference between your estimate and your measurement for **each** angle. Add all the differences together. This is your total error.
  b Repeat parts **i** to **iv** of part **a** for three obtuse angles.
  c Repeat parts **i** to **iv** of part **a** for three reflex angles.
  d Which type of angle are you most accurate with, and which type are you least accurate with?

4 Sketch the following triangles. Do not make any measurements, but try to get them as accurate as you can by estimating. The diagrams below are not to scale. Then use a ruler and a protractor to see how close you were.

a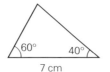
7 cm

b
6 cm

c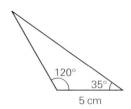
5 cm

Angle facts

Names of angles

You will already have met situations in which angles are described as being **acute**, **obtuse**, **right** or **reflex**.

The meaning of each of these terms is revisited below.

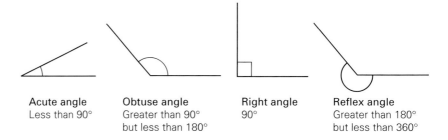

Acute angle	Obtuse angle	Right angle	Reflex angle
Less than 90°	Greater than 90° but less than 180°	90°	Greater than 180° but less than 360°

Angles on a line

The angles on a straight line add up to 180°, that is $a + b = 180°$.

Draw an example for yourself to show that the statement is true by measuring a and b.

This is true for any number of angles on a line. For example:
$$c + d + e + f = 180°$$

Angles around a point

The sum of the angles around a point
is 360°. For example:

$$a + b + c + d + e = 360°$$

Also check this for yourself by drawing an
example and measuring the angles.

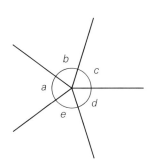

EXERCISE 15B

Calculate the size of the angle marked with a letter in each of these
examples.

1

2

3

4

5

6

7

8

9

10

11

12

13

14

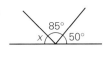

15

16

17

18

19  **20** **21**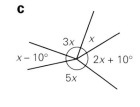

22

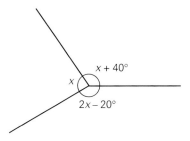

Solving angle problems

Sometimes we can use equations to solve angle problems.

Example 2

Find the value of x in the diagram.

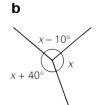

These angles are around a point, so they must add up to $360°$.

Therefore,
$$x + x + 40 + 2x - 20 = 360$$
$$4x + 20 = 360$$
$$4x = 340$$
$$x = 85°$$

EXERCISE 15C

1 Calculate the value of x in each of these examples.

a

60° 130°
70° x

b

$x - 10°$
x
$x + 40°$

c

$3x$ x
$x - 10°$ $2x + 10°$
$5x$

2 Calculate the value of *x* in each of these examples.

a 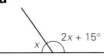 **b**  **c**

3 Calculate the value of *x* first and then find the size of angle *y* in each of these examples.

a 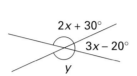 **b** 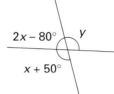 **c**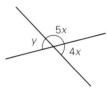

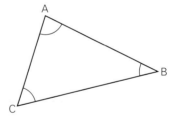

Activity

Angles in a triangle

You need a protractor.

Draw a triangle. Label the corners (vertices) A, B and C.

Use a ruler and make sure that the corners of your triangle form proper angles.

Like this.   Not like this…   … or this.

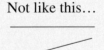

Measure each angle, A, B and C.

Write them down and add them up:

Angle A = ……°

Angle B = ……°

Angle C = ……°

Total   = ____

Repeat this for five more triangles, including at least one with an obtuse angle.

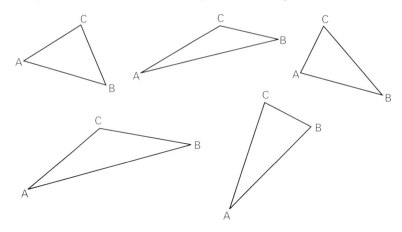

What conclusion can you draw about the sum of the angles in a triangle?

Remember You will not be able to measure with total accuracy.

Angles in a triangle

The three angles in a triangle add up to 180°. That is,

$$a + b + c = 180°$$

Again, check this for yourself by drawing a triangle and measuring its three angles

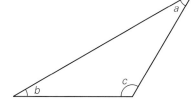

Special triangles

Equilateral triangle

An equilateral triangle is a triangle with all its sides equal. Therefore, all three interior angles are 60°.

Isosceles triangle

An isosceles triangle is a triangle with two equal sides, and therefore with two equal interior angles (at the foot of the equal sides).

Notice how we mark the equal sides and equal angles.

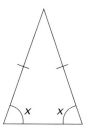

EXERCISE 15D

1 Find the size of the angle marked with a letter in each of these triangles.

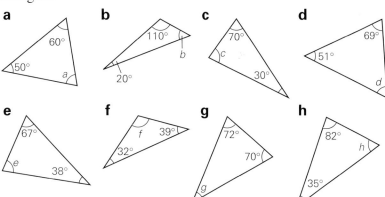

a (60°, 50°, a) **b** (110°, 20°, b) **c** (70°, 30°, c) **d** (69°, 51°, d)

e (67°, 38°, e) **f** (39°, 32°, f) **g** (72°, 70°, g) **h** (82°, 35°, h)

2 Are any of these sets of angles the three angles of a triangle? Explain your answer.

   a 35°, 75° and 80°   **b** 50°, 60° and 70°

   c 55°, 55° and 60°   **d** 60°, 60° and 60°

   e 35°, 35° and 110°   **f** 102°, 38° and 30°

3 The three interior angles of a triangle are given in each case. Find the angle indicated by a letter.

   a 20°, 80° and a°   **b** 52°, 61° and b°

   c 80°, 80° and c°   **d** 25°, 112° and d°

   e 120°, 50° and e°   **f** 122°, 57° and f°

4 In the triangle on the right, all the interior angles are the same.

   a What is each angle?

   b What is the special name of a triangle like this?

   c What is special about the sides of this triangle?

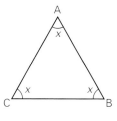

5 In the triangle on the right, two of the angles are the same.

   a Work out the size of the lettered angles.

   b What is the special name of a triangle like this?

   c What is special about the sides AC and AB of this triangle?

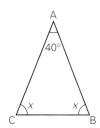

6 In the triangle on the right, the angles at B and C are the same. Work out the size of the lettered angles.

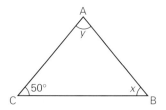

7 Find the size of the angle marked with a letter in each of these diagrams.

a

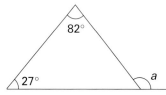

b

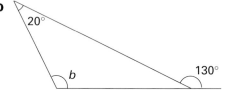

c

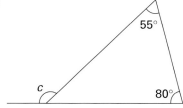

8 By using algebra, show that $x = a + b$.

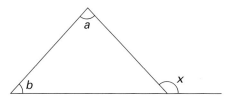

Angles in a polygon

Activity

Angle sums from triangles

Draw a quadrilateral (a four-sided shape).
Draw in a diagonal to make it into two triangles.

You should be able to copy and complete this statement:

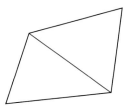

> The sum of the angles in a quadrilateral is equal to
> the sum of the angles in ...... triangles, which is
> ...... × 180° = ...°

Now draw a pentagon (a five-sided shape).

Draw in the diagonals to make it into three
triangles.

You should be able to copy and complete this
statement:

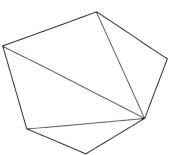

> The sum of the angles in a pentagon is equal
> to the sum of the angles in ...... triangles,
> which is ...... × 180° = ...°

Next, draw a hexagon (a six-sided shape).

Draw in the diagonals to make it into four triangles.

You should be able to copy and complete this
statement:

> The sum of the angles in a hexagon is equal
> to the sum of the angles in ...... triangles, which
> is ...... × 180° = ...°

Then, complete the table on page 302. Use the number pattern to carry on the
angle sum up to a decagon (ten-sided shape).

Shape	Sides	Triangles	Angle sum
Triangle	3	1	180°
Quadrilateral	4	2	
Pentagon	5	3	
Hexagon	6	4	
Heptagon	7		
Octagon	8		
Nonagon	9		
Decagon	10		

If you have spotted the number pattern, you should be able to copy and complete this statement:

The number of triangles in a 20-sided shape is ......, so the sum of the angles in a 20-sided shape is ...... × 180° = ...°

Angles in a quadrilateral

The four interior angles in a quadrilateral add up to 360°.
That is,
$$a + b + c + d = 360°$$

Again, check this for yourself by drawing a quadrilateral and measuring its four interior angles.

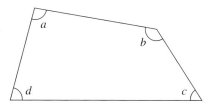

EXERCISE 15E

1 Find the size of the angle marked with a letter in each of these quadrilaterals.

a

b

c

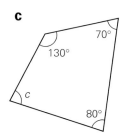

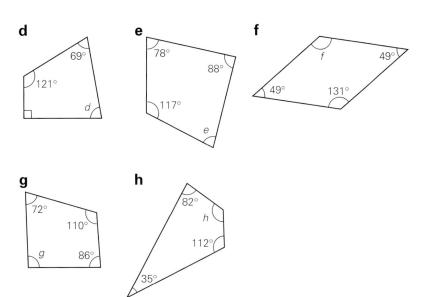

2 Are any of these sets of angles the four interior angles of a quadrilateral? Explain your answer.

    a 135°, 75°, 60° and 80°   **b** 150°, 60°, 80° and 70°

    c 85°, 85°, 120° and 60°   **d** 80°, 90°, 90° and 110°

    e 95°, 95°, 60° and 110°   **f** 102°, 138°, 90° and 30°

3 Three interior angles of a quadrilateral are given. Find the one indicated by a letter.

    a 120°, 80°, 60° and $a°$ **b** 102°, 101°, 90° and $b°$

    c 80°, 80°, 80° and $c°$ **d** 125°, 112°, 83° and $d°$

    e 120°, 150°, 50° and $e°$ **f** 122°, 157°, 80° and $f°$

4 In the quadrilateral on the right, all the angles are the same.

    a What is each angle?

    b What is the special name of a quadrilateral like this?

    c Is there another quadrilateral with all the angles the same? What is it called?

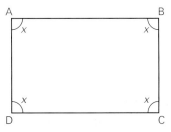

5 Work out the size of the angle marked with a letter in each of the polygons below. You may find the table you did on page 294 useful.

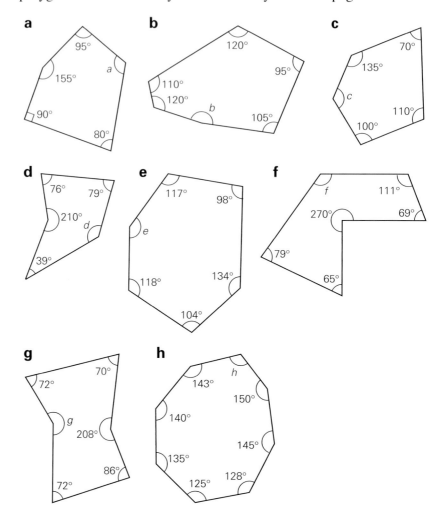

Activity

Regular polygons

To do these activities, you will need to have done those on pages 293–4.

You will also need a calculator.

Below are six **regular polygons**.

| Square 4 sides | Pentagon 5 sides | Hexagon 6 sides | Octagon 8 sides | Decagon 10 sides | Dodecagon 12 sides |

A polygon is regular if all its interior angles are equal and all its sides have the same length.

A square is a regular four-sided shape which has an angle sum of 360°. So, each angle is 360° ÷ 4 = 90°.

A **regular pentagon** has an angle sum of 540°. So, each angle is 540° ÷ 5 = 108°.

Copy and complete the table below.

Shape	Sides	Angle sum	Each angle
Square	4	360°	90°
Pentagon	5	540°	108°
Hexagon	6	720°	
Octagon	8		
Nonagon	9		
Decagon	10		
Dodecagon	12		

Using your results above and some of your results from the table on page 294, you should be able to copy and complete the following statements.

a In a regular 15-sided polygon, the angle sum is ......°
  Each angle is ......° ÷ 15 = ...°
b In a regular 18-sided polygon, the angle sum is ......°
  Each angle is ......° ÷ 18 = ...°
c In a regular 20-sided polygon, the angle sum is ......°
  Each angle is ......° ÷ 20 = ...°
d In a regular 30-sided polygon, the angle sum is ......°
  Each angle is ......° ÷ 30 = ...°
e In a regular n-sided polygon, the angle sum is ......°
  Each angle is ......° ÷ n = ...°

Interior and exterior angles

To do these activities you will need to have done the previous ones.

You will also need a calculator.

Look at these regular polygons.

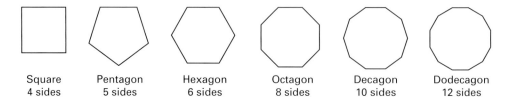

At each corner of each shape, there is an interior angle, *I*, and an exterior angle, *E*.

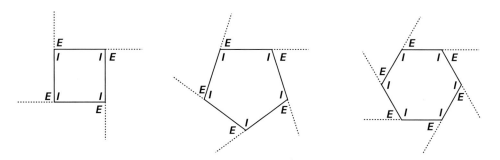

What can you say about *I* + *E* in each case?

Clearly, the exterior angles of a square are each 90°. So, the sum of the exterior angles of a square is

$$90° + 90° + 90° + 90° = 4 \times 90° = 360°.$$

You can calculate (or measure) the exterior angle of a regular pentagon.

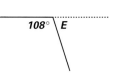

From page 305, you know that the interior angle is 108°. So, the exterior angle is 180° − 108° = 72°.

Therefore, the sum of the exterior angles is 5 × 72°.

Copy and complete the table on the next page.

Shape	Sides	Interior angle	Exterior angle	Sum of exterior angles
Square	4	90°	90°	$4 \times 90° = 360°$
Pentagon	5	108°	72°	$5 \times 72° =$
Hexagon	6	120°		
Octagon	8			
Nonagon	9			
Decagon	10			
Dodecagon	12			

Using your results above and some of your results from page 305, you should be able to copy and complete the following statements.

a In a regular 15-sided polygon, each interior angle is ......°
The exterior angle is $180° -$ ......° = ...°
The sum of the exterior angles is $15 \times$ ......° = ...°

b In a regular 18-sided polygon, each exterior angle is ......° $\div 18 =$ ......°
The interior angle is $180° -$ ......° = ...°

c In a regular 20-sided polygon, each exterior angle is ......° $\div 20 =$ ......°
The interior angle is $180° -$ ......° = ...°

d In a regular 30-sided polygon, each exterior angle is ......° $\div 30 =$ ......°
The interior angle is $180° -$ ......° = ...°

e In a regular n-sided polygon, each exterior angle is ......° $\div n =$ ......°
The interior angle is $180° -$ ......° = ...°

EXERCISE 15F

1 Each diagram shows just one corner (vertex) of a regular polygon. For each polygon:

  i What is its exterior angle?

  ii How many sides does it have?

  iii What is the sum of its interior angles?

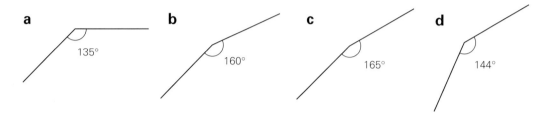

a 135° **b** 160° **c** 165° **d** 144°

2 Each diagram shows just one corner (vertex) of a regular polygon. For each polygon:

  i What is its interior angle?

  ii How many sides does it have?

  iii What is the sum of its interior angles?

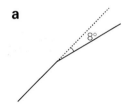

a 8° **b** 6° **c** 24° 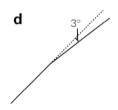 **d** 3°

3 Each of these cannot be the interior angle of a regular polygon. Explain why.

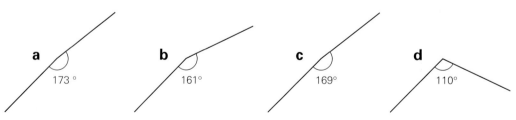

a 173 ° **b** 161° **c** 169° **d** 110°

4 Each of these cannot be the exterior angle of a regular polygon. Explain why.

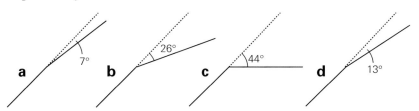

5 Take a regular octagon and join its corners (vertices) to its centre. Each angle is thus bisected (cut exactly in half).
Use this fact and the sum of the angles in a triangle to work out the value of the angle at the centre (marked x).
What connection does this have with the exterior angle?
Is this true for all regular polygons?

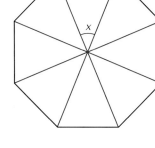

Activity

More angle names

You need tracing paper and/or a protractor.

Draw two parallel lines about 8 cm apart and a third line that crosses both of them. (The arrowheads indicate that the lines are parallel.)

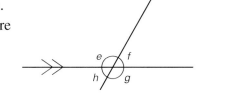

You should have eight angles.
Label these a, b, c, d, e, f and g.

Measure and/or trace angle a. Find all the angles on the diagram that are the same size as angle a.

Measure and/or trace angle b. Find all the angles on the diagram that are the same size as angle b.

What is the sum of $a + b$?

Find all the pairs of angles on the diagram that add up to $180°$.

Angles like these 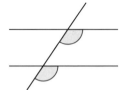 are called **corresponding angles** (also known as F angles).
Corresponding angles are **equal**.

Angles like these  are called **alternate angles** (also known as Z angles).
Alternate angles are **equal**.

Angles like these  are called **vertically opposite angles** (also known as X angles).
Vertically opposite angles are **equal**.

Angles like these 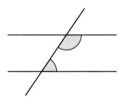 are called **interior angles** (also known as C angles).
Interior angles add to **180°**.

Copy and complete these statements to make them true.

1 *h* and ...... are corresponding angles.

2 *e* and ...... are vertically opposite angles.

3 *e* and ...... are alternate angles.

4 *e* and ...... are interior angles.

5 *b* and ...... are corresponding angles.

6 *b* and ...... are vertically opposite angles.

7 *d* and ...... are interior angles.

8 *a* and ...... are corresponding angles.

9 *g* and ...... are vertically opposite angles.

10 *c* and ...... are alternate angles.

EXERCISE 15G

1 State the size of the lettered angles in each diagram.

a 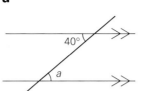 **b** 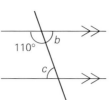 **c**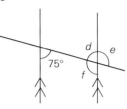

d 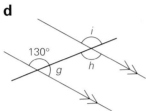 **e** 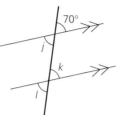 **f**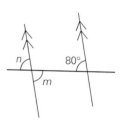

2 State the size of the lettered angles in each diagram.

a 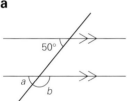 **b** 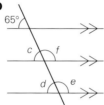 **c**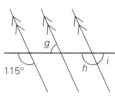

d 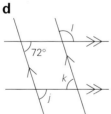 **e** 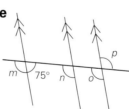 **f**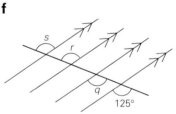

3 Two angles whose sum is 180° are
called **supplementary angles**. Write
down **all** the angles in the diagram
that are supplementary to angle *a*.

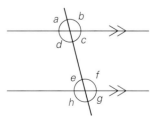

4 State the size of the lettered angles in these diagrams.

a

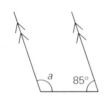

b

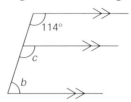

Special quadrilaterals

You should know the names of the following quadrilaterals, be familiar with their angle properties and know how to describe any angle using the three-letter notation.

Trapezium

- A trapezium has two parallel sides.
- The sum of the interior angles at the ends of each non-parallel side is 180°. That is,
  angle BAD + angle ADC = 180°
  angle ABC + angle BCD = 180°

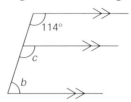

Parallelogram

- A parallelogram has opposite sides parallel.
- Its opposite sides are equal.
- Its diagonals bisect each other.
- Its opposite angles are equal. That is,
  angle BAD = angle BCD
  angle ABC = angle ADC

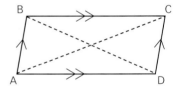

Rhombus

- A rhombus is a parallelogram with all its sides equal.
- Its diagonals bisect each other at right angles.
- Its diagonals also bisect the angles.

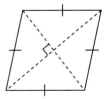

Kite

- A kite is a quadrilateral with two pairs of equal adjacent sides.
- Its longer diagonal bisects its shorter diagonal at right angles.
- The opposite angles between the sides of different lengths are equal.

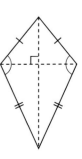

EXERCISE 15H

1 For each of these trapeziums, calculate the sizes of the lettered angles.

a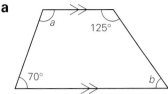

b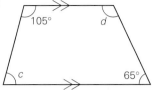

c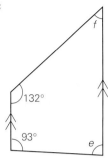

2 For each of these parallelograms, calculate the sizes of the lettered angles.

a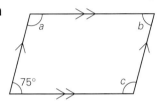

b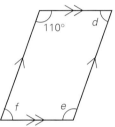

c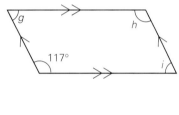

3 For each of these kites, calculate the sizes of the lettered angles.

a 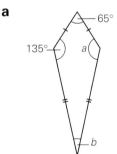 **b** 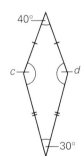 **c**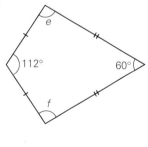

4 For each of these rhombuses, calculate the sizes of the lettered angles.

a 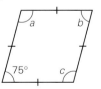 **b** **c**

5 For each of these shapes, calculate the sizes of the lettered angles.

a

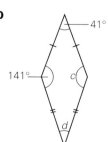

b

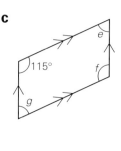

c

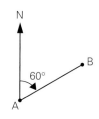

Bearings

The bearing of a point B from a point A is the angle through which you turn **clockwise** as you change direction from **due north** to the direction of B.

For example, in this diagram the bearing of B from A is 60°.

As a bearing can have any value from 0° to 360°, it is customary to give all bearings as **three-digit numbers**. So in the example above, the bearing becomes 060° using three digits. Here are three more examples.

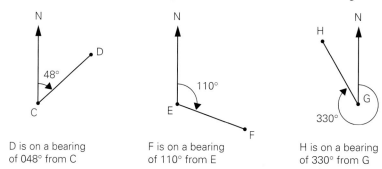

D is on a bearing of 048° from C

F is on a bearing of 110° from E

H is on a bearing of 330° from G

There are eight bearings with which you should be familiar. Here they are.

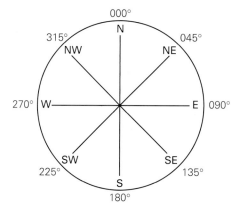

EXERCISE 15 I

1 Draw sketches to illustrate the following situations.
   a Rotherham is on a bearing of 025° from Sheffield.
   b Castleton is on a bearing of 170° from Hope.
   c Bude is on a bearing of 310° from Wadebridge.
   d Liverpool is on a bearing of 265° from Manchester.

2 A is due north from C. B is due east from A. B is on a bearing of 045° from C. Sketch the layout of the three points A, B and C.

3 Look at the following map.

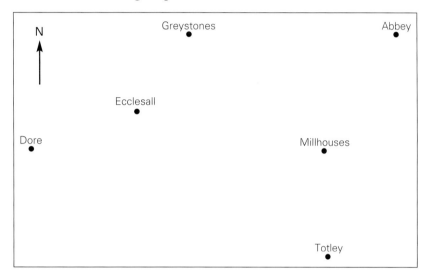

By measuring angles, find the bearing of
   a Totley from Dore
   b Dore from Ecclesall
   c Millhouses from Dore
   d Greystones from Abbey
   e Millhouses from Greystones
   f Totley from Millhouses

4 Captain Bird decided to sail his ship around the four sides of a square kilometre.
   a Assuming he started sailing due north, write down the further three bearings he would use in order to complete the square.
   b Assuming he started sailing on a bearing of 090°, write down the further three bearings he would use in order to complete the square.

Investigation

Measuring 22 Angles from Four!

Draw a triangle ABC. From B draw a line to meet the side AC at a point D.

Next, draw two lines parallel to AC, anywhere on the triangle.

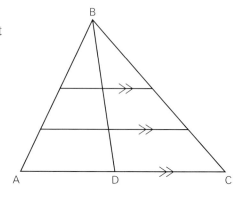

There are now 22 angles in the triangle.

Investigate how you can find them **all** by measuring just four angles.

Which combinations of four angles can you measure to give you all the other angles?

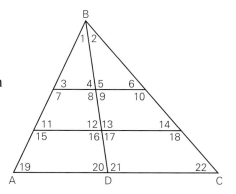

Examination questions

1

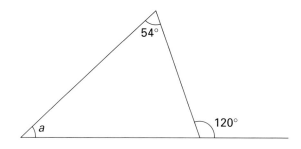

Work out the size of angle *a*.

OCR(SMP), Question 24, June 2000

2 **a** Find the size of the angle marked *x* in the triangle.

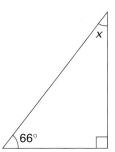

b Find the size of the angle marked *y* in the quadrilateral.

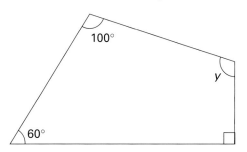

OCR, Question 14, Paper 1, June 2000

3 Find the sizes of the angles marked by letters in these diagrams.

Diagrams **not** drawn to scale

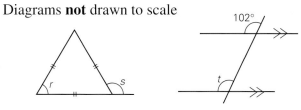

NEAB, Question 23, Specimen Paper 2F, 2000

4 Work out the sizes of the angles *p*, *q*, *r*, *s* and *t* in the diagrams below.

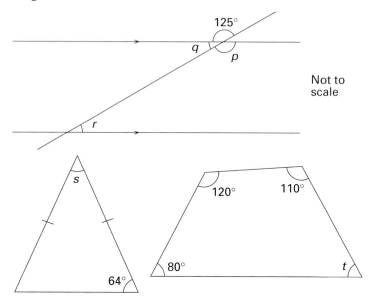

125°

q

p

Not to scale

r

s

120°   110°

80°   *t*

64°

MEG, Question 18, Paper 1, June 1998

5 a Triangle ABC is isosceles.
AB = AC.
Work out the size of angle *x*.

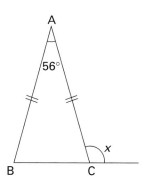

A

56°

B   C   *x*

b

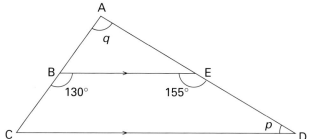

A

q

B   E

130°   155°

C   *p*   D

BE is parallel to CD.
   i   Write down the size of angle *p*.
   ii Work out the size of angle *q*.

AQA, Question 13, Paper 2, June 2000

6 a The diagram shows the frame of a rectangular gate with four parallel bars.

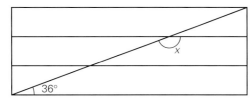

Not to scale

Write down the size of angle *x*. Give a reason for your answer.

b ABCD is a kite. Angle ABC = 90° and angle ADC = 54°. Calculate the size of angle BAD.

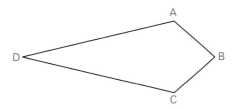

Not to scale

c The diagram shown has not been drawn accurately. When drawn accurately, POQ is a straight line, angle ROS is a right angle and *a* + *b* + *c* = 218°. Work out the sizes of angle *a* and angle *c*.

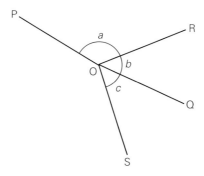

SEG, Question 18, Specimen Paper 5, 2000

> 7

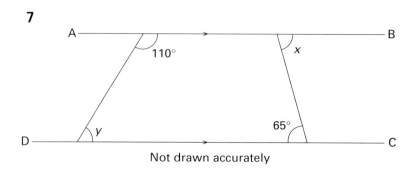

Not drawn accurately

AB is parallel to DC.

a Work out the size of angle x. Give a reason for your answer.

b Work out the size of angle y. Give a reason for your answer.

AQA, Question 15, Paper 2, June 1999

8 The angles of a triangle are $x°$, $(x + 20)°$ and $(2x – 40)°$.

i Write down an equation in x.

ii Solve your equation to find the value of x, and use this value to find the three angles of this triangle.

WJEC, Question 10, Specimen Paper 1F, 1998

9 a The Royal Mint designs a new coin in the shape of a regular pentagon.

i Draw a sketch of the coin.

ii What is the size of each of the interior angles of a regular pentagon?

b Write down the size of the angle marked x in each of the following diagrams.

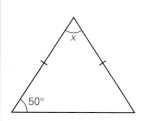

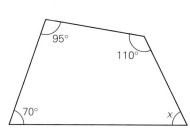

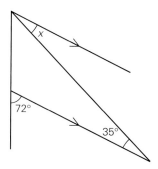

WJEC, Question 17, Specimen Paper 2F, 1998

10

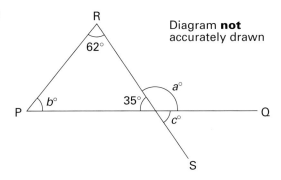

Diagram **not** accurately drawn

In the diagram PQ and RS are straight lines.
a **i** Work out the value of *a*.
    ii Give a reason for your answer.
b **i** Work out the value of *b*.
    ii Give a reason for your answer.
c **i** Work out the value of *c*.
    ii Give a reason for your answer.

EDEXCEL, Question 13, Paper 1, June 1999

11 The diagram shows three villages. Abshelf (A), Grasston (G), and Haswell (H). The North line through Grasston is shown.

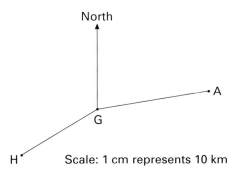

Scale: 1 cm represents 10 km

a What is the distance, in kilometres, between Abshelf and Grasston?
b Measure and write down the bearing of Abshelf from Grasston.
c Measure and write down the bearing of Haswell from Grasston.
d On the diagram, mark the village Wingly (W), which is 35 km from Grasston on a bearing of 320°

OCR, Question 15, Paper 1, June 1999

12 The bearing of a ship S, from a lighthouse L is 210°. The bearing of the ship, S, from a second lighthouse M is 285°. The positions of L and M are shown on the following diagram. Clearly drawing all necessary lines, mark the position of S on the diagram.

L

N

M

WJEC, Question 20, Paper 2, June 1999

What you should know after you have worked through Chapter 15

✔ The sum of the angles on a straight line is 180°.
✔ The sum of the angles around a point is 360°.
✔ The sum of the three interior angles in a triangle is 180°.
✔ An equilateral triangle has all its sides equal and all three interior angles equal to 60°.
✔ An isosceles triangle is a triangle with two equal sides and two equal interior angles.
✔ The names of the most common quadrilaterals and their properties.
✔ Vertically opposite angles are equal.
✔ How to recognise corresponding, alternate and interior angles.
✔ The sum of the angles in common polygons.
✔ How to find the interior and the exterior angles in regular polygons.

16 More about shapes

This chapter is going to ...

show you how to calculate the circumference and the area of a circle. It will also show you how to calculate the volume and surface area of a cuboid.

What you should already know

✔ What is meant by the terms 'radius', 'diameter' and 'circumference'
✔ How to round off decimal numbers
✔ How to square any number
✔ What is meant by the terms 'cube' and 'cuboid'
✔ What is meant by the term 'volume'
✔ How to find the area of a rectangle

Activity

Round and round

Find six cylindrical objects – bottles, cans, tubes, or piping will do.

You also need about 2 metres of string.

Copy the following table so that you can fill it in as you do this activity.

Object number	Diameter	Circumference	Circumference / Diameter
1			
2			
3			
4			
5			
6			

➤

Measure as accurately as you can the diameter of the first object. Write this measurement in your table.

Wrap the string around the object ten times, as shown in the diagram.

Make sure you start and finish along the **same line**. Mark clearly the point on the string where the tenth wrap ends.

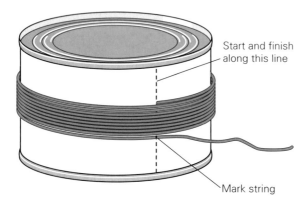

Start and finish along this line

Mark string

Then measure, as accurately as you can, the length of your ten wraps. This should be the distance from the starting end of the string to the mark you made on it.

Next, divide this length of string by 10. You have now found the length of the circumference of the first object. Write this in the table.

Repeat this procedure for each of the remaining objects.

Finally, complete the last column in the table by using your calculator to divide the circumference by the diameter. In each case, round off your answer to two decimal places.

If your measurements have been accurate, all the numbers you get should be about 3.14

This is the well-known number which is represented by the Greek letter π (pronounced pi). You can obtain a very accurate value for π by pressing the $\boxed{\pi}$ key on your calculator. Try it and see how close your numbers are to it.

Circumference of a circle

You calculate the circumference of a circle by multiplying its diameter by π, and then rounding off your answer to one or two decimal places.

The value of π is found on all scientific calculators ($\pi = 3.141\,592\,654$), but if it is not on yours then take $\pi = 3.142$.

The circumference of a circle is given by the formula:
Circumference $= \pi \times$ Diameter **or** $c = \pi d$

Example 1

Calculate the circumference of the circle with a diameter of 4 cm.

You can use at once the formula
Circumference $= \pi \times$ Diameter
$= \pi \times 4 = 12.6\,\text{cm}$ (rounded to 1dp)

Remember The length of the radius of a circle is half the length of its diameter. So, when you are given a radius in order to find a circumference, you must first **double** the radius to get the diameter.

Example 2

Calculate the circumference of the circle with a radius of 6 cm.

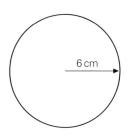

First, you need to double the radius to get the diameter:
Diameter $= 2 \times$ Radius $= 2 \times 6 = 12\,\text{cm}$

Then, calculate the circumference:
Circumference $= \pi \times 12 = 37.7\,\text{cm}$ (rounded to 1dp)

EXERCISE 16A

1 Calculate the circumference of each circle illustrated below.
Give your answers to one decimal place.

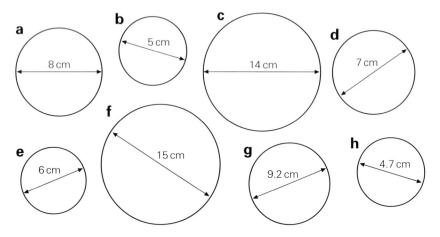

2 Find the circumference of each of the following coins. Give your
answers to one decimal place.
a 1p coin, diameter 2 cm
b 2p coin, diameter 2.6 cm
c 5p coin, diameter 1.7 cm
d 10p coin, diameter 2.4 cm

3 Calculate the circumference of each circle illustrated below.
Give your answers to one decimal place.

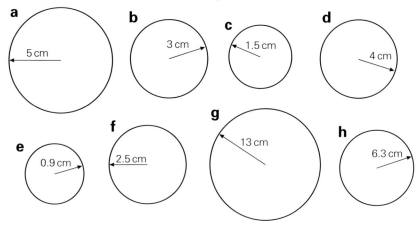

4 A bicycle wheel has a diameter of 32 cm. What is its circumference?

5 The diagram represents a race-track on a school playing field.
The diameter of each circle is shown below.

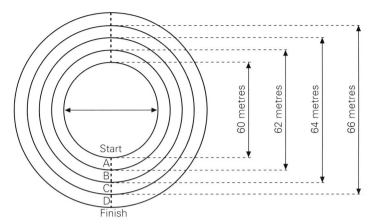

In a race with four runners, each runner starts and finishes on the
same inner circle of his/her lane after completing one circuit.

a Calculate the distance run by each runner in his/her lane.

b How much further than A does D have to run?

6 A rope is wrapped eight times round a capstan (cylindrical post), the
diameter of which is 35 cm. How long is the rope?

7 A hamster has a treadmill of diameter 12 cm.

a What is the circumference of the treadmill?

b How many centimetres has the hamster run when the wheel has
made 100 complete revolutions.

c Change into metres the answer to part **b**.

d One night, the hamster runs and runs and runs. He turns the wheel
100 000 times. How many kilometres will he have run?

8 A circle has a circumference of 314 cm. Calculate the diameter of the
circle.

9 What is the diameter of a circle whose circumference is 76 cm? Give
your answer to one decimal place.

10 What is the radius of a circle with a circumference of 100 cm? Give
your answer to one decimal place.

Area of a circle

The area of a circle is given by the formula:

$\text{Area} = \pi \times (\text{Radius})^2$ **or** $A = \pi \times r \times r$ **or** $A = \pi r^2$

Remember This formula uses radius. So, when you are given the diameter of a circle, you must **halve** it to get the radius.

Example 3

Radius given Calculate the area of a circle with a radius of 7 cm.

$$\begin{aligned}\text{Area} &= \pi \times (\text{Radius})^2 \\ &= \pi \times 7^2 = \pi \times 49 \\ &= 153.9\,\text{cm}^2 \quad (\text{rounded to 1dp})\end{aligned}$$

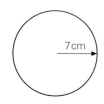

Example 4

Diameter given Calculate the area of a circle with a diameter of 12 cm.

First, halve the diameter to get the radius:

$\text{Radius} = 12 \div 2 = 6\,\text{cm}$

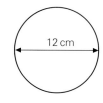

Then, find the area:

$$\begin{aligned}\text{Area} &= \pi \times (\text{Radius})^2 \\ &= \pi \times 6^2 = \pi \times 36 = 113.1\,\text{cm}^2 \quad (\text{rounded to 1dp})\end{aligned}$$

EXERCISE 16B

1 Calculate the area of each circle illustrated below. Give your answers to one decimal place.

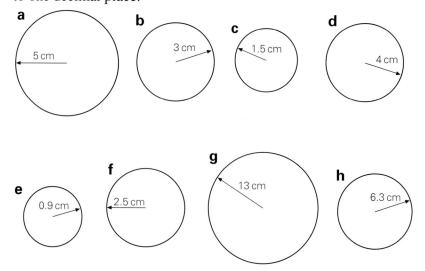

2 Find the area of one face of the following coins. Give your answers to one decimal place.
   a   1p coin, radius 1 cm
   b   2p coin, radius 1.3 cm
   c   5p coin, radius 0.85 cm
   d   10p coin, radius 1.2 cm

3 Calculate the area of each circle illustrated below. Give your answers to one decimal place.

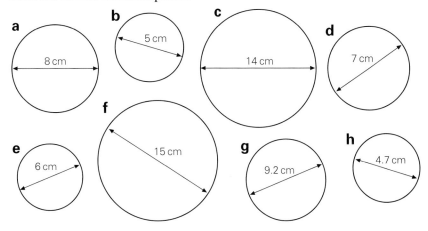

a   8 cm
b   5 cm
c   14 cm
d   7 cm
e   6 cm
f   15 cm
g   9.2 cm
h   4.7 cm

4 Milk-bottle tops are stamped from rectangular strips as shown.

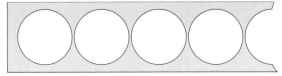

Each milk-bottle top is made from a circle of radius 1.7 cm.
Each rectangular strip measures 4 cm by 500 cm.
   a   What is the area of one milk-bottle top?
   b   How many milk-bottle tops can be stamped out of one strip 500 cm long when there is a 0.2 cm gap between each top?
   c   What is the area of the rectangular strip?
   d   What will be the total area of all the milk-bottle tops stamped out of the one strip?
   e   What waste is produced by one stamping?

5 A young athlete can throw the discus a distance of 35 metres, but is never too sure of the direction in which he will throw it. What area of field should be closed while he is throwing the discus?

6 Calculate **i** the circumference and **ii** the area of each of these circles. Give your answers to one decimal place.

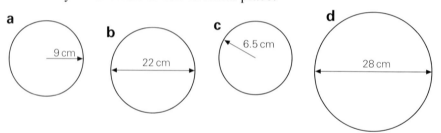

a 9 cm

b 22 cm

c 6.5 cm

d 28 cm

7 A circle has a circumference of 60 cm.

    a Calculate the diameter of the circle to one decimal place.

    b What is the radius of the circle to one decimal place?

    c Calculate the area of the circle to one decimal place.

8 Calculate the area of a circle with a circumference of 110 cm.

9 Calculate **i** the perimeter and **ii** the area of the following shapes. Give your answers to one decimal place.

a Semicircle

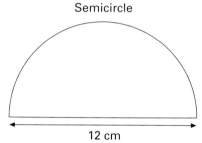

12 cm

b Quadrant

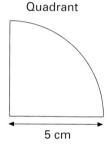

5 cm

Volume of cuboids

Cubes

A cube is a box shape, all six faces of which are squares. So, its 12 edges are all equal.

A cube with an edge length of 1 mm has a volume of 1 cubic millimetre (mm^3).

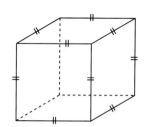

A cube with an edge length of 1 cm has a volume of 1 cubic centimetre (cm^3).

A cube with an edge length of 1 m has a volume of 1 cubic metre (m^3).

Note $1000\,mm^3 = 1\,cm^3$ and $1\,000\,000\,cm^3 = 1\,m^3$

Shapes made with cubes

Small children playing with wooden cubes or bricks make a variety of 3-D shapes with them, often trying to copy things they know.

Example 5

How many cubes, each 1 cm by 1 cm by 1 cm, have been used to make these steps? What volume do they occupy?

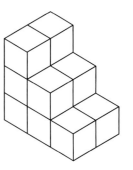

When you count the cubes, do not forget to include those hidden at the back.

You should count
$$6 + 4 + 2 = 12$$

The volume of each cube is $1\,cm^3$. So, the volume of the steps is
$$12 \times 1 = 12\,cm^3$$

EXERCISE 16C

Find the volume of each 3-D shape if the edge of each cube is 1 cm.

1

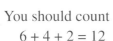

2

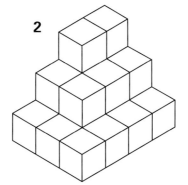

3

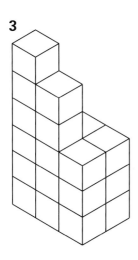

4

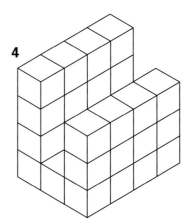

Cuboids

A cuboid is a box shape, all six faces of which are rectangles.

Every day you will come across many examples of cuboids, such as breakfast cereal packets, shoe boxes, video cassettes – and even this book.

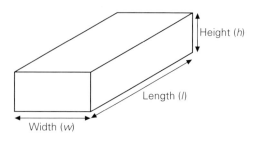

The volume of a cuboid is given by the formula:

Volume = Length × Width × Height   **or** $V = l \times w \times h$ **or** $V = lwh$

The surface area of a cuboid is calculated by finding the total area of the six faces, which are rectangles. Notice that each pair of opposite rectangles have the same area. So, from the diagram above, we have

Area of top and bottom rectangles = 2 × Length × Width = $2lw$
Area of front and back rectangles = 2 × Height × Width = $2hw$
Area of two side rectangles = 2 × Height × Length = $2hl$

Hence the surface area of a cuboid is given by the formula:

Surface area = $A = 2lw + 2hw + 2hl$

Example 6

Calculate the volume and surface area of this cuboid.

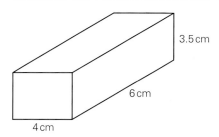

Volume = $6 \times 4 \times 3.5 = 84 \, \text{cm}^3$

Surface area = $(2 \times 6 \times 4) + (2 \times 3.5 \times 4) + (2 \times 3.5 \times 6)$
$= 48 + 28 + 42 = 118 \, \text{cm}^2$

EXERCISE 16D

1   Find **i** the volume and **ii** the surface area of each of these cuboids.

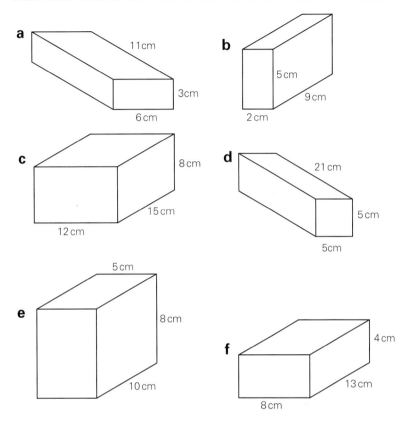

a   11cm   3cm   6cm

b   5cm   9cm   2cm

c   8cm   15cm   12cm

d   21cm   5cm   5cm

e   5cm   8cm   10cm

f   4cm   13cm   8cm

2   Find the capacity (volume of a liquid or a gas) of a fish-tank whose dimensions are: length 40 cm, width 30 cm and height 20 cm. Give your answer in litres. (1 litre = $1000 \, cm^3$)

3   Find the volume of the cuboid in each of the following cases.
   a   The area of the base is $40 \, cm^2$ and the height is 4 cm.
   b   The base has one side 10 cm, the other side 2 cm longer, and the height is 4 cm.
   c   The area of the top is $25 \, cm^2$ and the depth is 6 cm.

4   Calculate **i** the volume and **ii** the surface area of each of the cubes with these edge lengths.
   a   4 cm   **b**   7 cm   **c**   10 mm   **d**   5 m   **e**   12 m

5   The safety regulations say that in a room where people sleep there should be at least $12 \, m^3$ for each person. A dormitory is 20 m long, 13 m wide and 4 m high. What is the greatest number of people who can safely sleep in the dormitory?

6 Calculate the volume of each of these shapes.

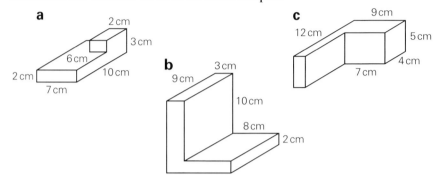

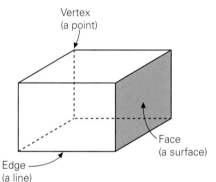

Investigation

Many-faced Shapes

All 3-D shapes have **faces**, **vertices** and **edges**. (Note: vertices is the plural of vertex.)

Look at the shapes in the table on the next page. Then copy the table and fill it in.

Vertex
(a point)

Face
(a surface)

Edge
(a line)

Remember that there are hidden faces, vertices and edges. These are shown with dashed lines.

Look at the numbers in the completed table.

■ For each shape, can you find the connection between the following properties?

 ☐ The number of faces, F.

 ☐ The number of vertices, V.

 ☐ The number of edges, E.

■ Find some other solid shapes. Does your connection hold for those also?

Shape	Name	Number of faces (F)	Number of vertices (V)	Number of edges (E)
	Cuboid			
	Square-based pyramid			
	Triangular-based pyramid (or tetrahedron)			
	Octahedron			
	Triangular prism			
	Hexagonal prism			
	Hexagon-based pyramid			

Examination questions

1 This box of herbs is a cuboid. Calculate the volume of the box.

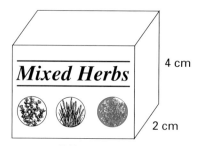

OCR(SMP), Question 21, June 1999

2

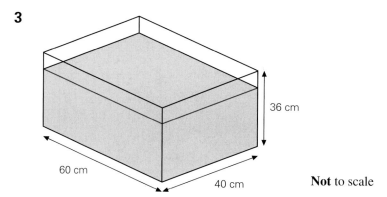

a What is the volume of the cuboid?

b What is the area of the shaded top of the cuboid?

OCR, Question 5, Paper 2, June 2000

3

A rectangular tank has length 60 cm, width 40 cm and height 36 cm. It is placed on a horizontal table. Water is poured into the tank until it is three-quarters full.

a Calculate the depth of the water in the tank.

b Calculate how many litres of water there are in the tank. [1 litre = 1000 cm³]

MEG, Question 17, Specimen Paper 1F, 1998

4 This container is a cuboid.

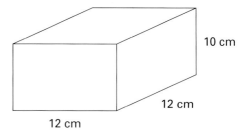

This jewellery box is also a cuboid. Jewellery boxes are packed into the container.

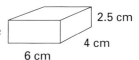

How many jewellery boxes fill the container?

OCR(SMP), Question 18, June 2000

5 The diagram represents a circular training track. The diameter of the track, AB, is 70 metres.

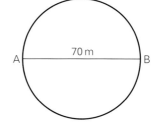

Alisa and Bryony have a race. Alisa runs along the diameter from A to B and back again. Bryony starts at A and runs all the way round the track to A again. Work out how much further Bryony runs than Alisa.

EDEXCEL, Question 22, Specimen Paper 2F, 1998

6 Water is stored in a tank in the shape of a cuboid with a square base. The sides of the base are 30 cm long. The depth of the water is 20 cm

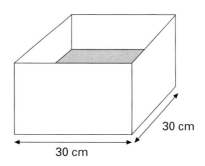

a Work out the volume of water

More water is put in the tank. The depth of the water rises to 21.6 cm.

b Calculate the percentage increase in the volume of water in the tank.

EDEXCEL, Question 15, Paper 2, June 1998

7 This flag is made from a coloured circle in a white rectangle. The radius of the circle is 5 cm. Calculate the area shown on the flag that is white.

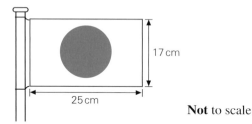

17 cm

25 cm

Not to scale

SEG, Question 21, Specimen Paper 6, 2000

8 A circular pond has a radius of 5.2 m. Calculate its area. Give your answer to an appropriate degree of accuracy.

OCR(SMP), Question 25, June 2000

9 A circle has a diameter of 7 cm.
    a Calculate the circumference of this circle.
    b Calculate the area of this circle.

NEAB, Question 19, Paper 2F, June 1997

10 a Work out the perimeter of the semicircle.

    b Work out the area of the semicircle.

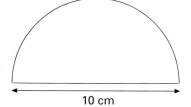

10 cm

EDEXCEL, Question 16, Paper 1, June 1998

11

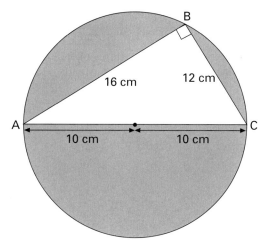

The diagram shows a right-angled triangle ABC and a circle. A, B, and C are points on the circumference of the circle. AC is a diameter of the circle. The radius of the circle is 10 cm. AB = 16 cm and BC = 12 cm.
Work out the area of the shaded part of the circle.
Give your answer correct to the nearest cm².

EDEXCEL, Question 22, Paper 1, June 1999

12

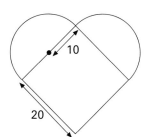

Instructions for making a heart-shaped cake.
• Bake a square cake of side 20 cm.
• Bake a round cake of radius 10 cm.
• Cut the round cake in half.
• Join the two halves to the square cake as shown in the diagram.

a Find the area of the heart-shape. State the units of your answer.

A red ribbon is fixed around the sides of the heart-shaped cake with ends overlapping by 3 cm.

b Find the length of the ribbon required.

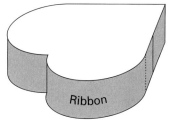

Ribbon

OCR, Question 14, Paper 2, June 2000

331

What you should know after you have worked through Chapter 16

✔ How to calculate the circumference of a circle.
✔ How to calculate the area of a circle.
✔ How to calculate the volume and surface area of a cuboid.

Revision for Chapters 1 to 16

- Answer all the questions
- Show your working
- Do **not** use a calculator for the first nine questions

1 **a** Write these numbers in order, smallest first.

  234   221   243   205   219   212

  b Add together all the numbers in part **a**.

  c Subtract the smallest number from the biggest.

  d Work out each of these.

i	5×9	**ii**	2×9	**iii**	5×4
iv	2×4	**v**	5×49	**vi**	2×49
vii	52×49	**viii**	4×37	**ix**	34×37

2 Work out each of these fraction sums.

  a $\frac{3}{7} + \frac{4}{7}$ **b** $\frac{5}{8} - \frac{3}{8}$ **c** $\frac{1}{4} + \frac{3}{8}$

  d $\frac{2}{3}$ of £27 **e** $\frac{3}{4}$ of 48 **f** $\frac{4}{5}$ of £125

3 What temperature (in °C) is shown on each of these thermometers?

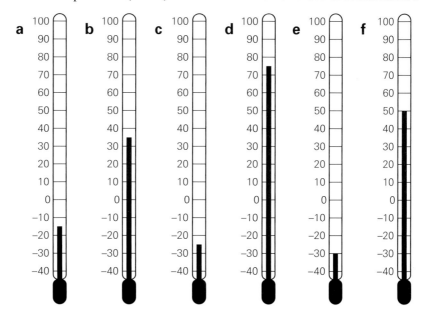

  g What is the difference between the largest and smallest values on these thermometers?

  h Which two temperatures are different by 50 degrees?

4 Find the missing number which makes each of these problems true.

a $7 - \square = 12$ **b** $\square + 3 = 1$ **c** $13 + \square = 7$

d $\square + 9 = 5$ **e** $\square - 2 = -2$ **f** $4 - \square = 1$

g $4 - \square = 11$ **h** $3 + \square - 5 = 0$ **i** $6 + \square = 0$

5 Look at this list of numbers.

     15   81   14   10   25   16   17

a Find a multiple of 7.

b Find an even square number.

c Find a square number **and** a multiple of 3.

d Find a factor of 30.

e Find a prime number.

f Find a triangular number.

g Find a number with exactly three factors.

6 These two bar charts show the marks scored in a maths test for two classes, Form 7J and Form 7K.

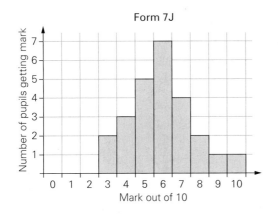

Form 7J

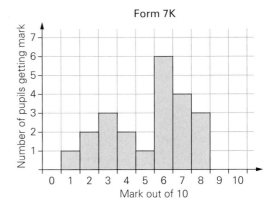

Form 7K

a How many pupils were in each class?

b How many scored 7 in each class?

c What was the most frequent score in each class?

d What was the range of marks in each class?

e Which class did better in the test? Give a reason for your answer.

7 Write each of these as algebraic expressions.

a 5 more than x **b** 6 less than y

c 7 times b **d** p times q

e Half of t **f** 2 times x plus 3

g $x + 3$, then times the answer by 2

h The perimeter of a rectangle $2t$ by $3t$ centimetres.

8 If $a = 2$, $b = 3$ and $c = 4$, work out the value of each of these expressions.

   a $3a + 4b$ **b** $4a + c$ **c** $a^2 + b^2$ **d** $2a + 3b - c$

   e $a(b + c)$ **f** $(6b - c) \div 2$ **g** $(a + b)^2$ **h** $(a + b + c)^2$

9 Waiting to get on the Eurotunnel train were 16 rows of cars. Each row had the same number of cars in it. In total, there were 544 cars. How many were in each row?

10 The Clintons are going to the USA on holiday.

   a   They want to change £2000 into US dollars. The exchange rate is $1.39 to each pound. How many dollars will they receive?

   b   A US gallon is 80% of a British gallon. The Clintons get 30 miles to a gallon out of their car. They get 22 miles to the gallon out of their US hire car. Which gives the most miles per gallon?

11 A small factory has 12 employees. Their annual salaries are
£100 000, £60 000, £40 000, £14 000, £12 000, £12 000, £12 000,
£12 000, £12 000, £12 000, £10 000, £4000

   a   What is the mean salary?

   b   What is the median salary?

   c   What is the modal salary?

   d   Which is the best average and why?

12 At break, there were five plates of biscuits on the staffroom table. Mr Sum, the maths teacher, noticed that there were six less biscuits on the second plate than on the first. Twice as many on the third plate as on the second. Six less on the fourth plate than on the third, and only six biscuits on the fifth plate. There were 60 biscuits out altogether.

   a   If there are x biscuits on the first plate, write down how many were on the second, third and fourth plates in terms of x.

   b   Set up an equation for the number of biscuits in total.

   c   Work out how many were on the first plate.

   d   Mr Sum took the plate that had exactly one-fifth of the biscuits. Which plate did he take?

Revision section

13 Copy and complete this cross-number puzzle. What percentage is each of these?

Clues across

  1   54 out of 200

  3   33 out of 50

  5   13 out of 25

  8   99 out of 100

 10 102 out of 200

 12 27 out of 50

 14 38 out of 200

Clues down

  2   300 out of 400

  4   134 out of 200

  6   87 out of 300

  7   100 out of 400

  9   19 out of 20

 11 110 out of 1000

 13 23 out of 50

14 Use the flow diagram to help you draw the graph of $y = 3x - 1$ for values of x from 0 to 5. Use axes as shown.

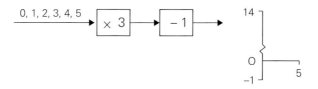

15 The graph shows Simon's journey home from school. Simon gets a lift to the station, catches a train, then a bus and finally walks home from the bus-stop.

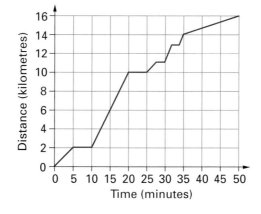

   a   **i**   How far is the station from the school?

        ii   How many minutes does he take to get to the station?

   b   **i**   How long does Simon wait for the train?

        ii   What is the average speed of the train?

16   The diagram shows a cuboid.

   a   Calculate the volume of the cuboid.

   b   Calculate the surface area of the cuboid.

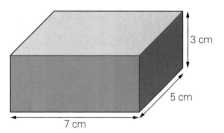

17   Calculate the size of each angle marked with a letter.

   a   **b**   **c**

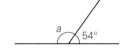 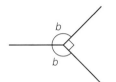 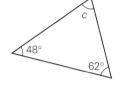

18   Solve the following equations.

   a $3x + 4 = 19$ **b** $2x + 7 = 1$ **c** $3(x + 4) = 18$

   d $5x + 7 = 2x - 5$

19   Calculate the circumference and the area of a circle whose radius is 6 cm. Give your answers to one decimal place.

20   Find the area of this garden patio. Give your answer to one decimal place.

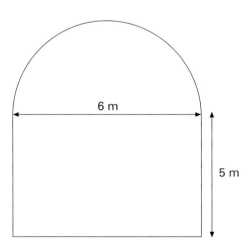

Revision section

17 Constructions

This chapter is going to ...

show you how to construct circles and triangles, using a ruler, a pair of compasses and a protractor. It will then introduce you to the idea of congruency.

What you should already know

✔ How to draw circles using a pair of compasses
✔ How to measure and draw angles using a protractor

Constructing circles

You need to know the following terms when dealing with circles:

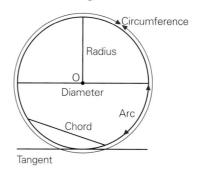

O	The centre of a circle.
Diameter	The 'width' of a circle. Any diameter passes through O.
Radius	The distance from O to the edge of a circle. The length of the diameter is twice the length of the radius.
Circumference	The distance all the way round a circle.
Chord	A line joining two points on the circumference.
Tangent	A line that touches the circumference at one point only.
Arc	A segment, or piece, of the circumference of a circle.

When drawing a circle, you first need to set your compasses to a given radius.

Example 1

Draw a circle with a radius of 3 cm.

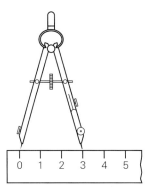

Set your compasses to a radius of 3 cm, as shown in the diagram.

Draw a circle and mark the centre O.

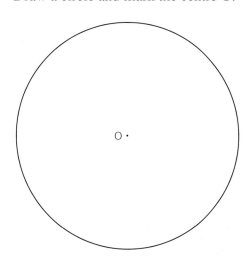

Activity

Circle patterns

You need a sharp pencil, a pair of compasses, a protractor and some coloured crayons or felt-tips.

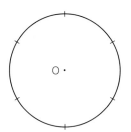

Draw a circle with a radius of 3 cm.

Put the centre of your protractor at the centre of the circle, and make a mark on the circumference for every 60°, as on the diagram.

(Notice that the six points form a regular hexagon.)

Using these marks as centres, draw circles still using a radius of 3 cm.

You should now get this circle pattern. Choose your own colours to make an impressive display.

Repeat the above, but mark the circumference every 30° or 45°.

EXERCISE 17A

1 Measure the radius of each of the following circles, giving your answers in centimetres. Write down the diameter of each circle.

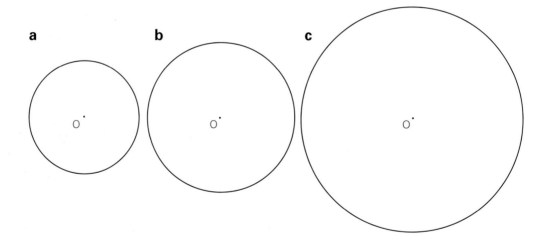

a   **b**   **c**

2 Draw circles with the following measurements.
   a Radius = 2 cm   **b** Radius = 3.5 cm
   c Diameter = 8 cm   **d** Diameter = 10.6 cm

3 Accurately draw the following shapes.

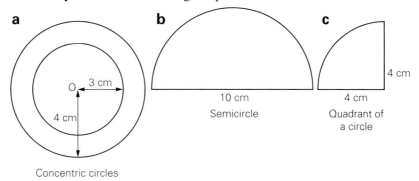

a

O ←3 cm→

4 cm

Concentric circles

b

10 cm

Semicircle

c

4 cm

4 cm

Quadrant of
a circle

4 Draw accurate copies of these diagrams.

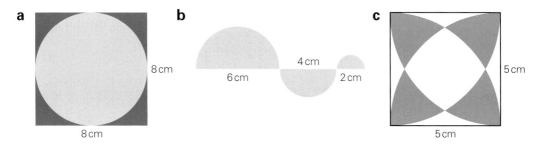

a

8 cm

8 cm

b

4 cm

6 cm   2 cm

c

5 cm

5 cm

5 **a** Draw a circle of radius 4 cm.

  b Keeping your compasses set with a radius 4 cm, go round the circle making marks on the circumference that are 4 cm apart.

  c Join the points with a ruler to make a polygon.

  d What name is given to the polygon you have drawn?

Constructing triangles

When you are asked to accurately draw a triangle, you will be expected either to copy a sketch or to construct it from given information.

Triangles are usually labelled in a particular way, so that you know which side or angle you are using.

The triangle ABC has three sides, AB, AC and BC, and three angles, $\angle A$, $\angle B$ and $\angle C$.

Sometimes, an angle is written using the two sides that form the angle, so that

  $\angle A$ is written as $\angle BAC$

  $\angle B$ is written as $\angle ABC$

  $\angle C$ is written as $\angle ACB$

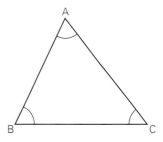

There are three ways of constructing a triangle. Which one we use depends on what information we are given about the triangle.

Two sides and the included angle known

Example 2

Draw a triangle ABC, where AB is 6 cm, BC is 5 cm and the included angle ABC is 55°. (The diagrams in this example are drawn at half-size.)

- First, draw the longest side, AB, as the base. Label the ends of the base A and B.

A ——————— B

- Next, place the protractor along AB with its centre on B, and make a point on the diagram at the 55° mark.

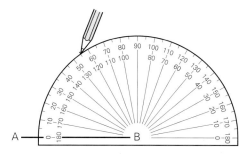

- Then draw a **feint** line from B through the 55° point. From B measure 5 cm along this line and mark the point. Label it C.

- Finally, join A and C and make AC and CB into bolder lines.

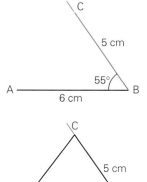

Note The construction lines are drawn lightly and left in to demonstrate how the triangle has been constructed.

Two angles and a side known

Example 3

Draw a triangle ABC, where AB is 7 cm, angle BAC is 40° and angle ABC is 65°.

- As before, start by drawing the base, which here has to be 7 cm. Label the ends A and B.

A ————————— B

- Next, centre the protractor on A and mark the angle of 40°. Draw a feint line from A through this point.

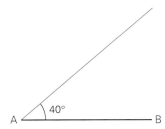

- Then centre the protractor on B and mark the

angle of 65°. Draw a feint line from B through this point, to intersect the 40° line drawn from A. Label the point of intersection as C.

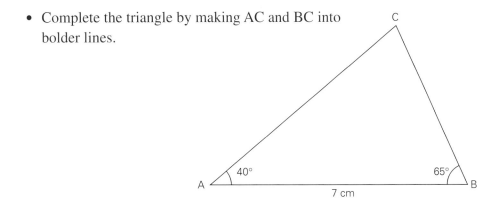

- Complete the triangle by making AC and BC into bolder lines.

343

Three sides known

Example 4

Draw a triangle ABC, where AB is 6 cm, AC is 5 cm and BC is 4 cm.

- First, draw the longest side, AB, as a base. Label the ends of the base A and B.

A ———————————— B
6 cm

- Next, set your compasses to a radius of 5 cm. With A as the centre, draw a large arc above AB.

A ———————————————— B
6 cm

- Then, set your compasses to a radius of 4 cm. With B as the centre, draw a large arc above AB, to intersect the other arc. Label the point of intersection C.

A ———————————————— B
6 cm

- Finally, using a ruler, join A to C and B to C to complete the triangle.

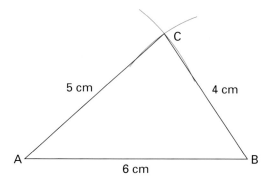

EXERCISE 17B

1   Accurately draw each of the following triangles and measure the sides and angles not given.

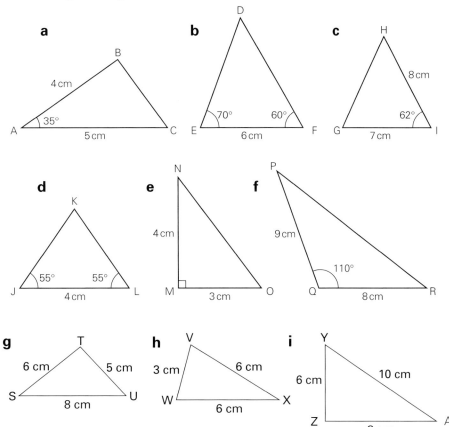

2   Draw a triangle ABC with AB = 8 cm, ∠A = 52° and ∠B = 68°.

3   Draw a triangle XYZ with XY = 9 cm, XZ = 7 cm and ∠X = 45°.

4   **a**   Accurately draw the shape on the right.
    b   What is the name of the shape you have drawn?

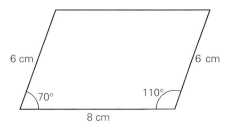

5 a Accurately draw the shape on the right.

b Measure the length of CD.

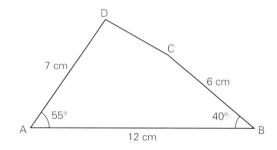

6 Draw an equilateral triangle with sides of 5 cm.

Congruent shapes

Figures which are exactly the **same** size and shape are said to be **congruent**. For example, although they are in different positions, these triangles are congruent, because they are all exactly the same size and shape.

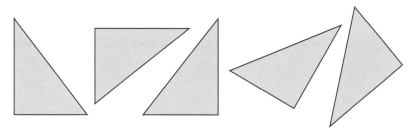

Congruent shapes fit exactly on top of each other. So, one way to see whether shapes are congruent is to trace one of them and check that it exactly covers the other shapes. For some of the shapes, you may have to turn over your tracing.

Example 5

Which of these shapes is not congruent to the others?

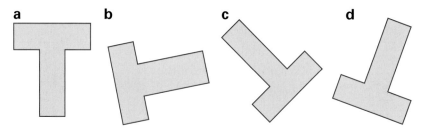

Trace shape **a** and check whether it fits exactly on top of the others.

You should find that shape **b** is not congruent to the others.

EXERCISE 17C

1 State whether each pair of shapes **a** to **f** are congruent or not.

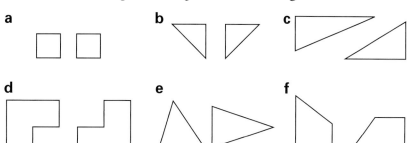

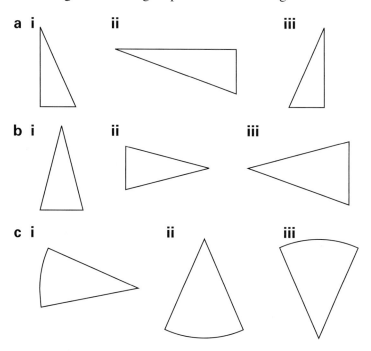

2 Which figure in each group **a** to **c** is not congruent to the other two?

3 For each of the following sets of shapes, write down the numbers of the shapes that are congruent to each other.

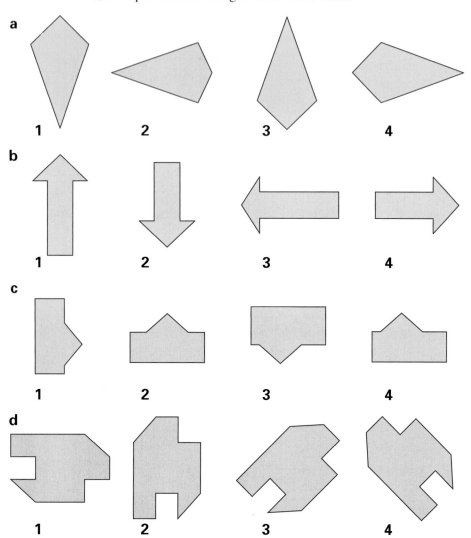

Investigation

Triangles

Draw as many different triangles as you can, using any three measurements taken from 40°, 60°, 7 cm and 8 cm.

Congruent Tees

In how many different ways will the T-shape fit inside the 3 × 3 grid?

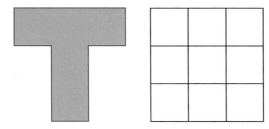

Here are two different ways. Can you find any other ways?

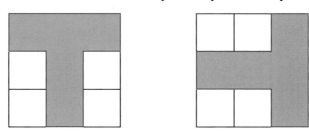

In how many different ways will the T-shape fit inside this 4 × 4 grid?

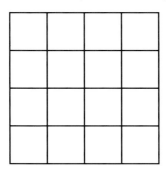

Find the number of ways the T-shape will fit inside a grid of **any** size.

Examination questions

1 a Draw a circle of radius 5 cm.

   b Draw a diameter on your circle. Label its ends A and B.

   c Mark a point, P, anywhere on the circumference of your circle. Join A to P and P to B.

   d Use your protractor to measure the angle APB.

NEAB, Question 9, Paper 2F, June 1998

2 From the six words below, pick the correct four and write them in the boxes on the diagram.

    Diameter

    Arc

    Chord

    Tangent

    Radius

    Circumference

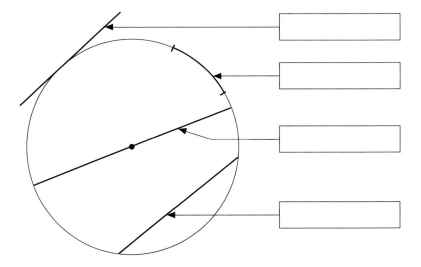

OCR, Question 2, Paper 1, June 2000

3 One of the triangles marked R, S and T is congruent to the triangle marked A. Which triangle is congruent to triangle A?

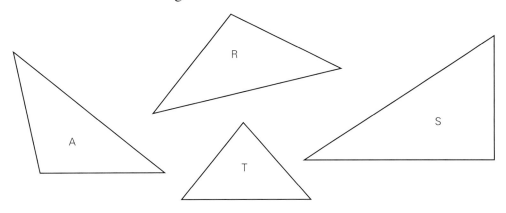

WJEC, Question 2, Specimen Paper 2F, 1998

4

Use your ruler, compasses and protractor to make an accurate construction of this triangle.

WJEC, Question 9, Specimen Paper 2F, 1998

5 Which **two** of the following shapes are congruent to each other?

a 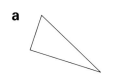 b 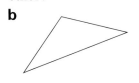 c 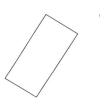 d

e f   g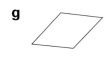

WJEC, Question 4, Paper 2, June 1999

6 Here is a sketch of a triangle. PR = 6.4 cm, QR = 7.7 cm, angle R = 35°.

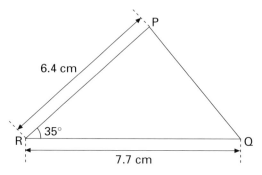

a Make an accurate drawing of the triangle.
b Measure the size of angle Q on your drawing.

EDEXCEL, Question 8, Paper 1, June 1999

7 C is the centre of the circle. PCS is a straight line which is a radius of the circle.

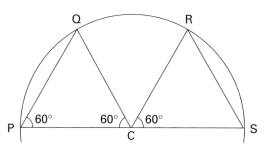

a Name every line which is a radius of the circle.
In the diagram, angle QPC = angle QCP = angle RCS = 60°.
b What type of triangle is PQC?
c Name two line which are parallel to each other.
d Make an accurate copy of the diagram. Start with a circle with its centre at C and with a radius 5 cm.

MEG, Question 19, Paper 1, June 1998

> ### What you should know after you have worked through Chapter 17
>
> ✔ How to draw a circle from given information.
> ✔ How to construct a triangle from given information.
> ✔ Two or more shapes are congruent if they fit exactly on each other.

PUZZLE PAGE

Going dotty

Join up these nine dots using **only four** straight lines, while keeping your pen on the paper.

Lillium gigantium

The *Lillium gigantium* is a plant which doubles its size everyday. It if completely covers a pond in 30 days, how long does it take to cover half of the pond?

Tricky crossing

Two men and two boys want to cross a river. They have only one boat between them, and it can carry only one man or two boys. How do they get across?

In the dark

A drawer contains ten white socks and ten black socks. You reach into the drawer in the dark. What is the smallest number of socks you must take out to be certain of getting a matching pair of socks?

Jill without Jack

Jill went to a well with two buckets. One held 3 litres and the other held 5 litres. She returned with 4 litres of water. How did she do it?

What a bargain!

Six costs 14p, seventeen costs 28p and three hundred and sixty cost 42p. What am I buying?

18 Probability

> ## This chapter is going to ...
> remind you of the basic definition of probability and show you how to calculate the probability of an event, expressing it as a fraction, a decimal or a percentage.
>
> ## What you should already know
> ✔ Basic ideas of probability
> ✔ The probability scale goes from 0 to 1
> ✔ How to add, subtract and cancel fractions

Probability scale

Almost daily, we hear somebody talking about the probability of whether this or that will happen. Only usually they use words like 'chance', 'likelihood' or 'risk' rather than 'probability'. For example:

'What is the likelihood of rain tomorrow?'

'What chance does she have of winning the 100 metres?'

'Is there a risk that his company will go bankrupt?'

We can give a value to the chance of any of these events happening – and millions of others, as well. We call this value the **probability**.

We know that some things are certain to happen, and that some things cannot happen. That is, the chance of something happening can be anywhere between **impossible** and **certain**. We represent this situation on a sliding scale, called the **probability scale**, as shown below.

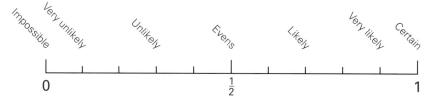

Note All probabilities lie between **0** and **1**.

An event which cannot happen (impossible) has a probability of 0. For example, the probability that pigs will fly is 0.

An event which is certain to happen has a probability of 1. For example, the probability that the sun will rise tomorrow is 1.

Example 1

Put arrows on the probability scale to show roughly the probability of the following events.

a You will get a head when throwing a coin.

b You will get a six when throwing a dice.

c You will have maths homework this week.

a This event is an even chance. (Commonly described as a fifty-fifty chance.)

b This event is fairly unlikely.

c This event is likely.

So, the arrows will be approximately in these positions on the probability scale:

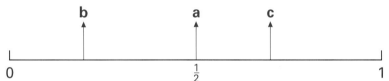

EXERCISE 18A

1 State whether each of the following events are impossible, very unlikely, unlikely, even, likely, very likely or certain.

   a Picking out a Heart from a well-shuffled pack of cards.

   b You have a maths lesson today.

   c Someone in your class is left-handed.

   d You will live to be 100.

   e A score of seven is obtained when throwing a dice.

   f You will watch some TV this evening.

   g A new-born baby will be a girl.

2   Draw a probability scale and put an arrow to show approximately the probability of each of the following events happening.
  a   The next car you see will have been made in Europe.
  b   A person in your class will have been born in the twentieth century.
  c   It will rain tomorrow.
  d   In the next Olympic Games, someone will run the 1500 m race in 3 minutes.
  e   During this week, you will have chips with a meal.

3   Give two events of your own where you think the probability is:
  a   impossible   **b**   very unlikely   **c**   unlikely
  d   evens   **e**   likely   **f**   very likely
  g   certain

Calculating probabilities

In Question **2** of Exercise 18A, you undoubtedly had difficulty in knowing exactly where to put some of the arrows on the probability scale. It would have been easier for you if each event could have been given a value between 0 and 1 to represent the probability for that event.

For some events, this can be done by first finding all the possibilities or **outcomes** for a particular event. For example, when you throw a coin there are two **equally likely** outcomes: heads or tails. If you want to calculate the probability of getting a head, there is only one outcome that is possible. So, we say there is a 1 in 2, or 1 out of 2, chance of getting a head. This is usually given as a **probability fraction**, namely $\frac{1}{2}$. So, we would write the event as

$\text{P(head)} = \frac{1}{2}$

Probabilities can also be written as decimals or percentages, so that

$\text{P(head)} = \frac{1}{2}$ or   0.5   or   50%

It is more usual to give probabilities as fractions in GCSE examinations, but you will frequently come across probabilities given as percentages: for example, in the weather forecasts on TV.

The probability of an event is defined as

$$\text{P(event)} = \frac{\text{Number of ways the event can happen}}{\text{Total number of all possible outcomes}}$$

This definition always leads to a fraction, which should be cancelled down to its simplest form.

Another probability term you will meet is **at random.** This means 'without looking' or 'not knowing what the outcome is in advance'.

Example 2

A bag contains 5 red balls and 3 blue balls. A ball is taken out at random. What is the probability that it is
a red   **b** blue   **c** green?

We use the above formula to work out these probabilities.

a There are 5 red balls out of a total of 8, so P(red) = $\frac{5}{8}$

b There are 3 blue balls out of a total of 8, so P(blue) = $\frac{3}{8}$

c There are no green balls, so this event is impossible: P(green) = 0

Example 3

The spinner shown below right is spun and the score on the side on which it lands is recorded. What is the probability that the score is
a 2   **b** odd   **c** less than 5?

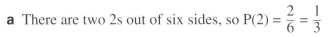

a There are two 2s out of six sides, so P(2) = $\frac{2}{6}$ = $\frac{1}{3}$

b There are four odd numbers, so P(odd) = $\frac{4}{6}$ = $\frac{2}{3}$

c All of the numbers are less than 5, so this is a certain event:
P(less than 5) = 1

1 What is the probability of each of the following events?
  a Throwing a 2 with a dice.
  b Throwing a 6 with a dice.
  c Tossing a coin and getting a tail.
  d Drawing a Queen from a pack of cards.
  e Drawing a Heart from a pack of cards.
  f Drawing a black card from a pack of cards.
  g Throwing a 2 or a 6 with a dice.
  h Drawing a black Queen from a pack of cards.
  i Drawing an Ace from a pack of cards.
  j Throwing a 7 with a dice.

2 What is the probability of each of the following events?

    a   Throwing an even number with a dice.

    b   Throwing a prime number with a dice.

    c   Getting a Heart or a Club from a pack of cards.

    d   Drawing the King of Hearts from a pack of cards.

    e   Drawing a picture card or an Ace from a pack of cards.

    f   Drawing the Seven of Diamonds from a pack of cards.

3 A bag contains only blue balls. If I take one out at random, what is the probability that

    a   I get a black ball   **b**   I get a blue ball?

4 The numbers 1 to 10 inclusive are placed in a hat. Bob takes a number out of the bag without looking. What is the probability that he draws

    a   the number 7   **b**   an even number

    c   a number greater than 6   **d**   a number less than 3

    e   a number between 3 and 8?

5 A bag contains 1 blue ball, 1 pink ball and 1 black ball. Joan takes a ball from the bag without looking. What is the probability that she takes out

    a   the blue ball   **b**   the pink ball

    c   a ball that is not black?

6 A pencil case contains 6 red pens and 5 blue pens. Geoff takes out a pen without looking at what it is. What is the probability that he takes out

    a   a red pen   **b**   a blue pen

    c   a pen that is not blue?

7 A bag contains 50 balls. Ten are green, 15 are red and the rest are white. Gemma takes a ball from the bag at random. What is the probability that she takes

    a   a green ball   **b**   a white ball

    c   a ball that is not white   **d**   a ball that is green or white?

8 A box contains 7 bags of cheese and onion crisps, 2 bags of beef crisps and 6 bags of plain crisps. Iklil takes out a bag of crisps at random. What is the probability that he gets

    a   a bag of cheese and onion crisps

    b   a bag of beef crisps

    c   a bag of crisps that are not cheese and onion

    d   a bag of prawn cracker crisps

    e   a bag of crisps that is either plain or beef?

9 In a Christmas raffle, 2500 tickets are sold. One family has 50 tickets. What is the probability that that family wins the first prize?

10 Arthur, Brenda, Charles, Doris and Eliza are in the same class. Their teacher wants two pupils to do a special job.

    a Write down all the possible combinations of two people. For example, Arthur and Brenda, Arthur and Charles (there are 10 combinations altogether).

    b How many pairs give two boys?

    c What is the probability of choosing two boys?

    d How many pairs give a boy and a girl?

    e What is the probability of choosing a boy and a girl?

    f What is the probability of choosing two girls?

11 In a sale at the supermarket, there is a box of 10 unlabelled tins. On the side it says: 4 Tins of Creamed Rice and 6 Tins of Chicken Soup. Malcolm buys this box. When he gets home he wants to have a lunch of chicken soup followed by creamed rice.

    a What is the smallest number of tins he could open to get his lunch?

    b What is the largest number of tins he could open to get his lunch?

    c The first tin he opens is soup. What is the chance that the second tin he opens is

        i soup   **ii** rice?

12 What is the probability of each of the following events?

    a Drawing a Jack from a pack of cards.

    b Drawing a 10 from a pack of cards.

    c Drawing a red card from a pack of cards.

    d Drawing a 10 or a Jack from a pack of cards.

    e Drawing a Jack or a red card from a pack of cards.

    f Drawing a red Jack from a pack of cards.

13 A bag contains 25 coloured balls. Twelve are red, seven are blue and the rest are green. Martin takes a ball at random from the bag.

    a Find

        i P (he chooses a red)   **ii** P (he chooses a blue)

        iii P(he chooses a green)

    b Add together the three probabilities. What do you notice?

    c Explain your answer to part **b**.

14 The weather tomorrow will be sunny, cloudy or raining. If P(sunny) = 40%, P(cloudy) = 25%, what is P(raining)?

15 At morning break, Pauline has a choice of coffee, tea or hot chocolate. If P(she chooses coffee) = 0.3 and P(she chooses hot chocolate) = 0.2, what is P(she chooses tea)?

Probability that an event will not happen

The probability of throwing a six on a dice is $P(6) = \frac{1}{6}$

The probability of not throwing a six on a dice is

$$P(\text{not a 6}) = \frac{5}{6}$$

since there are five outcomes that are not sixes: $\{1, 2, 3, 4, 5\}$

Notice that

$$P(6) = \frac{1}{6} \quad \text{and} \quad P(\text{not a 6}) = \frac{5}{6}$$

If we know that $P(6) = \frac{1}{6}$, then $P(\text{not a 6})$ is

$$1 - \frac{1}{6} = \frac{5}{6}$$

So, if we know P(event happening), then
P(event not happening) = 1 − P(event happening)

Example 4

What is the probability of not picking an Ace from a pack of cards?

First, find the probability of picking an Ace:
P(picking an Ace from a pack of cards) $= \frac{4}{52} = \frac{1}{13}$

Therefore,
P(not picking an Ace from a pack of cards) $= 1 - \frac{1}{13} = \frac{12}{13}$

EXERCISE 18C

1 a The probability of winning a prize in a raffle is $\frac{1}{20}$. What is the probability of not winning a prize in the raffle?

b The probability that snow will fall during the Christmas holidays is 45%. What is the probability that it will not snow?

c The probability that Paddy wins a game of chess is 0.7, and the probability that he draws the game is 0.1. What is the probability that he loses the game?

2 Millicent picks a card from a pack of well-shuffled playing cards. Find the probability that she picks:

a i a picture card	**ii** a card that is not a picture
b i a Club	**ii** not a Club
c i an Ace or a King	**ii** neither an Ace nor a King.

3 The following letters are put into a bag.

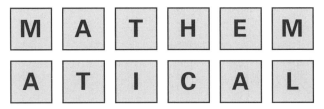

    a Steve takes a letter at random.
        i What is the probability he takes a letter A?
        ii What is the probability he does not take a letter A?
    b Richard picks an M and keeps it. Sue now takes a letter from those remaining.
        i What is the probability she takes a letter A?
        ii What is the probability she does not take a letter A?

Activity

Heads or tails?

Toss a coin 10 times and record the results like this.

Record how many heads you obtained.

Now repeat the above so that altogether you toss the coin 50 times. Record your results and count how many heads you obtained. Now toss the coin another 50 times and once again record your results and count the heads.

It helps if you work with a partner. First, your partner records while you toss the coin. Then you swap over and record, while your partner tosses the coin. Add the number of heads you obtained to the number your partner obtained.

Now find three more people to do the same activity and add together the number of heads that all five of you obtained.

Now find five more people and add their results to the previous total.

Combine as many results together as possible.

You should now be able to fill in a table like the one below. The first column is the number of times coins were tossed. The second column is the number of heads obtained. The third column is the first column divided by the second column.

➤

The results below are from a group who did the same experiment.

Number of tosses	Number of heads	Heads ÷ tosses
10	6	0.6
50	24	0.48
100	47	0.47
200	92	0.46
500	237	0.474
1000	488	0.488
2000	960	0.48
5000	2482	0.4964

If we drew a graph of these results, plotting the first column against the last column, it would look like this.

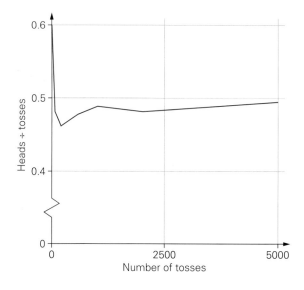

Your results should look very similar.

What happens to the value of heads ÷ tosses as the total number of tosses increases?

You should find that it gets closer and closer to 0.5

Experimental probability

The value of number of heads ÷ number of tosses is called an **experimental probability.** As the number of trials or experiments increases, the value of the experimental probability gets closer to the true or theoretical probability.

Experimental probability is also known as the **relative frequency** of an event. The relative frequency of an event is an estimate for the theoretical probability. It is given by

$$\text{Relative frequency of an event} = \frac{\text{Frequency of the event}}{\text{Total number of trials}}$$

Example 5

The frequency table shows the speeds of 160 vehicles which pass a radar speed check on a dual carriageway.

Speed (mph)	20–29	30–39	40–49	50–59	60–69	70+
Frequency	14	23	28	35	52	8

a What is the experimental probability that a car is travelling faster than 70 mph?

b If 500 vehicles pass the speed check, estimate how many will be travelling faster than 70 mph.

a The experimental probability is the relative frequency, which is
$\frac{8}{160} = \frac{1}{20}$

b The number of vehicles travelling faster than 70 mph will be $\frac{1}{20}$ of 500. That is, $500 \div 20 = 25$

EXERCISE 18D

1 Naseer throws a dice and records the number of sixes that he gets after various numbers of throws. The table shows his results.

Number of throws	10	50	100	200	500	1000	2000
Number of sixes	2	4	10	21	74	163	329

a Calculate the experimental probability of a six at each stage that Naseer recorded his results.

b How many ways can a dice land?

c How many of these ways give a six?

d What is the theoretical probability of throwing a six with a dice?

e If Naseer threw the dice a total of 6000 times, how many sixes would you expect him to get?

2 Marie made a five-sided spinner, like the one shown in the diagram. She used it to play a board game with her friend Sarah. The girls thought that the spinner wasn't very fair as it seemed to land on some numbers more than others. They threw the spinner 200 times and recorded the results. The results are shown in the table.

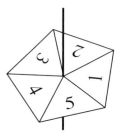

Side spinner lands on	1	2	3	4	5
Number of times	19	27	32	53	69

   a Work out the experimental probability of each number.

   b How many times would you expect each number to occur if the spinner is fair?

   c Do you think that the spinner is fair? Give a reason for your answer.

3 A sampling bottle contains 20 balls. The balls are either black or white. (A sampling bottle is a sealed bottle with a clear plastic tube at one end into which one of the balls can be tipped.) Kenny conducts an experiment to see how many black balls are in the bottle. He takes various numbers of samples and records how many of them showed a black ball. The results are shown in the table.

Number of samples	Number of black balls	Experimental probability
10	2	
100	25	
200	76	
500	210	
1000	385	
5000	1987	

   a Copy the table and calculate the experimental probability of getting a black ball at each stage.

   b Using this information, how many black balls do you think are in the bottle?

4 Use a set of number cards from 1 to 10 (or make your own set) and work with a partner. Take it in turns to choose a card and keep a record each time of what card you get. Shuffle the cards each time and repeat the experiment 60 times. Put your results in a copy of this table.

Score	1	2	3	4	5	6	7	8	9	10
Total										

  a How many times would you expect to get each number?

  b Do you think you and your partner conducted this experiment fairly?

  c Explain your answer to part **b**.

5 A four-sided dice has faces numbered 1, 2, 3 and 4. The 'score' is the face on which it lands. Five pupils throw the dice to see if it is biased. They each throw it a different number of times. Their results are shown in the table.

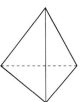

Pupil	Total number of throws	Score			
		1	**2**	**3**	**4**
Alfred	20	7	6	3	4
Brian	50	19	16	8	7
Caryl	250	102	76	42	30
Deema	80	25	25	12	18
Emma	150	61	46	26	17

  a Which pupil will have the most reliable set of results? Why?

  b Add up all the score columns and work out the relative frequency of each score. Give your answers to two decimal places.

  c Is the dice biased? Explain your answer.

Activity

Biased spinner

You need a piece of stiff card, a cocktail stick and some Blu-tack.

You may find that it is easier to work in pairs.

Make a copy of this hexagon on the card and push the cocktail stick through its centre to make a six-sided spinner. The size of the hexagon doesn't really matter, but it does need to be **accurately** drawn.

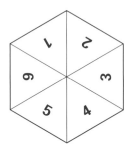

Stick a small piece of Blu-tack underneath one of the numbers. You now have a **biased** spinner.

Spin it 100 times and record your results in a frequency table.

Estimate the experimental probability of getting each number.

How can you tell that your spinner is biased?

Put Blu-tack underneath a different number and see whether your partner can predict towards which number the spinner is biased.

Combined events

There are many situations where two events occur together. Four examples are given below.

Throwing two dice

Imagine that two dice, one red and one blue, are thrown. The red dice can land with any one of six scores: 1, 2, 3, 4, 5 or 6. The blue dice can also land with any one of six scores. This gives a total of 36 possible combinations. These are shown in the left-hand diagram on the top of the next page, where each combination is given as (2, 3) etc. The first number is the score on the blue dice and the second number is the score on the red dice.

The combination (2, 3) gives a total of 5. The total scores for all the combinations are shown in the right-hand diagram at the top of the next page.

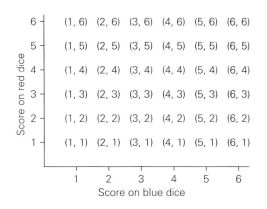

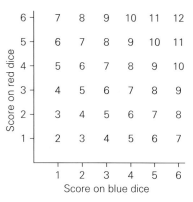

Diagram showing the outcomes of throwing two dice as 'co-ordinates'

Diagram showing the outcomes of throwing two dice as 'total scores'

From the diagram on the right, we can see that there are two ways to get a score of 3. This gives a probability of

$$P(3) = \frac{2}{36} = \frac{1}{18}$$

From the diagram on the left, we can see that there are six ways to get a 'double'. This gives a probability of

$$P(double) = \frac{6}{36} = \frac{1}{6}$$

Throwing coins

Throwing one coin

There are two equally likely outcomes, head or tail: (H) (T)

Throwing two coins together

There are four equally likely outcomes:

$$P(2 \text{ heads}) = \frac{1}{4}$$

P(head and tail) = 2 ways out of 4 = $\frac{2}{4} = \frac{1}{2}$

Dice and coins

Throwing a dice and a coin

Outcome on coin

H   (1, H) (2, H) (3, H) (4, H) (5, H) (6, H)

T   (1, T) (2, T) (3, T) (4, T) (5, T) (6, T)

      1   2   3   4   5   6

Score on dice

P (head and an even number) = 3 ways out of 12 = $\frac{3}{12} = \frac{1}{4}$

EXERCISE 18E

1 To answer these questions, use the diagram on page 375 for the total scores when two dice are thrown together.
   a What is the most likely score?
   b Which two scores are least likely?
   c Write down the probabilities of all scores from 2 to 12.
   d What is the probability of a score that is
     i bigger than 10   **ii** between 3 and 7
     iii even   **iv** a square number
     v a prime number   **vi** a triangle number?

2 Using the diagram on page 375 that shows, as co-ordinates, the outcomes when two dice are thrown together, what is the probability that
   a the score is an even 'double'
   b at least one of the dice shows 2
   c the score on one dice is twice the score on the other dice
   d at least one of the dice shows a multiple of 3?

3 Using the diagram on page 375 that shows, as co-ordinates, the outcomes when two dice are thrown together, what is the probability that
   a both dice show a 6
   b at least one of the dice will show a six
   c exactly one dice shows a six?

4 The diagram shows the score for the event 'the difference between the scores when two dice are thrown'. Copy and complete the diagram.

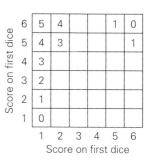

For the event described above, what is the probability of a difference of

a 1   **b** 0   **c** 4

d 6   **e** an odd number?

5 When two coins are thrown together, what is the probability of

a 2 heads   **b** a head and a tail

c at least 1 tail   **d** no tails

Use the diagram of the outcomes when two coins are thrown together, on page 375.

6 Two five-sided spinners are spun together and the total score of the faces that they land on is worked out. Copy and complete the probability space diagram below.

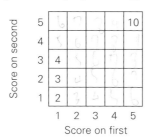

a What is the most likely score?

b When two five-sided spinners are spun together, what is the probability that

i the total score is 5

ii the total score is an even number

iii the score is a 'double'

iv the score is less than 7?

Examination questions

1 a On a combination lock there are two rings.

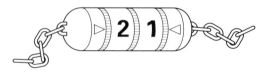

There are three digits on each ring: **1**, **2** and **3**. Each combination is a two-digit number, for example **2**, **1**

  i List **all** the possible combinations.

  ii What is the probability that a lock has a combination of **2, 1**?

  iii What is the probability that the two digits of a combination are the same?

b On a combination lock with **three** rings, the probability that the three digits are the same is $\frac{1}{9}$. What is the probability that the three digits are **not** the same?

SEG, Question 13, Specimen Paper 5, 2000

2 Richard has a box of 15 coloured light bulbs. Seven are pink, six are blue and two are white. Richard chooses a bulb at random.

a What is the probability that it is white?

b What is the probability that it is either blue or white?

SEG, Question 14, Specimen Paper 5, 2000

3 The line below is a probability line.

a On a copy of the probability line, show an estimate of the probability that a person chosen at random is left-handed.

b On a different probability line, show an estimate of the probability that a person chosen at random is **not** left-handed.

c A class has 30 pupils. There are 14 boys in the class. Eight of the girls in the class wear glasses. A girl is chosen. What is the probability that the girl chosen wears glasses?

SEG, Question 7, Specimen Paper 6, 2000

4 A bag contains 4 green balls, 8 blue balls, 15 yellow balls and 6 black balls. A ball is taken at random from the bag. Find the probablity that it is

a blue   **b** green or black

c not yellow

MEG, Question 5, Paper 1, June 1998

5 In a school fête, contestants throw two dice and add the two numbers showing. Contestants who score ten or more win a prize.

a Copy and complete the following table to show all possible outcomes for the game.

6	......	......	......	......	......	......
5	......	......	......	......	......	......
4	5	......	......	......	......	......
3	4	5	......	......	......	......
2	3	4	......	......	......	......
1	2	3	4	5	6	7
0	1	2	3	4	5	6

b Jeremy has one turn at the game. What is the probability that he will win a prize?

c At the fête, 270 people each play the game once. Approximately how many are likely to win a prize?

WJEC, Question 7, Specimen Paper 2F, 1998

6 Polly has kept records of the weather for five years. She works out that the probability that it will rain on any day in September is 0.2.

a What is the probability that it will not rain on September 15th?

b On how many September days could it be expected to rain?

September 1998			
	6	13	20	27
	7	14	21	28
1	8	15	22	29
2	9	16	23	30
3	10	17	24	
4	11	18	25	
5	12	19	26	

MEG, Question 12, Paper 2, June 1998

7 Two fair spinners are used for a game. The scores from each spinner are added together.

For example: The total score from these two spinners is 4 + 5 = 9

a Copy and complete this table to show all the possible totals for the two spinners.

	1	2	3	4	5
2	3	4			
3	4	5			
4					
5					
6					

b What is the probability of scoring
   i a total of 3
   ii a total of more than 8?

NEAB, Question 12, Paper 1F, June 1998

8 Five children guess the score on the next throw
of a fair six-sided dice.

The scale below shows the probability of each statement
being correct.

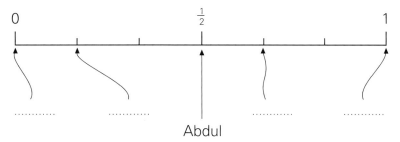

Copy the line and put the name of each child in its correct
place. Abdul's has been done for you.

NEAB, Question 10, Paper 2F, June 1998

9 Amy throws a fair coin and rolls a fair dice. She works out her score as follows.

> If she gets a head, she doubles the number on the dice.
> If she gets a tail, she adds 2 to the number on the dice.

a Complete the table of Amy's possible scores.

Number on the dice

Coin		1	2	3	4	5	6
	Head	2	4				
	Tail	3	4				

b **i** List the scores which are prime numbers.

ii Write down the probability of getting a score which is a prime number.

iii Write down the probability that the score is **not** prime.

AQA, Question 15, Paper 1, June 2000

10 **a** A bag contains 3 red beads, 2 blue beads and 5 yellow beads. A bead is taken from the bag at random.

i What is the probability that it is a blue bead?

ii What is the probability that it is not a blue bead?

b In a game at a fête a player rolls a coin onto a squared board. The squares on which the coin may land are coloured red, blue, green, yellow or orange. If the coin lands completely on one of the coloured squares the player wins. If it does not land completely on one of the coloured squares the player loses.

The table below shows the probabilities of the coin landing on the winning colours.

Colour	Red	Blue	Green	Yellow	Orange
Probability	0.23	0.15	0.06	0.03	0.20

i 400 people each have one turn on the game. About how many coins would you expect to land on a blue square?

ii What is the probability that the coin does not land completely on one of the coloured squares?

WJEC, Question 14, Paper 2, June 1999

**What you should know after you
have worked through Chapter 18**

✔ How to put events in order of likelihood.
✔ How approximately to place events on the probability scale from 0 to 1.
✔ How to calculate the experimental probability of an event from data supplied.
✔ How to calculate the theoretical probability of an event from considerations of all outcomes of the event.
✔ That as the number of trials of an event increases, the experimental probability of the event gets closer to its theoretical probability.
✔ How to calculate the probability of combined events.

19 Transformations

This chapter is going to ...

show you how to transform shapes by using translations, reflections, rotations and enlargements. It will also show you how to tessellate simple shapes.

What you should already know

✔ How to find the lines of symmetry of a 2-D shape
✔ How to find the order of rotational symmetry of a 2-D shape

A **transformation** changes the position or the size of a plane shape in a particular way. We shall deal with the four basic ways of using transformations to change a shape: **translation, reflection, rotation** and **enlargement**.

When we carry out a transformation, the shape's original position is called the **object** and its 'new' position is called the **image**.

Activity

Chess moves

You need a chessboard and the various pieces.

Find out all the different moves that each chess piece is allowed to make, and write them down.

Describe the movements of each piece in terms of the number of squares that it moves in a particular direction, using words such as 'forwards', 'backwards', 'left' and 'right'.

Translation

A translation is the movement of a shape from one position to another without reflecting it or rotating it. It is sometimes called a 'sliding' movement, since the shape appears to slide from one position to another.

Every point in the shape moves in the same direction and through the same distance.

Example 1

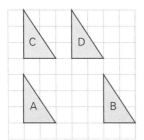

Triangle A has been transformed into triangle B by a translation of
5 squares right.

Triangle A has been transformed into triangle C by a translation of
4 squares up.

Triangle A has been transformed into triangle D by a translation of
3 squares right and 4 squares up.

Example 2

Draw the image of triangle ABC after a translation of 3 squares left and 4 squares down.

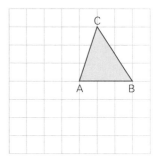

In a translation, all the points move the same distance. So, to draw the image of triangle ABC, first translate each vertex 3 squares left and 4 squares down. Then join the points to get the image triangle A'B'C'.

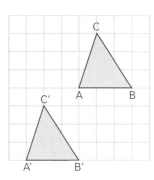

EXERCISE 19A

1 Copy each of these shapes on squared paper and draw its image by using the given translation.

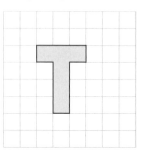

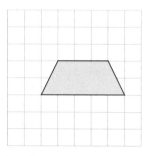

a 3 squares right

b 3 squares up

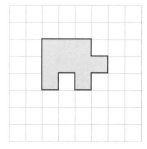

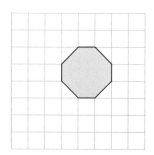

c 3 squares down

d 3 squares left

2 Copy each of these shapes on squared paper and draw its image by using the given translation.

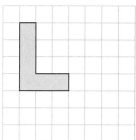

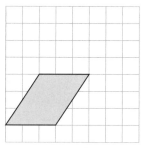

a 4 squares right
and 3 squares down

b 3 squares right
and 3 squares up

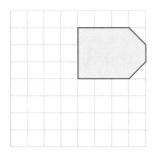

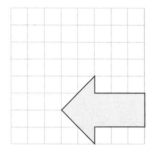

c 4 squares left
and 3 squares down

d 1 square left
and 4 squares up

3 Look at the diagram below, then describe these translations.

a **i** A to B   **ii** A to C   **iii** A to D   **iv** A to E   **v** A to F
  vi A to G

b **i** B to A   **ii** B to C   **iii** B to D   **iv** B to E   **v** B to F
  vi B to G

c **i** C to A   **ii** C to B   **iii** C to D   **iv** C to E   **v** C to F
  vi C to G

d **i** D to E   **ii** E to B   **iii** F to C   **iv** G to D   **v** F to G
  vi G to E

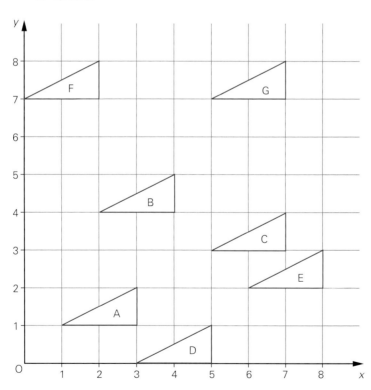

4 Draw a triangle whose vertices have co-ordinates A(1, 1), B(3, 1) and C(3, 2). Translate the triangle 5 squares right and 4 squares up to form the image triangle A′B′C′. Write down the co-ordinates of A′, B′ and C′.

Reflection

Reflection is the movement of a shape so that it becomes a mirror image of itself.

Notice that each point on the image is the same distance from the mirror line as the corresponding point on the object.

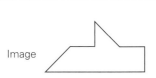

So, if you could 'fold' the whole diagram along the mirror line, every point on the object would coincide with its reflection.

Example 3

Reflect the triangle in the mirror line.

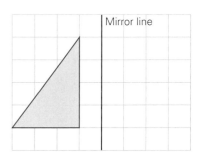

Each vertex on the image will be the same distance from the mirror line as the corresponding vertex on the object. So, the reflection of the original will be as shown on the right.

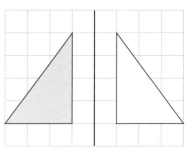

Example 4

a Reflect the triangle ABC in the *x*-axis. Label the image P.

b Reflect the triangle ABC in the *y*-axis. Label the image Q.

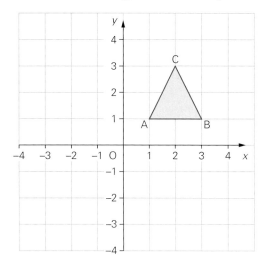

a The mirror line is the *x*-axis. So, each vertex on triangle P will be the same distance from the *x*-axis as the corresponding vertex on the object.

b The mirror line is the *y*-axis. So, each vertex on triangle Q will be the same distance from the *y*-axis as the corresponding vertex on the object.

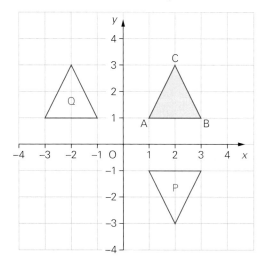

EXERCISE 19B

1 Copy each shape on squared paper and draw its image after a reflection in the given mirror line.

a 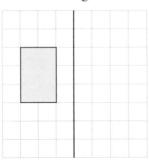 b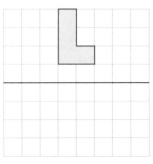

c 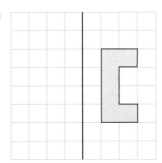 d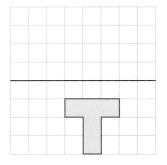

2 Draw each of these figures on squared paper, leaving plenty of space on the opposite side of the given mirror line. Then draw the reflection of the figure in the mirror line.

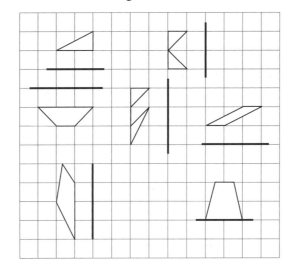

3 Draw these figures on squared paper and then draw the reflection of each in the given mirror line.

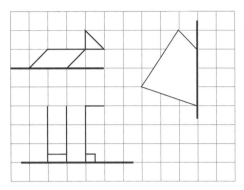

4 Copy this diagram on squared paper.

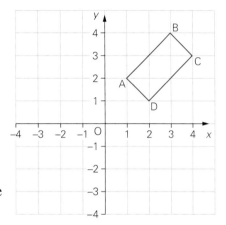

  a Reflect the rectangle ABCD in the *x*-axis. Label the image R.

  b Reflect the rectangle ABCD in the *y*-axis. Label the image S.

  c What special name is given to figures that are exactly the same shape and size?

5 a Draw a pair of axes, *x*-axis from –5 to 5, *y*-axis from –5 to 5.

  b Draw the triangle with co-ordinates A(1, 1), B(3, 1), C(4, 5).

  c Reflect triangle ABC in the *x*-axis. Label the image P.

  d Reflect triangle P in the *y*-axis. Label the image Q.

  e Reflect triangle Q in the *x*-axis. Label the image R.

  f Describe the reflection that will transform triangle ABC onto triangle R.

6 a Repeat the steps of Question **5** but start with any shape you like.

  b Is your answer to part **f** the same as before?

  c Would the final answer always be the same no matter what shape you started with?

7 Draw each of these figures on squared paper, leaving plenty of space on the opposite side of the given mirror line. Then draw the reflection of the figure in the mirror line.

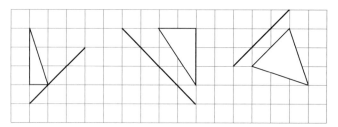

Rotation

Rotation moves a shape to a new position by turning it about a fixed point called the **centre of rotation**.

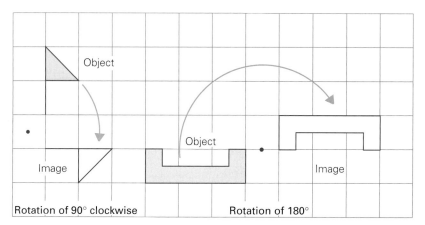

Notice
- The direction of turn (angle of rotation) is expressed as **clockwise** or **anticlockwise**.
- The position of the centre of rotation is **always specified**.
- The amounts of turn (angles of rotation) which occur in GCSE examinations are a $\frac{1}{4}$ turn or 90°, a $\frac{1}{2}$ turn or 180°, and a $\frac{3}{4}$ turn or 270°.
- The rotations $\frac{1}{2}$ turn clockwise and $\frac{1}{2}$ turn anticlockwise are the **same**.

Example 5

Draw the image of this shape after it has been rotated $\frac{1}{4}$ turn clockwise about the point X.

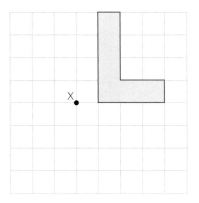

Using tracing paper is always the easiest way of doing rotations.

First trace the shape and fix the centre of rotation with a pencil point. Then rotate the tracing paper through a $\frac{1}{4}$ turn clockwise.

The tracing now shows the position of the image.

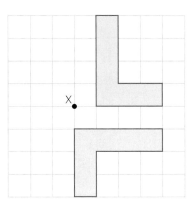

EXERCISE 19C

1 Copy each of these diagrams on squared paper. Draw its image using the given rotation about the centre of rotation, X.

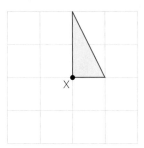

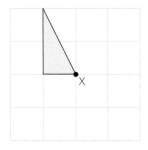

a $\frac{1}{2}$ turn　　　　**b** $\frac{1}{4}$ turn clockwise

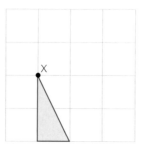

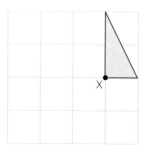

c $\frac{1}{4}$ turn anticlockwise   **d** $\frac{3}{4}$ turn clockwise

2 Copy each of these diagrams on squared paper. Draw its image using the given rotation about the centre of rotation, X.

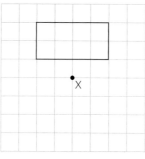

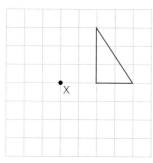

a $\frac{1}{2}$ turn   **b** $\frac{1}{4}$ turn clockwise

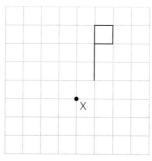

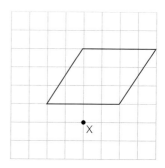

c $\frac{1}{4}$ turn anticlockwise   **d** $\frac{3}{4}$ turn clockwise

3 Copy this diagram on squared paper.

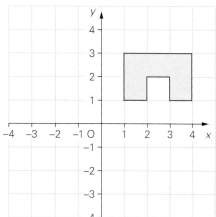

   a Rotate the shape $\frac{1}{4}$ turn clockwise about the origin O. Label the image P.

   b Rotate the shape $\frac{1}{2}$ turn clockwise about the origin O. Label the image Q.

   c Rotate the shape $\frac{3}{4}$ turn clockwise about the origin O. Label the image R.

   d What rotation takes R back to the original shape?

4 Copy this diagram on squared paper.

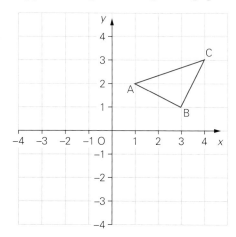

   a Write down the co-ordinates of the triangle ABC.

   b Rotate the triangle ABC through 90° clockwise about the origin O. Label the image S.
Write down the co-ordinates of triangle S.

   c Rotate the triangle ABC through 180° clockwise about the origin O. Label the image T.
Write down the co-ordinates of triangle T.

   d Rotate the triangle ABC through 270° clockwise about the origin O. Label the image U.
Write down the co-ordinates of triangle U.

   e What do you notice about the coordinates of the four triangles?

5 On squared paper, draw these shapes and centres of rotation.

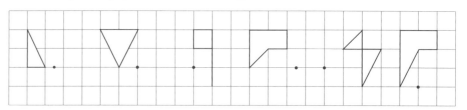

    a Rotate each shape about its centre of rotation
      i first by 90° clockwise   **ii** then by a further 180°
    b Describe, in each case, the transformation that would take the original shape to the final image.

6 On squared paper, draw these shapes and centres of rotation.

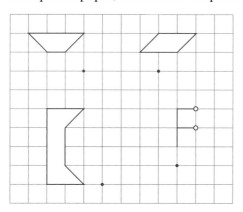

    a Rotate each shape about its centre of rotation
      i first by 90° anticlockwise   **ii** then by a further 180°
    b Describe, in each case, the transformation that would take the original shape to the final image.

Enlargement

Enlargement changes the size of a shape to give a similar image. It always has a **centre of enlargement** and a **scale factor**.

Every length of the enlargement will be
    Original length × Scale factor

The distance of each image point on the enlargement from the centre of enlargement will be
    Distance of original point from centre of enlargement × Scale factor

For example, this diagram shows an enlargement by scale factor 3 of a triangle ABC.

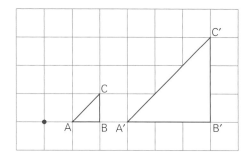

Notice

- Each length on the enlargement A'B'C' is three times the corresponding length on the original shape, so that the sides are in the ratio 1 : 3.
- The distance of any point on the enlargement from the centre of enlargement is three times longer than the corresponding distance on the original shape.

There are two distinct ways to enlarge a shape: the **ray method** and the **co-ordinate method**.

Ray method

This is the **only** way to construct an enlargement when the diagram is not on a grid. The example below shows an enlargement by scale factor 3 made by the ray method.

Notice that the rays have been drawn from the centre of enlargement, O, to each vertex and beyond.

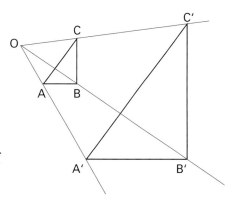

The distance from each vertex on triangle ABC to the centre of enlargement was measured and multiplied by 3 to give the distance of each image vertex from the centre of enlargement. Once each image vertex has been found, the whole image shape can then be drawn.

Check the measurements and see for yourself how the calculations have been done. Notice again that each line is three times longer in the enlargement.

Co-ordinate method

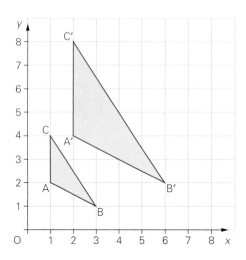

Triangle A′B′C′ is an enlargement of triangle ABC by scale factor 2, with the origin, O, as the centre of enlargement.

The co-ordinates of A are (1, 2) and the co-ordinates of A′ are (2, 4). Notice that the co-ordinates of A′ are the co-ordinates of A multiplied by 2, which is the scale factor of enlargement.

Check that the same happens for the other vertices.

This is a useful method for enlarging shapes on a co-ordinate grid, when the origin, O, is the centre of enlargement.

Example 6

Enlarge the square by scale factor 3, using the origin as the centre of enlargement.

The co-ordinates of the original square are (1, 1), (2, 1), (2, 2) and (1, 2). The enlarged square will have these co-ordinates multiplied by 3.

The co-ordinates are, therefore, (3, 3), (6, 3) (6, 6) and (3, 6), as shown in the diagram.

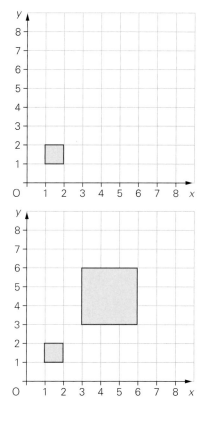

EXERCISE 19D

1   Copy each of these figures with its centre of enlargement. Then enlarge it by the given scale factor, using the ray method.

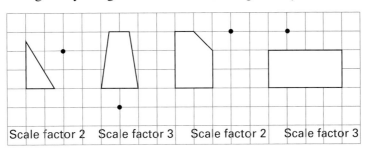

Scale factor 2   Scale factor 3   Scale factor 2   Scale factor 3

2   Copy each of these diagrams on squared paper and enlarge it by scale factor 2, using the origin as the centre of enlargement.

a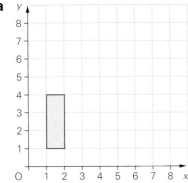

b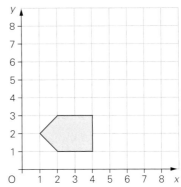

c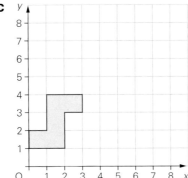

3 Copy each of these diagrams on squared paper and enlarge it by scale factor 2, using the origin as the centre of enlargement.

a
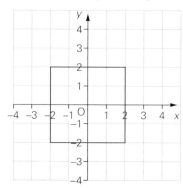

b
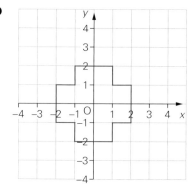

Tessellations

Activity

Tiling patterns

You need 1-cm squared paper and some card in several different colours.

Make a template for each of the following shapes on the 1-cm squared paper.

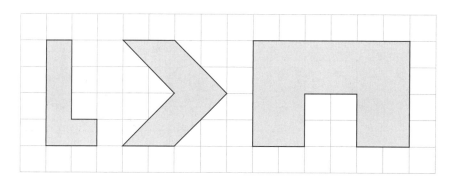

Use your template to make about 20 card tiles for each shape, using different colours.

For each shape, put all the tiles together to create a tiling pattern without any gaps.

What do you find?

From this activity you should have found that you could cover as much space as you wanted using the **same** shape in a **repeating pattern**. We say that the shape **tessellates**.

So, a tessellation is a regular pattern made with identical plane shapes which fit together exactly, without overlapping and leaving no gaps.

For example, these three patterns are tessellations.

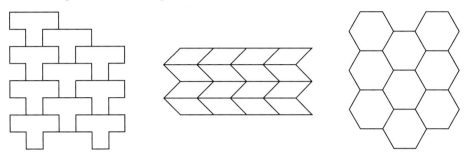

EXERCISE 19E

1   On squared paper, show how each of these shapes tessellate.

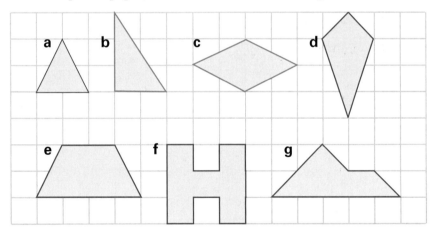

2   Invent some of your own tessellating patterns.

3   'Every quadrilateral will form a tessellation'. Investigate this statement to see whether it is true.

Investigation

Keep Turning Left

This shape is made by following the instructions.

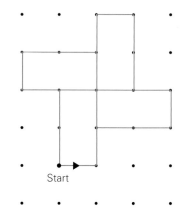

- Draw a line 1 cm long.
** ■ Rotate left 90° and draw a line 3 cm long.
- Rotate left 90° and draw a line 2 cm long.
- Rotate left 90° and draw a line 1 cm long.
- Go back to **.

Call this pattern (1, 3, 2). What other patterns can you make using different numbers?

Growing Squares

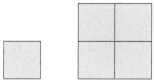

The large square is an enlargement of the small square by scale factor 2.

Four small squares can be fitted into the enlargement.

Draw enlargements of the small square using different scale factors.

Investigate how many small squares can be fitted into each enlargement.

Find the rule connecting the scale factor and the number of small squares in each enlargement.

Pentomino Patterns

A **pentomino** is a shape made from five squares which touch edge to edge.

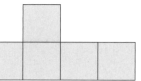

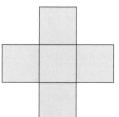

These are two examples of different pentominoes.

How many different pentominoes can you find?

Examination questions

1 a

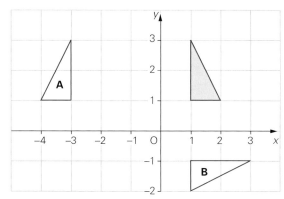

Triangle A is a reflection of the shaded triangle.
Copy the diagram and indicate the mirror line for this
reflection.

b Describe fully the single transformation that maps the
shaded triangle onto triangle B.

NEAB, Question 14, Paper 1F, June 1998

2 a

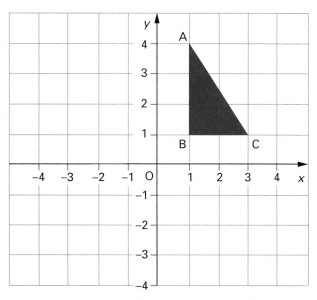

Write down the coordinates of point A. Copy the
diagram for answers to parts **b** and **c**.

b Rotate triangle ABC 90° clockwise about (0, 0). Label
the new triangle A′B′C′.

c Reflect triangle A′B′C′ in the *x*-axis. Label the new
triangle A″B″C″.

WJEC, Question 15, Paper 2F, June 1998

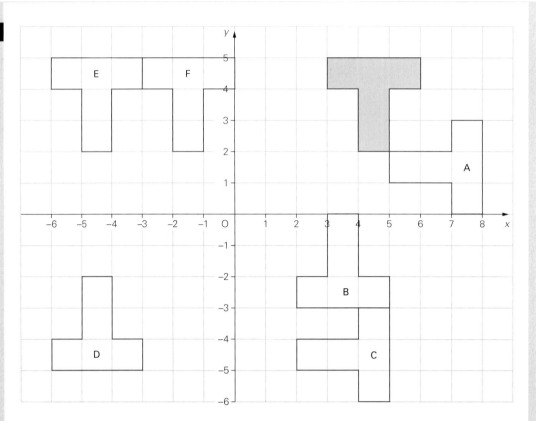

3 a Give the letter of the finishing point after

    i the shaded T-shape has been reflected in the *y*-axis

    ii the shaded T-shape has been rotated $\frac{1}{4}$ turn clockwise about O

    iii the shaded T-shape has been translated 6 units to the left.

b Describe the single transformation which will map the shaded T-shape onto shape D.

NEAB, Question 8, Specimen Paper 1F, 2000

4 Use squared paper to copy the diagram on the right, and to enlarge the shaded figure, using scale factor 3 and centre of enlargement E.

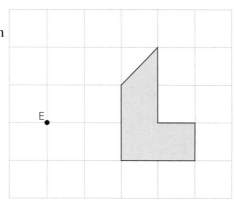

MEG, Question 20, Specimen Paper 1F, 1998

5

The diagram shows a shape.

a What are the coordinates of A?

b Each square on the diagram has an area of 1 cm². What is the area of the shape?

c The shape is reflected in the mirror line PQ. Copy the diagram and draw the reflected shape.

SEG, Question 4, Specimen Paper 5, 2000

6 Copy the diagrams.

   a Reflect the L shape in the *x*-axis.

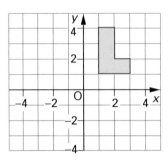

   b Rotate the L shape 90° anticlockwise, centre (0, 0).

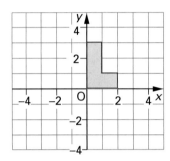

   c Translate the L shape 3 units to the right and 2 units up.

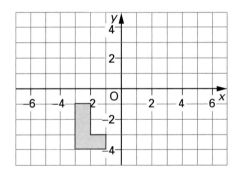

MEG, Question 15, Paper 1, June 1998

7 Copy the diagrams.

    a Draw the reflection of the diagram in the mirror line.

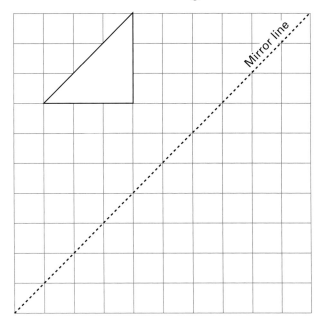

    b Draw accurately the position of the shape after it has been rotated through a $\frac{3}{4}$ turn clockwise about the dot on the grid.

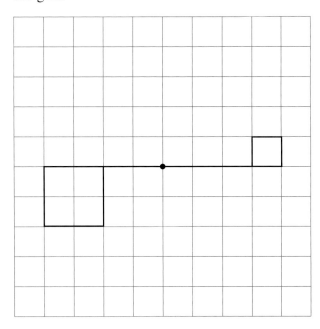

OCR, Question 15, Paper 2, June 2000

8 Copy the diagrams.

a Reflect the triangle in the mirror line.

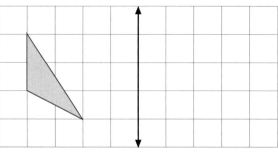

Mirror line

b Rotate the triangle through 180° about centre A.

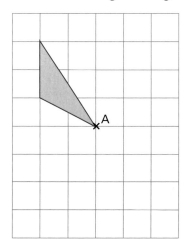

c Enlarge the triangle by scale factor 2, centre B.

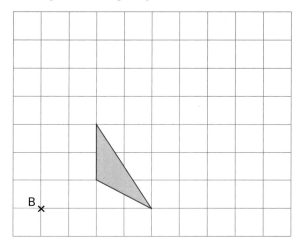

OCR, Question 11, Paper 1, June 2000

9 **a** Write down the co-ordinates of the point labelled C.
  b Copy the diagram and mark clearly with a star (*) the
     obtuse angle in the triangle ABC.
  c Draw an enlargement of ABC with scale factor 2. Use O
     as the centre of your enlargement.

OCR, Question 25, Paper 1, June 2000

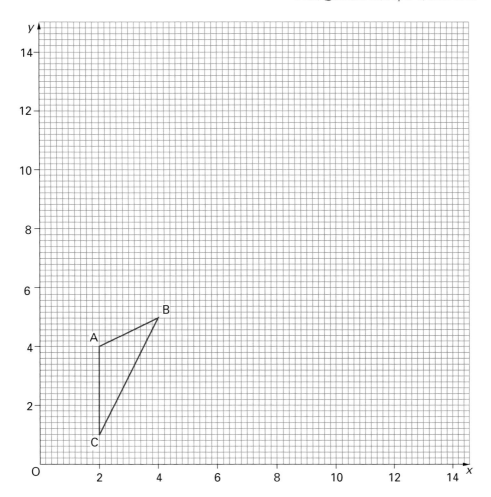

10 Copy the grid below and show how this kite will tessellate. You should draw at least 6 kites.

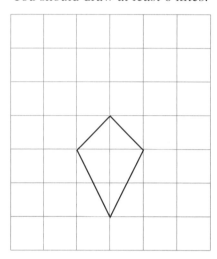

EDEXCEL, Question 14, Paper 1, 1998

What you should know after you have worked through Chapter 19

✔ What is meant by the terms translation, reflection, rotation and enlargement.
✔ How to change shapes by using translations, reflections, rotations and enlargements.
✔ What is meant by the term tessellate.
✔ How to show that a shape tessellates.

Scale

This chapter is going to ...

show you how to use scale drawings to solve problems, how to construct nets for 3-D shapes, how to draw 3-D shapes on an isometric grid and how to draw plans and elevations of 3-D shapes.

What you should already know

✔ The names of the common 3-D shapes
✔ How to measure the lengths of lines
✔ How to draw an accurate triangle using a pair of compasses

Scale drawings

A scale drawing is an accurate representation of a real object.

Scale drawings are usually smaller in size than the original objects. But in certain cases they have to be enlargements, typical examples of which are miniature electronic circuits and very small watch movements.

In a scale drawing:
• all the measurements must be in proportion to the corresponding measurements on the original object, and
• all the angles must be equal to the corresponding angles on the original object.

To obtain the measurements for a scale drawing, all the actual measurements are multiplied by a common scale factor, usually referred to as a **scale**. (See the section on enlargements, pages 388–90.)

Scales are often given as ratios: for example, 1 cm : 1 m.

When the units in a ratio are the **same,** they are normally not given. For example, a scale of 1 cm : 1000 cm is written as 1 : 1000.

Beware When you are making a scale drawing, take care to express **all measurements** in the **same unit**.

Example 1

The diagram (right) shows the front of

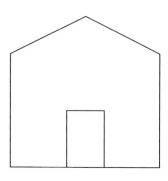

a kennel. It is drawn to a scale of 1 : 30.

This means that a measurement of 1 cm on the diagram represents a measurement of 30 cm on the actual kennel.

So, the actual width of the front is

4 cm × 30 = 120 cm

And the actual height of the doorway is

1.5 cm × 30 = 45 cm

Map scales are usually expressed as ratios, such as 1 : 50 000 or 1 : 200 000. The first ratio means that 1 cm on the map represents 50 000 cm or 500 m on the land. The second ratio means that 1 cm represents 200 000 cm or 2 km.

Example 2

The map on the right is drawn to a scale of 1 cm to 20 km. This means that a distance of 1 cm on the map represents a distance of 20 km on the land.

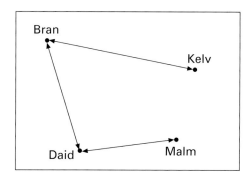

The actual distance between

Bran and Kelv is 4 × 20 km = 80 km
Bran and Daid is 3 × 20 km = 60 km
Daid and Malm is 2.5 × 20 km = 50 km

EXERCISE 20A

1   Look at this plan of a garden, drawn to a scale of 1 cm to 10 m.

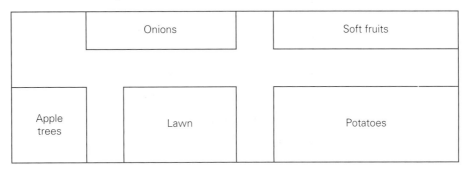

   a   State the actual dimensions of each plot of the garden.
   b   Calculate the actual area of each plot.

2   On the right is a plan for a
   mouse mat. It is drawn to a
   scale of 1 to 6.

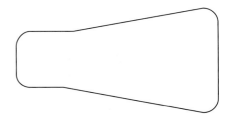

   a   How long is the actual
         mouse mat?
   b   How wide is the narrowest
         part of the mouse mat?

3   Look at the map below, drawn to a scale of 1: 200 000.

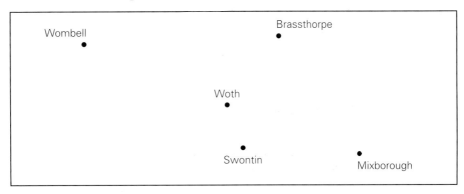

   To the nearest kilometre, state the actual distances from:
   a   Wombell to Woth   **b**   Woth to Brassthorpe
   c   Brassthorpe to Swontin   **d**   Swontin to Mixborough
   e   Mixborough to Woth   **f**   Woth to Swontin

4 This map is drawn to a scale of 1 cm to 40 km.

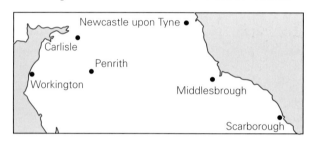

Give the approximate direct distances of:

a Penrith to:

    i Workington   **ii** Scarborough

    iii Newcastle upon Tyne   **iv** Carlisle

b Middlesbrough to:

    i Scarborough   **ii** Workington

    iii Carlisle   **iv** Penrith

5 This map is drawn to a scale of 1 cm to 20 kilometres.

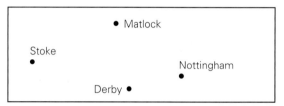

State the direct distance, to the nearest 5 kilometres, from Matlock to:

a Stoke   **b** Derby   **c** Nottingham

6 Below is a scale plan of the top of Derek's desk, scale 1 : 10.

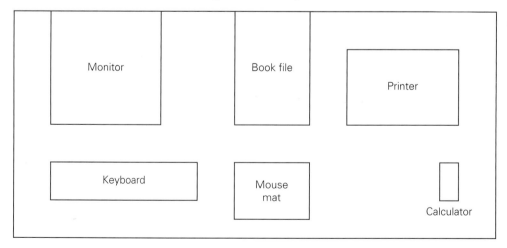

What are the actual dimensions of each of these articles?

a Monitor   **b** Keyboard   **c** Mouse mat

d Book file   **e** Printer   **f** Calculator

Activity

Little & Large!

Find a map of Great Britain. Note the scale on the map.

Find:

- the distance on the map and
- the actual distance
  - between Sheffield and Birmingham
  - between Manchester and York
  - between Glasgow and Bristol

Take some measurements of your school buildings so that you can make a scale drawing of them.

Nets

Many of the 3-D shapes that you come across can be made from **nets**.

A net is a flat shape that can be folded into a 3-D shape.

Example 3

This is a sketch of a net for a cube.

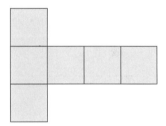

This is a sketch of a net for a square-based pyramid.

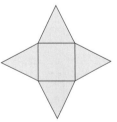

EXERCISE 20B

1 Sketch three nets for a cuboid, each one being different.

2 Draw, on squared paper, an accurate net for each of these cuboids.

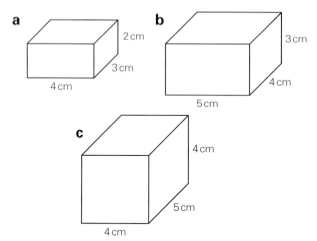

3 Draw an accurate net for each of these pyramids. For each pyramid, its base is a rectangle, and its sloping edges are all the same length. (Remember: you will have to use your compasses to draw the triangles accurately.)

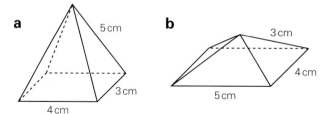

4 The shape on the right is a triangular prism. Its ends are isosceles triangles, and its other faces are rectangles. Draw an accurate net for this prism.

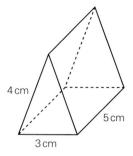

5 The tetrahedron on the right is made up of four equilateral triangles, all lengths being 4 cm. Draw an accurate net for this prism.

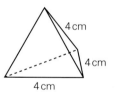

6 Sketch the nets of these shapes.

a

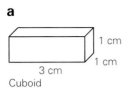

Cuboid

b

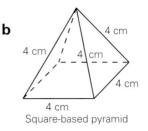

Square-based pyramid

c

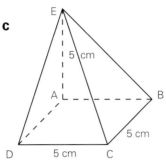

Square-based pyramid, with
point E directly above point A

d

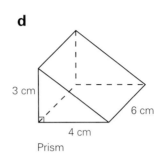

Prism

Using an isometric grid

Isometric grids

The problem with drawing a 3-D shape is that we have to draw it on a flat
(2-D) surface so that it looks like the original 3-D shape. We somehow
have to give the drawing the appearance of depth by slanting the view.

One easy way to draw a 3-D shape is to use an **isometric grid** (a grid of
equilateral triangles).

Below are two drawings of the same cuboid, one on squared paper, the
other on isometric paper. The cuboid measures $5 \times 4 \times 2$ units.

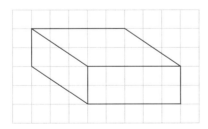

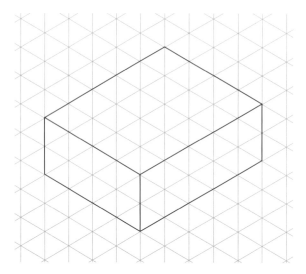

Notice The dimensions of the cuboid can be **taken straight from** the isometric drawing, whereas they can't be from the other drawing on squared paper.

You can use a triangular dot grid instead of an isometric grid, but you **must** make sure that it is the **correct way round** – as shown here.

Plans and elevations

A **plan** is the view of a 3-D shape when it is looked at from above.

An **elevation** is the view of a 3-D shape when it is looked at from the front or from another side.

The 3-D shape below is drawn on an isometric grid.

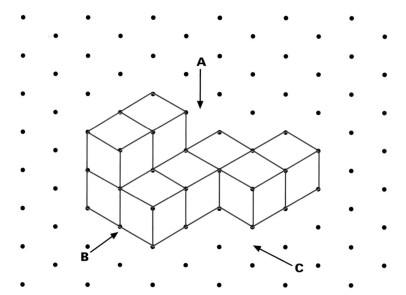

Its plan, front elevation and side elevation can be drawn on squared paper.

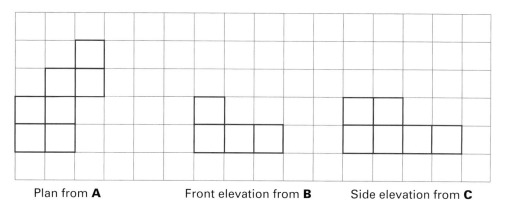

Plan from **A**   Front elevation from **B**   Side elevation from **C**

EXERCISE 20C

1 Draw each of these cuboids on an isometric grid.

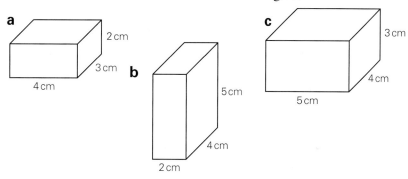

a 2 cm 3 cm 4 cm

b 5 cm 4 cm 2 cm

c 3 cm 4 cm 5 cm

2 Draw each of these shapes on an isometric grid.

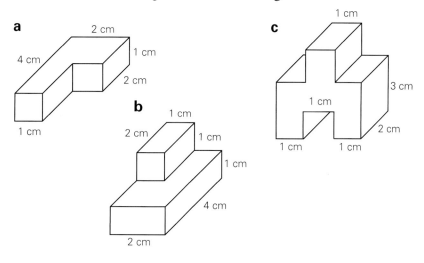

a 2 cm 4 cm 1 cm 2 cm 1 cm

b 1 cm 2 cm 1 cm 1 cm 4 cm 2 cm

c 1 cm 3 cm 1 cm 2 cm 1 cm 1 cm

3 Imagine that this shape falls and lands on the side shaded. Draw, on isometric paper, the position of the shape after it has landed.

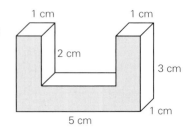

4 The firm TIL want their name made into a solid shape from 1 m^3 blocks of concrete. Draw, on isometric paper, a representation of these letters made from the blocks.

5 For each of the following 3-D shapes, draw
 i the plan
 ii the front elevation
 iii the side elevation.

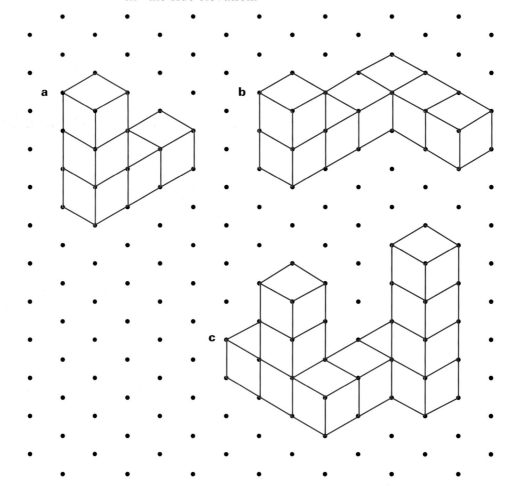

Investigation

Hexomino cubes

A **hexomino** is a shape made from six squares which touch edge to edge. These are two examples of hexominoes.

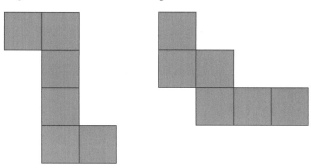

■ Draw as many different hexominoes as you can.
■ Which of these hexominoes are nets for a cube?

Examination questions

1 Write down which of the following are nets of a cube.

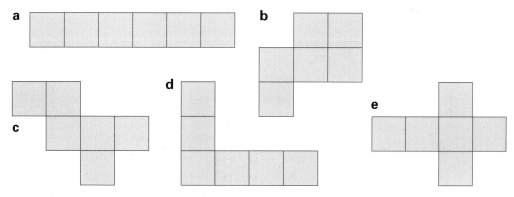

WJEC, Question 14, Specimen Paper 2F, 1998

413

2 The recommended angle that a ladder should make with the ground is 70°. The ladder is leaning at this angle, with its top against a vertical wall. The bottom of the ladder is 2 m from the wall.

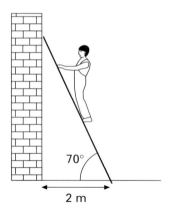

a Make a scale drawing of the ladder in this position. Use a scale of 2 cm to 1 m.

b Use your scale diagram to find the length of the ladder.

OCR, Question 9, Paper 2, June 2000

3 This chocolate box is a triangular prism.

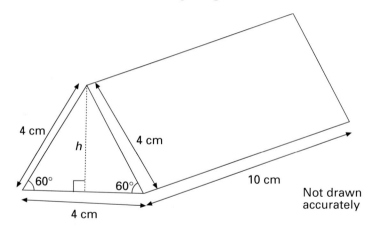

Not drawn accurately

a The end of the box is a triangle. What special name is given to the triangle?

b How many faces, edges and vertices has the triangular prism?

c Draw an accurate net for this triangular prism.

d Use your net to find the height, *h*, of the prism.

AQA, Question 12, Paper 2, June 2000

4 The diagram shows a block of Starlight soap. Its volume is 24 cm³.

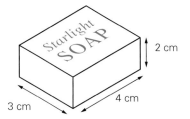

 a On an isometric grid, draw another block of soap, with different dimensions, which also has a volume of 24 cm³.

 b On an isometric grid, draw a diagram of a box whose dimensions are twice those of the Starlight soap.

NEAB, Question 24, Specimen Paper 1F, 2000

5 Here is a sketch of a matchbox tray. Draw an accurate net for the matchbox tray.

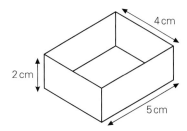

NEAB, Question 17, Specimen Paper 1F, 2000

6 The diagram shows an accurate plan of a bungalow drawn to a scale of 1 : 150.

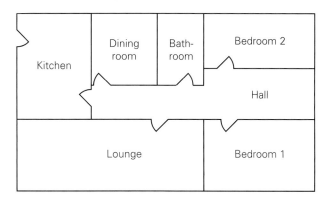

Find the actual length and width of the lounge in metres.

SEG, Question 10, Specimen Paper 6, 2000

7 These drawings show two views of the same solid made with centimetre cubes. The base of the solid is horizontal.

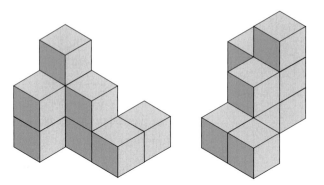

    a How many centimetre cubes are there in the solid?

    b Draw an accurate full-sized plan view of the solid on a centimetre grid.

MEG, Question 10, Paper 2, June 1998

8 This is a sketch of a park seat. It is made from three rectangular concrete slabs.

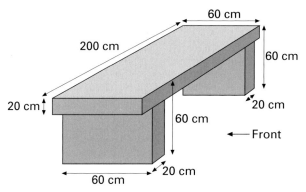

The front of the seat is drawn on the grid at the top of the next page. The scale is 1 cm to 20 cm. Draw to scale

a the plan view

b the side view.

Label each view.

Front view

OCR, Question 14, Paper 2, June 1999

9 Below left is a plan view of a solid made from four cubes.

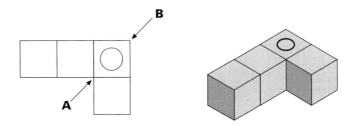

Above right is a view of the solid from direction **A**.
Copy and complete the drawing below to show the view
from direction **B**.

MEG, Question 24, Paper 2, June 1998

10 Mary has some cubes of side 1 centimetre.

Not drawn to scale

She makes this shape with her cubes.

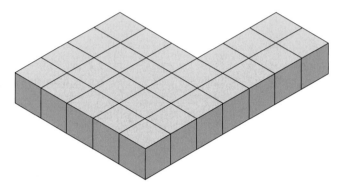

a What is the volume of this shape? Remember to state the units.

b 24 of Mary's cubes just fill this box.

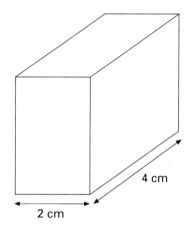

Not drawn to scale

4 cm

2 cm

What is the height of the box?

c Copy and complete the full-sized drawing of the box.

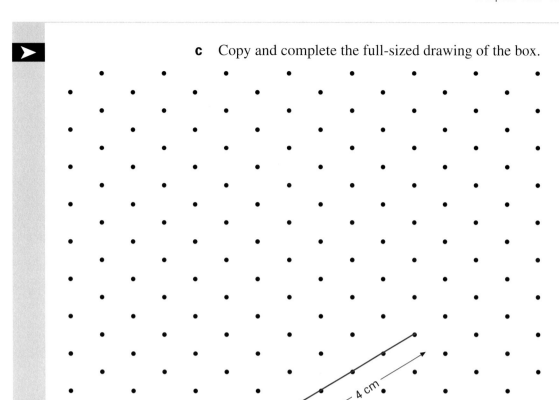

NEAB, Question 14, Paper 2, June 1998

What you should know after you have worked through Chapter 20

✔ How to read and use a scale from a scale drawing.
✔ How to construct a net for any common 3-D shape.
✔ How to draw any common 3-D shape on an isometric grid.
✔ How to draw a plan and an elevation of a 3-D shape.

Revision for Chapters 1 to 20

- Answer all the questions
- Show your working
- Do not use your calculator for the first eight questions

1 Put a bracket in each of these to make the answer correct.

    a $7 + 2 \times 4 = 15$ **b** $1 + 5 \times 7 - 3 = 24$

2   **a**   How long will it take me to save £312, if I save £13 a week?

       b   How many days are there in 27 weeks?

3 Calculate each of the following

    a $\frac{2}{5} + \frac{1}{5}$ **b** $\frac{5}{8} + \frac{3}{8}$ **c** $\frac{7}{8} - \frac{5}{8}$

    d $\frac{4}{5} + \frac{1}{5}$ **e** $\frac{3}{4} + \frac{3}{4}$ **f** $\frac{3}{4}$ of £160

    g $\frac{2}{3}$ of 120 m   **h** $\frac{5}{8}$ of 48 minutes   **i** $\frac{5}{6}$ of 3 hours

    j $\frac{4}{5}$ of 45 weeks

4 Write down the answer to each of the following.

    a $3 - 9$ **b** $-5 - 12$ **c** $-3 + 9$ **d** $-6 + 4$

    e $5 - -1$ **f** $2 - -15$ **g** $-10 - -7$ **h** $-4 + -8$

    i $-8 + 16$ **j** $-31 + -14$

5 For each of the following shapes calculate

    i   the perimeter   **ii**   the area

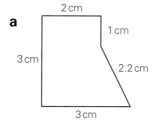
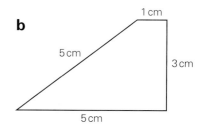

a   2 cm, 1 cm, 3 cm, 2.2 cm, 3 cm

b   1 cm, 5 cm, 3 cm, 5 cm

6 Express the perimeter of each of the following shapes as simply as possible.

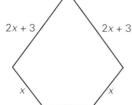
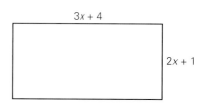

a $2x + 3$, $2x + 3$, x, x, x

b $3x + 4$, $2x + 1$

7 The pictogram below illustrates the number of milk bottles delivered by Graham on a particular day.

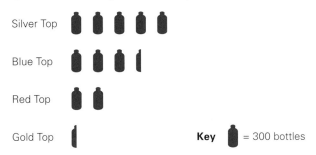

Silver Top

Blue Top

Red Top

Gold Top   **Key** = 300 bottles

a How many milk bottles did Graham deliver altogether on this day?
b Draw a fully labelled bar chart to illustrate this information.

8 James and Helen share £1600 in the ratio 3 : 5. How much does each of them receive?

9 I drove from my home to Villa Park in 1 hour 45 minutes. My average speed was 50 mph.
a Change the 1 hour 45 minutes to decimal time.
b How far is it from my home to Villa Park?

10 Make a copy of each shape below.

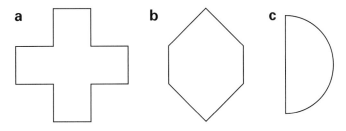

a   **b**   **c**

i Draw in all the lines of symmetry.
ii State the order of rotational symmetry for each shape.

11 I counted the number of passengers in cars going past my house one morning.

Number of passengers	Frequency
0	24
1	15
2	8
3	2
4	1

Calculate the mean number of passengers per car.

Revision section

12 **a** What fraction of this diagram is shaded?

     b What percentage of this diagram is shaded?

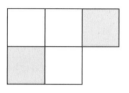

13 Solve each of these equations.

     a $x + 5 = 19$ **b** $5x = 35$ **c** $4x - 3 = 9$

14 Given that $y = 3x - 1$

     a Complete the table below.

x	1	2	3	4	5	6
y			8			17

     b Plot these points on a grid and hence draw the graph of $y = 3x - 1$.
         Draw the x-axis as 2 cm to 1 unit and the y-axis as 1 cm to 2 units.

15 The three angles of a triangle are given as x, $4x$ and $7x$.

     a Calculate the value of x.

     b What type of triangle is this?

16 A circle has a diameter of 8 cm.

     a Calculate the circumference of this circle.

     b Calculate the area of this circle.

     Give your answers to one decimal place.

17 Use your ruler, compasses and protractor
to make an accurate construction of this
triangle.

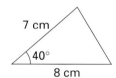

18 After a flood, the labels have come off all the cans in a shop. The
manager knew that he had 24 cans of soup, 15 cans of rice pudding
and 11 cans of beans. All the cans look the same. What is the
probability of choosing correctly:

     a a can of soup   **b** a can that is **not** rice pudding?

19 **a** Draw a pair of axes, both showing –5 to 5. Then draw triangle
         ABC with co-ordinates A(1, 1), B(3, 1) and C(1, 2)

     b Reflect ABC in the y-axis, and label it A′B′C′.

     c Reflect ABC in the x-axis, and label it A″B″C″.

     d Describe fully the single transformation that will map A′B′C′ to
         A″B″C″.

20 **a** Draw on squared paper an accurate net of a cuboid with
     dimensions 2 cm × 3 cm × 5 cm

     b Draw an accurate diagram of the cuboid on an isometric grid.

21 Units

This chapter is going to ...

show you which units to use to measure length, weight, volume and capacity in everyday situations. It will also show you how to convert from one metric unit to another, and how to change between metric and imperial units.

What you should already know

✔ The basic units of length, weight, volume and capacity
✔ The approximate size of these units

Systems of measurement

There are two systems of measurement currently in use in Britain: the imperial system and the metric system.

The imperial system is based on traditional units of measurement, many of which were first introduced several hundred years ago. It is gradually being replaced by the metric system, which is used throughout Europe and in many other parts of the world.

The main disadvantage of the imperial system is that it has a lot of awkward conversions, such as 12 inches = 1 foot. The metric system has the advantage that it is based on powers of 10, namely 10, 100, 1000 and so on, so is much easier to use and calculate with.

It will be many years before all the units of the imperial system disappear, so you have to know units in both systems.

System	Unit	How to estimate it
Metric system	*Length* 1 metre	A long stride for an average person
	1 kilometre	Two and a half times round a school running track
	1 centimetre	The distance across a fingernail
Imperial system	1 foot	The length of an A4 sheet of paper
	1 yard	From your nose to your fingertips when you stretch out your arm
	1 inch	The length of the top joint of an adult's thumb
Metric system	*Weight* 1 gram	A 1p coin is about 4 grams
	1 kilogram	A bag of sugar
	1 tonne	A saloon car
Imperial system	1 pound	A jar full of jam
	1 stone	A bucket three-quarters full of water
	1 ton	A saloon car
Metric system	*Volume/ Capacity* 1 litre	A full carton of orange juice
	1 centilitre	A small wine glass
	1 millilitre	A full teaspoon is about 5 millilitres
Imperial system	1 pint	A bottle full of milk
	1 gallon	A half-full bucket

Volume and capacity

The term **capacity** is normally used to refer to the volume occupied, or to be occupied, by a liquid or a gas.

For example, when referring to the volume of petrol that a car's fuel tank will hold, we say its capacity is 60 litres or 13 gallons.

In the metric system, there is an equivalence between the units of capacity and volume, as you can see on page 426.

Metric units

You should be able to estimate a reasonable length or distance in metric units. For example, you should be able to make a sensible estimate in metric units for the following quantities, and know which is the appropriate unit to use for each.

    Your own height   metres or centimetres

    The length of your pen   centimetres

    The thickness of this book   millimetres

    The length of your classroom   metres

    The distance from home to school   kilometres

You should know which is the appropriate unit to use to measure quantities such as these:

    Your own weight   kilograms

    The weight of a coin   grams

    The weight of a bus   tonnes

You should also know which is the appropriate unit to use to measure quantities such as these:

    A large bottle of lemonade   litres

    A dose of medicine   millilitres

    A bottle of wine   centilitres

EXERCISE 21A

Decide in which metric unit you would most likely measure each of the following amounts.

1 The height of your classroom.

2 The distance from London to Barnsley.

3 The thickness of your little finger.

4 The weight of this book.

5 The amount of water in a fish tank.

6 The weight of water in a fish tank.

7 The weight of an aircraft.

8 The amount of medicine you get on one spoon.

9 The amount of wine in a standard bottle.

10 The length of a football pitch.

11   The weight of your head teacher.

12   The amount of water in a bath.

13   The weight of a mouse.

14   The amount of tea in a teapot.

15   The thickness of a piece of wire.

Estimate the approximate metric length, weight or capacity of each of the following.

16   This book (both length and weight).

17   The length of your school hall. (You do **not** need to look at it.)

18   The capacity of a milk bottle (metric measure).

19   A brick (length, width and weight).

20   The diameter of a 10p coin, and its weight.

21   The distance from your school to Manchester.

22   The weight of a cat.

23   The amount of water in one raindrop.

24   The dimensions of the room you are in.

25   Your own height and weight. (You can check this later and keep it to yourself.)

Metric relationships

You should already know the relationships between these metric units.

Length   10 millimetres = 1 centimetre
1000 millimetres = 100 centimetres = 1 metre
1000 metres = 1 kilometre

Weight   1000 grams = 1 kilogram
1000 kilograms = 1 tonne

Capacity   10 millilitres = 1 centilitre
1000 millilitres = 100 centilitres = 1 litre

Volume   1000 litres = 1 metre^3
1 millilitre = 1 centimetre^3

Note the equivalence between the units of capacity and volume:
   1 litre = 1000 cm^3 which means   1 mℓ = 1 cm^3

You need to be able, with confidence, to convert from one unit to another. Since the metric system is based on powers of 10, you should be able easily to multiply or divide to change units. Follow through these examples.

To change **small** units to **larger** units, always **divide**.

Change
a 732 cm to metres $\rightarrow$ 732 ÷ 100 = 7.32 m
b 410 mm to centimetres $\rightarrow$ 410 ÷ 10 = 41 cm
c 840 mm to metres $\rightarrow$ 840 ÷ 1000 = 0.84 m
d 5300 m to kilometres $\rightarrow$ 5300 ÷ 1000 = 5.3 km
e 650 g to kilograms $\rightarrow$ 650 ÷ 1000 = 0.65 kg
f 75 kg to tonnes $\rightarrow$ 75 ÷ 1000 = 0.075 t
g 85 mℓ to centilitres $\rightarrow$ 85 ÷ 10 = 8.5 cℓ
h 3250 mℓ to litres $\rightarrow$ 3250 ÷ 1000 = 3.25 ℓ
i 450 cℓ to litres $\rightarrow$ 450 ÷ 100 = 4.5 ℓ
j 7150 ℓ to metres^3 $\rightarrow$ 7150 ÷ 1000 = 7.15 m^3

To change **large** units to **smaller** units, always **multiply**.

Change
a 1.2 m to centimetres $\rightarrow$ 1.2 × 100 = 120 cm
b 0.62 cm to millimetres $\rightarrow$ 0.62 × 10 = 6.2 mm
c 3 m to millimetres $\rightarrow$ 3 × 1000 = 3000 mm
d 2.75 km to metres $\rightarrow$ 2.75 × 1000 = 2750 m
e 5.1 kg to grams $\rightarrow$ 5.1 × 1000 = 5100 g
f 7.02 t to kilograms $\rightarrow$ 7.02 × 1000 = 7020 kg
g 75 cℓ to millilitres $\rightarrow$ 75 × 10 = 750 mℓ
h 0.85 ℓ to millilitres $\rightarrow$ 0.85 × 1000 = 850 mℓ
i 1.2 ℓ to centilitres $\rightarrow$ 1.2 × 100 = 120 cℓ
j 20 000 m^3 to litres $\rightarrow$ 20 000 × 1000 = 20 000 000 ℓ

EXERCISE 21B

Fill in the gaps using the conversion factors given on page 426.

1 125 cm = m	**2** 82 mm = cm	**3** 550 mm = m
4 2100 m = km	**5** 208 cm = m	**6** 1240 mm = m
7 142 mm = cm	**8** 3560 m = km	**9** 3550 mm = m
10 94 cm = m	**11** 650 m = km	**12** 45 mm = m
13 805 mm = cm	**14** 1250 cm = m	**15** 2060 m = km
16 4200 g = kg	**17** 5750 kg = t	**18** 85 mℓ = cℓ
19 2580 mℓ = ℓ	**20** 340 cℓ = ℓ	**21** 600 kg = t
22 755 g = kg	**23** 800 mℓ = ℓ	**24** 200 cℓ = ℓ

25 630 mℓ =　cℓ　**26** 1020 kg =　t　**27** 4500 mℓ =　ℓ

28 2040 g =　kg　**29** 450 cℓ =　ℓ　**30** 55 mℓ =　ℓ

31 8400 ℓ =　m³　**32** 35 mℓ =　cm³　**33** 1035 ℓ =　m³

34 530 ℓ =　m³　**35** 5.3 m =　cm　**36** 34 km =　m

37 3.4 m =　mm　**38** 13.5 cm =　mm　**39** 0.67 m =　cm

40 7.03 km =　m　**41** 0.72 cm =　mm　**42** 0.25 m =　cm

43 0.05 m =　cm　**44** 0.64 km =　m　**45** 0.11 m =　mm

46 2.4 ℓ =　mℓ　**47** 5.9 ℓ=　cℓ　**48** 8.4 cℓ =　mℓ

49 5.2 m³ =　ℓ　**50** 0.58 kg =　g　**51** 3.75 t =　kg

52 0.74 ℓ =　cℓ　**53** 0.94 cm³ =　ℓ　**54** 45.8 kg =　g

55 12.5 ℓ =　mℓ　**56** 21.6 ℓ =　cℓ　**57** 15.2 kg =　g

58 14 m³ =　ℓ　**59** 1.56 t =　kg　**60** 0.19 cm³ =　mℓ

Imperial units

You need to be familiar with imperial units which are still in daily use. The main ones are:

Length　12 inches = 1 foot
3 feet = 1 yard
1760 yards = 1 mile

Weight　16 ounces = 1 pound
14 pounds = 1 stone
2240 pounds = 1 ton

Capacity　8 pints = 1 gallon

- To change **large** units to **smaller** units, always **multiply**.
- To change **small** units to **larger** units, always **divide**.

Examples of the everyday use of imperial measures are:
miles for distances by road
pints for milk
gallons of petrol (in conversation)
pounds for the weight of babies (in conversation)
ounces for the weight of food ingredients in a food recipe
feet for people's heights

EXERCISE 21C

Fill in the gaps using the information on page 428.

1 2 feet = inches   **2** 4 yards = feet

3 2 miles = yards   **4** 5 pounds = ounces

5 4 stone = pounds   **6** 3 tons = pounds

7 5 gallons = pints   **8** 4 feet = inches

9 1 yard = inches   **10** 10 yards = feet

11 4 pounds = ounces   **12** 60 inches = feet

13 5 stone = pounds   **14** 36 feet = yards

15 1 stone = ounces   **16** 8800 yards = miles

17 15 gallons = pints   **18** 1 mile = feet

19 96 inches = feet   **20** 98 pounds = stones

21 56 pints = gallons   **22** 32 ounces = pounds

23 15 feet = yards   **24** 11 200 pounds = tons

25 1 mile = inches   **26** 128 ounces = pounds

27 72 pints = gallons   **28** 140 pounds = stones

29 15 840 feet = miles   **30** 1 ton = ounces

Conversion factors

You need to know the relationships between certain metric and imperial units.

The conversion factors you should be familiar with are given below (the symbol ≈ means 'is approximately equal to'). Those you do need to know for your examinations are in **bold** type.

Length   **1 inch ≈ 2.5 centimetres**
           1 mile ≈ 1.6 kilometres
           5 miles ≈ 8 kilometres

Weight   1 pound ≈ 450 grams
           1 kilogram ≈ 2.2 pounds

Capacity   1 pint ≈ 570 millilitres
           1 gallon ≈ 4.5 litres
           1 litre ≈ $1\frac{3}{4}$ pints

Follow through these examples.

Change

a   5 gallons to litres $5 \times 4.5 = 22.5$ litres

b   36 litres to gallons $36 \div 4.5 = 8$ gallons

c   45 miles to kilometres 9×5 miles $= 9 \times 8$ kilometres $=$
72 kilometres

d   160 kilometres to miles 8×20 kilometres $= 5 \times 20 = 100$ miles

e   25 kilograms to pounds $25 \times 2.2 = 55$ pounds

f   5 pounds to kilograms $5 \div 2.2 = 2.3$ kilograms (rounded to 1 dp)

Note An answer should be rounded off when it has several decimal places, since it is only an approximation.

Exercises 21D to 21H will give you practice in all conversion factors that you **need to know**.

EXERCISE 21D

> **1 kilogram ≈ 2.2 pounds**

1   Change each of these weights in kilograms to pounds.

a	10	**b**	13	**c**	24	**d**	40
e	55	**f**	78	**g**	100	**h**	1000

2   Change each of these weights in pounds to kilograms. (Give each answer to the nearest kilogram.)

a	33	**b**	44	**c**	66	**d**	49
e	55	**f**	77	**g**	110	**h**	1000

In Questions **3** to **11**, you must show all your working to back up each answer.

3   A children's ride has a weight limit of 70 pounds. Dave weighs 32 kg. Will he be allowed on the ride?

4   An airline's luggage allowance is 20 kg. My luggage weighs 45 pounds. Will I have to pay for excess baggage?

5   Beryl weighs 65 kg. Cynthia weighs 140 pounds. Who is heavier?

6   Donna weighs 42 kg. Ethel weighs 95 pounds. Who is lighter?

7   A lift has a sign saying: 'Maximum weight 2500 pounds'. A rugby team with a total weight of 1210 kg gets in. Is it safe in the lift?

8 A slimming club gives a prize to any member who loses 5 pounds or more in a week. Martha loses 2.3 kg in a week. Does she get a prize?

9 To tow a caravan, the AA recommends that your car weighs at least two and a half times as much as your caravan. My car weighs 2400 pounds. My caravan weighs 450 kg. Is this a safe combination?

10 The Eiffel Tower weighs 80 000 tonnes (1 tonne = 1000 kg). Blackpool Tower weighs 75 000 tons (1 ton = 2240 pounds). Which is heavier and by how much (in pounds)?

11 On the label of a jam jar is this information: '1 pound or 454 grams'
   a How many grams is 2.2 pounds?
   b Why is the answer not exactly 1000 grams?

EXERCISE 21E

$$1 \text{ litre} \approx 1\tfrac{3}{4} \text{ pints} = 1.75 \text{ pints}$$

1 Change each of these capacities (volumes) in litres to pints.
   a 10   **b** 13   **c** 24   **d** 40
   e 55   **f** 78   **g** 100   **h** 1000

2 Change each of these capacities in pints to litres. (Give each answer to the nearest litre.)
   a 35   **b** 51   **c** 70   **d** 49
   e 56   **f** 77   **g** 110   **h** 1000

In Questions **3** to **12**, you must show all your working to back up each answer.

3 A bucket has a capacity of 3 litres. Dave wants to carry 5 pints of water. Can he do it in one bucketful?

4 A barrel of beer holds 200 litres. I want 360 pints of beer for a party. Will I have enough if I get a barrel?

5 Container A holds 65 litres. Container B holds 110 pints. Which holds more?

6 Container D holds 42 litres. Container E holds 75 pints. Which holds less?

7 An oil tank has a sign saying: 'Maximum capacity 1500 litres'. John pumps a total of 2500 pints of oil into the empty tank. Will the tank overflow?

8 An automatic tap allows 5 pints of water an hour to flow. Fred's flowers need 2.8 litres of water an hour. Should Fred install this tap?

9 A shop sells five half-litre cans of coke for £1.80. The same shop sells nine half-pint cans of coke for £1.80. Which is the better buy?

10 **a** A gallon is 8 pints. How many litres are in a gallon?
  b Petrol used to be £2.62 a gallon. Overnight it was repriced at 59p per litre. If there had been no rise in fuel tax, was the garage owner pulling a fast one?

11 A swimming pool has a volume of 1 million litres.
  a It fills at the rate of 200 000 pints an hour. How long will it take to fill?
  b It drains at a rate of 250 000 pints an hour. How long does it take to drain?

12 A litre of water weighs 1 kilogram. How much does a gallon weigh? (1 gallon = 8 pints). Give your answer in **a** kilograms and **b** pounds. Is it a good estimate to say a gallon of water weighs 10 pounds?

EXERCISE 21F

8 kilometres ≈ 5 miles

1 Change each of these distances in miles to kilometres.
  a 10 **b** 15 **c** 25 **d** 40
  e 55 **f** 75 **g** 100 **h** 1000

2 Change each of these distances in kilometres to miles.
  a 32 **b** 48 **c** 68 **d** 50
  e 56 **f** 80 **g** 104 **h** 1000

In Questions **3** to **10**, you must show all your working to back up each answer.

3 The distance from Leeds to London is 200 miles. Dave has enough petrol to travel 330 km. Can he drive from Leeds to London without having to put petrol in his car?

4 Fred is going on an airline journey of 2000 km. He needs another 1300 Air Miles to get a free camera. Will he have enough Air Miles after this trip?

5 A to B is 65 km. C to D is 40 miles. Which is the greater distance?

6 D to E is 42 km. F to G is 25 miles. Which is the shorter distance?

7 As I am driving along a road, I see a sign saying: 'Little Chief Restaurant 20 miles.' Immediately after is another sign saying: 'Happy Feeder Restaurant 30 km.' I am really hungry. Which restaurant will I get to first?

8 My AA book says that from Le Havre to Paris is 210 miles. My RAC book says from Cherbourg to Paris is 350 km. Which is the shorter journey?

9 The handbook for my new car recommends the car is serviced every 9000 miles. The car is French and the odometer (distance recorder) measures in kilometres. At what distance in kilometres should I have it serviced?

10 The table on the right shows the distance, in miles, between four towns in South Yorkshire. Copy the table, without the numbers, and then fill it in with the equivalent distances in kilometres.

Leeds	35	40	25
	Sheffield	20	15
		Doncaster	15
			Barnsley

EXERCISE 21G

> **1 gallon ≈ 4.5 litres**

1 Change each of these capacities (volumes) in gallons to litres.
a	10	**b**	15	**c**	25	**d**	40
e	55	**f**	75	**g**	100	**h**	1000

2 Change each of these capacities in litres to gallons.
a	36	**b**	54	**c**	63	**d**	81
e	70	**f**	90	**g**	108	**h**	1000

In Questions **3** to **9**, you must show all your working to back up each answer.

3 'Capacity 2 gallons' is stamped on the side of my bucket. I need 10 litres of water to make some concrete. Can I get enough water in one bucketful?

4 The fuel tanks on an aircraft can hold 30 000 gallons. The tanks are just about empty. Can they be filled from a tanker holding 140 000 litres of fuel?

5 Tank A holds 49 gallons of oil. Tank B holds 210 litres of oil. Which tank holds more oil?

6 My car does 32 miles to a gallon of petrol. My neighbour's car does 8 miles to a litre of petrol. Whose car has better petrol consumption?

7 My garden pond holds 32 gallons of water. I bought a bottle of bactericidal liquid to add to the pond. The label on it says: 'Enough to treat 130 litres'. Is this bottle big enough to treat my pond against bacteria?

8 A farmer has a slurry tank holding 12 000 gallons. His new French-made slurry spreader has a capacity of 6000 litres. How many trips to the slurry tank will he need to make if he plans to spread all the slurry in the tank?

9 The Ladybower reservoir holds 230 million gallons. Water is used at the rate of 14 million litres a day. Assuming that there is a drought and that no water is going into the reservoir, how many days will the store of water last?

EXERCISE 21H

> **1 metre ≈ 39.37 inches**
> **1 foot ≈ 30.5 cm**
> **1 foot = 12 inches**

1 Change each of these distances in metres to inches. (Give each answer to the nearest inch.)
a	10	**b**	15	**c**	25	**d**	40
e	55	**f**	75	**g**	100	**h**	1000

2 Change each of these distances in feet to centimetres. (Give each answer to the nearest centimetre.)
a	36	**b**	54	**c**	63	**d**	81
e	70	**f**	90	**g**	108	**h**	1000

3 Change each of these distances in inches to metres. (Give each answer to the nearest metre.)
a	80	**b**	120	**c**	630	**d**	790
e	705	**f**	905	**g**	1100	**h**	2050

4 Change each of these distances in centimetres to feet. (Give each answer to the nearest foot.)
a	90	**b**	120	**c**	640	**d**	790
e	830	**f**	940	**g**	1070	**h**	2040

In Questions **5** to **11,** you must show all your working to back up each answer.

5 Which is longer, 10 feet of string or 300 cm of string?

6 Which is shorter, a stick of 24 inches or a stick of 60 cm?

7 Which is longer, 25 feet of ribbon or 7 m of ribbon?

8 Which is shorter, a pencil of 8 inches or a pencil of 20 cm?

9 Workmen have delivered 50 m of fence. I need 165 feet to surround the school garden. Will I have enough?

10 My kitchen plan needs a worktop that is 10 feet long. The biggest I can buy from the local DIY shop is 2.8 m. Can I have a continuous worktop or will I need to have a join?

11 A metre trundle wheel made 200 turns from one end of the school playground to the other. How many turns would be made by a trundle wheel that measures in yards (1 yard = 3 feet)?

Examination questions

1 Write down the **metric** unit you would use to measure
  a the length of a person's hand
  b the weight of a mouse
  c the distance from Manchester to London
  d a teaspoon of medicine.

EDEXCEL, Question 5, Paper 2, June 1998

2 Sarah's father sends her to the shops to buy 5 pounds of potatoes and 2 pints of milk. She buys a 3-kilogram bag of potatoes and a litre carton of milk. Does she buy enough potatoes and milk?

WJEC, Question 11, Specimen Paper 2F, 1998

3 **a** How many grams are there in $1\frac{1}{2}$ kilograms?
  b How many centimetres are there in 2 metres?
  c How many millilitres are there in 3 litres?
  d Which **metric** unit would be the most useful to measure
    i the area of a football pitch
    ii the capacity of a car's petrol tank?

OCR, Question 2, Paper 1, June 1999

4 It takes 100 g of flour to make 15 shortbread biscuits.

  a How many shortbread biscuits can be made from 1 kg of flour?

  b Calculate the weight of flour needed to make 24 biscuits.

MEG(SMP), Question 10, Specimen Paper 2F, 1998

5 This diagram shows some of the tallest buildings in the world and the years when they were built.

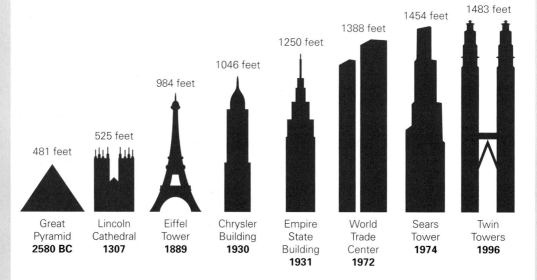

  a How much taller is the Sears Tower than the Great Pyramid?

  b Which building is about 175 metres high?
(3 feet is approximately 1 metre)

NEAB, Question 3, Paper 1F, June 1998

6 Here is a rough rule for changing kilometres into miles.

> **Multiply the number of kilometres by five and divide the answer by eight**

Use the rule to change 347 kilometres into miles. Give your answer to a sensible degree of accuracy.

OCR, Question 18, Paper 1, June 1999

7 **a** Darren claims that 6 pounds of potatoes are heavier than 3 kilograms of sugar. Is he correct? **You must give a reason for your answer.**

   b Mary pours three pints of milk into a jug which has a volume of 2 litres. Will the milk overflow? **You must give a reason for your answer.**

WJEC, Question 7, Paper 2, June 1998

8 Fiona weighs 10 stone 3 pounds.

   a There are 14 pounds in one stone. Estimate her weight in kilograms.

   Fiona is 5 feet 2 inches tall.

   b There are 12 inches in one foot. Take one inch as 2.5 centimetres. Work out her height in metres.

OCR, Question 16, Paper 1, June 2000

9 **a** **Show all your working.**
       Tom cycled a distance of 12 miles. Mary cycled a distance of 20 kilometres. Tom claimed that he had cycled further than Mary. Is he correct?

   b **Show all your working.**
       Sasha claims that 12 lb of potatoes will balance 5 kg of sugar. Is she correct?

WJEC, Question 11, Paper 2, June 1999

What you should know after you have worked through Chapter 21

✔ The approximate size of metric units and imperial units.
✔ Which units to use to measure length, weight, volume and capacity in everyday situations.
✔ The relationship between metric units.
✔ The conversion factors between the metric and imperial units in daily use.

> ## This chapter is going to ...
>
> show you how to draw and interpret pie charts and how to draw scatter diagrams and lines of best fit. It will also show you how to conduct surveys and design questionnaires.
>
> ## What you should already know
>
> ✔ How to draw and interpret pictograms, bar charts and line graphs
> ✔ How to draw and measure angles
> ✔ How to plot co-ordinates

Pie charts

Pictograms, bar charts and line graphs (see pages 103–9) are easy to draw, but they can be difficult to interpret when there is a big difference between the frequencies or there are only a few categories. In these cases, it is often more convenient to illustrate the data on a **pie chart**.

In a pie chart, the whole data is represented by a circle (the 'pie'), and each category of it is represented by a sector of the circle (a 'slice of the pie'). The angle of each sector is proportional to the frequency of the category it represents.

So, a pie chart cannot show individual frequencies like a bar chart, for example. It can only show proportions.

Example 1

In a survey on holidays, 120 people were asked to state which type of transport they used on their last holiday. This table shows the results of the survey. Draw a pie chart to illustrate the data.

Type of transport	Train	Coach	Car	Ship	Plane
Frequency	24	12	59	11	14

We need to find the fraction of 360° which represents each type of transport. This is usually done in a table, as shown below.

Type of transport	Frequency	Calculation	Angle
Train	24	$\frac{24}{120} \times 360 = 72°$	72°
Coach	12	$\frac{12}{120} \times 360 = 36°$	36°
Car	59	$\frac{59}{120} \times 360 = 177°$	177°
Ship	11	$\frac{11}{120} \times 360 = 33°$	33°
Plane	14	$\frac{14}{120} \times 360 = 42°$	42°
Totals	120		360°

Notice

- Use the frequency total (120 in this case) to calculate each fraction.
- Check that the sum of all the angles is 360°.
- Label each sector.
- The angles or frequencies do not have to be shown on the pie chart.

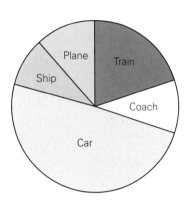

EXERCISE 22A

1 Draw a pie chart to represent each of the following sets of data.

a The number of children in 40 families.

No. of children	0	1	2	3	4
Frequency	4	10	14	9	3

b The favourite soap-opera of 60 students.

Programme	Home and Away	Neighbours	Coronation Street	Eastenders	Brookside
Frequency	15	18	10	13	4

c How 90 students get to school.

Journey to school	Walk	Car	Bus	Cycle
Frequency	42	13	25	10

2 Pat asked 24 of her friends which sport they preferred to play. Her data is shown in this frequency table.

Sport	Rugby	Football	Tennis	Squash	Basketball
Frequency	4	11	3	1	5

Illustrate her data on a pie chart.

3 Andy wrote down the number of lessons he had per week in each subject on his school timetable.

Mathematics 5   English 5   Science 8   Languages 6
Humanities 6   Arts 4   Games 2

a How many lessons did Andy have on his timetable?
b Draw a pie chart to show the data.
c Draw a bar chart to show the data.
d Which diagram best illustrates the data? Give a reason for your answer.

4 In the run up to an election, 720 people were asked in a poll which political party they would vote for. The results are given in the table.

Conservative	248
Labour	264
Liberal-Democrat	152
Green Party	56

a Draw a pie chart to illustrate the data.
b Why do you think pie charts are used to show this sort of information during elections?

5 This pie chart illustrates the favourite lessons of the 120 pupils in Y10 in a Cornish school.

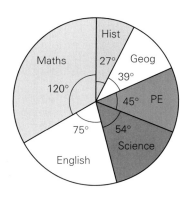

a How many pupils had as their favourite lesson
 i Mathematics
 ii PE
 iii English?
b What percentage of pupils chose science as their favourite lesson?

6 This pie chart shows the proportions of the different shoe sizes worn by 144 pupils in Y11 in a London school.

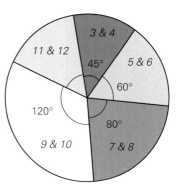

    a What is the angle of the sector representing shoe sizes 11 and 12?

    b How many pupils had a shoe size of 11 or 12?

    c What percentage of pupils wore the modal size?

Scatter diagrams

A scatter diagram (also called a scattergraph, or scattergram) is a method of comparing two variables by plotting on a graph their corresponding values (usually taken from a table).

In other words, treating them just like a set of (x, y) co-ordinates, as shown in the scatter diagram below, in which the marks scored in an English test are plotted against the marks scored in a mathematics test.

This graph shows **positive correlation.** This means that pupils who get high marks in mathematics tests also tend to get high marks in English tests.

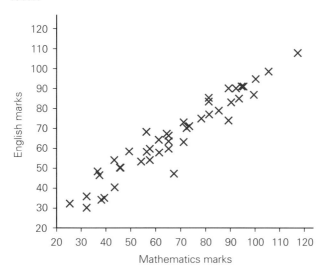

Correlation

Here are three statements that may or may not be true.

   The taller people are, the wider their arm span is likely to be.

   The older a car is, the lower its value will be.

   The distance you live from your place of work will affect how much you earn.

These relationships could be tested by collecting data and plotting the data on a scatter diagram. For example, the first statement may give a scatter diagram like the diagram on the right. This has **positive correlation**.

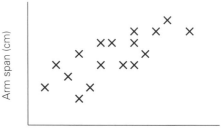

The diagram has positive correlation because as one quantity increases so does the other.

From such a scatter diagram we could say that the taller someone is, the wider the arm span.

Testing the second statement may give a scatter diagram like the diagram on the right. This has **negative correlation**. The diagram has negative correlation because as one quantity increases, the other quantity decreases.

From such a scatter diagram we could say that as a car gets older, its value decreases.

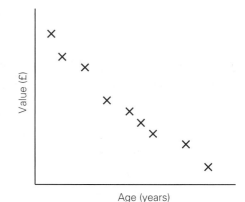

Testing the third statement may give a scatter diagram like the diagram on the right. This scatter diagram has **no correlation.**

There is no relationship between the distance a person lives from his or her work and how much the person earns.

Example 2

The graphs below show the relationship between the temperature and the amount of ice-cream sold, and that between the age of people and the amount of ice-cream they eat.

a Comment on the correlation of each graph.

b What does each graph tell you?

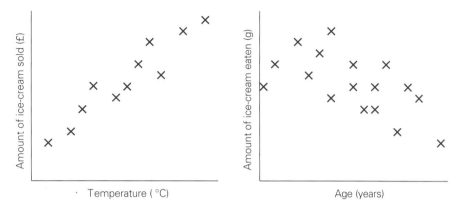

The first graph has positive correlation and tells us that as the temperature increases, the amount of ice-cream sold increases.

The second graph has negative correlation and tells us that as people get older, they eat less ice-cream.

Line of best fit

This is a straight line that goes between all the points on a scatter diagram, passing as close as possible to all of them. You should try to have the same number of points on both sides of the line. Because you are drawing this line by eye, examiners make a generous allowance around the correct answer. The line of best fit for the scatter diagram on page 441 is shown below.

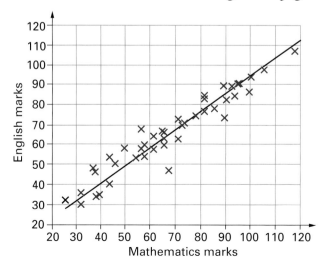

The line of best fit can be used to answer the following type of question: 'A girl took the mathematics test and scored 75 marks, but was ill for the English test. How many marks was she likely to have scored?'

The answer is found by drawing a line up from 75 on the Mathematics axis to the line of best fit and then drawing a line across to the English axis. This gives 73, which is the mark she is likely to have scored in the English test.

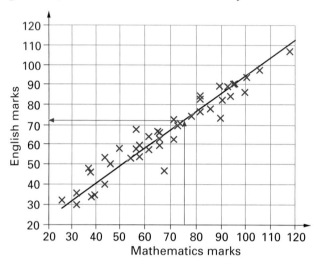

EXERCISE 22B

1 Describe the correlation of each of these four graphs.

a   **b**

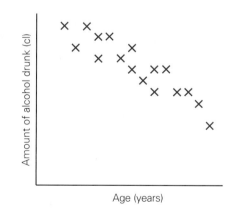

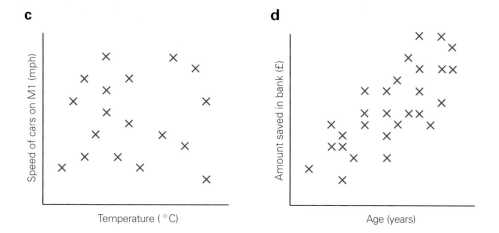

c Speed of cars on M1 (mph) / Temperature (°C)

d Amount saved in bank (£) / Age (years)

2 Write in words what graph **1a** tells you.

3 Write in words what graph **1b** tells you.

4 Write in words what graph **1c** tells you.

5 Write in words what graph **1d** tells you.

6 The table below shows the results of a science experiment in which a ball is rolled along a desk top. The speed of the ball is measured at various points.

Distance from start (cm)	10	20	30	40	50	60	70	80
Speed (cm/s)	18	16	13	10	7	5	3	0

    a Plot the data on a scatter diagram.

    b Draw the line of best fit.

    c If the ball's speed had been measured at 5 cm from the start, what is it likely to have been?

    d How far from the start was the ball when its speed was 12 cm/s?

7 The table below shows the marks for ten pupils in their mathematics and geography examinations.

Pupil	Anna	Beryl	Cath	Dema	Ethel	Fatima	Greta	Hannah	Imogen	Joan
Maths	57	65	34	87	42	35	59	61	25	35
Geog	45	61	30	78	41	36	35	57	23	34

    a Plot the data on a scatter diagram. Take the x-axis for the mathematics scores and mark it from 20 to 100. Take the y-axis for the geography scores and mark it from 20 to 100.

    b Draw the line of best fit.

    c One of the pupils was ill when she took the geography examination. Which pupil was it most likely to be?

d If another pupil, Kate, was absent for the geography examination but scored 75 in mathematics, what mark would you expect her to have got in geography?

e If another pupil, Lynne, was absent for the mathematics examination but scored 65 in geography, what mark would you expect her to have got in mathematics?

8 The heights, in centimetres, of 20 mothers and their 15-year-old daughters were measured. These are the results.

Mother	153	162	147	183	174	169	152	164	186	178
Daughter	145	155	142	167	167	151	145	152	163	168
Mother	175	173	158	168	181	173	166	162	180	156
Daughter	172	167	160	154	170	164	156	150	160	152

a Plot these results on a scatter diagram. Take the x-axis for the mothers' heights from 140 to 200. Take the y-axis for the daughters' heights from 140 to 200.

b Is it true that the tall mothers have tall daughters?

9 The government wanted to see how much the prices of houses had risen over the last ten years in different areas of Britain. They surveyed ten houses that had been sold ten years ago and had them valued at today's prices. The table shows the value of the houses (in thousands of pounds) ten years ago and today.

House	A	B	C	D	E	F	G	H	I	J
Value 10 years ago	32	54	89	25	43	58	38	47	95	39
Value today	43	61	94	34	56	67	46	56	105	48

a Plot the data on a scatter diagram. Take the x-axis as the price ten years ago and mark it from 20 to 100. Take the y-axis as the price today and mark it from 20 to 110.

b Draw the line of best fit.

c What would you expect a house worth £65 000 ten years ago to be worth today?

d Apart from inflation, what other factors could have affected the rise or fall in the value of a house?

e Would you say that there was a correlation between the value of a house ten years ago and the value of the same house today?

10 A form teacher carried out a survey of his class and asked them to say how many hours per week they spent playing sport and how many hours per week they spent watching TV. This table shows the results of the survey.

Pupil	1	2	3	4	5	6	7	8	9	10
Hours playing sport	12	3	5	15	11	0	9	7	6	12
Hours watching TV	18	26	24	16	19	27	12	13	17	14

Pupil	11	12	13	14	15	16	17	18	19	20
Hours playing sport	12	10	7	6	7	3	1	2	0	12
Hours watching TV	22	16	18	22	12	28	18	20	25	13

a Plot these results on a scatter diagram. Take the *x*-axis as the number of hours playing sport and mark it from 0 to 20. Take the *y*-axis as the number of hours watching TV and mark it from 0 to 30.

b If you knew that another pupil from the form watched 8 hours of TV a week, would you be able to predict how long she or he spent playing sport? Explain why.

Activity

Body data

You need graph paper, a metric tape measure and scales.

Survey

Height _____ cm

Weight _____ kg

Arm span _____ cm

Head circumference _____ cm

Shoe size _____

Ask about 40 people of widely different ages to complete this data collection sheet.

On graph paper, draw scatter diagrams to compare different pairs of variables. For example, height and weight, height and arm span, weight and shoe size.

Write a report on what each of your scatter diagrams tells you.

Surveys

A survey is an organised way of asking a lot of people a few, well-constructed questions, or of making a lot of observations in an experiment, in order to reach a conclusion about something.

We use surveys to test out people's opinions or to test a hypothesis.

Simple data collection sheet

If you need just to collect some data to analyse, you will have to design a simple data collection sheet.

For example: 'Where do you want to go for the Y10 trip at the end of term – Blackpool, Alton Towers, The Great Western Show or London?'

You would put this question on the same day to a lot of Y10 students, and enter their answers straight onto a data collection sheet, as below.

Place	Tally	Frequency
Blackpool	ЖТ ЖТ ЖТ ЖТ III	23
Alton Towers	ЖТ ЖТ ЖТ ЖТ ЖТ ЖТ ЖТ ЖТ ЖТ I	46
The Great Western Show	ЖТ ЖТ IIII	14
London	ЖТ ЖТ ЖТ ЖТ II	22

Notice how plenty of space is made for the tally marks, and how the tallies are 'gated' in groups of five to make counting easier when the survey is complete.

This is a good, simple data collection sheet because:
- only one question ('Where do you want to go?') has to be asked
- all the possible venues are listed
- the answer from each interviewee can be easily and quickly tallied, then on to the next interviewee.

Notice, too, that since the question listed specific places, they must appear on the data collection sheet. You would lose many marks in an examination if you just asked the open question: 'Where do you want to go?'

Data sometimes needs to be collected to obtain responses for two different categories. The data collection sheet is then in the form of a two-way table.

Example 3

The head of a school carries out a survey to find out how much time students in different year groups spend on their homework during a particular week. He asks a sample of 60 students and fills in a two-way table as follows.

	Up to 5 hours	Up to 10 hours	Up to 20 hours	More than 20 hours
Year 7	ЖЖ II	ЖЖ		
Year 8	ЖЖ	ЖЖ II		
Year 9	III	ЖЖ II	II	
Year 10	III	ЖЖ	III	I
Year 11	II	IIII	IIII	II

This gives a clearer picture of the amount of homework done in each year group

Using your computer

Once the data has been collected for your survey, it can be put into a computer database. This allows the data to be stored and amended or updated at a later date if necessary.

From the database, suitable statistical diagrams can easily be drawn within the software, and averages calculated for you. Your results can then be published in, for example, the school magazine.

EXERCISE 22C

1 'People like the supermarket to open on Sundays.'
   a To see whether this statement is true, design a data collection sheet which will allow you to capture data while standing outside a supermarket.
   b Does it matter on which day you collect data outside the supermarket?

2 The school tuck shop wanted to know which types of chocolate it should get in to sell – plain, milk, fruit and nut, wholenut or white chocolate.
   a Design a data collection sheet which you could use to ask the pupils in your school which of these chocolate types are their favourite.
   b Invent the first 30 entries on the chart.

3 What types of television programme do your age group watch the most? Is it crime, romance, comedy, documentary, sport or something else? Design a data collection sheet to be used in a survey of your age group.

4 What do people of your age tend to spend their money on? It is sport, magazines, clubs, cinema, sweets, clothes or something else? Design a data collection sheet to be used in a survey of your age group.

5 Design two-way tables to show the following. Invent about 40 entries for each one.

    a How students in different year groups travel to school in the morning.

    b The type of programme which different age groups prefer to watch on TV.

    c The favourite sport of boys and girls.

    d How much time students in different year groups spend on the computer in the evening.

Questionnaires

When you are putting together a questionnaire, you must think very carefully about the sorts of question you are going to ask. Here are four rules that you should **always** follow.

- Never ask a leading question designed to get a particular response.
- Never ask a personal, irrelevant question.
- Keep each question as simple as possible.
- Include questions that will get a response from whomever is asked.

The following questions are **badly constructed** and should **never** appear in any questionnaire.

What is your age?　　This is personal. Many people will not want to answer.

Slaughtering animals for food is cruel to the poor defenceless animals. Don't you agree?　　This is a leading question, designed to get a 'yes'.

Do you go to discos when abroad?　　This can be answered only by those who have been abroad.

When you first get up in a morning and decide to have some sort of breakfast that might be made by somebody else, do you feel obliged to eat it all or not?　　This is a too complicated question.

The following questions are **well constructed**.

Which age group are you in? 0–20 21–30 31–50 over 50

Do you think it is cruel to kill animals for meat to feed humans?

If you went abroad would you consider going to a disco?

Do you eat all your breakfast?

A questionnaire is usually put together to test a hypothesis or a statement. For example: 'People buy cheaper milk from the supermarket as they don't mind not getting it on their doorstep. They'd rather go out to buy it.'

A questionnaire designed to test whether this statement is true or not should include these questions:

'Do you have milk delivered to your doorstep?'
'Do you buy cheaper milk from the supermarket?'
'Would you buy your milk only from the supermarket?'

Once these questions have been answered, they can be looked at to see whether or not the majority of people hold views that agree with the statement.

EXERCISE 22D

1 Design a questionnaire to test the following statement.
'People under 16 do not know what is meant by all the jargon used in the business news on TV, but the over twenties do.'

2 'The under twenties feel quite at ease with computers, while the over forties would rather not bother with them. The 20–40s always try to look good with computers.'
Design a questionnaire to test this statement.

3 Design a questionnaire to test the following hypothesis.
'The older you get, the less sleep you need.'

Activity

Using the Internet

Through the Internet you have access to a vast amount of data on many topics, which you can use to carry out surveys. This data will enable you to draw statistical diagrams, answer a variety of questions and test all manner of hypotheses.

Here are some examples of what you can do.

Analyse football results of various teams
Analyse the numbers from the National Lottery
Compare GCSE examination results
Show the population growth of countries
Compare election results
Show the general index of retail prices
Find information from the National Census
Show how income tax is calculated

The following websites are a useful source of data for some of the above.

www.statistics.gov.uk
www.lufc.co.uk
www.national-lottery.co.uk
www.doh.gov.uk

Investigation

Watching TV is Bad for Your Maths

'Young people today watch too much television. This is bound to affect their test results in mathematics.'

Draw up a suitable questionnaire to test the validity of this statement.

Get Up!

Do a survey of your class to find out at what time your classmates get up in the morning on school days.

Is there a relationship between the getting-up time and the time it takes to get to school?

➤

For these coursework tasks, you may find it helpful to design a questionnaire of your own using a computer. Statistical diagrams can also be drawn using computer databases. Their use will improve the presentation of your work.

Examination questions

1 Rachel and Teri were collecting information on the type of meal bought by students in the school canteen. Draw a suitable data collection sheet for the information.

EDEXCEL, Question 21, Paper 1, June 1998

2 The table gives information about the age, in years, and the value, in £, of a number of cars of the same type.

Age	1	3	$4\frac{1}{2}$	6	3	5	2	$5\frac{1}{2}$	4	7
Value	8200	5900	4900	3800	6200	4500	7600	2200	5200	3200

    a Use this information to draw a scatter diagram.

    b What does the graph tell you about the value of these cars as they get older?

SEG, Question 18, Specimen Paper 6, 2000

3 Nazia is going to carry out a survey of the types of video her friends have watched. Draw a suitable data collection sheet that Nazia could use.

EDEXCEL, Question 22, Paper 1, June 2000

4 Jane does a survey about vehicles passing her school. She wants to know about the types of vehicle and their colours. Design a suitable observation sheet to record this information. Fill in your observation sheet as if you had carried out this survey. You should invent suitable data for about 25 vehicles.

NEAB, Question 13, Paper 2F, June 1998

5 Annie asked a group of teenagers to say how much time they spent doing homework one evening and how much time they spent watching TV. Here is a scatter diagram to show the results.

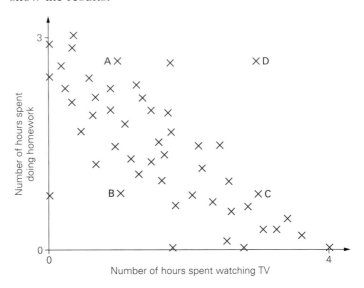

a Which of the four points A, B, C, or D represents each of the statements shown below?

Amy: 'I watched a lot of TV last night and I also did a lot of homework.'

Joe: 'I spent most of my evening doing homework. I watched only one programme on TV.'

Helen: 'I went out last night. I didn't do much homework or watch much TV.'

b Make up a statement which matches the fourth point.

c What does the graph tell you about the relationship between time spent watching TV and time spent doing homework?

d Annie also drew scatter diagrams which showed that:

i Older students tend to spend more time doing homework than younger students.

ii There is no relationship between the time students spend watching TV and the time they spend sleeping.

Sketch two scatter diagrams to illustrate the above statements.

NEAB, Question 18, Specimen Paper 2F, 2000

6 In one week Ronnie rents out 90 items from his shop, as shown in the table below.

Item	Frequency
Television	35
Video	30
Computer	17
Other equipment	8

Draw a pie chart for all the week's rentals.

NEAB, Question 20, Paper 2F, June 1998

7 This table gives you the marks scored by pupils in a French test and in a German test.

French	15	35	34	23	35	27	36	34	23	24	30	40	25	35	20
German	20	37	35	25	33	30	39	36	27	20	33	35	27	32	28

a Draw a scatter diagram of the marks scored in the French and German tests.

b Describe the relationship between the marks scored in the two tests.

Abigail scored 32 on the French test.

c Use the scatter diagram to estimate the mark she scored on the German test.

EDEXCEL, Question 18, Specimen Paper 2F, 1998

8 As part of a survey, Susan recorded the colours of the cars in a car park. The table shows the percentage of each colour of car.

Colour	Percentage
Red	46
White	22
Blue	18
Black	14

a Show this information on a labelled pie chart.

b There was a total of 350 cars on the car park.
Calculate how many were black.

OCR(SMP), Question 15, June 1999

9 Annie is doing a survey of all the pupils in her class. She is interested in finding out whether there is a connection between the colour of their hair and the colour of their eyes. Design a suitable observation sheet to record the information she needs.

OCR, Question 13, Paper 1, June 2000

10 Some members of a youth group went on a camping holiday to France. The pie chart shows how they spent their money while they were on holiday.

The cost of the food was £240.

a What was the total cost of the holiday?

b How much did they spend on transport?

MEG(SMP), Question 18, June 1998

11 This statement is made on a television programme about health.

a A school has 584 pupils. According to the television programme, how many pupils do not take any exercise outside school?

b Clare says, 'I go to the gym twice a week after school.' She decides to do a survey to investigate what exercise other pupils do outside school. Write down **two** questions she should ask.

AQA, Question 16, Paper 1, June 2000

12 The scatter diagram shows the heights of sixteen Year 9 boys and their fathers.

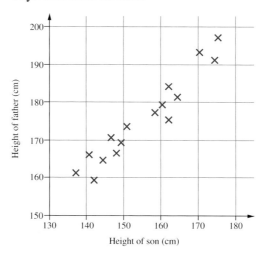

a What does the scatter diagram tell you about the relationship between the heights of these boys and their fathers?

b Copy the diagram and draw a line of best fit on it.

c Bill, another Year 9 boy, is 155 cm tall. Use the diagram to estimate the height of Bill's father. Explain clearly how you obtained your answer.

NEAB, Question 13, Paper 2I, June 1998

13 Bridgit and Pong K'I are two Chinese games. Each game is for two players. A class of children played each other at these games. The table on the next page shows the number of wins obtained by some of the children.

Child	Ann	Ben	Ciri	Dawn	Erin	Fay	Gil	Hue	Ian	Jo
Number of wins at Bridgit	14	7	10	5	12	7	10	3	5	12
Number of wins at Pong K'I	1	10	5	14	3	12	7	16	12	5

a Plot these results as a scatter diagram on a copy of the grid.

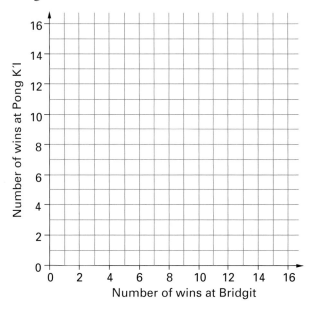

b What does the scatter diagram tell you?

c Draw a line of best fit on the scatter diagram.

d Sue won six games of Bridgit. Use the scatter diagram to estimate the number of games of Pong K'I that Sue won.

AQA, Question 14, Paper 1I, June 1999

What you should know after you have worked through Chapter 22

✔ How to draw and interpret pie charts.
✔ How to draw a scatter diagram.
✔ How to draw a line of best fit on a scatter diagram and use it to predict.
✔ What correlation means.
✔ How to design and use a data collection sheet.
✔ How to design and use a questionnaire.

23 Pattern

This chapter is going to ...

show you how to recognise rules for sequences and how to express these rules in formulae. It will then show you what is meant by the nth term, and how to find it for simple sequences.

What you should already know

✔ How to use letters for numbers
✔ How to solve simple linear equations

Patterns in number

Look at these number patterns.

$0 \times 9 + 1 = 1$	$1 \times 8 + 1 = 9$
$1 \times 9 + 2 = 11$	$12 \times 8 + 2 = 98$
$12 \times 9 + 3 = 111$	$123 \times 8 + 3 = 987$
$123 \times 9 + 4 = 1111$	$1234 \times 8 + 4 = 9876$
$1234 \times 9 + 5 = 11111$	$12345 \times 8 + 5 = 98765$

$1 \times 3 \times 37 = 111$	$7 \times 7 = 49$
$2 \times 3 \times 37 = 222$	$67 \times 67 = 4489$
$3 \times 3 \times 37 = 333$	$667 \times 667 = 444889$
$4 \times 3 \times 37 = 444$	$6667 \times 6667 = 44448889$

Check that the patterns you see there are correct and then try to continue each pattern without using a calculator. Check them with a calculator afterwards.

Spotting patterns is an important part of mathematics. It helps us to see rules for making calculations.

EXERCISE 23A

Look for the pattern and then write the next two lines. Check your answers with a calculator afterwards.

You might find that some of the answers are too big to fit in a calculator display. This is one of the reasons why spotting patterns is important.

1
$$1 \times 1 = 1$$
$$11 \times 11 = 121$$
$$111 \times 111 = 12321$$
$$1111 \times 1111 = 1234321$$

2
$$9 \times 9 = 81$$
$$99 \times 99 = 9801$$
$$999 \times 999 = 998001$$
$$9999 \times 9999 = 99980001$$

3
$$3 \times 4 = 3^2 + 3$$
$$4 \times 5 = 4^2 + 4$$
$$5 \times 6 = 5^2 + 5$$
$$6 \times 7 = 6^2 + 6$$

4
$$10 \times 11 = 110$$
$$20 \times 21 = 420$$
$$30 \times 31 = 930$$
$$40 \times 41 = 1640$$

5
$$1 = \ 1 = 1^2$$
$$1 + 2 + 1 = \ 4 = 2^2$$
$$1 + 2 + 3 + 2 + 1 = \ 9 = 3^2$$
$$1 + 2 + 3 + 4 + 3 + 2 + 1 = 16 = 4^2$$

6
$$1 = \ 1 = 1^3$$
$$3 + 5 = \ 8 = 2^3$$
$$7 + 9 + 11 = 27 = 3^3$$
$$13 + 15 + 17 + 19 = 64 = 4^3$$

7
$$1 \qquad\qquad = 1$$
$$1 + 1 \qquad\qquad = 2$$
$$1 + 2 + 1 \qquad\quad = 4$$
$$1 + 3 + 3 + 1 \qquad = 8$$
$$1 + 4 + 6 + 4 + 1 \quad = 16$$
$$1 + 5 + 10 + 10 + 5 + 1 \ = 32$$

8
$$12\,345\,679 \times \ 9 = 111\,111\,111$$
$$12\,345\,679 \times 18 = 222\,222\,222$$
$$12\,345\,679 \times 27 = 333\,333\,333$$
$$12\,345\,679 \times 36 = 444\,444\,444$$

9
$$1^3 \qquad\qquad = 1^2 \qquad\qquad = 1$$
$$1^3 + 2^3 \qquad\ = (1 + 2)^2 \qquad = 9$$
$$1^3 + 2^3 + 3^3 \ = (1 + 2 + 3)^2 \ = 36$$

10
$$3^2 + 4^2 = 5^2$$
$$10^2 + 11^2 + 12^2 = 13^2 + 14^2$$
$$21^2 + 22^2 + 23^2 + 24^2 = 25^2 + 26^2 + 27^2$$

Hint:
$$4 + 5 = 9 = 3^2$$
$$12 + 13 = 25 = 5^2$$
$$24 + 25 = 49 = 7^2$$

From your observations on the number patterns in Questions **1** to **10**, answer Questions **11** to **19** without using a calculator.

11 $111\ 111\ 111 \times 111\ 111\ 111 =$

12 $999\ 999\ 999 \times 999\ 999\ 999 =$

13 $12 \times 13 =$

14 $90 \times 91 =$

15 $1 + 2 + 3 + 4 + 5 + 6 + 7 + 8 + 9 + 8 + 7 + 6 + 5 + 4 + 3 + 2 + 1 =$

16 $57 + 59 + 61 + 63 + 65 + 67 + 69 + 71 =$

17 $1 + 9 + 36 + 84 + 126 + 126 + 84 + 36 + 9 + 1 =$

18 $12\ 345\ 679 \times 81 =$

19 $1^3 + 2^3 + 3^3 + 4^3 + 5^3 + 6^3 + 7^3 + 8^3 + 9^3 =$

Number sequences

A number sequence is an ordered set of numbers with a rule to find every number in the sequence. The rule which takes you from one number to the next could be a simple addition or multiplication, but often it is more tricky than that. So you need to look most carefully at the pattern of a sequence.

Each number in a sequence is called a **term** and is in a certain position in the sequence.

Look at these sequences and their rules.

3, 6, 12, 24 … doubling the last term each time … 48, 96, …

2, 5, 8, 11, … adding 3 to the last term each time … 14, 17, …

1, 10, 100, 1000, … multiplying the last term by 10 each time … 10 000, 100 000

1, 8, 15, 22, … adding 7 to the last term each time … 29, 36, …

These are all quite straightforward once you have looked for the link from one term to the next (consecutive terms).

Differences

For some sequences we need to look at the differences between consecutive terms to determine the pattern.

Example 1

Find the next two terms of the sequence 1, 3, 6, 10, 15, ...

Looking at the differences between each pair of consecutive terms, we notice

```
1   3   6   10   15
 ↑   ↑   ↑   ↑
 2   3   4   5
```

So, we can continue the sequence as follows:

```
1   3   6   10   15      21       28
 ↑   ↑   ↑   ↑    └   ┘└    ┘
 2   3   4   5   └ +6 ┘└ +7 ┘
```

The differences usually form a number sequence of their own, so you need to find out the sequence of the differences before you can expand the original sequence.

EXERCISE 23B

1 Look at the following number sequences. Write down the next three terms in each and explain how each sequence is found.

   a 1, 3, 5, 7, ...
                                         b 2, 4, 6, 8, ...
   c 5, 10, 20, 40, ...
                                         d 1, 3, 9, 27, ...
   e 4, 10, 16, 22, ...
                                         f 3, 8, 13, 18, ...
   g 2, 20, 200, 2000, ...
                                h 7, 10, 13, 16, ...
   i 10, 19, 28, 37, ...
                                j 5, 15, 45, 135, ...
   k 2, 6, 10, 14, ...
                                      l 1, 5, 25, 125, ...

2 By considering the differences in the following sequences, write down the next two terms in each case.

   a 1, 2, 4, 7, 11, ...
                                   b 1, 2, 5, 10, 17, ...
   c 1, 3, 7, 13, 21, ...
                                 d 1, 4, 10, 19, 31, ...
   e 1, 9, 25, 49, 81, ...
                                 f 1, 2, 7, 32, 157, ...
   g 1, 3, 23, 223, 2223, ...
                         h 1, 2, 4, 5, 7, 8, 10, ...
   i 2, 3, 5, 9, 17, ...
                                 j 3, 8, 18, 33, 53, ...

3 Look carefully at each number sequence below. Find the next two numbers in the sequence and try to explain the pattern.

a 1, 1, 2, 3, 5, 8, 13, ...   **b** 1, 4, 9, 16, 25, 36, ...
c 3, 4, 7, 11, 18, 29, ...

4 Triangle numbers are found as follows.

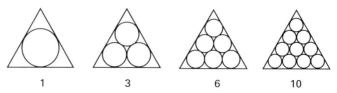

Find the next four triangle numbers.

5 Hexagon numbers are found as follows.

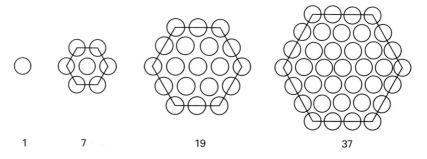

Find the next three hexagon numbers.

6 Look at the sequences below. Find the rule for each sequence and write down its next three terms.

a 3, 6, 12, 24, ...   **b** 3, 9, 15, 21, 27, ...
c 1, 3, 4, 7, 11, 18, ...   **d** 50, 47, 44, 41, ...
e 2, 5, 10, 17, 26, ...   **f** 5, 6, 8, 11, 15, 20, ...
g 5, 7, 8, 10, 11, 13, ...   **h** 4, 7, 10, 13, 16, ...
i 1, 3, 6, 10, 15, 21, ...   **j** 1, 2, 3, 4, ...
k 100, 20, 4, 0.8, ...   **l** 1, 0.5, 0.25, 0.125, ...

Finding the rule

When using a number sequence, we sometimes need to know, say, its 50th term, or even a bigger number in the sequence. To do so, we need to find the rule which produces the sequence in its general form.

Let's first look at the problem backwards. That is, we'll take a rule and see how it produces a sequence.

Example 2

A sequence is formed by the rule $3n + 1$, where $n = 1, 2, 3, 4, 5, 6, \ldots$. Write down the first five terms of the sequence.

Substituting $n = 1, 2, 3, 4, 5$ in turn, we get

$$(3 \times 1 + 1), \quad (3 \times 2 + 1), \quad (3 \times 3 + 1), \quad (3 \times 4 + 1), \quad (3 \times 5 + 1), \quad \ldots$$
$$\quad\quad 4 \quad\quad\quad\quad 7 \quad\quad\quad\quad 10 \quad\quad\quad\quad 13 \quad\quad\quad\quad 16$$

So the sequence is 4, 7, 10, 13, 16, …

Notice that the difference between each term and the next is always 3, which is the coefficient of n (the number attached to n).

Example 3

The nth term of a sequence is $4n - 3$. Write down the first five terms of the sequence.

Substituting $n = 1, 2, 3, 4, 5$ in turn, we get

$$(4 \times 1 - 3), \quad (4 \times 2 - 3), \quad (4 \times 3 - 3), \quad (4 \times 4 - 3), \quad (4 \times 5 - 3)$$
$$\quad 1 \quad\quad\quad\quad 5 \quad\quad\quad\quad 9 \quad\quad\quad\quad 13 \quad\quad\quad\quad 17$$

So the sequence is 1, 5, 9, 13, 17, …

Notice that the difference between each term and the next is always 4, which is the coefficient of n.

EXERCISE 23C

1 Use each of the following rules to write down the first five terms of a sequence.

  a $2n + 1$ for $n = 1, 2, 3, 4, 5$ **b** $3n - 2$ for $n = 1, 2, 3, 4, 5$
  c $5n + 2$ for $n = 1, 2, 3, 4, 5$ **d** n^2 for $n = 1, 2, 3, 4, 5$
  e $n^2 + 3$ for $n = 1, 2, 3, 4, 5$

2 Write down the first five terms of the sequence which has its nth term as

  a $n + 3$ **b** $3n - 1$ **c** $5n - 2$ **d** $n^2 - 1$ **e** $4n + 5$

3 The first two terms of the sequence of fractions $\dfrac{n-1}{n+1}$ are

$$n = 1: \quad \frac{1-1}{1+1} = \frac{0}{2} = 0$$

$$n = 2: \quad \frac{2-1}{2+1} = \frac{1}{3}$$

Work out the next five terms of the sequence.

4 A sequence is formed by the rule $\frac{1}{2} \times n \times (n + 1)$ for $n = 1, 2, 3, 4, \ldots$
The first term is given by $n = 1$: $\frac{1}{2} \times 1 \times (1 + 1) = 1$
The second term is given by $n = 2$: $\frac{1}{2} \times 2 \times (2 + 1) = 3$

   a Work out the next five terms of this sequence.

   b This is a well-known sequence you have met before. What is it?

5 5! means factorial 5, which is $5 \times 4 \times 3 \times 2 \times 1 = 120$
In the same way 7! means $7 \times 6 \times 5 \times 4 \times 3 \times 2 \times 1 = 5040$

   a Calculate 2!, 3!, 4! and 6!

   b If your calculator has a factorial button, check that it gives the same answers as you get for part **a**. What is the largest factorial you can work out with your calculator before you get an error?

Finding the *n*th term of a linear sequence

Note This type of question will **not** appear in your examination papers, but you will find the method useful in your coursework tasks.

A linear sequence has the **same difference** between each term and the next.

For example:
   $2, 5, 8, 11, 14, \ldots$ difference of 3

The *n*th term of this sequence is given by $3n - 1$.

Here is another linear sequence:
   $5, 7, 9, 11, 13, \ldots$ difference of 2

The *n*th term of this sequence is given by $2n + 3$.

So, you can see that the *n*th term of a linear sequence is **always** of the form $An + b$, where

• A, the coefficient of n, is the difference between each term and the next term (consecutive terms).

• b is the difference between the first term and A.

Example 4

Find the *n*th term of the sequence $5, 7, 9, 11, 13, \ldots$

The difference between consecutive terms is 2. So the first part of the *n*th term is $2n$.

Subtract the difference 2 from the first term 5, which gives $5 - 2 = 3$

So the *n*th term is given by $2n + 3$

(You can test it by substituting $n = 1, 2, 3, 4, \ldots$.)

Example 5

Find the nth term of the sequence 3, 7, 11, 15, 19, …

The difference between consecutive terms is 4. So the first part of the nth term is $4n$.

Subtract the difference 4 from the first term 3, which gives $3 - 4 = -1$

So the nth term is given by $4n - 1$

Example 6

From the sequence 5, 12, 19, 26, 33, … find
a the nth term   **b** the 50th term

a The difference between consecutive terms is 7. So the first part of the nth term is $7n$.

Subtract the difference 7 from the first term 5, which gives $5 - 7 = -2$

So the nth term is given by $7n - 2$

b The 50th term is found by substituting $n = 50$ into the rule, $7n - 2$. So
50th term $= 7 \times 50 - 2 = 350 - 2$
$= 348$

EXERCISE 23D

1 Find the next two terms and the nth term in each of these linear sequences.

    a 3, 5, 7, 9, 11, …   **b** 5, 9, 13, 17, 21, …

    c 8, 13, 18, 23, 28, …   **d** 2, 8, 14, 20, 26, …

    e 5, 8, 11, 14, 17, …   **f** 2, 9, 16, 23, 30, …

    g 1, 5, 9, 13, 17, …   **h** 3, 7, 11, 15, 19, …

    i 2, 5, 8, 11, 14, …   **j** 2, 12, 22, 32, …

    k 8, 12, 16, 20, …   **l** 4, 9, 14, 19, 24, …

2 Find the nth term and the 50th term in each of these linear sequences.

    a 4, 7, 10, 13, 16, …   **b** 7, 9, 11, 13, 15, …

    c 3, 8, 13, 18, 23, …   **d** 1, 5, 9, 13, 17, …

    e 2, 10, 18, 26, …   **f** 5, 6, 7, 8, 9, …

    g 6, 11, 16, 21, 26, …   **h** 3, 11, 19, 27, 35, …

    i 1, 4, 7, 10, 13, …   **j** 21, 24, 27, 30, 33, …

    k 12, 19, 26, 33, 40, … **l** 1, 9, 17, 25, 33, …

3 For each sequence **a** to **j**, find
  i the nth term   **ii** the 100th term
  a 5, 9, 13, 17, 21, …   **b** 3, 5, 7, 9, 11, 13, …
  c 4, 7, 10, 13, 16, …   **d** 8, 10, 12, 14, 16, …
  e 9, 13, 17, 21, …   **f** 6, 11, 16, 21, …
  g 0, 3, 6, 9, 12, …   **h** 2, 8, 14, 20, 26, …
  i 7, 15, 23, 31, …   **j** 25, 27, 29, 31, …

General rules from given patterns

Many problem-solving situations that you are likely to meet in your coursework tasks involve number sequences. So you do need to be able to formulate general rules from given number patterns.

Example 7

The diagram shows a pattern of squares building up.
a How many squares will be on the base of the nth pattern?
b Which pattern has 99 squares in its base?

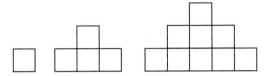

a First, we build up the following table for the patterns.

Pattern number	1	2	3	4	5
Number of squares in base	1	3	5	7	9

Looking at the difference between consecutive patterns, we see it is always 2 squares. So, we use $2n$.

Subtract the difference 2 from the first number, which gives $1 - 2 = -1$

So the number of squares in the nth pattern is $2n - 1$

b We have to find n when $2n - 1 = 99$:
$$2n - 1 = 99$$
$$2n = 99 + 1 = 100$$
$$n = 100 \div 2 = 50$$

The pattern with 99 squares in its base is the 50th.

EXERCISE 23E

1 A pattern of squares is built up from matchsticks as shown.

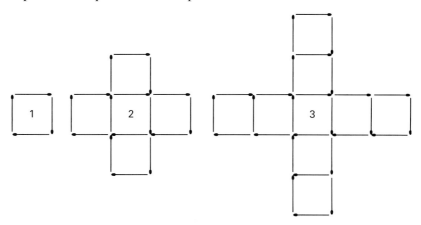

a Draw the 4th diagram.
b How many squares are in the nth diagram?
c How many squares are in the 25th diagram?
d With 200 squares, which is the biggest diagram that could be made?

2 A pattern of triangles is built up from matchsticks.

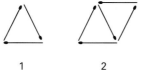 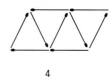

a Draw the 5th set of triangles in this pattern.
b How many matchsticks are needed for the nth set of triangles?
c How many matchsticks are needed to make the 60th set of triangles?
d If there are only 100 matchsticks, which is the largest set of triangles that could be made?

3 A conference centre had tables each of which could sit six people. When put together, the tables could seat people as shown.

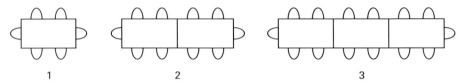

1   2   3

    a How many people could be seated at 4 tables?
    b How many people could be seated at *n* tables put together in this way?
    c A conference had 50 people who wished to use the tables in this way. How many tables would they need?

4 A pattern of squares is put together as shown.

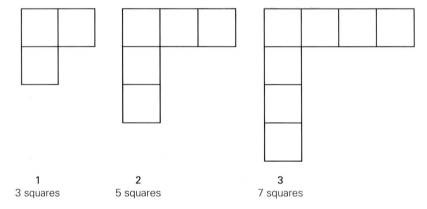

    1   2   3
   3 squares   5 squares   7 squares

    a Draw the 4th diagram.
    b How many squares are in the *n*th diagram?
    c How many squares are in the 50th diagram?
    d With 300 squares, what is the biggest diagram that could be made?

5 Regular pentagons of side length 1 cm are joined together to make a pattern as shown.

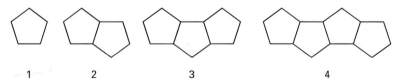

   1   2   3   4

Copy this pattern and write down the perimeter of each shape.
    a What is the perimeter of patterns like this made from
       i 6 pentagons   **ii** *n* pentagons   **iii** 50 pentagons?
    b What is the largest number of pentagons that can be put together like this to have a perimeter less than 1000 cm?

6 Lamp-posts are put at the end of every 100 m stretch of a motorway, as shown,

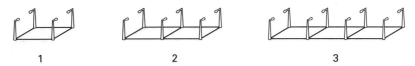

1   2   3

a How many lamp-posts are needed for
   i 900 m of this motorway   **ii** 8 km of this motorway?
b The M99 is a motorway being built. The contractor has ordered 1598 lamp-posts. How long is this motorway?

Examination questions

1 A supermarket sells four different sized bottles of Cola.

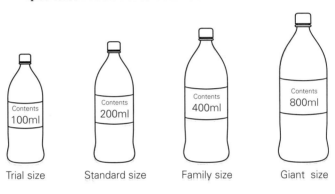

Contents 100ml — Trial size
Contents 200ml — Standard size
Contents 400ml — Family size
Contents 800ml — Giant size

a Describe the number pattern that the contents follow.
b The supermarket introduces a super giant size, which is the next sized bottle in the pattern. How much is the contents of this bottle?

NEAB, Question 20, Specimen Paper 1F, 2000

2 Sticks are used to make a sequence of patterns. The first four patterns are shown.

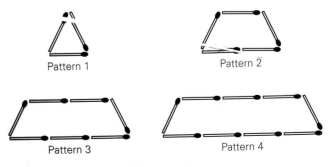

Pattern 1   Pattern 2

Pattern 3   Pattern 4

a i How many sticks are needed for Pattern 5?

ii How many extra sticks are needed to make Pattern 6 from Pattern 5 ?

Shape 1

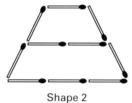

Shape 2

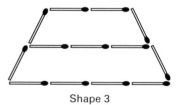

Shape 3

b The patterns are used to make a sequence of shapes as shown.

i How many sticks will Shape 4 have?

The rule for finding the number of sticks, s, needed for Shape n, is $s = 3n + 4$

ii Find the number of sticks for Shape n, when $n = 50$.

c Solve the equation $3n + 4 = 22$

SEG, Question 8, Specimen Paper 5, 2000

3 In a table tennis league, a team only scores points for a win,

a Copy and complete the table to show the number of games won and the number of points scored by teams A, B, C, D.

Team	A	B	C	D
Won	1		4	6
Points	3	6		18

b In the first six weeks of the league, Team D won every game. The running total of points scored formed a pattern: 3, 6, 9, 12, 15, 18. Describe this pattern.

SEG, Question 3, Specimen Paper 6, 2000

4 a Copy and fill in the missing numbers in this pattern:

$11^2 - 10^2 = 21$

$10^2 - 9^2 = \ldots$

$9^2 - \quad \ldots$

ι write down the next line of the pattern.

NEAB, Question 4, Paper 1F, June 1998

5 **a** Here are the first five odd numbers: 1, 3, 5, 7, 9
     i Write down the tenth odd number
     ii What is the twentieth odd number?

   b Here are the first four terms of a sequence: 21, 20, 17, 12, ... Write down the next two terms in the sequence.

NEAB, Question 5, Paper 1F, June 1998

6 **a** Copy and complete the following number pattern.
$$1^3 = 1 \times 1 \times 1 = 1$$
$$2^3 = 2 \times 2 \times 2 = 8$$
$$3^3 = \qquad\qquad = 27$$
$$4^3 = \qquad\qquad = \ldots$$

   b Use your answers to part **a** to complete this pattern.
$$1^3 = 1 = 1^2$$
$$1^3 + 2^3 = 9 = 3^2$$
$$1^3 + 2^3 + 3^3 = 36 = 6^2$$
$$1^3 + 2^3 + 3^3 + 4^3 = \ldots = \ldots$$

   c A line of the pattern in part **b** is shown below. Copy and fill in the missing parts of this line.
$$\ldots = 441 = \ldots$$

NEAB, Question 16, Paper 2F, June 1998

7 The diagram shows patterns made from square tiles.

Diagram	**Number of tiles**
	2
	6
	12
	20

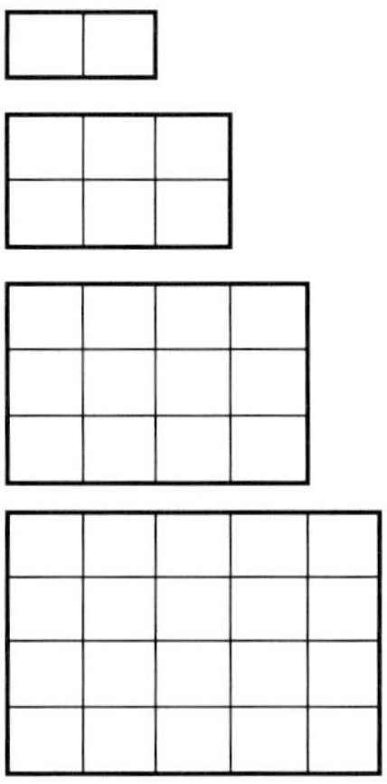

The numbers 2, 6, 12, 20, ... form a number sequence.
Work out the eighth number in this sequence.

EDEXCEL, Paper 1, June 2000

8 Ivan builds fences in different lengths using pieces of wood.

Fence length 1

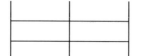

Fence length 2

Fence length 3

a Sketch fence length 5.

Ivan counted how many pieces he needed to make each fence length. He then drew up the table below.

Fence length	1	2	3	4	5	6
Number of pieces	4	7	10			

b Complete the table to show how many pieces of wood he would use for fence lengths 4, 5 and 6.

c Explain how you would work out the number of pieces needed for fence length 25.

EDEXCEL, Question 15, Specimen Paper 1F, 1998

9 Look at these matchstick shapes.

 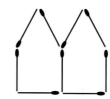 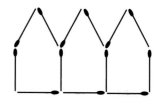

5 matchsticks   9 matchsticks

a Complete this table.

Shape number	1	2	3	4	5
Number of matchsticks	5	9	...	...	...

b How many matchsticks are there in Shape 12? Explain how you work this out without drawing a diagram.

OCR(SMP), Question 1, June 2000

10 Here are four patterns in a sequence.

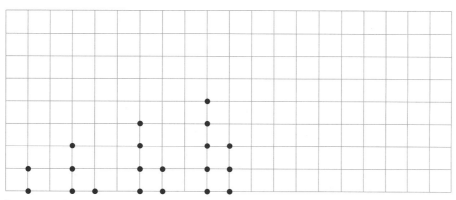

Pattern 1   Pattern 2   Pattern 3   Pattern 4

a   On a copy of the grid, draw the next pattern in the sequence.

b   Fill in this table.

Pattern		1	2	3	4	5
Number of dots in the pattern						

c   How many dots are there in pattern 100?.

OCR(SMP), Question 1, June 2000

What you should know after you have worked through Chapter 23

✔   Be able to recognise a number pattern and explain how the pattern is made.

✔   Be able to recognise a linear pattern and find its nth term.

Practice examination paper 1: Non-calculator

- You **cannot use** a calculator to do this paper.
- Allow **one hour** in which to do this paper

1 This is the timetable for trains from Doncaster to Sheffield, via Rotherham and Meadowhall.

Doncaster–Rotherham– Meadowhall–Sheffield				
Sundays				
Doncaster	09 55	10 55	11 35	11 47
Conisbrough	10 02	11 02	......	......
Mexborough	10 06	11 06	......	......
Swinton	10 09	11 09	......	......
Rotherham	10 17	11 17	......	......
Meadowhall	10 24	11 24	......	12 14
Sheffield	10 37	11 37	12 01	12 26
Doncaster	12 05	13 06	14 00	14 12
Conisbrough	12 12	13 13	......	14 19
Mexborough	12 16	13 17	......	14 23
Swinton	12 19	13 21	......	14 26
Rotherham	12 27	13 29	......	14 34
Meadowhall	12 34	13 35	......	14 41
Sheffield	12 48	13 50	14 25	14 52

Rose and Javid decide to get the train that arrives at Meadowhall at 13 35, to go to an athletics event at Don Valley Stadium, which is near Meadowhall.

a What time does this train leave Doncaster? [1]

b How long does the journey take? [1]

c The event starts at 2 pm. How long will they have to get from Meadowhall to the stadium? [1]

d The 11 47 train from Doncaster arrives at Meadowhall at 12 14. How long does the journey take? [1]

Examination practice

2

> # Don Valley Stadium
> # Britain's Premier Athletics
> # Venue!
>
> ## 24 536 spectators at the last event!

a Write the number 24 536 to the nearest 100. [1]

b What does the number 4 represent in 24 536? [1]

c They overheard a steward speaking.

> We had forty-seven thousand, two hundred and three people at the Rolling Stones concert last year.

Write this number in figures. [1]

d There were 502 stewards at the Rolling Stones concert.
There were 347 stewards at the athletics event.
How many more stewards were at the Rolling Stones concert than at the athletics event? [1]

3 The picture shows a family standing by the score board.

a Estimate the height h of the scoreboard. **Show all your working**. [2]

b The scoreboard has 120 rows of lights. Each row contains 192 bulbs. How many bulbs are there on the scoreboard altogether? [2]

4 For a crowd of 3000 people the stadium would order:

1800 hot dogs
1500 cans of pop
1300 cups of coffee
2100 bags of chips

A crowd of 22 000 people is expected. Malcolm has filled in the order form.

To Acme Caterers Ltd	
Please supply for June 9th	
13 500	hot dogs
11 000	cans of pop
9500	cups of coffee
19 000	bags of chips

One of the values is wrong. Use estimation to check which it is. Show clearly how you got your answer. [2]

5 This is a sketch of a triangular vegetable plot.

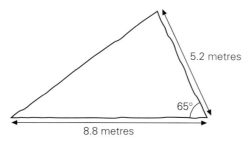

Make an accurate drawing of the plot using a scale of 1 centimetre to 1 metre. [3]

6 Pam and Dave sell small paving slabs for making garden paths. Here is one slab called the 'Diamond'.

a Explain why the angle at A must be exactly 60°.

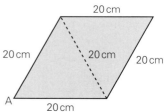

[1]

b Pam and Dave make this design using seven 'Diamond' slabs.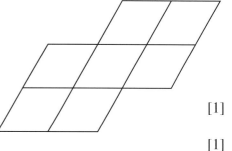

    i Work out the full-size perimeter of their design. [1]

    ii Draw the lines of symmetry on the design. [1]

c They have started to make another design, shown right. Draw one more diamond slab on their design to give it rotational symmetry. [1]

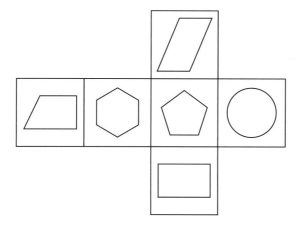

d On the drawing, mark clearly:

    i An acute angle. Label it *a*.

    ii A reflex angle. Label it *r*.

    iii An obtuse angle. Label it *o*.

    iv Two parallel edges. Label each of them *p*. [4]

7 This is the net for a dice.

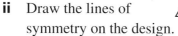

When the dice is made, what shape would be on the opposite face to the circle?

You can mark the face on the diagram and give the name of the shape. [2]

Examination practice

8

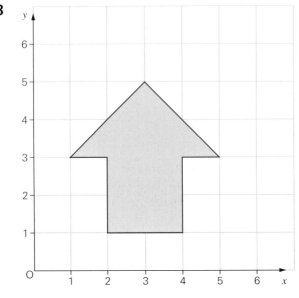

a Write down the co-ordinates of the vertices of the arrow.

(3, 5); (5, 3); (…, …); (…, …); (…, …); (…, …); (…, …) [2]

b The squares on the grid are each 1 cm by 1 cm. What is the
area of the arrow? [1]

9 Beryl is fitting a new bathroom.

The bath costs £168
The side panel for the bath costs £17.35
The washbasin costs £129
The taps cost £172.86

How much change will Beryl get from £500? [2]

10

A   B   C   D

E   F   G   H

a Which designs have rotational symmetry? [2]

b Which designs have lines of symmetry? Draw in these lines on the diagrams. [2]

11 Jane makes these rows of triangles.

  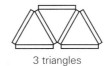 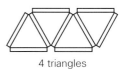

1 triangle   2 triangles   3 triangles   4 triangles

Number of triangles in the row	1	2	3	4	5	6	7	8
Number of matchsticks needed	3	5	7	9				

[1]

b Explain why she cannot make a row of triangles with exactly 30 matchsticks. [1]

c Jane has found a rule to work out the number of matchsticks she needs for any number of triangles. Jane writes her rule as a formula. She uses m for the number of matchsticks and t for the number of triangles in the row. Write down her formula [2]

d Use Jane's rule to work out how many matchsticks she needs to make a row of 100 triangles. [1]

12 a Complete the table to show all the possible totals for two throws of a dice. [1]

Second throw

6	7	8				
5	6	7				
4	5	6				
3	4	5				
2	3	4	5	6	7	8
1	2	3	4	5	6	7
	1	2	3	4	5	6

First throw

b List all the ways of getting a total of 7 when you throw the dice twice. [1]

c i What is the probability of getting a total of 7? [1]

ii What is the probability of getting a double? [1]

13 Emma has the following rule for working out how much it costs to make plaster gnomes.

To find the cost, in £, of making the models:
First, you write down the number of models you want to make.
Next, you add 25 to this number.
Then, you divide your answer by 5.

a Complete the table below to show how the cost depends on the number of models she makes.

Number of models Emma makes	5	20	50
Total cost in £	6		

[2]

b Draw a graph to show this information. [2]

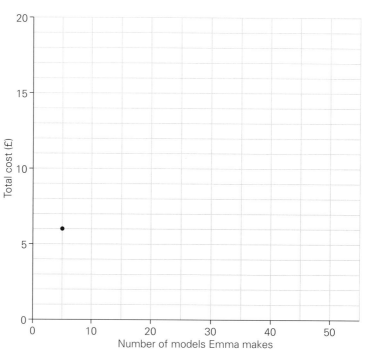

c Use your graph to find the cost of making 15 models. Show clearly how you got your answer. [1]

14 Solve these equations.
a $4x + 3 = 23$ [2]
b $5x + 3 = x + 5$ [3]

15 Work out each of these.

    a $\sqrt{25} + \sqrt{64}$ [2]

    b 2^5 [1]

16 This is a rule for a sequence of numbers.

    When the number is even, halve it.

    When the number is odd, multiply it by 3 and subtract 1.

    These are the first four terms of the sequence:

    18, 9, 26, 13

    Write down the next three terms.   [2]

Total: 60 marks

Practice examination paper 2: Calculator

- You **can use** a calculator to do this paper.
- Allow **one hour** in which to complete this paper.

1 Beryl is designing a bathroom. This is her design.

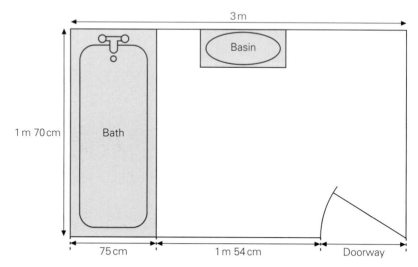

Diagram **not** drawn to scale

a Calculate the width of the doorway. [2]

b What fraction of the room does the bath take up? [1]

2 An old fence is slightly pushed over. There are two horizontal rails.

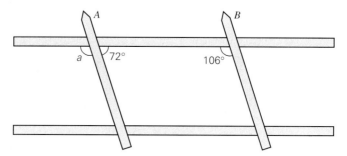

a Calculate the size of angle *a*. [1]

b Is post B parallel to post A? Give a reason for your answer. [1]

Examination practice

3 What is the volume, in cm³, of this box? Show all your working.

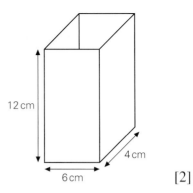

12 cm

4 cm

6 cm

[2]

4 This is a plan of an allotment.

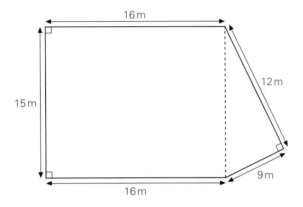

16 m

15 m

12 m

16 m

9 m

a Calculate the perimeter of the allotment. [1]

b Calculate the area of the allotment. [2]

5 A circular flower bed has a diameter of 8 metres.

a What is the circumference of the flower bed? [2]

b What is the area of the flower bed? [2]

6 Fred makes biscuits to help raise money. In a shop, biscuits are sold at 60p per pound.

a About how much do the shop biscuits cost per kilogram? (1 kilogram ≈ 2.2 pounds) [2]

b Fred wants to sell his biscuits 15% cheaper than the shop. How much will Fred's biscuits cost per pound? [2]

Examination practice

7 On the Liverpool-to-Belfast ferry, some of the crew are talking.

a

There are 600 vehicles on board.

Three-fifths of them are cars.

  i   What fraction of the vehicles are **not** cars? [1]

  ii How many cars are on the ferry? [1]

b

There are 600 vehicles on the ferry of which 30 are coaches.

What percentage of the vehicles are coaches? [2]

c

There are 1500 people on board.

The ratio of Irish people to non-Irish people is 2 : 3

How many Irish people are on board? [2]

d

On yesterday's sailing 75% of the passengers were Irish.

What fraction is 75%? Give your answer in its lowest terms. [1]

8 In a moderate breeze, the weight that a hang-glider will lift is given by the formula

$w = 5(a - 3)$

where w kilograms is the weight of the person

           a square metres is the area of the sail

Solve the equation to find the area of sail that will lift a person weighing 70 kilograms. [2]

Examination practice

9 Suzie runs a lottery.

> She sells tickets like this for £1 each.
>
> | 1 | 2 | 3 |
> |---|---|---|
> | 4 | 5 | 6 |
>
>
>
> Each player must cross out two numbers on a ticket and hand it in.
>
> At the end of the week Suzie will draw out two numbered balls from a bag.

    a   List all the different pairs of numbers that could be crossed out. [2]

    b   The probability that a player wins a prize is approximately 0.07. What is the probability that a player doesn't win a prize? [2]

10

> **To make 10 biscuits, you will need:**
> 120 g   plain flour
> 30 g   sugar
> 40 g   margarine
> 10 g   water

Fred wants to make a trial batch of 25 biscuits. Write down the quantities he will need. [2]

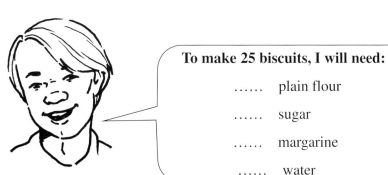

> **To make 25 biscuits, I will need:**
>   ......   plain flour
>   ......   sugar
>   ......   margarine
>   ......   water

11 The frequency chart below shows the distances of the deliveries requested by the first 40 customers of a furniture shop.

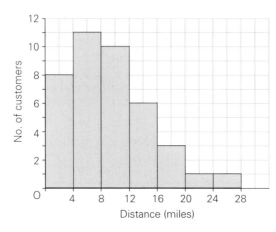

a How many of the customers' deliveries were less than 16 miles? [1]

b What percentage of the deliveries was less than 16 miles? [2]

c Estimate the probability of the next customer asking for a delivery of more than 20 miles. [2]

12 Jill decides to buy some perfume.

a There is a special offer of 12% off the marked price.
How much will she **pay** for a bottle of perfume with a marked price of £15.00?

[2]

b There is a perfume tester that is two-thirds full. Shade the bottle on the right to show that it is about two-thirds full.

[1]

13 Every Saturday morning Brenda and Dennis go shopping in Redford.

Brenda lives in a village north of Redford.

Dennis lives in a village east of Redford.

Over several weeks, they time their journeys each Saturday.

My time had a mean of 18.4 minutes and a range of 10 minutes.

My times, in minutes, were: 13, 29, 20, 14, 20, 19, 13, 15, 28, 19, 19, 14.

  a **i** Find the mean of Brenda's journey times. [2]

     ii Find the range of Brenda's journey times. [1]

  b Compare Brenda's times with Dennis' times. What do the mean and range tell you about their journeys to Redford? [2]

14 Melanie is thinking of running a minibus service which will pick people up from their homes and take them to Redford.

  a She conducts a survey of 60 people who travel to Redford to go shopping. Here are the replies to her question: 'How long do you spend shopping on a Saturday?'

Time spent shopping	Number of people
0 to 1 hour	6
1 to 2 hours	9
2 to 3 hours	24
3 to 4 hours	21
4 to 5 hours	0

2 to 3 hours

    Complete the pie chart to show this information. [2]

  b Melanie wants to decide on a route and a timetable for her minibus. Write down **two** other questions she should ask. [2]

Examination practice

15 **a** Work out $\dfrac{4.8 \times 21.2}{6.3 - 2.4}$. Write down your full calculator display. [2]

    b Use estimation to check your answer. Show your working. [2]

16

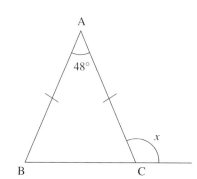

Triangle ABC is an isosceles triangle with AB = AC. Calculate the size of angle *x*.

[2]

17 **a** Phil drives 135 miles by car and his journey takes $2\frac{1}{4}$ hours. What is his average speed? [2]

    b Sandra travels 135 miles by train at an average speed of 90 mph. How long does the journey take? [2]

Total: 60 marks

Examination practice

Answers

Note Answers are not provided for the following features: Activities, Investigations and Puzzle Pages.

Exercise 1A

1 a 45 **b** 43 **c** 40 **d** 45 **e** 45 **f** 36 **g** 43 **h** 42 **i** 41 **2 a** 0, 4, 8 **b** 6, 2, 9 **c** 1, 0, 6
d 9, 1, 7, 6 **e** 4, 9, 0, 10, 3, 8 **f** 6, 5, 7, 18, 8, 17, 45 **g** 8, 6, 12, 1, 7, 22 **h** 1, 8, 0, 13, 5, 19, 43
i 1, 6, 5, 0, 7, 3, 7, 14, 11 or 1, 6, 5, 7, 14, 3, 0, 7, 11

Exercise 1B

1 a 20 **b** 21 **c** 24 **d** 15 **e** 16 **f** 12 **g** 10 **h** 42 **i** 24 **j** 18 **k** 30 **l** 28 **m** 18 **n** 56 **o** 25
p 45 **q** 27 **r** 30 **s** 49 **t** 24 **u** 36 **v** 35 **w** 32 **x** 36 **y** 48 **2 a** 5 **b** 4 **c** 6 **d** 6 **e** 5 **f** 4
g 7 **h** 6 **i** 2 **j** 3 **k** 7 **l** 8 **m** 9 **n** 5 **o** 8 **p** 9 **q** 4 **r** 7 **s** 7 **t** 9 **u** 5 **v** 4 **w** 5 **x** 7
y 6 **3 a** 12 **b** 15 **c** 21 **d** 13 **e** 8 **f** 7 **g** 14 **h** 3 **i** 30 **j** 6 **k** 35 **l** 5 **m** 16 **n** 7 **o** 16
p 15 **q** 27 **r** 6 **s** 15 **t** 24 **u** 40 **v** 6 **w** 17 **x** 72 **y** 46 **4 a** 30 **b** 50 **c** 80 **d** 100 **e** 120
f 180 **g** 240 **h** 400 **i** 700 **j** 900 **k** 1000 **l** 1400 **m** 2400 **n** 7200 **o** 10000 **p** 2 **q** 7 **r** 9
s 17 **t** 30 **u** 3 **v** 8 **w** 12 **x** 29 **y** 50

Exercise 1C

1 a 11 **b** 6 **c** 10 **d** 12 **e** 11 **f** 13 **g** 11 **h** 12 **i** 12 **j** 4 **k** 13 **l** 3 **2 a** 16 **b** 2 **c** 10
d 10 **e** 6 **f** 18 **g** 6 **h** 15 **i** 9 **j** 12 **k** 3 **l** 8 **3 b** 11 **c** 1 **d** 7 **e** 13 **f** 11 **g** 0 **h** 8
i 17 **j** 31 **k** 9 **l** 10 **4 a** 38 **b** 48 **c** 3 **d** 2 **e** 5 **f** 14 **g** 10 **h** 2 **i** 5 **j** 19 **k** 15 **l** 2
m 20 **n** 19 **o** 54 **p** 7 **q** 2 **r** 7 **s** 7 **t** 38 **u** 42 **v** 10 **w** 2 **x** 10 **y** 10 **z** 24 **5 a** $(4+1)$
b $(6 \div 2)$ **c** $(2+1)$ **d** $(4 \div 4)$ **e** $(4+4)$ **f** $(16-4)$ **g** (3×4) **h** $(6 \div 3)$ **i** $(20-10)$ **j** $(10 \div 2)$ **k** $(5+5)$
l $(4+2)$ **m** $(15-5)$ **n** $(7-2)$ **o** $(3+3)$ **p** $(12 \div 3)$ **q** $(24 \div 8)$ **r** $(8-2)$ **6 a** 8 **b** 6 **c** 6 **d** 13
e 11 **f** 9 **g** 12 **h** 8 **i** 15 **j** 16 **k** 1 **l** 7 **7 a** $2 \times 3 + 5$ **b** $2 \times (3+5)$ **c** $2+3 \times 5$
d $5-(3-2)$ and $(5+3) \div 2$ **e** $5 \times 3 - 2$ **f** $5 \times 3 \times 2$

Exercise 1D

1 a 40 **b** 5 units **c** 100 **d** 90 **e** 80 **f** 9 units **g** 80 **h** 500 **i** 0 **j** 5000 **k** 0 **l** 4 units
m 300 **n** 90 **o** 80 000 **2 a** Forty–three, two hundred **b** One hundred and thirty–six, four thousand and ninety–nine
c Two hundred and seventy–one, ten thousand, seven hundred and fourty–four **3 a** Five million, six hundred thousand
b Four million, seventy–five thousand, two hundred **c** Three million, seven thousand, nine hundred and fifty
d Two million, seven hundred and eight–two **4 a** 8 200 058 **b** 9 406 107 **c** 1 000 502 **d** 2 076 040
5 a 9, 15, 21, 23, 48, 54, 56, 85 **b** 25, 62, 86, 151, 219, 310, 400, 501 **c** 97, 357, 368, 740, 888, 2053, 4366
6 a 95, 89, 73, 52, 34, 25, 23, 7 **b** 700, 401, 174, 117, 80, 65, 18, 2 **c** 6227, 3928, 2034, 762, 480, 395, 89, 59 **7 a** Larger
b Larger **c** Smaller **d** Larger **e** Larger **f** Smaller **g** Larger **h** Smaller **i** Smaller
8 a Six different numbers **b** 368 **c** 863 **9** 408, 480, 804, 840 **10** 33, 35, 38, 53, 55, 58, 83, 85, 88

Exercise 1E

1 a 20 **b** 60 **c** 80 **d** 50 **e** 100 **f** 20 **g** 90 **h** 70 **i** 10 **j** 30 **k** 30 **l** 50 **m** 80 **n** 50 **o** 90
p 40 **q** 70 **r** 20 **s** 100 **t** 110 **2 a** 200 **b** 600 **c** 800 **d** 500 **e** 1000 **f** 100 **g** 600 **h** 400
i 1000 **j** 1100 **k** 300 **l** 500 **m** 800 **n** 500 **o** 900 **p** 400 **q** 700 **r** 800 **s** 1000 **t** 1100 **3 a** 1
b 2 **c** 1 **d** 1 **e** 3 **f** 2 **g** 3 **h** 2 **i** 1 **j** 1 **k** 3 **l** 2 **m** 74 **n** 126 **o** 184 **4 a** 2000 **b** 6000
c 8000 **d** 5000 **e** 10000 **f** 1000 **g** 6000 **h** 3000 **i** 9000 **j** 2000 **k** 3000 **l** 5000 **m** 8000 **n** 5000
o 9000 **p** 4000 **q** 7000 **r** 8000 **s** 1000 **t** 2000 **5 a** 230 **b** 570 **c** 720 **d** 520 **e** 910 **f** 230
g 880 **h** 630 **i** 110 **j** 300 **k** 280 **l** 540 **m** 770 **n** 500 **o** 940 **p** 380 **q** 630 **r** 350 **s** 1010
t 1070 **6 a** True **b** False **c** True **d** True **e** True **f** False **7 a** Man Utd v Liverpool **b** Bolton v QPR
c 17 000, 31 000, 21 000, 34 000, 29 000, 26 000, 25 000, 33 000, 35 000 **d** 17 400, 31 000, 21 000, 34 100, 29 500, 25 600, 25 300,
33 100, 34 900 **8 a** 35 min **b** 55 min **c** 15 min **d** 50 min **e** 10 min **f** 15 min **g** 45 min **h** 35 min
i 5 min **j** 0 min

Exercise 1F

1 a 713 **b** 151 **c** 6381 **d** 968 **e** 622 **f** 1315 **g** 8260 **h** 818 **i** 451 **j** 852 **2 a** 646 **b** 826
c 3818 **d** 755 **e** 2596 **f** 891 **g** 350 **h** 2766 **i** 8858 **j** 841 **k** 6831 **l** 7016 **m** 1003 **n** 4450
o 9944 **3 a** 450 **b** 563 **c** 482 **d** 414 **e** 285 **f** 486 **g** 244 **h** 284 **i** 333 **j** 216 **k** 2892 **l** 4417
m 3767 **n** 4087 **o** 1828 **4 a** 128 **b** 29 **c** 334 **d** 178 **e** 277 **f** 285 **g** 335 **h** 399 **i** 4032
j 4765 **k** 3795 **l** 5437 **5 a** 6, 7 **b** 4, 7 **c** 4, 8 **d** 7, 4, 9 **e** 6, 9, 7 **f** 6, 2, 7 **g** 2, 6, 6 **h** 4, 5, 9

i 4, 8, 8   **j** 4, 4, 9, 8   **6 a** 3, 5   **b** 8, 3   **c** 5, 8   **d** 8, 5, 4   **e** 6, 7, 5   **f** 1, 2, 1   **g** 2, 7, 7   **h** 5, 5, 6   **i** 8, 3, 8
j 1, 8, 8, 9

Exercise 1G

1 a 56   **b** 65   **c** 51   **d** 38   **e** 108   **f** 115   **g** 204   **h** 294   **i** 212   **j** 425   **k** 150   **l** 800   **m** 960
n 1360   **o** 1518   **2 a** 294   **b** 370   **c** 288   **d** 832   **e** 2163   **f** 2520   **g** 1644   **h** 3215   **i** 3000   **j** 2652
k 3696   **l** 1880   **m** 54 387   **n** 21 935   **o** 48 888   **3 a** 119   **b** 96   **c** 144   **d** 210   **e** 210   **4 a** 219   **b** 317
c 315   **d** 106   **e** 99   **f** 121   **g** 252   **h** 141   **i** 144   **j** 86   **k** 63   **l** 2909   **m** 416   **n** 251   **o** 1284
5 a 13   **b** 37   **c** 43   **d** 36   **e** 45

Examination questions (Chapter 1)

1 a 12, 47   **b** 4   **2 a i** 52 406   **ii** 52 000   **b i** ten thousand two hundred and ninety two   **ii** 10 300
3 a Four million, twenty–three thousand, five hundred and forty–eight   **b** 400 000   **4 a** $(2 + 4) \times 3 = 18$ and $2 + (4 \times 3) = 14$
5 a i 1500   **ii** 150 000   **b i** 10   **ii** 10 000   **6 a** Ben Nevis, Snowdon, Scafell Pike, Clisham, Sawell, Yes Tor
b Between 800 m and 978 m   **7 a** 34 650   **b** 34 749   **8 a** True: same numbers multiplied together   **b** False: switching
numbers changes result   **c** True: LHS = RHS   **9 a i** 7431   **ii** 1347   **iii** $34 = 2 \times 17$ **b** 0   **c** 6

Exercise 2A

1 a $\frac{1}{4}$ b $\frac{1}{3}$ c $\frac{5}{8}$ d $\frac{7}{12}$ e $\frac{4}{9}$ f $\frac{3}{10}$ g $\frac{3}{8}$ h $\frac{15}{16}$ i $\frac{5}{12}$ j $\frac{7}{18}$ k $\frac{4}{8}=\frac{1}{2}$ l $\frac{4}{12}=\frac{1}{3}$ m $\frac{6}{9}=\frac{2}{3}$ n $\frac{6}{10}=\frac{3}{5}$ o $\frac{4}{8}=\frac{1}{2}$
p $\frac{5}{64}$

Exercise 2B

1 a $\frac{3}{4}$ b $\frac{4}{8}=\frac{1}{2}$ c $\frac{3}{5}$ d $\frac{8}{10}=\frac{4}{5}$ e $\frac{2}{3}$ f $\frac{5}{7}$ g $\frac{7}{9}$ h $\frac{5}{6}$ i $\frac{4}{5}$ j $\frac{7}{8}$ k $\frac{5}{10}=\frac{1}{2}$ l $\frac{5}{7}$ m $\frac{4}{5}$ n $\frac{5}{6}$ o $\frac{5}{9}$ p $\frac{7}{11}$
2 a $\frac{2}{4}=\frac{1}{2}$ b $\frac{3}{5}$ c $\frac{3}{8}$ d $\frac{3}{10}$ e $\frac{1}{3}$ f $\frac{4}{6}=\frac{2}{3}$ g $\frac{3}{7}$ h $\frac{5}{9}$ i $\frac{4}{5}$ j $\frac{3}{7}$ k $\frac{3}{9}=\frac{1}{3}$ l $\frac{6}{10}=\frac{3}{5}$ m $\frac{3}{6}=\frac{1}{2}$ n $\frac{2}{8}=\frac{1}{4}$ o $\frac{2}{11}$
p $\frac{4}{10}=\frac{2}{5}$ 3 a 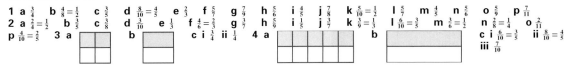 b c i $\frac{3}{4}$ ii $\frac{1}{4}$ 4 a b c i $\frac{6}{10}=\frac{3}{5}$ ii $\frac{8}{10}=\frac{4}{5}$
iii $\frac{7}{10}$

Exercise 2C

1 a $\frac{4}{24}$ b $\frac{8}{24}$ c $\frac{3}{24}$ d $\frac{16}{24}$ e $\frac{20}{24}$ f $\frac{18}{24}$ g $\frac{9}{24}$ h $\frac{15}{24}$ i $\frac{21}{24}$ j $\frac{12}{24}$ 2 a $\frac{11}{24}$ b $\frac{9}{24}$ c $\frac{7}{24}$ d $\frac{19}{24}$ e $\frac{23}{24}$ f $\frac{23}{24}$ g $\frac{21}{24}$
h $\frac{22}{24}$ i $\frac{19}{24}$ j $\frac{23}{24}$ 3 a $\frac{5}{20}$ b $\frac{5}{20}$ c $\frac{15}{20}$ d $\frac{16}{20}$ e $\frac{2}{20}$ f $\frac{10}{20}$ g $\frac{12}{20}$ h $\frac{8}{20}$ i $\frac{14}{20}$ j $\frac{6}{20}$ 4 a $\frac{9}{20}$ b $\frac{14}{20}$ c $\frac{11}{20}$ d $\frac{13}{20}$
e $\frac{19}{20}$

Exercise 2D

1 a $\frac{8}{20}$ b $\frac{3}{12}$ c $\frac{15}{40}$ d $\frac{12}{15}$ e $\frac{15}{18}$ f $\frac{12}{28}$ g $\times2,\ \frac{6}{20}$ h $\times3,\ \frac{3}{9}$ i $\times4,\ \frac{12}{20}$ j) $\times6,\ \frac{12}{18}$ k $\times3,\ \frac{9}{12}$ l $\times5,\ \frac{25}{40}$ m $\times2,\ \frac{14}{20}$
n $\times4,\ \frac{4}{24}$ o $\times5,\ \frac{15}{40}$ 2 a $\frac{1}{2}=\frac{2}{4}=\frac{3}{6}=\frac{4}{8}=\frac{5}{10}=\frac{6}{12}$ b $\frac{1}{3}=\frac{2}{6}=\frac{3}{9}=\frac{4}{12}=\frac{5}{15}=\frac{6}{18}$ c $\frac{3}{4}=\frac{6}{8}=\frac{9}{12}=\frac{12}{16}=\frac{15}{20}=\frac{18}{24}$ d $\frac{2}{5}=\frac{4}{10}=\frac{6}{15}=\frac{8}{20}=\frac{10}{25}=\frac{12}{30}$
e $\frac{3}{7}=\frac{6}{14}=\frac{9}{21}=\frac{12}{28}=\frac{15}{35}=\frac{18}{42}$ 3 a $\frac{2}{3}$ b $\frac{4}{5}$ c $\frac{5}{7}$ d $\div6,\ \frac{2}{3}$ e $\frac{2}{5}$ f $\div3,\ \frac{7}{10}$ 4 a $\frac{2}{3}$ b $\frac{1}{3}$ c $\frac{2}{3}$ d $\frac{3}{4}$ e $\frac{1}{2}$ f $\frac{1}{2}$ g $\frac{7}{8}$
h $\frac{4}{5}$ i $\frac{1}{2}$ j $\frac{1}{4}$ k $\frac{5}{7}$ l $\frac{5}{7}$ m $\frac{5}{7}$ n $\frac{2}{3}$ o $\frac{2}{5}$ p $\frac{3}{4}$ q $\frac{2}{3}$ r $\frac{7}{10}$ s $\frac{3}{4}$ t $\frac{3}{5}$ u $\frac{2}{3}$ v $\frac{3}{4}$ w $\frac{3}{2}$ x $\frac{3}{2}$ y $\frac{7}{2}$
5 a $\frac{1}{2}, \frac{2}{3}, \frac{5}{6}$ b $\frac{1}{3}, \frac{5}{8}, \frac{3}{4}$ c $\frac{2}{5}, \frac{1}{2}, \frac{7}{10}$ d $\frac{7}{12}, \frac{2}{3}, \frac{3}{4}$ e $\frac{1}{6}, \frac{1}{4}, \frac{1}{3}$ f $\frac{3}{4}, \frac{4}{5}, \frac{9}{10}$ g $\frac{7}{10}, \frac{3}{5}, \frac{1}{2}$ h $\frac{7}{10}, \frac{1}{3}, \frac{3}{5}$

Exercise 2E

1 $2\frac{1}{3}$ 2 $2\frac{2}{3}$ 3 $2\frac{1}{4}$ 4 $1\frac{3}{7}$ 5 $2\frac{2}{5}$ 6 $1\frac{2}{3}$ 7 $2\frac{3}{4}$ 8 $3\frac{3}{4}$ 9 $3\frac{1}{3}$ 10 $2\frac{1}{7}$ 11 $2\frac{5}{6}$ 12 $3\frac{3}{5}$ 13 $4\frac{3}{4}$ 14 $3\frac{1}{7}$ 15 $1\frac{3}{11}$
16 $1\frac{1}{11}$ 17 $5\frac{3}{5}$ 18 $2\frac{5}{8}$ 19 $5\frac{5}{7}$ 20 $8\frac{2}{5}$ 21 $2\frac{1}{10}$ 22 $2\frac{1}{2}$ 23 $1\frac{2}{3}$ 24 $3\frac{1}{8}$ 25 $2\frac{3}{10}$ 26 $2\frac{1}{11}$ 27 $7\frac{3}{8}$ 28 $5\frac{3}{7}$
29 5 30 2 31 $\frac{10}{3}$ 32 $\frac{35}{9}$ 33 $\frac{9}{5}$ 34 $\frac{37}{7}$ 35 $\frac{41}{10}$ 36 $\frac{17}{9}$ 37 $\frac{5}{2}$ 38 $\frac{13}{3}$ 39 $\frac{43}{9}$ 40 $\frac{29}{8}$ 41 $\frac{19}{3}$ 42 $\frac{89}{9}$ 43 $\frac{59}{7}$
44 $\frac{16}{5}$ 45 $\frac{35}{9}$ 46 $\frac{28}{9}$ 47 $\frac{26}{5}$ 48 $\frac{11}{4}$ 49 $\frac{30}{7}$ 50 $\frac{49}{6}$ 51 $\frac{26}{5}$ 52 $\frac{37}{6}$ 53 $\frac{61}{5}$ 54 $\frac{13}{8}$ 55 $\frac{71}{10}$ 56 $\frac{73}{9}$ 57 $\frac{61}{8}$ 58 $\frac{21}{2}$
59 $\frac{17}{16}$ 60 $\frac{19}{4}$

Exercise 2F

1 a $\frac{6}{8}=\frac{3}{4}$ b $\frac{10}{4}=\frac{5}{2}$ c $\frac{6}{9}=\frac{2}{3}$ d $\frac{3}{4}$ e $\frac{6}{10}=\frac{3}{5}$ f $\frac{6}{12}=\frac{1}{2}$ g $\frac{8}{16}=\frac{1}{2}$ h $\frac{10}{16}=\frac{5}{8}$ 2 a $\frac{12}{10}=\frac{6}{5}=1\frac{1}{5}$ b $\frac{9}{8}=1\frac{1}{8}$ c $\frac{9}{8}=1\frac{1}{8}$
d $\frac{13}{8}=1\frac{5}{8}$ e $\frac{11}{8}=1\frac{3}{8}$ f $\frac{7}{6}=1\frac{1}{6}$ g $\frac{9}{6}=\frac{3}{2}=1\frac{1}{2}$ h $\frac{5}{4}=1\frac{1}{4}$ 3 a $\frac{10}{8}=\frac{5}{4}=1\frac{1}{4}$ b $\frac{6}{4}=\frac{3}{2}=1\frac{1}{2}$ c $\frac{5}{5}=1$ d $\frac{16}{8}=\frac{5}{8}=1\frac{3}{8}$
e $\frac{10}{8}=\frac{5}{4}=1\frac{1}{4}$ f $\frac{22}{16}=\frac{11}{8}=1\frac{3}{8}$ g $\frac{16}{12}=\frac{4}{3}=1\frac{1}{3}$ h $\frac{18}{16}=\frac{9}{8}=1\frac{1}{8}$ i $1\frac{3}{4}$ j $3\frac{1}{4}$ k $6\frac{1}{4}$ l $3\frac{5}{6}$ 4 a $\frac{4}{8}=\frac{1}{2}$ b $\frac{6}{10}=\frac{3}{5}$ c $\frac{1}{4}$ d $\frac{3}{8}$
e $\frac{1}{4}$ f $\frac{3}{8}$ g $\frac{4}{10}=\frac{2}{5}$ h $\frac{5}{16}$ i $1\frac{1}{4}$ j $1\frac{1}{3}$ k $2\frac{1}{4}$ l $2\frac{1}{8}$

Exercise 2G

1 $\frac{1}{8}$ 2 a $\frac{1}{4}$ b $\frac{3}{8}$ c Brenda 3 $\frac{4}{6}=\frac{2}{3}$ 4 $\frac{3}{8}$ 5 $\frac{2}{5}$ 6 $\frac{3}{8}$ 7 $\frac{4}{11}$ 8 $\frac{1}{6}$ 9 $\frac{5}{8}$

Exercise 2H

1 a 18 b 10 c 18 d 28 e 15 f 18 g 48 h 45 2 a £1800 b 128g c 160kg d £116
e 65 litres f 90 min g 292 d h 21h i 18h j 2370 miles 3 a $\frac{5}{8}$ of 40 = 25 b $\frac{3}{4}$ of 280 = 210 c $\frac{4}{5}$ of 70 = 56
d $\frac{5}{6}$ of 72 = 60 e $\frac{3}{5}$ of 95 = 57 f $\frac{3}{4}$ of 340 = 255 4 £6080 5 £3150 6 23 000 7 52 kg 8 a 856 b 187 675
9 a £50 b £550 10 a 180g b 900g 11 a £120 b £240 12 £6400

Exercise 2I

1 a $\frac{1}{3}$ b $\frac{1}{5}$ c $\frac{1}{5}$ d $\frac{5}{24}$ e $\frac{2}{5}$ f $\frac{1}{6}$ g $\frac{2}{7}$ h $\frac{1}{3}$ 2 $\frac{3}{5}$ 3 $\frac{12}{31}$ 4 $\frac{7}{12}$

Exercise 2J

1 $\frac{1}{6}$ 2 $\frac{3}{20}$ 3 $\frac{2}{9}$ 4 $\frac{1}{6}$ 5 $\frac{1}{4}$ 6 $\frac{2}{5}$ 7 $\frac{1}{2}$ 8 $\frac{1}{2}$ 9 $\frac{3}{14}$ 10 $\frac{35}{48}$

Examination questions (Chapter 2)

1 $\frac{3}{8}$ 2 $3\frac{7}{8}$ 3 100 g 4 £3.60 5 a Shade 16 squares b i $\frac{20}{24}=\frac{5}{6}$ ii $\frac{4}{24}=\frac{1}{6}$ 6 28 kg 7 a $\frac{3}{8}$ b 4 8 780g
9 $1\frac{1}{2}$ inches

Answers

Exercise 3A

1 –£5 **2** –£9 **3** Profit **4** –200 m **5** – 50 m **6** Above **7** –3 h **8** –5 h **9** After **10** –2 °C **11** –8 °C
12 Above **13** –70 km **14** –200 km **15** North **16** +5 m **17** –5 mph **18** –2

Exercise 3B

1 Many different correct answers to each part **2** Many different answers to each part **3 a** Is smaller than
b Is bigger than **c** Is smaller than **d** Is smaller than **e** Is bigger than **f** Is smaller than **g** Is smaller than
h Is bigger than **i** Is bigger than **j** Is smaller than **k** Is smaller than **l** Is bigger than **4 a** Is smaller than
b Is smaller than **c** Is smaller than **d** Is bigger than **e** Is smaller than **f** Is smaller than
5 a < **b** > **c** < **d** < **e** < **f** > **g** < **h** > **i** > **j** > **k** < **l** < **m** > **n** > **o** < **p** >

6 a

–5	–4	–3	–2	–1	O	1	2	3	4	5

b

–25	–20	–15	–10	–5	O	5	10	15	20	25

c

–10	–8	–6	–4	–2	O	2	4	6	8	10

d

–50	–40	–30	–20	–10	O	10	20	30	40	50

e

–15	–12	–9	–6	–3	O	3	6	9	12	15

f

–20	–16	–12	–8	–4	O	4	8	12	16	20

g

$-2\frac{1}{2}$	–2	$-1\frac{1}{2}$	–1	$-\frac{1}{2}$	O	$\frac{1}{2}$	1	$1\frac{1}{2}$	2	$2\frac{1}{2}$

h

–100	–80	–60	–40	–20	O	20	40	60	80	100

i

–250	–200	–150	–100	–50	O	50	100	150	200	250

Exercise 3C

1 a –2° **b** –3° **c** –2° **d** –3° **e** –2° **f** –3° **g** 3 **h** 3 **i** –1 **j** –1 **k** 2 **l** –3 **m** –4 **n** –6 **o** –6
p –1 **q** –5 **r** –4 **s** 4 **t** –1 **u** –5 **v** –4 **w** –5 **x** –5 **2 a** –4 **b** –4 **c** –10 **d** 2 **e** 8 **f** –5
g 2 **h** 5 **i** –7 **j** –12 **k** 13 **l** 25 **m** –32 **n** –30 **o** –5 **p** –8 **q** –12 **r** 10 **s** –36 **t** –14 **u** 41
v 12 **w** –40 **x** –101 **3 a** 6 **b** –5 **c** 6 **d** –1 **e** –2 **f** –6 **g** –6 **h** –2 **i** 3 **j** 0 **k** –6 **l** –6
m 8 **n** 1 **o** –9 **p** –9 **q** –5 **r** –80 **s** –7 **t** –1 **u** –47

Exercise 3D

1 a 6 **b** 7 **c** 8 **d** 6 **e** 8 **f** 10 **g** 2 **h** –3 **i** 1 **j** +2 **k** –1 **l** –7 **m** 2 **n** –3 **o** 1 **p** –5
q 3 **r** –4 **s** –3 **t** –8 **u** –10 **v** –9 **w** –4 **x** –9 **2 a** –8 **b** –10 **c** –11 **d** –3 **e** 2 **f** –5 **g** 1
h 4 **i** 7 **j** –8 **k** –5 **l** –11 **m** 11 **n** 6 **o** 8 **p** 8 **q** –2 **r** –1 **s** –9 **t** –5 **u** 5 **v** –9 **w** 8
x 0 **3 a** 3 °C **b** 0 °C **c** –3 °C **d** –5 °C **e** –11 °C **4 a** 10 °C **b** 7 °C **c** 9 °C **5** –9, –6, –5, –1, 1, 2, 3, 8
6 a –3 **b** –4 **c** –2 **d** –7 **e** –14 **f** –6 **g** –12 **h** –10 **i** 4 **j** –4 **k** 14 **l** 11 **m** –4 **n** –1
o –10 **p** –5 **q** –3 **r** 5 **s** –4 **t** –8 **7 a** 2 **b** –3 **c** –5 **d** –7 **e** –10 **f** –20 **8 a** 2 **b** 4 **c** –1
d –5 **e** –11 **f** 8 **9 a** 13 **b** 2 **c** 5 **d** 4 **e** 11 **f** –2 **10 a** –10 **b** –5 **c** –2 **d** 4 **e** 7 **f** –4
13 a –5 **b** 6 **c** 0 **d** 2 **e** 13 **f** 0 **g** –6 **h** –2 **i** 212 **j** 5 **k** 3 **l** 3 **m** –67 **n** 7 **o** 25
14 a –1, 0, 1, 2, 3 **b** –6, –5, –4, –3, –2 **c** –3, –2, –1, 0, 1 **d** –8, –7, –6, –5, –4 **e** –9, –8, –7, –6, –5 **f** 3, 4, 5, 6, 7
g –12, –11, –10, –9. –8 **h** –16, –15, –14, –13, –12 **i** –2, –1, 0, 1, 2, 3; –4, –3, –2, –1, 0, 1
j –12, –11, –10, –9, –8, –7; –14, –13, –12, –11, –10, –9 **k** –2, –1, 0, 1, 2, 3; 0, 1, 2, 3, 4, 5
l –8, –7, –6, –5, –4, –3, –2; –5, –4, –3, –2, –1, 0, 1 **m** –10, –9, –8, –7, –6, –5, –4; –1, 0, 1, 2, 3, 4, 5
n 3, 4, 5, 6, 7, 8, 9; –5, –4, –3, –2, –1, 0, 1 **15 a** +5 + +5 = +10 **b** +5 + –9 = –4 **c** +5 – –9 = +14 **d** +5 – +5 = 0
16 a +5 + +7 – –9 = +21 **b** +5 + –9 – +7 = –11 **c** +7 + –7, +4 + –4 **17 a** –4 **b** 3 **c** 4 **d** –6 **e** 7 **f** 2
g 7 **h** –6 **i** –7 **j** 0 **k** 0 **l** –6 **m** –7 **n** –9 **o** 4 **p** 0 **q** 5 **r** 0 **s** 10 **t** –5 **u** 3 **v** –3
w –9 **x** 0 **y** –3 **z** –3

Exercise 3E

1
-1	-9	-2
-5	-4	-3
-6	1	-7

−12

2
1	-4	3
2	0	-2
-3	4	-1

0

3
0	-14	-1
-6	-5	-4
-9	4	-10

−15

4
2	-12	1
-4	-3	-2
-7	6	-8

−9

5
-3	-6	-9
-12	-6	0
-3	-6	-9

−18

6
-2	-18	-1
-6	-7	-8
-13	4	-12

−21

7
-4	-12	-5
-8	-7	-6
-9	-2	-10

−21

8
2	1	-3
-5	0	5
3	-1	-2

0

9
-2	-10	-3
-6	-5	-4
-7	0	-8

−15

10
-8	-1	-3	-14
-8	-9	-7	-2
-11	-6	-4	-5
1	-10	-12	-5

−26

11
-7	5	2	-16
-6	-8	-5	3
-11	-3	0	-2
8	-10	-13	-1

−16

Examination questions (Chapter 3)

1 a +124 °C   **b i** Any answer greater than −62 °C   **ii** Any answer between −273 °C and −186 °C   **2 a** −6 °C   **b** 9 °C
c −2 °C   **3 a** Glasgow   **b** 6 °C   **c** Cardiff   **d** Hull

4 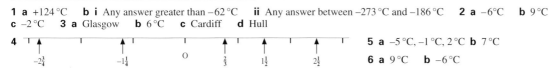   **5 a** −5 °C, −1 °C, 2 °C   **b** 7 °C

6 a 9 °C   **b** −6 °C

Exercise 4A

1 a 3, 6, 9, 12, 15   **b** 7, 14, 21, 28, 35   **c** 9, 18, 27, 36, 45   **d** 11, 22, 33, 44, 55   **e** 16, 32, 48, 64, 80
2 a 254, 108, 68, 162, 98, 812, 102, 270   **b** 111, 255, 108, 162, 711, 615, 102, 75, 270   **c** 255, 615, 75, 270
d 108, 162, 711, 270   **3. a** 72, 132, 216, 312, 168, 144   **b** 161, 91, 168, 294   **c** 72, 102, 132, 78, 216, 312, 168, 144, 294
4 a 98   **b** 99   **c** 96   **d** 95   **e** 98   **5 a** 1002   **b** 1008   **c** 1008

Exercise 4B

1 a 1, 2, 5, 10   **b** 1, 2, 4, 7, 14, 28   **c** 1, 2, 3, 6, 9, 18   **d** 1, 17   **e** 1, 5, 25   **f** 1, 2, 4, 5, 8, 10, 20, 40
g 1, 2, 3, 5, 6, 10, 15, 30   **h** 1, 3, 5, 9, 15, 45   **i** 1, 2, 3, 4, 6, 8, 12, 24   **j** 1, 2, 4, 8, 16
2 a 1, 2, 3, 4, 5, 6, 8, 10, 12, 15, 20, 24, 30, 40, 60, 120   **b** 1, 2, 3, 5, 6, 10, 15, 25, 30, 50, 75, 150
c 1, 2, 3, 4, 6, 8, 9, 12, 16, 18, 24, 36, 48, 72, 144   **d** 1, 2, 3, 4, 5, 6, 9, 10, 12, 15, 18, 20, 30, 36, 45, 60, 90, 180
e 1, 13, 169   **f** 1, 2, 3, 4, 6, 9, 12, 18, 27, 36, 54, 108   **g** 1, 2, 4, 7, 14, 28, 49, 98, 196   **h** 1, 3, 9, 17, 51, 153
i 1, 2, 3, 6, 9, 11, 18, 22, 33, 66, 99, 198   **j** 1, 199   **3 a** 55   **b** 67   **c** 29   **d** 39   **e** 65   **f** 80   **g** 80   **h** 70   **i** 81
j 50   **4 a** 2 **b** 2 **c** 3 **d** 5 **e** 3 **f** 3 **g** 7 **h** 5 **i** 10 **j** 11

Exercise 4C

1 36, 49, 64, 81, 100, 121, 144, 169, 196, 225, 256, 289, 324, 361, 400   **2** 4, 9, 16, 25, 36, 49   **3 c** 3   **e** 5   **f** 7
g Odd numbers   **4 a** 50, 65, 82   **b** 98, 128, 162   **c** 51, 66, 83   **d** 48, 63, 80   **e** 149, 164, 181   **5 a** 529 **b** 3249 **c** 5929
d 15129 **e** 23104 **f** 10.24 **g** 90.25 **h** 566.44 **i** 16 **j** 144   **6 a** 25, 169, 625, 1681, 3721   **b** Answers in each row are the same.

Exercise 4D

1 a 2   **b** 5   **c** 7   **d** 1   **e** 9   **f** 10   **g** 8   **h** 3   **i** 6   **j** 4   **k** 11   **l** 12   **m** 20   **n** 30   **o** 13
2 a 5   **b** 6   **c** 10   **d** 7   **e** 8   **f** 4   **g** 3   **h** 9   **i** 1   **j** 12   **3 a** 81   **b** 40   **c** 100   **d** 14   **e** 36   **f** 15
g 49   **h** 12   **i** 25   **j** 21   **k** 121   **l** 16   **m** 64   **n** 17   **o** 441   **4 a** 24   **b** 31   **c** 45   **d** 40   **e** 67   **f** 101
g 3.6   **h** 6.5   **i** 13.9   **j** 22.2

Exercise 4E

1 a 27   **b** 125   **c** 216   **d** 1728   **e** 16   **f** 256   **a** 625   **h** 32   **i** 2187   **j** 1024
2 a 100   **b** 1000   **c** 10 000   **d** 100 000   **e** 1 000 000   **f** The power is the same as the number of zeros   **i** 100 000 000
ii 10 000 000 000   **iii** 1 000 000 000 000 000

Examination questions (Chapter 4)

1 a 10, 25   **b** 16, 25   **c** 7, 13, 19   **2 a** 9, 64   **b** 8, 64   **c** 3, 41   **d** 8, 28   **3 a i**   1, 4, 9, 16, 25, 36, 49
ii Any one of 2, 4, 5, 10, 20, 25   **iii** Any one of 5, 10, 15, 20, 25, 30, 35, 40, 45
iv Any one of 2, 3, 5, 7, 11, 13, 17, 19, 23, 29, 31, 37, 41, 43, 47   **b i** 49   **ii** 2   **iii** 42   **4 a** 5, 10, 15, 20, 25
b 30, 45, 60, 75, 90, …, 300, 600 …   **c** For example: 105, 120, 135 …   **5 a** 6   **b** 2, 3, 5   **6** 384   **7 i** 8, 16, 24, 32, 40
ii 36   **iii** $2 \times 5 \times 7$ **iv a** 9   **b** 5   **8 i** 8   **ii** 3, 9   **iii** 2, 3   **iv**

8	3	4
1	5	9
6	7	2

9 a 73   **b** 0   **c** 96
10 a $3 \times 3 \times 3$, $4 \times 4 \times 4 = 64$ **b** $100 = 10^2$
c $1^3 + 2^3 + 3^3 + 4^3 + 5^3 + 6^3 = 441 = 21^2$

Revision for Chapters 1 to 4

1 a 14   **b** 14   **c** 28   **d** 16   **e** 7   **f** 9   **g** 13   **h** 4   **i** 42   **j** 5   **k** 40   **l** 3   **m** 15   **n** 6   **o** 17   **p** 14
q 37   **r** 8   **s** 25   **t** 54   **u** 35   **v** 7   **w** 27   **x** 72   **y** 36   **2 a** Three million, eighty-five thousand, two hundred
b Twelve million, seven thousand, eight hundred and six   **3** 22, 25, 27, 52, 55, 57, 72, 75, 77   **4 a** $(3+5) \times 6 = 48$
b $30 - 2 \times (3 + 1) = 22$ **5 a** 105 **d b** 216   **c** 288   **6 a** 34   **b** 23 weeks   **c** 23 m   **d** 24 d   **7 a** 1   **b** $\frac{3}{5}$ **c** $\frac{11}{8} = 1\frac{3}{8}$
d $\frac{13}{10} = 1\frac{3}{10}$ **e** $\frac{1}{3}$ **f** $\frac{4}{6} = \frac{2}{3}$ **g** 1   **h** $\frac{3}{9} = \frac{1}{3}$ **i** $\frac{1}{5}$ **j** $\frac{5}{7}$ **k** $\frac{3}{9} = \frac{1}{3}$ **l** $\frac{4}{10} = \frac{2}{5}$ **m** $\frac{5}{6}$ **n** $\frac{9}{8} = 1\frac{1}{4}$ **o** $\frac{12}{11} = 1\frac{1}{11}$ **p** $\frac{12}{10} = \frac{6}{5} = 1\frac{1}{5}$
8 a $\frac{13}{8} = 1\frac{5}{8}$ **b** $\frac{5}{10} = \frac{1}{2}$ **c** $\frac{5}{4} = 1\frac{1}{4}$ **d** $\frac{3}{8}$ **e** $\frac{3}{4}$ **f** $\frac{1}{8}$ **g** $\frac{14}{10} = \frac{7}{5} = 1\frac{2}{5}$ **h** $\frac{3}{16}$ **9 a** £8   **b** 42 kg   **c** 48 min   **d** 56 cm
10 a $3\frac{7}{8}$ **b** $9\frac{1}{4}$ **c** $3\frac{3}{8}$ **d** $5\frac{1}{8}$ **11 a** -4 **b** -5 **c** -3 **d** -5 **e** -4 **f** -7 **g** -11 **h** -11 **i** 3   **j** -14
k 14   **l** 10   **m** -5 **n** -3 **o** -11 **p** -4 **q** -2 **r** 4   **s** -3 **t** -18 **12 a** $5°$ **b** $-7°C$
13 a 294, 207, 75, 78, 261, 117, 402, 720, 222   **b** 145, 75, 305, 815, 65, 720   **c** 207, 261, 117, 720   **14 a** 1, 2, 3, 4, 6, 12
b 1, 2, 4, 7, 14, 28   **c** 1, 2, 4, 8, 16   **d** 1, 19   **e** 1, 5, 7, 35   **f** 1, 2, 3, 5, 6, 10, 15, 30   **g** 1, 2, 3, 4, 6, 9, 12, 18, 36
h 1, 3, 5, 9, 15, 45   **i** 1, 2, 3, 4, 6, 8, 12, 24   **j** 1, 2, 3, 6, 9, 18   **15 a** 25   **b** 50   **c** 64   **d** 14   **e** 49   **f** 15   **g** 81
h 11   **i** 1   **j** 21   **k** 144   **l** 16   **m** 9   **n** 17   **o** 484   **16** 23, 29, 31, 37, 41, 43, 47   **17 a** 7, 13, 19   **b** 4, 10, 16
c 4, 16   **d** 21

Exercise 5A

1 10 cm   **2** 8 cm   **3** 14 cm   **4** 12 cm   **5** 16 cm   **6** 6 cm   **7** 10 cm   **8** 12 cm   **9** 12 cm   **10** 14 cm   **11** 12 cm
12 12 cm

Exercise 5B

1 a 10 cm^2 **b** 11 cm^2 **c** 13 cm^2 **d** 12 cm^2 (Estimates only)

Exercise 5C

1 35 cm^2, 24 cm   **2** 33 cm^2, 28 cm   **3** 45 cm^2, 36 cm   **4** 70 cm^2, 34 cm   **5** 56 cm^2, 30 cm   **6** 10 cm^2, 14 cm
7 48 cm^2, 28 cm   **8** 77 cm^2, 36 cm   **9 a** 20 cm, 21 cm^2 **b** 18 cm, 20 cm^2 **c** 2 cm, 8 cm^2 **d** 3 cm, 15 cm^2
e 3 cm, 18 cm   **f** 4 cm, 22 cm   **g** 5 cm, 10 cm^2 **h** 7 cm, 24 cm   **10** A = 1 m^2, B = 10 000 cm^2, 1 m^2 = 10 000 cm^2,

Exercise 5D

1 30 cm^2 **2** 40 cm^2 **3** 51 cm^2 **4** 35 cm^2 **5** 43 cm^2 **6** 51 cm^2 **7** 48 cm^2 **8** 33 cm^2

Exercise 5E

1 a 6 cm^2, 12 cm   **b** 120 cm^2, 60 cm   **c** 30 cm^2, 30 cm   **2 a** 21 cm^2 **b** 55 cm^2 **c** 165 cm^2 **3** 84 m^2 **4** 40 cm^2
b 49 cm^2 **c** 36 cm^2 **5 c** 75 cm^2

Exercise 5F

1 a 21 cm^2 **b** 12 cm^2 **c** 14 cm^2 **d** 55 cm^2 **e** 90 cm^2 **f** 140 cm^2 **2 a** 28 cm^2 **b** 8 cm   **c** 4 cm   **d** 3 cm
e 7 cm   **f** 44 cm^2 **3 a** 40 cm^2 **b** 65 m^2 **c** 80 cm^2 **4 a** 65 cm^2 **b** 50 m^2 **5** For example: height 10 cm,
base 10 cm; height 5 cm, base 20 cm; height 25 cm, base 4 cm; height 50 cm, base 2 cm

Exercise 5G

1 96 cm^2 **2** 70 cm^2 **3** 20 m^2 **4** 125 cm^2 **5** 10 cm^2 **6** 112 m^2

Examination questions (Chapter 5)

1 About 18 km^2 **2 a** 30 cm   **b** 27 cm^2 **3 a** 26 cm   **b** 6 cm^2 **4 a** 24 m   **b** 22 m^2 **5 a** 35 cm^2 **b** 27$\frac{1}{2}$ m^2
6 300 km^2 **7** 34 cm^2 **8** 33 cm^2 **9 a** 21 m   **b** 23$\frac{1}{2}$ m^2 **10 a** 8   **b** 800 cm^2 **c** 1.4 m

Exercise 6A

1 a Observation   **b** Sampling   **c** Observation   **d** Sampling   **e** Observation   **f** Experiment

2 a

Goals	0	1	2	3
Frequency	6	8	4	2

b 1 goal   **c** 22

3 a

Score	1	2	3	4	5	6
Frequency	5	6	6	6	3	4

b 30   **c** Yes, frequencies are similar

4 a

Temperature (°C)	14–16	17–19	20–22	23–25	26–28
Frequency	5	10	8	5	2

b 17–19 °C

c Getting warmer in the first half and then getting cooler towards the end.

5 a

Height (cm)	151–155	156–160	161–165	166–170	171–175	176–180	181–185	186–190
Frequency	2	5	5	7	5	4	3	1

b 166 – 170 cm

Exercise 6B

1 a May 9 h, Jun 11 h, Jul 12 h, Aug 11 h, Sep 10 h   **b** July   **c** Visual impact, easy to understand   **2 a** Simon   **b** £165
c Difficult to show fractions of a symbol   **3** 1 symbol = 5 cars   **4** 1 symbol = 1 pint

Exercise 6C

1 a Swimming   **b** 74   **c** For example: limited facilities   **d** No. It may not include people who are not fit

2 a

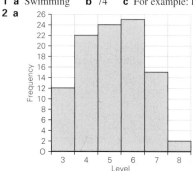

b $\frac{2}{5}$ **c** Easier to read the exact frequency

3 a

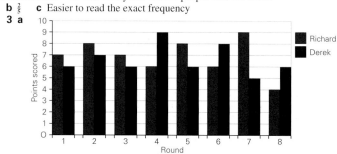

b Richard got the most points, but Derek was more consistent

4 a

Time (min)	1–10	11–20	21–30	31–40	41–50	51–60
Frequency	4	7	5	5	7	2

b

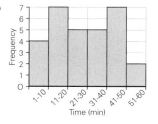

c Some live close to the school. Some live a good distance away and probably travel to school by bus

5 b

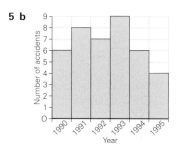

c Use the pictogram because an appropriate symbol makes more impact

Exercise 6D

1 a Tuesday, 52p   **b** 2p   **c** Friday   **d** £90   **2 a**   **b** About 16 500   **c** 1971 and 1981
d No. Do not know the reason why
the population started to decrease after 1981
3 a

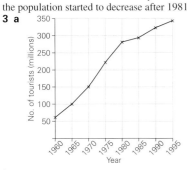

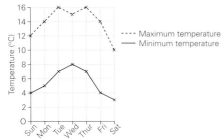

b Between 178 and 180 million   **c** 1970 and 1975
d Increasing. Better communications, cheaper air travel, more advertising, better living standards

4 a

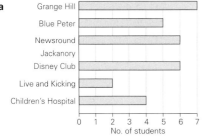

b 7 °C and 10 °C

Examination questions (Chapter 6)

1 a 144 cm   **b**

Height (cm)	140–149	150–159	160–169	170–179	180–189
Frequency	3	9	12	5	1

c i 30   **ii** 6

2 a Rolling Stones   **b** 80   **c** Ages of sample would be similar, so need more than one time period

3 a i 80   **ii** 50   **b i** ●●●●●   **ii** ●●◀   **c**

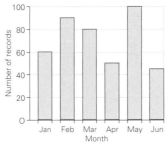

4 a

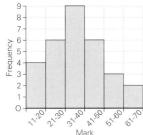

b Jackanory

5 a

Mark	11–20	21–30	31–40	41–50	51–60	61–70
Frequency	4	6	9	6	3	2

b

c i Second   **ii** More than half the students got over 40 marks in second test
6 a India   **b** New Zealand   **c** New Zealand, Britain, Canada
d Greece and Spain   **7 a** Friday   **b** More shop at weekend in 2000
c True, 51% is about $\frac{1}{2}$ **8 a** 27.5%   **c** 1993, line has steepest gradient

Exercise 7A

1 a $2 + x$ **b** $x - 6$ **c** $k + x$ **d** $x - t$ **e** $x + 3$ **f** $d + m$ **g** $b - y$ **h** $p + t + w$ **i** $8x$ **j** hj **k** $x \div 4$ or $\frac{x}{4}$
l $2 \div x$ or $\frac{2}{x}$ **m** $y \div t$, or $\frac{y}{t}$ **n** wt **o** a^2 **p** g^2 **2 a i** $P = 4, A = 1$ **ii** $P = 4x, A = x^2$ **iii** $P = 12, A = 9$
iv $P = 4t, A = t^2$ **b i** $P = 4s$ cm **ii** $A = s^2$ cm^2 **3** $x + 3$ yr **b** $x - 4$ yr **4** $F = 2C + 30$ **5** Rule **a** **6 a** $C = 100M$
b $N = 12F$ **c** $W = 4C$ **d** $H = P$ **7 a** $3n$ **b** $3n + 3$ **c** $n + 1$ **d** $n - 1$ **8** Rob: $2n$, Tom: $n + 2$, Vic: $n - 3$,
Wes: $2n + 3$ **9 a** $P = 8n, A = 9n^2$ **b** $P = 24n, A = 36n^2$ **10 a** £4 **b** £$(10 - x)$ **c** £$(y - x)$ **d** £$2x$ **11 a** 75p
b $15x$ p **c** $4A$ p **d** Ay p **12** £$(A - B)$ **13** £$A \div 5$, $\frac{£A}{5}$ **14** Dad: $(72 + x)$ yr, Me: $(T + x)$ yr **15 a** $T \div 2$, or $\frac{T}{2}$
b $T \div 2 + 4$, or $\frac{T}{2} + 4$ **c** $T - x$ **16 a** $8x$ **b** $12m$ **c** $18t$ **17** $3n - 3, 3n - 1, 3n - 6, 0, 2n, 3n - 3m$

Exercise 7B

1 a £t **b** £$(3t + 3)$ **2 a** $10x + 2y$ **b** $7x + y$ **c** $6x + y$ **3 a** $5a$ **b** $4b$ **c** $6c$ **d** $5d$ **e** $9e$ **f** $6f$ **g** $3g$
h h **i** $4i$ **j** $4j$ **k** $7k$ **l** $5l$ **m** $2m$ **n** 0 **o** $34x$ **p** $18p$ **q** $3q$ **r** 0 **s** $3s$ **t** $15t$ **u** $3u$ **v** $-v$
w $-w$ **x** $6x^2$ **y** $5y^2$ **z** 0 **4 a** $7x$ **b** $6y$ **c** $3t$ **d** $2m$ **e** $8k$ **f** $-2x$ **g** $-3t$ **h** $-5x$ **i** $-5k$ **j** $4x$
k $9a$ **l** $5t$ **m** $2m^2$ **n** 0 **o** f^2 **5 a** $5x + 9y$ **b** $2m + 5p$ **c** $7x + 5$ **d** $5x + 6$ **e** $5p$ **f** $5x + 6$ **g** $4p - 6$
h $6x + 2y$ **i** $5p + t + 5$ **j** $8w - 5k$ **k** $3 - 2x$ **l** 5 **m** c **n** $8k - 6y + 10$ **6 a** $3a + 2b$ **b** $2b + 3c$ **c** $2c + 3d$
d $5d + 2e$ **e** $5e + 7f$ **f** $f + 3g + 4h$ **g** $g + 2h$ **h** $h + j$ **i** $2i + 3k$ **j** $3j + 7k$ **k** $2k + 9p$ **l** $3k + 2m + 5p$
m $7m - 7n$ **n** $6n - 3p$ **o** $20x + 14y$ **p** $17p + 9q$ **q** $16q - 6r$ **r** 0 **s** $7s - 4t$ **t** $10t + 5s$ **u** $6u - 3v$ **v** $2v$
w $2w - 3y$ **x** $11x^2 - 5y$ **y** $-y^2 - 2z$ **z** $x^2 - z^2$ **7 a** $8x + 6$ **b** $3x + 16$ **c** $2x + 2y + 8$ **8 a** $2f + 6$ **b** $3k - 12$
c $4t + 4$ **d** $6d + 9$ **e** $12t - 8$ **f** $10m + 6$ **g** $20 + 8w$ **h** $6 - 8x$ **i** $12 + 15p$ **j** $10t + 15w$ **k** $12m - 8d$
l $6x + 15y$ **m** $8f + 6$ **n** $40 - 10t$ **o** $12g + 6t$ **p** $x^2 + 5x$ **q** $t^2 + 8t$ **r** $4s - s^2$ **9 a** $3(x + 2)$ **b** $5(x + 3)$
c $3(2x + 3)$ **d** $2(2x - 3)$ **e** $4(4y - 3)$ **f** $5(5t - 1)$ **g** $4(2z - 5)$ **h** $5(3 + 2t)$ **i** $7(3 - 4m)$ **j** $x(x + 8)$ **k** $t(t + 5)$
l $y(y - 7)$

Exercise 7C

1 i 8 **ii** 17 **iii** 32 **2 i** 3 **ii** 11 **iii** 43 **3 i** 9 **ii** 15 **iii** 29 **4 i** 9 **ii** 5 **iii** -1 **5 i** 13 **ii** 33
iii 78 **6 i** 10 **ii** 13 **iii** 58 **7 i** 32 **ii** 64 **iii** 224 **8 i** 6.5 **ii** 0.5 **iii** -2.5 **9 i** 2 **ii** 8 **iii** -10
10 i 3 **ii** 2.5 **iii** -5 **11 i** 6 **ii** 3 **iii** 2 **12 i** 12 **ii** 8 **iii** $1\frac{1}{2}$

Exercise 7D

1 a 11 **b** 17 **c** 13 **2 a** 7 **b** 14 **c** -2 **3 a** 7 **b** 32 **c** -3 **4 a** 27 **b** 5 **c** 0 **5 a** 75 **b** 8
c -6 **6 a** 900 **b** 180 **c** 0 **7 a** 5 **b** 8 **c** 1 **8 a** 4.4 **b** 2.6 **c** -1.6

Examination questions (Chapter 7)

1 12 cm^2 **2** 20 **3 a** $F = 2C + 30$ **b i** 138 **ii** 12 **4 a** 6 **b** $10 - x$ **c** $y - z$ **5 a** $8y$ **b** $6y + 6$ **c** $y = 3$
6 a $16q$ **b** $8n + 4p$ **7 a** $3b + 5g$ **b** $12a - 8$ **8 a** £60 **b** 1.5 **9 a i** $3f + 2g$ **ii** $3yt$ **iii** r^2 **b** $6t + 15$
10 a £4.40 **b** 20 words **11** 7 **12 a** $3a, 9a + 2b + 6c$ **b** 57

Exercise 8A

1 12 138　**2** 45 612　**3** 29 988　**4** 20 654　**5** 51 732　**6** 25 012　**7** 19 359　**8** 12 673　**9** 19 943　**10** 26 235
11 31 535　**12** 78 399　**13** 17 238　**14** 43 740　**15** 66 065　**16** 103 320　**17** 140 224　**18** 92 851　**19** 520 585
20 78 660

Exercise 8B

1 25　**2** 15　**3** 37　**4** 43　**5** 27　**6** 48　**7** 53　**8** 52　**9** 32　**10** 57　**11** 37 rem 15　**12** 25 rem 5
13 34 rem 11　**14** 54 rem 9　**15** 36 rem 11　**16** 17 rem 4　**17** 23　**18** 61 rem 14　**19** 42　**20** 27 rem 2

Exercise 8C

1 6000　**2** 312　**3** 68　**4** 38　**5** 57 600 m or 57.6 km　**6** 60 200　**7** 5819 litres　**8** £302.40　**9** 33　**10** 34 h
11 £1.75　**12** £136.80

Exercise 8D

1 a 4.8　**b** 3.8　**c** 2.2　**d** 8.3　**e** 3.7　**f** 46.9　**g** 23.9　**h** 9.5　**i** 11.1　**j** 33.5　**k** 7.1　**l** 46.8　**m** 0.1
n 0.1　**o** 0.6　**p** 65.0　**q** 213.9　**r** 76.1　**s** 455.2　**t** 51.0　**2 a** 5.78　**b** 2.36　**c** 0.98　**d** 33.09　**e** 6.01
f 23.57　**g** 91.79　**h** 8.00　**i** 2.31　**j** 23.92　**k** 6.00　**l** 1.01　**m** 3.51　**n** 96.51　**o** 0.01　**p** 0.07　**q** 7.81
r 569.90　**s** 300.00　**t** 0.01　**3 a** 4.6　**b** 0.08　**c** 45.716　**d** 94.85　**e** 602.1　**f** 671.76　**g** 7.1　**h** 6.904
i 13.78　**j** 0.1　**k** 4.002　**l** 60.0　**m** 11.99　**n** 899.996　**o** 0.1　**p** 0.01　**q** 6.1　**r** 78.393　**s** 200.00　**t** 5.1
4 a 9　**b** 9　**c** 3　**d** 7　**e** 3　**f** 8　**g** 3　**h** 8　**i** 6　**j** 4　**k** 7　**l** 2　**m** 47　**n** 23　**o** 96　**p** 33
q 154　**r** 343　**s** 704　**t** 910

Exercise 8E

1 a 49.8　**b** 21.3　**c** 48.3　**d** 33.3　**e** 5.99　**f** 8.08　**g** 90.2　**h** 21.2　**i** 12.15　**j** 13.08　**k** 13.26　**l** 24.36
2 a 1.4　**b** 1.8　**c** 4.8　**d** 3.8　**e** 3.75　**f** 5.9　**g** 3.7　**h** 3.77　**i** 3.7　**j** 1.4　**k** 11.8　**l** 15.3　**3 a** 30.7
b 6.6　**c** 3.8　**d** 16.7　**e** 11.8　**f** 30.2　**g** 43.3　**h** 6.73　**i** 37.95　**j** 4.7　**k** 3.8　**l** 210.5

Exercise 8F

1 a 7.2　**b** 7.6　**c** 18.8　**d** 37.1　**e** 32.5　**f** 28.8　**g** 10.0　**h** 55.2　**i** 61.5　**j** 170.8　**k** 81.6　**l** 96.5 **2 a** 9.36
b 10.35　**c** 25.85　**d** 12.78　**e** 1.82　**f** 3.28　**g** 2.80　**h** 5.52　**i** 42.21　**j** 56.16　**k** 7.65　**l** 48.96　**3 a** 1.8
b 1.4　**c** 1.4　**d** 1.2　**e** 2.13　**f** 0.69　**g** 2.79　**h** 1.21　**i** 1.89　**j** 1.81　**k** 0.33　**l** 1.9　**4 a** 1.75　**b** 1.28
c 1.85　**d** 3.65　**e** 1.66　**f** 1.45　**g** 1.42　**h** 1.15　**i** 3.35　**j** 0.98　**k** 2.3　**l** 1.46　**5 a** 1.89　**b** 1.51
c 0.264　**d** 4.265　**e** 1.224　**f** 0.182　**g** 0.093　**h** 2.042　**i** 1.908　**j** 2.8　**k** 4.25　**l** 18.5
6 Pack of 8 at £0.625 each pack　**7** £49.90　**8** Yes. She needed 8

Exercise 8G

1 a 89.28　**b** 298.39　**c** 66.04　**d** 167.98　**e** 2352.0　**f** 322.4　**g** 1117.8　**h** 4471.5　**i** 464.94　**j** 25.55
k 1047.2　**l** 1890.5　**2 a** £224.10　**b** £223.75　**c** £29.90　**3** £54.20　**4** £120.75

Exercise 8H

1 a 0.48　**b** 2.92　**c** 1.12　**d** 0.12　**e** 0.028　**f** 0.09　**g** 0.192　**h** 3.0264　**i** 7.134　**j** 50.96　**k** 3.0625
l 46.512　**2 a** 35, 35.04, 0.04　**b** 16, 18.24, 2.24　**c** 60, 59.67, 0.33　**d** 180, 172.86, 7.14　**e** 12, 12.18, 0.18
f 24, 26.016, 2.016　**g** 40, 40.664, 0.664　**h** 140, 140.58, 0.58

Exercise 8I

1 a $\frac{7}{10}$　**b** $\frac{2}{5}$　**c** $\frac{1}{2}$　**d** $\frac{3}{100}$　**e** $\frac{3}{50}$　**f** $\frac{13}{100}$　**g** $\frac{1}{4}$　**h** $\frac{19}{50}$　**i** $\frac{11}{20}$　**j** $\frac{16}{25}$　**2 a** 0.5　**b** 0.75　**c** 0.6　**d** 0.9　**e** 0.333
f 0.625　**g** 0.667　**h** 0.35　**i** 0.636　**j** 0.444　**3 a** 0.3, $\frac{1}{2}$, 0.6　**b** 0.3, $\frac{2}{5}$, 0.8　**c** 0.15, $\frac{1}{4}$, 0.35　**d** $\frac{7}{10}$, 0.71, 0.72
e 0.7, $\frac{3}{4}$, 0.8　**f** $\frac{1}{20}$, 0.08, 0.1　**g** 0.4, $\frac{1}{2}$, 0.55　**h** 1.2, 1.23, $1\frac{1}{4}$

Examination questions (Chapter 8)

1 £363.40　**2 i** £5.21　**ii** £4.79　**iii** 6　**3** 364　**4 a** 1488　**b** 50 × 30 = 1500　**5 a** 2.8　**b** 75 ÷ 25 = 3
6 a £20 × 150 = 3000　**b** £2664　**7 a** £6.87　**b** £3.13　**8 a** 12　**b** £1020　**9** 20 250　**10** £2.08　**11** £14
12 a 0.375　**b** $\frac{3}{8}$　**13** 13 boxes, 32 left over　**14** £3.85

Answers

1 a 14   **b** 25   **c** 28   **d** 9   **e** 31   **f** 13   **g** 24   **h** 8   **i** 54   **j** 17   **2 a** $16 - (2 + 3) = 11$
b $5 + (4 \times 3) - 1 = 16$ **3 a** 196   **b** 37 weeks   **c i** 78   **ii** 23   **4 a** 1   **b** $\frac{2}{8} = \frac{1}{4}$ **c** $\frac{9}{8} = 1\frac{1}{8}$ **d** $\frac{3}{5}$ **e** $\frac{5}{7}$
f $\frac{11}{10} = 1\frac{1}{10}$ **g** $\frac{4}{8} = \frac{1}{2}$ **h** $\frac{7}{5} = 1\frac{2}{5}$ **i** $\frac{4}{6} = \frac{2}{3}$ **j** $\frac{12}{9} = \frac{4}{3} = 1\frac{1}{3}$ **5 a** 4 days   **b** £15   **c** 12 weeks   **d** 20 cm   **e** 15 min
f 50 min   **g** 10 cm   **h** £35   **6 a** -4 **b** -5 **c** -7 **d** -7 **e** 8   **f** 9   **g** 1   **h** 2   **i** -5 **j** -5
7 a 7, 14, 21, 28, 35   **b** 1, 2, 3, 4, 6, 8, 12, 24   **c** 2, 3, 5, 7, 11, 13, 17, 19, 23, 29   **d** 1, 4, 9, 16, 25, 36, 49, 64, 81, 100
8 9^2 **9 a** 62 cm   **b** 52 cm   **10 a** 40.5 cm^2 **b** 21 cm^2 **c** 22 cm^2
11 a £1.83   **b**

Cost (£)	Tally(£)	Frequency(£)
1.50–1.59		5
1.60–1.69		3
1.70–1.79		6
1.80–1.89		2

c £1.50 – £1.59 ⊟⊟⊟⊟⊟
£1.60 – £1.69 ⊟⊟⊟
£1.70 – £1.79 ⊟⊟⊟⊟⊟⊟
£1.80 – £1.89 ⊟⊟

12

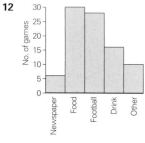

13 a 4 m   **b** $9 - x$ **c** $y - z$ **14 a** 40   **b** 16   **c** -6.5
15 a 6   **b i** $2a + 3b$ **ii** $21x + 15y$ **16 a i** $4 \times 5 \approx 20$ **ii** 20.14
b i $3 \times 7 \approx 21$ **ii** 18.25   **c i** $40 \times 4 \approx 160$ **ii** 134.52
d i $25 \times 10 \approx 250$ **ii** 219.24   **17** £807.10   **18** 16 boxes with 16 left over

Exercise 9A

1 a 1:3 **b** 3:4 **c** 2:3 **d** 2:3 **e** 2:5 **f** 2:5 **g** 5:8 **h** 25:6 **i** 3:2 **j** 8:3 **k** 7:3 **l** 5:2 **m** 1:6
n 3:8 **o** 5:3 **p** 4:5 **2 a** 1:3 **b** 3:2 **c** 5:12 **d** 8:1 **e** 17:15 **f** 25:7 **g** 4:1 **h** 5:6 **i** 1:24
j 48:1 **k** 5:2 **l** 3:14 **m** 2:1 **n** 3:10 **o** 31:200 **p** 5:8 **3** $\frac{7}{10}$ **4** $\frac{10}{25} = \frac{2}{5}$ **5 a** $\frac{3}{5}$ **b** $\frac{2}{5}$ **6 a** $\frac{7}{10}$ **b** $\frac{3}{10}$
7 John $\frac{2}{3}$, Joseph $\frac{1}{3}$ **8** Sugar $= \frac{5}{12}$, fruit $= \frac{7}{12}$

Exercise 9B

1 a 160 g : 240 g **b** 80 kg : 200 kg **c** 150 : 350 **d** 950 m : 50 m **e** 175 min : 125 min **f** £40 : £60 **g** £90 : £150
h 100 g : 500 g **i** £3.40 : £1.60 **j** 180 kg : 20 kg **2 a** 160 **b** 96 **3** 250 kg **4** 21 **5 a** Mott: No, Wright: Yes,
Brennan: No, Smith: No, Kaye: Yes **b** For example: 26, 30; 31, 38; 33, 37 **6 a** 1 : 400 000 **b** 1 : 125 000 **c** 1 : 250 000
d 1 : 25 000 **e** 1 : 20 000 **f** 1 : 40 000 **g** 1 : 62 500 **h** 1 : 10 000 **i** 1 : 60 000 **7 a** 1 : 1 000 000 **b** 47 km
c 8 mm **8 a** 1 : 250 000 **b** 2 km **c** 4.8 cm **9 a** 1 : 20 000 **b** 0.54 km **c** 40 cm **10 a** 1 : 1.6 **b** 1 : 3.25
c 1 : 1.125 **d** 1 : 1.44 **e** 1 : 5.4 **f** 1 : 1.5 **g** 1 : 4.8 **h** 1 : 42 **i** 1 : 1.25

Exercise 9C

1 a 3:2 **b** 32 **c** 80 **2 a** 100 **b** 160 **3** 0.5 litre **4** 102 **5** 1000 g **6** 10 125 **7** 5 **8** £2040
9 5.5 litres **10 a** 14 min **b** 75 min

Exercise 9D

1 18 mph **2** 280 miles **3** 52.5 mph **4** 11.50 am **5** 250 s **6 a** 75 mph **b** 6.5 h **c** 175 miles **d** 240 km
e 64 km/h **f** 325 km **g** 4.3 h (4 h 18 min) **7 a** 120 km **b** 48 km/h **8 a** 30 min **b** 6 mph **9 a** 7.75 h
b 52.9 mph **10 a** 2.25 **b** 99 miles **11 a** 1.25 h **b** 1 h 15 min **12 a** 48 mph **b** 6 h 40 min

Exercise 9E

1 60 g **2** £5.22 **3** 45 **4** £6.72 **5 a** £312.50 **b** 8 **6 a** 56 litres **b** 350 miles **7 a** 300 kg **b** 9 weeks **8** 40 s
9 a i 100 g, 200 g, 250 g, 150 g **ii** 150 g, 300 g, 375 g, 225 g **iii** 250 g, 500 g, 625 g, 375 g **b** 24

Exercise 9F

1 a Large jar **b** 600 g tin **c** 5 kg bag **d** 75 ml tube **e** Large box **f** Large box **g** 400 ml bottle **2** Large tin

Examination questions (Chapter 9)

1 1 £25:£225 **2** 180 **3** Ann £250, Bill £150 **4 a** 4 g **b** 8 g **5 a** £1000 **b** £900 **6** 12 **7** 175 miles
8 7 hours 30 min **9** 75 **10 a** 90 mph **b** 4½ hours **11** 9, 3, 1½, 225 g, 15 g **12** 345 g, 225 g, 150 g, 3
13 750 g packet **14 a** 6.25 ml **b** 330 ml can **15** £60 million **16 a** 200 miles **b** 30 min

Exercise 10A

1 a **b** **c** **d** **e** **f** 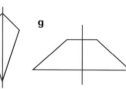 **g**

2 a i 5 **ii** 6 **iii** 8 **b** 10 **3 a** **b** **c**
4 a

b **c** **d** 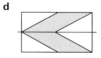 **e** **f**

5 2, 1, 1, 2, 0 **6 a**

7 a 1 **b** 5 **c** 1 **d** 6
8 c Infinite number

Exercise 10B

1 a 4 **b** 2 **c** 2 **d** 3 **e** 6 **2 a** 4 **b** 5 **c** 6 **d** 4 **e** 6 **3 a** 2 **b** 2 **c** 2 **d** 2 **e** 2 **4 a** 4
b 3 **c** 8 **d** 2 **e** 4 **f** 2 **5** A, B, C, D, E, F, G, J, K, L, M, P, Q, R, T, U, V, W, Y **6** Infinite number

Exercise 10C

1 a 9 **b** 4 **c** 4 **3 a** Sphere **4 a** 3 **b** 1 **c** 1 **d** 1 **e** Infinite **f** 1

Examination questions (chapter 10)

1 a, b, d **2 a** 4 **b** 2 **c** 1 **3 a i** 2 **ii** 3 **b**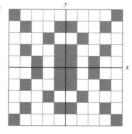

4 a 2 **b** 6 **c** 3 **5 a** 8 **b** 16 **c** 2
6 **7 a** M, A, T, H **b** H, S **8 a i** **ii** Hexagon **b i** 0 **ii** 3

504

Exercise 11A

1 a 4   **b** 48   **c** –1   **d** $\frac{1}{4}$ **e** No mode   **f** 3.21   **2 a** Red   **b** Sun   **c** ß   **d** ★   **3 a** 5   **b** No. More than half the form got a higher mark   **4 a** 32   **b** 6   **c** No   **d** No. Boys generally take larger shoe sizes

5 a

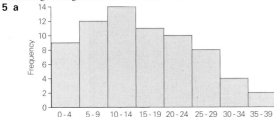

b 70   **c** 24.   **d** Cannot tell. Know only that 9 households had between 0 and 4 letters   **e** 10–14
6 The mode will be the most popular item or brand sold in a shop

Exercise 11B

1 a 5   **b** 33   **c** $7\frac{1}{2}$ **d** 24   **e** $8\frac{1}{2}$ **f** 0   **g** 5.25   **2 a** 5   **b i** 15   **ii** 215   **iii** 10   **iv** 10
3 a £2.20   **b** £2.25   **c** The median, because it is the central value   **4 a** 13, Ella   **b** 162 cm, Pat   **c** 40 kg, Elisa
d Ella, because she is closest to the 3 medians   **6** 12, 14, 14, 16, 20, 22, 24   **7 a** 21   **b** 16   **c** 15   **8** 50

Exercise 11C

1 a 6   **b** 24   **c** 45   **d** 1.57   **e** 2   **2 a** 55.1   **b** 324.7   **c** 58.5   **d** 44.9   **e** 2.3   **3 a** 61   **b** 60   **c** 59
d Brian   **e** 2   **4** 42 min   **5** 14 oz   **6 a** £200   **b** £260   **c** £278   **d** The median, because the extreme value of £480 is not taken into account   **7 a** 35   **b** 36   **8** 24   **9 a** 6   **b** 16   All the numbers and the mean are 10 more than those in part **a**   **c i** 56   **ii** 106   **iii** 7

Exercise 11D

1 a 7   **b** 26   **c** 5   **d** 2.4   **e** 7   **2 a** 8 °F, 5 °F, 2 °F, 12 °F, 5 °F   **b** Variable weather over England   **3 a** 82 and 83
b 20 and 12   **c** Margaret, because her scores are more consistent   **4 a** £31, £28, £33   **b** £8, £14, £4
c Not particularly consistent   **5 a** 5 min and 4 min   **b** 9 min and 13 min   **c** Number 50, because its times are more consistent

Exercise 11E

1 a i Mode 3, median 4, mean 5,   **ii** 6, 7, $7\frac{1}{2}$ **iii** 4, 6, 8   **b i** Mean: balanced data   **ii** Mode: 6 appears five times
iii Median: 28 is an extreme value   **2 a** Mode 73, median 76, mean 80   **b** The mean, because it is the highest average
3 a Mean   **b** Median   **c** Mode   **d** Median   **e** Mode   **f** Mean   **4** No. Mode is 31, median is 31, and mean is $31\frac{1}{2}$
5 a 29   **b** 28   **c** 27.1   **d** 14   **6 a** 150   **b** 20   **7 a i** £18 000   **ii** £24 000
iii £23 778   **b** The 6% rise, because it gives a greater increase in salary for the higher paid employees   **8 a** Median   **b** Mode
c Mean

Exercise 11F

1 a i 7   **ii** 6   **iii** 6.4   **b i** 4   **ii** 4   **iii** 3.7   **c i** 8   **ii** 8.5   **iii** 8.2   **d i** 0   **ii** 0   **iii** 0.3
2 a 668   **b** 1.9   **c** 0   **d** 328   **3 a** 2.2, 1.7, 1.3   **b** Better dental care   **4 a** 0   **b** 1.0   **5 a** 7   **b**   6.5   **c** 6.5
6 a 1   **b** 1   **c** 1.0   **7 a** Roger 5, Brian 4   **b** Roger 3, Brian 8   **c** Roger 5, Brian 4   **d** Roger 5.4, Brian 4.5   **e** Roger, because he has the smaller range   **f** Brian, because he has the better mean

Examination questions (Chapter 11)

1 a 56   **b** 53   **c**   25   **2 a** 5.3   **b** 5   **c**   9   **3 a** 1   **b** 2.2   **c** 2   **4 a** 7   **b** 6   **c**   Boys. The range shows they are more consistent   **5 a i** 94 kg   **ii** 53 kg   **iii** 87.4 kg   **b** Median. Not affected by the one extreme value
6 a 6   **b** 4   **c**   3   **7 a** 9   **b** 8   **c**   7.7   **8 a** 12 cm   **b** 30 cm   **c** Some beans either longer or shorter
9 a i 6.1 s   **ii** 13.7 s   **b** The boys were generally faster than, but not as consistent as, the girls   **10 a i** 7 min
ii 3 min   **b** Thompson bus   **11 a** 26   **b** 2   **c**   2.1   **12 a** 69   **b** 15   **c**   Increase   **13** 21 to 25
14 a Frequencies: 3, 7, 9, 4, 2   **b** $10 \le t < 15$

Exercise 12A

1 a $\frac{2}{25}$ **b** $\frac{1}{2}$ **c** $\frac{1}{5}$ **d** $\frac{1}{20}$ **e** $\frac{1}{10}$ **f** $\frac{3}{4}$ **g** $\frac{1}{4}$ **h** $\frac{9}{20}$ **i** $\frac{3}{5}$ **j** $\frac{2}{5}$ **k** $\frac{7}{20}$ **l** $\frac{9}{10}$ **m** $\frac{1}{25}$ **n** $\frac{3}{10}$ **o** 1 **p** $\frac{7}{10}$ **q** $\frac{3}{20}$ **r** $\frac{13}{20}$
2 a 0.27 **b** 0.85 **c** 0.13 **d** 0.06 **e** 0.08 **f** 0.02 **g** 0.346 **h** 0.125 **i** 0.984 **j** 2.0 **k** 1.25 **l** 1.75
m 0.34 **n** 0.268 **o** 1.12 **p** 0.72 **q** 0.175 **r** 0.9 **3** 150 **4** None **5** 20 **6 a** 77% **b** 39% **c** 63%
7 27% **8** 61.5% **9 a** 50% **b** 20% **c** 80% **10 a** 87.5%, 75%, 62.5%, 50%, 25% **b** 12.5%, 12.5%, 12.5%, 12.5%, 25%

Exercise 12B

1 a £45 **b** £6.30 **c** 128.8 kg **d** 1.125 kg **e** 1.08 h **f** 37.8 cm **g** £0.12 **h** 2.94 m **i** £7.60 **j** 33.88 min
k 136 kg **l** £162 **2** 96 **3** £1205 **4 a** 86% **b** 215 **5** 8520 **6** 287 **7** Each team: 22 500, referees: 750, other
teams: 7500, FA: 15 000, celebrities: 6750 **8** 114 **9** Mon: 816, Tue: 833, Wed: 850, Thu: 799, Fri: 748 **10** Lead 150 g,
tin 87.5 g, bismuth 12.5 g **11 a** £3.25 **b** 2.21 kg **c** £562.80 **d** £6.51 **e** 42.93 m **f** £24 **12** 480 cm³ nitrogen,
120 cm³ oxygen **13** 13 **14** £270

Exercise 12C

1 a £62.40 **b** 12.96 kg **c** 472.5 g **d** 599.5 m **e** £38.08 **f** £90 **g** 391 kg **h** 824.1 cm **i** 253.5 g
j £143.50 **k** 736 m **l** £30.24 **2** £29 425 **3** 1 690 200 **4 a** Bob: £17 325, Anne: £18 165, Jean: £20 475,
Brian: £26 565 **b** No **5** £411.95 **6** 7560 **7** 575 g **8** 918 **9** 60 **10** TV: £287.88, microwave: £84.60,
CD: £135.13, stereo: £34.66

Exercise 12D

1 a £9.40 **b** 23 kg **c** 212.4 g **d** 339.5 m **e** £4.90 **f** 39.6 m **g** 731 m **h** 83.52 g **i** 360 cm **j** 117 min
k 81.7 kg **l** £37.70 **2** £5525 **3 a** 52.8 kg **b** 66 kg **c** 45.76 kg **4** Mr Speed: £56, Mrs Speed: £297.50, James:
£126.50, John: £337.50 **5** 448 **6** 705 **7** £18 975 **8 a** 66.5 mph **b** 73.5 mph **9** £16.72, £22.88 **10** 524.8

Exercise 12E

1 a 20% **b** 25% **c** 75% **d** 45% **e** 87.5% **f** 50% **g** 60% **h** 17.5% **i** 55% **j** 30% **2 a** 33.3%
b 16.7% **c** 66.7% **d** 83.3% **e** 28.6% **f** 78.3% **g** 68.9% **h** 88.9% **i** 81.1% **j** 20.9 **3 a** 7% **b** 80%
c 66% **d** 25% **e** 54.5% **f** 82% **g** 30% **h** 89.1% **i** 120% **j** 278% **4 a** $\frac{24}{40} = \frac{3}{5}$ **b** 0.6 **c** 60% **5** 63%,
83%, 37%, 62%, 77% **6 a** 80% **b** 20% **7** 6.7% **8** 25.5%

Exercise 12F

1 a 25% **b** 60.6% **c** 46.3% **d** 12.5% **e** 41.7% **f** 60% **g** 20.8% **h** 10% **i** 1.9% **j** 8.3% **k** 45.5%
l 10.5% **m** 31.25% **n** 40% **o** 2.2% **p** 8.3% **q** 7.2% **r** 0.05% **s** 0.09% **t** 12.5% **2 a** 48.3%
b 64.3% **c** 10.5% **d** 81.8% **e** 26.3% **3** 32% **4** 17.9% **5** 4.9% **6** 6.5% **7** 2.2% **8** 33.7% **9** 90.5%
10 Brit Com: 20.9%, USA: 26.5%, France: 10.3%, Other 42.3%

Examination questions (Chapter 12)

1 0.25, 25%; $\frac{3}{10}$, 30% **2** 117 cm **3 a** $\frac{12}{25}$ **b** 35% **4** 60% **5 a** 77 **b** 57.75 **c** 25% **6** 40% **7** £11.99
8 £77.35 **9** £998.75 **10** £20 709 **11 a** 55% **b** 210 **12** 45% **13 a** 50% **b** $\frac{3}{4}$ **c** 0.07 **14 a** 40%
b Simon Smith **c** 14 000 **15 a** £9240 **b i** 80% **ii** 20%

Revision for Chapters 1 to 12

1 a $(9-2) \times 3 = 21$ **b** $7 + 5 \times (4-2) = 17$ **2 a** 32 weeks, **b** 224 d **3** **a** $\frac{4}{5}$ **b** $\frac{2}{8} = \frac{1}{4}$ **c** $\frac{12}{8} = \frac{3}{2} = 1\frac{1}{2}$ **d** 1
e $\frac{9}{7} = 1\frac{2}{7}$ **f** £45 **g** 40 m **h** 25 min **i** 100 min **j** 28 weeks **4 a** −5 **b** −17 **c** 5 **d** −5 **e** 8 **f** 20 **g** −4
h −12 **i** 5 **j** −34 **5 a** 8, 16, 24, 32, 40, 48, 56, 64, 72 **b** 1, 2, 3, 4, 6, 8, 12, 16, 24, 48 **c** 11, 13, 17, 19, 23, 29, 31, 37
d 81 **6 a i** 26 m **ii** 36 m² **b i** 29 cm **ii** $38\frac{1}{2}$ cm² **7 a** 103
b

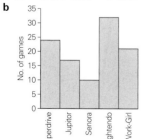

8 a $6m + 4t$ **b** $12p$ **9 a** 29 **b** $9\frac{1}{2}$ **c** 4 **10 a** 10 191 **b** 34 **c** 3.68
d 25.44 **11** George £375, Jo £225 **12 a** 15 m² **b** $\frac{1}{2}$ **13 a** 1.25 h
b 50 miles **14 a** 2 huts **b** 8 h
15 a i   **ii**   **iii**

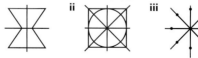

b i 2 **ii** 4 **iii** 8 **16 a** Mode 5 **b** Median 4 **c** Mean 3,7
17 a Range 4 eggs **b** Mean 2.08 eggs **18 a** 25% **b** $\frac{1}{2}$, 50% **c** 0.13, 13%
19 a $\frac{7}{20}$ **b** 35% **20 a** 14 **b** £90.30

Exercise 13A

1 $\leftarrow \div 3 \leftarrow -5 \leftarrow, x = 2$ **2** $\leftarrow \div 3 \leftarrow +13 \leftarrow, x = 13$ **3** $\leftarrow \div 3 \leftarrow +7 \leftarrow, x = 13$ **4** $\leftarrow \div 4 \leftarrow +19 \leftarrow, y = 6$
5 $\div 3 \leftarrow -8, a = 1$ **6** $\leftarrow \div 2 \leftarrow -8 \leftarrow, x = 3$ **7** $\leftarrow \div 2 \leftarrow -6 \leftarrow, y = 6$ **8** $\leftarrow \div 8 \leftarrow -4 \leftarrow, x = 1$ **9** $\leftarrow \div 2 \leftarrow +10 \leftarrow, x = 9$
10 $\leftarrow \times 2 \leftarrow -2 \leftarrow, x = 5$ **11** $\leftarrow \times 3 \leftarrow +4 \leftarrow, t = 18$ **12** $\leftarrow \times 4 \leftarrow -1 \leftarrow, y = 24$ **13** $\leftarrow \times 2 \leftarrow +6 \leftarrow, k = 18$
14 $\leftarrow \times 8 \leftarrow +4 \leftarrow, h = 40$ **15** $\leftarrow \times 6 \leftarrow -1 \leftarrow, w = 18$ **16** $\leftarrow \times 4 \leftarrow -5 \leftarrow, x = 8$ **17** $\leftarrow \times 2 \leftarrow +3 \leftarrow, y = 16$
18 $\leftarrow \times 5 \leftarrow -2 \leftarrow, f = 30$

Exercise 13B

1 56 **2** 2 **3** 6 **4** 3 **5** 4 **6** $2\frac{1}{2}$ **7** $3\frac{1}{2}$ **8** $2\frac{1}{2}$ **9** 4 **10** 21 **11** 72 **12** 56 **13** 0 **14** –7 **15** –18
16 36 **17** 36 **18** 60

Exercise 13C

1 1 **2** 3 **3** 2 **4** 2 **5** 9 **6** 5 **7** 6 **8** 24 **9** 10 **10** 21 **11** 72 **12** 56 **13** 5 **14** 28 **15** 5
16 35 **17** 33 **18** 23 **19** 4 **20** 2 **21** –2

Exercise 13D

1 3 **2** 7 **3** 5 **4** 3 **5** 4 **6** 6 **7** 8 **8** 1 **9** 1.5 **10** 2.5 **11** 0.5 **12** 1.2 **13** 2.4 **14** 4.5 **15** 3.5
16 2 **17** –2 **18** –1 **19** –2 **20** –2 **21** –1 **22** –4 **23** –2 **24** –1.5

Exercise 13E

1 2 **2** 1 **3** 7 **4** 4 **5** 2 **6** –1 **7** 3 **8** –2 **9** 5 **10** 4 **11** –2 **12** 2 **13** 6 **14** 11 **15** 1 **16** 4
17 9 **18** 6

Exercise 13F

1 6 yr **2** 9 yr **3** 3 cm **4** 55p **5 a** 1.5 **b** 2 **6 a** 1.5 cm **b** 6.75 cm^2 **7** 17 **8** 5

Examination questions (Chapter 13)

1 a 3 **b** –20 **c** 11 **2 a** 7 **b** $2\frac{1}{2}$ **c** 13 **3 a** 3 **b** 1.4 **c** –4 **d** 7 **4 a** 5 **b** $\frac{1}{2}$ **5 a** –6 **b** 8
c $1\frac{1}{2}$ **6 a** 55 **b** 7 **7 a** $3x + 2$ **b** 7 **8 a** $17n + 380$ **b** 48 **9 a** $x + 4$ **b** $4x + 10$ **c** 6m **10 a** $y + 5$
b $4y + 5$ **c** 14p **11** 3.36 **12** 10.5

Answers

Exercise 14A

1 a i $8\frac{1}{4}$ kg   **ii** $2\frac{1}{4}$ kg   **iii** 9 lb   **iv** 22 lb   **b** 2.2 lb   **2 a i** 10 cm   **ii** $22\frac{1}{2}$ cm   **iii** 2 in   **iv** $8\frac{3}{4}$ in   **b** $2\frac{1}{2}$ cm
3 a i \$320   **ii** \$100   **iii** £45   **iv** £78   **b** \$3.2   **4 a i** £120   **ii** £82   **b i** 32   **ii** 48   **5 a i** £100   **ii** £325
b i 500   **ii** 250   **6 a i** £70   **ii** £29   **b i** £85   **ii** £38   **7 a i** 40 km   **ii** 16 km   **iii** 25 miles   **iv** $9\frac{1}{2}$ miles
b 8 km   **8 a i** 95 °F   **ii** 68 °F   **iii** 10 °C   **iv** 32 °C   **b** 32 °F   **9 b** 2.15 pm   **10 b** £50   **11 a i** 3 m^3
ii $8\frac{1}{4}$ m^3 **iii** 13 yd^3 **iv** $6\frac{3}{4}$ yd^3 **b** 1.3   **12 b** $6\frac{3}{4}$ m

Exercise 14B

1 a i 9 am   **ii** 10 am   **iii** 12 noon   **b i** 40 km/h   **ii** 120 km/h   **iii** 40 km/h   **2 a i** 125 km   **ii** 125 km/h
b i Between 2 and 3 pm   **ii** 25 km/h   **3 a** 30 km   **b** 40 km   **c** 200 km/h   **4 a** He fell over or stopped to tie up a shoe
lace   **b i** 333 m/min   **ii** 180 s   **iii** 5.6 m/s   **c i** About $8\frac{1}{2}$ min into the race   **ii** About 30 s
5 a i Because it stopped several times   **ii** Ravinder   **b** Ravinder at 3.57 pm or 3.58 pm, Sue at 4.20 pm, Michael at 4.35 pm
c i 24 km/h   **ii** 20 km/h   **iii** 5   **6 a** Araf ran the race at a constant pace, taking 5 minutes to cover the 1000 metres. Sean
started slowly, covering the first 500 metres in 4 minutes. He then went faster, covering the last 500 metres in
$1\frac{1}{2}$ minutes, giving a total time of $5\frac{1}{2}$ minutes for the race   **b i** 20 km/h   **ii** 12 km/h   **iii** 10.9 km/h

Exercise 14C

1 a A(1, 2), B(3, 0), C(0, 1), D(–2, 4), E(–3, 2), F(–2, 0), G(–4, –1), H(–3, –3), I(1, –3), J(4, –2)   **b i** (2, 1)   **ii** (–1, –3)
iii (1, 1)   **c** $x = -3, x = 2, y = 3, y = -4$ **d i** $x = -\frac{1}{2}$ **ii** $y = -\frac{1}{2}$ **2** Values of y: 2, 3, 4, 5, 6   **3** Values of y: –2, 0, 2, 4, 6
4 Values of y: 1, 2, 3, 4, 5   **5** Values of y: –4, –3, –2, –1, 0   **6 a** Values of y: –3, –2, –1, 0, 1 and –6, –4, –2, 0, 2   **b** (3, 0)
7 a Values of y: 0, 4, 8, 12, 16 and 6, 8, 10, 12, 14   **b** (6, 12)   **8 a** Values of y: –1, 5, 11, 17, 23 and 4, 5, 6, 7, 8
b (2, 5)   **9** Points could be (0, –1), (1, 4), (2, 9), (3, 14), (4, 19), (5, 24) etc

Exercise 14D

1 Extreme points are (0, 4), (5, 19)   **2** Extreme points are (0, –5), (5, 5)   **3** Extreme points are (0, –3), (10, 2)
4 Extreme points are (–3, –4), (3, 14)   **5** Extreme points are (–6, 2), (6, 6)   **6 a** Extreme points are (0, –2), (5, 13) and (0, 1),
(5,11)   **b** (3, 7)   **7 a** Extreme points are (0, –5), (5, 15) and (0, 3), (5,13)   **b** (4, 11)   **8 a** Extreme points are (0, –1),
(12, 3) and (0, –2), (12,4)   **b** (6, 1)   **9 a** Extreme points are (0, 1), (4, 13) and (0, –2), (4,10)   **b** Do not cross because they are
parallel   **10 a** Values of y: 5, 4, 3, 2, 1, 0. Extreme points are (0, 5), (5, 0)   **b** Extreme points are (0, 7), (7, 0)

Examination questions (Chapter 14)

1 a P(3, 1), Q(1, –3), R(–5, 0), S(–3, 4)   **b** Side RS   **2 b ii** 80 hectares   **3 a** 2.2 km   **b** 7 min   **c** Stopped
d C to D   **4 b i** 10 °C   **ii** 34–38 °C   **c** 87–90 s   **5 a i** 40 miles   **ii** Stopped   **b** $2\frac{1}{2}$ h
6 a Values of y: –3, –1, 1, 3   **c** 1.75   **7 a** Values of y: –3, –1, 1, 3, 5, 7   **c i** 6   **ii** –1.75 **8 a** Values of y: –3, –1, 1, –1
9 a 2   **b i** 2 km   **ii** 12 km/h   **c** DE   **10 a** Values of l: 16, 20, 24, 28, 32, 36   **c** $6\frac{1}{2}$ kg   **11 a** 68 m   **b** $28\frac{1}{2}$ s
c $27\frac{1}{2}$ s   **d** $1\frac{1}{2}$ s and $26\frac{3}{4}$ s

Exercise 15A

1 a 40° **b** 30° **c** 35° **d** 43° **e** 100° **f** 125° **g** 340° **h** 225°

Exercise 15B

1 48° **2** 307° **3** 108° **4** 52° **5** 59° **6** 81° **7** 139° **8** 51° **9** 138° **10** 128° **11** 47° **12** 117°
13 27° **14** 45° **15** 108° **16** 69° **17** 135° **18** 58° **19** 74° **20** 23° **21** 55° **22** 56°

Exercise 15C

1 a 100° **b** 110° **c** 30° **2 a** 55° **b** 45° **c** $12\frac{1}{2}$° **3 a** $x = 34°, y = 98°$ **b** $x = 70°, y = 120°$ **c** $x = 20°, y = 80°$

Exercise 15D

1 a 70° **b** 50° **c** 80° **d** 60° **e** 75° **f** 109° **g** 38° **h** 63° **2 a** No, total is 190° **b** Yes, total is 180°
c No, total is 170° **d** Yes, total is 180° **e** Yes, total is 180° **f** No, total is 170° **3 a** 80° **b** 67° **c** 20° **d** 43°
e 10° **f** 1° **4 a** 60° **b** Equilateral triangle **c** Same length **5 a** 70° each **b** Isosceles triangle **c** Same length
6 $x = 50°, y = 80°$ **7 a** 109° **b** 110° **c** 135° **8 a** Missing angle = y, $x + y = 180°$, so $x = a + b$

Exercise 15E

1 a 90° **b** 150° **c** 80° **d** 80° **e** 77° **f** 131° **g** 92° **h** 131° **2 a** No, total is 350° **b** Yes, total is 360°
c No, total is 350° **d** No, total is 370° **e** Yes, total is 360° **f** Yes, total is 360° **3 a** 100° **b** 67° **c** 120° **d** 40°
e 40° **f** 1° **4 a** 90° **b** Rectangle **c** Square **5 a** 120° **b** 170° **c** 125° **d** 136° **e** 149° **f** 126°
g 212° **h** 114°

Exercise 15F

1 a i 45° **ii** 8 **iii** 1080° **b i** 20° **ii** 18 **iii** 2880° **c i** 15° **ii** 24 **iii** 3960° **d i** 36° **ii** 10 **iii** 1440°
2 a i 172° **ii** 45 **iii** 7740° **b i** 174° **ii** 60 **iii** 10440° **c i** 156° **ii** 15 **iii** 2340° **d i** 177° **ii** 120
iii 21240° **3 a** Exterior angle is 7°, which does not divide exactly into 360°. **b** Exterior angle is 19°, which does not divide
exactly into 360°. **c** Exterior angle is 11°, which does divide exactly into 360°. **d** Exterior angle is 70°, which does not divide
exactly into 360°. **4 a** 7° does not divide exactly into 360°. **b** 26° does not divide exactly into 360°. **c** 44° does not divide
exactly into 360°. **d** 13° does not divide exactly into 360°. **5** Bisected interior angle is 67.5°. Angle at centre is 45°. This is the
same as the exterior angle. This is true for all regular polygons

Exercise 15G

1 a 40° **b** $b = c = 70°$ **c** $d = 75°, e = f = 105°$ **d** $g = 50°, h = i = 130°$ **e** $j = k = l = 70°$ **f** $n = m = 80°$
2 a $a = 50°, b = 130°$ **b** $c = d = 65°, e = f = 115°$ **c** $g = i = 65°, h = 115°$ **d** $j = k = 72°, l = 108°$ **e** $m = n = o = p = 105°$
f $q = r = s = 125°$ **3** b, d, f, h **4 a** $a = 95°$ **b** $b = 66°$ **c** $c = 114°$

Exercise 15H

1 a $a = 110°, b = 55°$ **b** $c = 75°, d = 115°$ **b** $e = 87°, f = 48°$ **2 a** $a = c = 105°, b = 75°$ **b** $d = f = 70°, e = 110°$
c $g = i = 63°, h = 117°$ **3 a** $a = 135°, b = 25°$ **b** $c = d = 145°, e = f = 94°$ **4 a** $a = c = 105°, b = 75°$ **b** $d = f = 93°$,
$e = 87°$ **c** $g = i = 49°, h = 131°$ **5 a** $a = 58°, b = 47°$ **b** $c = 141°, d = 37°$ **c** $e = g = 65°, f = 115°$

Exercise 15 I

3 a 110° **b** 250° **c** 091° **d** 270° **e** 130° **f** 180° **4 a** 090°, 180°, 270° **b** 000°, 270°, 180°

Examination questions (Chapter 15)

1 66° **2 a** 24° **b** 110° **3** $p = 56°, q = 124°, r = 60°, s = 120°, t = 102°$ **4** $p = 125°, q = 55°, r = 55°, s = 52°, t = 50°$
5 a 118° **b i** 25° **ii** 105° **6 a** 144° **b** 108° **c** $a = 128°, c = 38°$ **7 a** 65°, alternate angles **b** 70°, interior
angles = 360° **8 i** $4x - 20° = 180°$ **ii** $x = 50°; 50°, 70°, 60°$ **9 a ii** 108° **b** 80°, 85°, 35° **10 a i** 145° **ii** Angles
on a line = 180° **b i** 83° **ii** Angles in a triangle = 180° **c i** 35° **ii** Vertically opposite angles are equal **11 a** 30 km
b 080° **c** 240°

Exercise 16A

1 a 25.1 cm   **b** 15.7 cm   **c** 44.0 cm   **d** 22.0 cm   **e** 18.8 cm   **f** 47.1 cm   **g** 28.9 cm   **h** 14.8 cm   **2 a** 6.3 cm
b 8.2 cm   **c** 5.3 cm   **d** 7.5 cm   **3 a** 31.4 cm   **b** 18.8 cm   **c** 9.4 cm   **d** 25.1 cm   **e** 5.7 cm   **f** 15.7 cm   **g** 81.7 cm
h 39.6 cm   **4** 100.5 cm   **5 a** A 188.5 m, B 194.8 m, C 201.1 m, D 207.3 m   **b** 18.7 m   **6** 879.6 or 880 cm   **7 a** 37.7 cm
b 3770 cm   **c** 37.7 m   **d** 37.7 km   **8** 100 cm   **9** 24.2 cm   **10** 15.9 cm

Exercise 16B

1 a 78.5 cm^2 **b** 28.3 cm^2 **c** 7.1 cm^2 **d** 50.3 cm^2 **e** 2.5 cm^2 **f** 19.6 cm^2 **g** 530.9 cm^2 **h** 124.7 cm^2
2 a 3.1 cm^2 **b** 5.3 cm^2 **c** 2.3 cm^2 **d** 4.5 cm^2 **3 a** 50.3 cm^2 **b** 19.6 cm^2 **c** 153.9 cm^2 **d** 38.5 cm^2 **e** 28.3 cm^2
f 176.7 cm^2 **g** 66.5 cm^2 **h** 17.3 cm^2 **4 a** 9.1 cm^2 **b** 138   **c** 2000 cm^2 **d** 1255.8 cm^2 **e** 744.2 cm^2
5 3848.5 m^2 **6 a i** 56.5 cm   **ii** 254.5 cm^2 **b i** 69.1 cm   **ii** 380.1 cm^2 **c i** 40.8 cm   **ii** 132.7 cm^2 **d i** 88.0 cm
ii 615.8 cm^2 **7 a** 19.1 cm   **b** 9.5 cm   **c** 286.5 cm^2 (or 283.5 cm^2)   **8** 962.9 cm^2 (or 962.1 cm^2)   **9 a i** 30.8 cm
ii 56.5 cm^2 **b i** 17.9 cm   **ii** 19.6 cm^2

Exercise 16C

1 12 cm^2 **2** 20 cm^2 **3** 23 cm^2 **4** 32 cm^2

Exercise 16D

1 a i 198 cm^3 **ii** 234 cm^2 **b i** 90 cm^3 **ii** 146 cm^2 **c i** 1440 cm^3 **ii** 792 cm^2 **d i** 525 cm^3 **ii** 470 cm^2
e i 400 cm^3 **ii** 340 cm^2 **f i** 416 cm^3 **ii** 376 cm^2 **2** 24 litres   **3 a** 160 cm^3 **b** 480 cm^3 **c** 150 cm^3
4 a i 64 cm^3 **ii** 96 cm^2 **b i** 343 cm^3 **ii** 294 cm^2 **c i** 1000 cm^3 **ii** 600 cm^2 **d i** 125 m^3 **ii** 150 m^2
e i 1728 m^3 **ii** 864 m^2 **5** 86   **6 a** 148 cm^3 **b** 468 cm^3 **c** 260 cm^3

Examination questions (Chapter 16)

1 44 cm^3 **2 a** 40 cm^3 **b** 20 cm^2 **3 a** 27 cm   **b** 64.8 litres   **4** 24   **5** 79.9 m   **6 a** 18 000 cm^3 **b** 8%
7 346.5 cm^2 **8** 84.9 m^2 **9 a** 22 cm   **b** 38.5 cm^2 **10 a** 25.7 cm   **b** 39.3 cm^2 **11** 218 cm^2 **12 a** 714.2 cm^2
b 105.8 cm

Revision for Chapters 1 to 16

1   **a** 205, 212, 219, 221, 234, 243   **b** 1334   **c** 38   **d i** 45   **ii** 18   **iii** 20   **iv** 8   **v** 245   **vi** 98   **vii** 2548
viii 148   **ix** 1258   **2 a** 1   **b** $\frac{2}{8} = \frac{1}{4}$ **c** $\frac{5}{8}$ **d** £18   **e** 36   **f** £100   **3**   **a** −15 °C   **b** 35 °C   **c** −25 °C
d 75 °C   **e** −30 °C   **f** 50 °C   **g** 105 °C   **h** 35 °C and −15 °C   **4 a** −5   **b** −2   **c** −6   **d** −4   **e** 0   **f** 3   **g** −7
h 2   **i** −6   **5 a** 14   **b** 16   **c** 81   **d** 10 or 15   **e** 17   **f** 10 or 15   **g** 14 or 25   **6**   **a** 7J : 25, 7K : 22   **b** 7J : 4,
7K : 4   **c** 7J : 6, 7K : 6   **d** 7J : 7, 7K : 7   **e** 7J, because they had higher scores   **7 a** $5 + x$ **b** $y − 6$ **c** $7b$ **d** pq
e $\frac{t}{2}$ **f** $2x + 3$ **g** $2(x + 3)$ **h** $10t$ cm   **8 a** 18   **b** 12   **c** 13   **d** 9   **e** 14   **f** 7   **g** 25   **h** 81

9 34   **10 a** $2780   **b** Clintons' own car (80% of 30 is 24)   **11 a** £25 000   **b** £12 000   **c** £12 000   **d** The mode or the
median, because the mean is distorted by the very high salary   **12 a** $x − 6, 2x − 12, 2x − 18$ **b** $6x − 30 = 60$ **c** $x = 15$
d Fourth plate, which had 12 biscuits   **13**

2	7		6	6
	5	2		7
2		9	9	
5	1		5	4
	1	9		6

14 Points are (0, −1), (1,2), (2, 5), (3,8),
(4, 11), (5, 14)   **15 a i** 2 km   **ii** 5 min   **b i** 5 min
ii 48 km/h   **16 a** 105 cm^3 **b** 142 cm^2 **17 a** 126°
b 135°   **c** 70°   **18 a** 5   **b** −3   **c** 2   **d** −4
19 a 37.7 cm   **b** 113.1 cm^2 **20** 44.1 m^2

Exercise 17A

1 a $1\frac{1}{2}$ cm, 3 cm   **b** 2 cm, 4 cm   **c** 3 cm, 6 cm   **5 d** Regular hexagon

Exercise 17B

1 a $a = 2.9$ cm, $\angle B = 92°$, $\angle C = 53°$ **b** $e = 7.4$ cm, $f = 6.8$ cm, $\angle D = 50°$ **c** $i = 7.8$ cm, $\angle G = 65°$, $\angle H = 53°$
d $j = 3.5$ cm, $l = 3.5$ cm, $\angle K = 70°$ **e** $m = 5$ cm, $\angle N = 37°$, $\angle O = 53°$ **f** $q = 13.9$ cm, $\angle P = 33°$, $\angle R = 37°$ **g** $\angle S = 39°$,
$\angle T = 94°$, $\angle U = 47°$ **h** $\angle V = 74°$, $\angle W = 77°$, $\angle X = 29°$ **i** $\angle A = 37°$, $\angle Y = 53°$, $\angle Z = 90°$ **4 b** Parallelogram   **5 b** 4 cm

Exercise 17C

1 a Yes   **b** Yes   **c** No   **d** Yes   **e** No   **f** Yes   **2 a** Triangle **ii**   **b** Triangle **iii**   **c** Sector **i**   **3 a** 1, 3, 4   **b** 2, 4
c 1, 4   **d** 1, 2, 3, 4

Examination questions (Chapter 17)

1 d 90°   **2** Tangent, arc, diameter, chord   **3** R   **5 a** and **d**   **6 b** 56°   **7 a** CP, CQ, CR, CS   **b** Equilateral
c PQ and CR or CQ and SR

Answers

Exercise 18A

1 a Unlikely **b** Certain **c** Likely **d** Very unlikely **e** Impossible **f** Very likely **g** even

2

Exercise 18B

1 a $\frac{1}{6}$ **b** $\frac{1}{6}$ **c** $\frac{1}{2}$ **d** $\frac{1}{13}$ **e** $\frac{1}{4}$ **f** $\frac{1}{2}$ **g** $\frac{1}{3}$ **h** $\frac{1}{26}$ **i** $\frac{1}{13}$ **j** 0 **2 a** $\frac{1}{2}$ **b** $\frac{1}{2}$ **c** $\frac{1}{2}$ **d** $\frac{1}{52}$ **e** $\frac{4}{13}$ **f** $\frac{1}{52}$ **3 a** 0 **b** 1 **4 a** $\frac{1}{10}$ **b** $\frac{1}{2}$ **c** $\frac{2}{5}$ **d** $\frac{1}{5}$ **e** $\frac{2}{5}$ **5 a** $\frac{1}{3}$ **b** $\frac{1}{3}$ **c** $\frac{2}{3}$ **6 a** $\frac{6}{11}$ **b** $\frac{5}{11}$ **c** $\frac{6}{11}$ **7 a** $\frac{1}{5}$ **b** $\frac{1}{2}$ **c** $\frac{1}{2}$ **d** $\frac{7}{10}$ **8 a** $\frac{7}{15}$ **b** $\frac{2}{15}$ **c** $\frac{8}{15}$ **d** 0 **e** $\frac{8}{15}$ **9** $\frac{1}{50}$ **10 a** AB, AC, AD, AE, BC, BD, BE, CD, CE, DE **b** 1 **c** $\frac{1}{10}$ **d** 6 **e** $\frac{3}{5}$ **f** $\frac{3}{10}$ **11 a** 2 **b** 10 **c i** $\frac{5}{9}$ **ii** $\frac{4}{9}$ **12 a** $\frac{1}{13}$ **b** $\frac{1}{13}$ **c** $\frac{1}{2}$ **d** $\frac{2}{13}$ **e** $\frac{7}{13}$ **f** $\frac{1}{26}$ **13 a i** $\frac{12}{25}$ **ii** $\frac{7}{25}$ **iii** $\frac{6}{25}$ **b** They add up to 1 **c** All possible outcomes used **14** 35% **15** 0.5

Exercise 18C

1 a $\frac{19}{20}$ **b** 55% **c** 0.2 **2 a i** $\frac{3}{13}$ **ii** $\frac{10}{13}$ **b i** $\frac{1}{4}$ **ii** $\frac{3}{4}$ **c i** $\frac{2}{13}$ **ii** $\frac{11}{13}$ **3 a i** $\frac{1}{4}$ **ii** $\frac{3}{4}$ **b i** $\frac{3}{11}$ **ii** $\frac{8}{11}$

Exercise 18D

1 a $\frac{1}{5}, \frac{2}{25}, \frac{1}{10}, \frac{21}{100}, \frac{37}{250}, \frac{163}{1000}, \frac{329}{2000}$ **b** 6 **c** 1 **d** $\frac{1}{6}$ **e** 1000 **2 a** $\frac{19}{200}, \frac{27}{200}, \frac{4}{25}, \frac{53}{200}, \frac{69}{200}$ **b** 40 **c** No **3 a** $\frac{1}{5}, \frac{1}{4}, \frac{19}{50}, \frac{21}{50}, \frac{77}{200}, \frac{1987}{5000}$ **b** 8 **4 a** 6 **5 a** Caryl threw most number of times **b** 0.39, 0.31, 0.17, 0.14 **c** Yes. All answers should be close to 0.25

Exercise 18E

1 a 7 **b** 2 and 12 **c** $\frac{1}{36}, \frac{1}{18}, \frac{1}{12}, \frac{1}{9}, \frac{5}{36}, \frac{1}{6}, \frac{5}{36}, \frac{1}{9}, \frac{1}{12}, \frac{1}{18}, \frac{1}{36}$ **d i** $\frac{1}{12}$ **ii** $\frac{1}{3}$ **iii** $\frac{1}{2}$ **iv** $\frac{7}{36}$ **v** $\frac{15}{36}$ **vi** $\frac{5}{18}$ **2 a** $\frac{1}{12}$ **b** $\frac{11}{36}$ **c** $\frac{1}{6}$ **d** $\frac{5}{9}$ **3 a** $\frac{1}{36}$ **b** $\frac{11}{36}$ **c** $\frac{5}{18}$ **4 a** $\frac{5}{18}$ **b** $\frac{1}{2}$ **c** $\frac{1}{9}$ **d** 0 **e** $\frac{1}{2}$ **5 a** $\frac{1}{4}$ **b** $\frac{1}{2}$ **c** $\frac{3}{4}$ **d** $\frac{1}{4}$ **6 a** 6 **b i** $\frac{4}{25}$ **ii** $\frac{13}{25}$ **iii** $\frac{1}{5}$ **iv** $\frac{3}{5}$

Examination questions (Chapter 18)

1 a i 11, 12, 13, 21, 22, 23, 31, 32, 33 **ii** $\frac{1}{9}$ **iii** $\frac{1}{3}$ **b** $\frac{8}{9}$ **2 a** $\frac{2}{15}$ **b** $\frac{8}{15}$ **3 a** **b** **c** $\frac{1}{2}$ **4 a** $\frac{8}{33}$ **b** $\frac{10}{33}$ **c** $\frac{6}{11}$ **5 b** $\frac{1}{6}$ **c** 45 **6 a** 0.8 **b** 6 **c** 1, certain **7 b i** $\frac{1}{25}$ **ii** $\frac{6}{25}$ **8** David, Barbara, Abdul, Cathy, Ewan

9 a

2	4	6	8	10	12
3	4	5	6	7	8

b i 2, 3, 5, 7 **ii** $\frac{1}{3}$ **iii** $\frac{2}{3}$ **10 a i** $\frac{1}{5}$ **ii** $\frac{4}{5}$ **b i** 60 **ii** 0.33

Exercise 19A

[D down, L left, R Right, U up] **3 a i** 1R and 3U   **ii** 4R and 2U   **iii** 2R and 1D   **iv** 5R and 1U   **v** 1L and 6U
vi 4R and 6U   **b i** 1L and 3D   **ii** 3R and 1D   **iii** 1R and 4D   **iv** 4R and 2D   **v** 2 L and 3U   **vi** 3R and 3U
c i 4L and 2D   **ii** 3L and 1U   **iii** 2L and 3D   **iv** 1R and 1D   **v** 5L and 4U   **vi** 4U   **d i** 3R and 2U   **ii** 4L and 2U
iii 5R and 4D   **iv** 2L and 7D   **v** 5R   **vi** 1R and 5D   **4**   A′ (6, 5), B′(8, 5), C′ (8, 6)

Exercise 19B

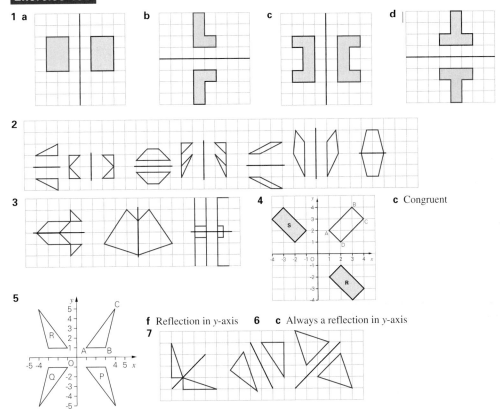

4   **c** Congruent

5

f Reflection in *y*-axis   **6**   **c** Always a reflection in *y*-axis
7

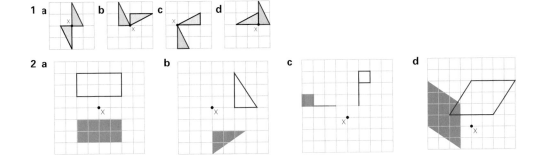

Exercise 19C

1 a   **b**   **c**   **d**

2 a   **b**   **c**   **d**

3
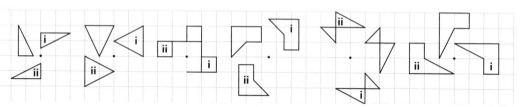

d ¼ turn clockwise about O
4 a   A(1, 2), B(3, 1), C(4, 3)
b (2, −1), (1, −3), (3, −4)   **c** (−1, −2), (−3, −1), (−4, −3)
d (−2, 1), (−1, 3), (−3, 4)
e   Corresponding vertices have same pairs of numbers switching round and changing signs

5 a
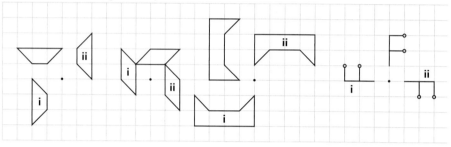

b Rotation 90° anticlockwise *or* rotation 270° clockwise
6 a
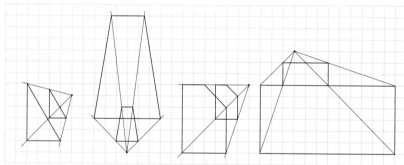

b Rotation 90° clockwise

Exercise 19D

1

2 a **b** **c**

3 a **b**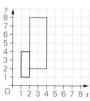

Examination questions (Chapter 19)

1 a Line $x = -1$ **b** Rotation 90° clockwise about (0, 0) **2 a** (1, 4) **b–c**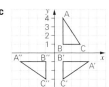

3 a i E **ii** C **iii** F **b** Rotation 180° about (0, 0)

4

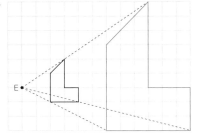

5 a (3,4) **b** 10 cm² **c** 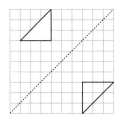 **6 a** 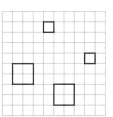 **b**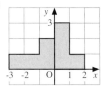

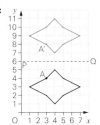

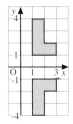

c 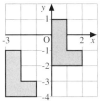 **7 a** 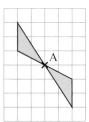 **b**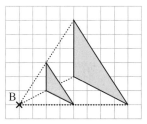

8 a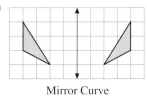

Mirror Curve

b **c**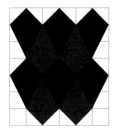

9 a (2, 1) **b** ∠BAC **c** 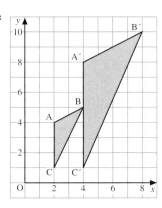 **10**

Exercise 20A

1 a Onions: 40 m × 10 m, soft fruit: 50 m × 10 m, apple trees: 20 m × 20 m, lawn: 30 m × 20 m, potatoes: 50 m × 20 m
b Onions: 400 m², soft fruit: 500 m², apple trees: 400 m², lawn: 600 m², potatoes: 1000 m²   **2 a** 33 cm   **b** 9 cm
3 a 8 km   **b** 4 km   **c** 6 km   **d** 6 km   **e** 7 km   **f** 2 km   **4 a i** 60 km   **ii** 200 km   **iii** 120 km   **iv** 40 km
b i 80 km   **ii** 200 km   **iii** 160 km   **iv** 120 km   **5 a** 50 km   **b** 35 km   **c** 45 km   **6 a** 30 cm × 30 cm
b 40 cm × 10 cm   **c** 20 cm × 15 cm   **d** 30 cm × 20 cm   **e** 30 cm × 20 cm   **f** 10 cm × 5 cm

Examination questions (Chapter 20)

1 c and **e**   **2 b**   5.8 m   **3 a** Equilateral   **b** 5, 9, 6   **d** 3.5 cm   **6** 7.5 m, 3 m   **7 a** 9   **10 a** 26 cm³   **b** 3 cm

Revision for Chapters 1 to 20

1 a $7 + (2 \times 4) = 15$ **b** $(1 + 5) \times (7 - 3) = 24$ **2 a** 24 weeks   **b** 189 days   **3 a** $\frac{3}{5}$ **b** 1   **c** $\frac{1}{4}$ **d** 1   **e** $1\frac{1}{2}$ **f**
£120   **g** 80 m   **h** 30 min   **i** $2\frac{1}{2}$ h   **j** 36 weeks   **4 a** −6   **b** −17   **c** 6   **d** −2   **e** 6   **f** 17   **g** −3   **h** −12   **i** 8
j −45   **5 a i** 11.2 cm   **ii** 7 cm²   **b i** 14 cm   **ii** 9 cm²   **6 a** $7x + 6$ **b** $10x + 10$ **7 a** 3300   **8** James £600,
Helen £1000   **9 a** 1.75   **b** 87.5 m   **10 a i**   **ii** 4   **b i**   **ii** 2   **c i**
ii 1   **11** 0.82   **12 a** $\frac{2}{5}$ **b** 40%   **13 a**
14   **b** 7   **c** 3   **14 a** 2, 5, 8, 11, 14, 17
15 a 15°
 b Obtuse–angled or scalene   **16 a** 25.1 cm
 b 50.3 cm²   **18 a** $\frac{24}{50} = \frac{12}{25}$ **b** $\frac{35}{50} = \frac{7}{10}$
 19 d Rotation of 180° about O

Exercise 21A

1 Metres **2** Kilometres **3** Millimetres **4** Kilograms or grams **5** Litres **6** Kilograms **7** Tonnes **8** Millilitres **9** Centilitres **10** Metres **11** Kilograms **12** Litres **13** Grams **14** Centilitres **15** Millimetres

Exercise 21B

1 1.25 m **2** 8.2 cm **3** 0.55 m **4** 2.1 km **5** 2.08 cm **6** 1.24 m **7** 14.2 cm **8** 3.56 km **9** 3.55 m **10** 0.94 m **11** 0.65 km **12** 0.045 m **13** 80.5 cm **14** 12.5 m **15** 2.06 km **16** 4.2 kg **17** 5.75 t **18** 8.5 cl **19** 2.58 l **20** 3.4 l **21** 0.6 t **22** 0.755 kg **23** 0.8 l **24** 2 l **25** 63 cl **26** 1.02 t **27** 4.5 l **28** 2.04 kg **29** 4.5 l **30** 0.055 l **31** 8.4 m³ **32** 35 cm³ **33** 1.035 m³ **34** 0.53 m³ **35** 530 cm **36** 34 000 m **37** 3400 mm **38** 135 mm **39** 67 cm **40** 7030 m **41** 7.2 mm **42** 25 cm **43** 5 cm **44** 640 m **45** 110 mm **46** 2400 ml **47** 590 cl **48** 84 ml **49** 5200 l **50** 580 g **51** 3750 kg **52** 74 cl **53** 0.000 94 l **54** 45 800 g **55** 12 500 ml **56** 2160 cl **57** 15 200 g **58** 14 000 l **59** 1560 kg **60** 0.19 ml

Exercise 21C

1 24 in **2** 12 ft **3** 3520 yd **4** 80 oz **5** 56 lb **6** 6720 lb **7** 40 pt **8** 48 in **9** 36 in **10** 30 ft **11** 64 oz **12** 5 ft **13** 70 lb **14** 12 yd **15** 224 oz **16** 5 miles **17** 120 pt **18** 5280 ft **19** 8 ft **20** 7 st **21** 7 gal **22** 2 lb **23** 5 yd **24** 5 tons **25** 63 360 in **26** 8 lb **27** 9 gal **28** 10 st **29** 3 miles **30** 35 840 oz

Exercise 21D

1 a 22 lb **b** 28.6 lb (or 29 lb) **c** 52.8 lb (or 53 lb) **d** 88 lb **e** 121 lb **f** 171.6 lb (or 172 lb) **g** 220 lb **h** 2200 lb **2 a** 15 kg **b** 20 kg **c** 30 kg **d** 22 kg **e** 25 kg **f** 35 kg **g** 50 kg **h** 455 kg **3** No, Dave weighs 70.4 lb **4** Yes, because my luggage weighs 20.45 kg **5** Beryl, because she weighs 143 lb **6** Donna, because she weighs 92.4 lb **7** No, because the team weighs 2662 lb **8** Yes, because she loses 5.06 lb **9** No, because my caravan weighs 1990 lb **10** Eiffel tower is 8 million lb heavier **11 a** 998.8 g **b** Because it is an approximation

Exercise 21E

1 a 17.5 pt **b** 22.75 pt (or 23 pt) **c** 42 pt **d** 70 pt **e** 96.25 pt (or 96 pt) **f** 136.5 pt (or 137 pt) **g** 175 pt **h** 1750 pt **2 a** 20 l **b** 29 l **c** 40 l **d** 28 l **e** 32 l **f** 44 l **g** 63 l **h** 571 l **3** Yes, because the bucket holds 5.25 pints **4** No, because the barrel holds only 350 pints **5** A, because it holds 3.75 pints more. **6** D, because it holds 73.5 pints **7** No. Assuming the tank is empty, it will hold 2625 pints **8** Yes, the plants need only 4.9 l **9** Half-pint cans **10 a** 4.5 l **b** Yes, now £2.68 per gallon **11 a** 8.75 h **b** 7 h **12 a** 4½ kg **b** 9.9 lb Yes

Exercise 21F

1 a 16 km **b** 24 km **c** 40 km **d** 64 km **e** 88 km **f** 120 km **g** 160 km **h** 1600 km **2 a** 20 miles **b** 30 miles **c** 42.5 miles **d** 31.25 miles **e** 35 miles **f** 50 miles **g** 65 miles **h** 625 miles **3** Yes, because the distance is 320 km **4** No, because the journey is only 1250 miles **5** A to B **6** F to G **7** Happy Feeder **8** Le Havre to Paris **9** Every 14 400 km **10** Top row: 56, 64, 40, second row: 32, 24, last row: 24

Exercise 21G

1 a 45 l **b** 67.5 l **c** 112.5 l **d** 180 l **e** 247.5 l **f** 337.5 l **g** 450 l **h** 4500 l **2 a** 8 gal **b** 12 gal **c** 14 gal **d** 18 gal **e** 16 gal **f** 20 gal **g** 24 gal **h** 222 gal **3** No, because the bucket holds only 9 l **4** Yes, because the fuel tank hold 135 000 l **5** Tank A **6** My neighbour **7** No, because the pond holds 144 l **8** Nine trips **9** About 74 days

Exercise 21H

1 a 394 in **b** 591 in **c** 984 in **d** 1575 in **e** 2165 in **f** 2953 in **g** 3937 in **h** 39 370 in **2 a** 1098 cm **b** 1647 cm **c** 1922 cm **d** 2471 cm **e** 2135 cm **f** 2745 cm **g** 3294 cm **h** 30 500 cm **3 a** 2 m **b** 3 m **c** 16 m **d** 20 m **e** 18 m **f** 23 m **g** 28 m **h** 52 m **4 a** 3 ft **b** 4 ft **c** 21 ft **d** 26 ft **e** 27 ft **f** 31 ft **g** 35 ft **h** 67 ft **5** 10 ft of string **6** 60 cm stick **7** 25 ft of ribbon **8** 20 cm pencil **9** No, because I need 50.3 m **10** No, a join will be needed **11** About 219 turns

Examination questions (Chapter 21)

1 a Centimetres **b** Grams **c** Kilometres **d** Millilitres **2** Enough potatoes (6.6 lb), but not enough milk (1¾ pt) **3 a** 1500 g **b** 200 cm **c** 3000 ml **d i** m² **ii** litres **4 a** 150 **b** 160 g **5 a** 973 ft **b** Lincoln Cathedral **6** 217 miles **7 a** No, 6.6 lb sugar **b** No, 2 l ≈ 3½ pt **8 a** 65 kg **b** 1.55 m **9 a** No, 20 km ≈ 12½ miles **b** No, 5 kg ≈ 11 lb

Exercise 22A

1 a 36°, 90°, 126°, 81°, 27°　**b** 90°, 108°, 60°, 78°, 24°　**c** 168°, 52°, 100°, 40°　**2** 60°, 165°, 45°, 15°, 75°
3 a 36　**b** 50°, 50°, 80°, 60°, 60°, 40°, 20°　**d** Bar chart, because easier to make comparisons　**4 a** 124°, 132°, 76°, 28°
b Split of total data seen at a glance　**5 a i** 40　**ii** 15　**iii** 25　**b** 15%　**6 a** 55°　**b** 22　**c** 33⅓%

Exercise 22B

1 a Positive correlation　**b** Negative correlation　**c** No correlation　**d** Positive correlation　**2** A person's reaction time
increases as more alcohol is consumed　**3** As people get older, they consume less alcohol　**4** No relationship between
temperature and speed of cars on M1　**5** As people get older, they have more money in the bank　**6 c** About 20 cm/s
d about 35 cm　**7 c** Greta　**d** About 70　**e** About 72　**8 b** Yes, usually (good correlation)　**9 c** About £75 000
d Locality, improvements　**e** Yes, positive correlation　**10 b** No correlation

Examination questions (Chapter 22)

2b As cars get older, their value decreases　**4** Draw a two-way table showing vehicle type and colour　**5 a i** D　**ii** A
iii B　**b** Watches a lot of TV and spends little time on homework　**c** As students watch more TV, they spend less time on homework
d

6 140°, 120°, 68°, 32°　**7 b** Positive correlation　**c** 29–35
8 a 166°, 79°, 65°, 50°　**b** 49
9 Draw a two-way table showing colour of hair and colour of eyes
10 a £960　**b** £192　**11 a** 219　**b** For example: What sports do
you play? and How often do you exercise?　**12 a** Positive correlation
c About 175 cm　**13 b** Negative correlation　**d** 12

Exercise 23A

1 $11111 \times 11111 = 123454321$, $111111 \times 111111 = 12345654321$
2 $99999 \times 99999 = 9999800001$, $999999 \times 999999 = 999998000001$ **3** $7 \times 8 = 7^2 + 7$, $8 \times 9 = 8^2 + 8$
4 $50 \times 51 = 2550$, $60 \times 61 = 3660$ **5** $1 + 2 + 3 + 4 + 5 + 4 + 3 + 2 + 1 = 25 = 5^2$, $1 + 2 + 3 + 4 + 5 + 6 + 5 + 4 + 3 + 2 + 1 = 36 = 6^2$
6 $21 + 23 + 25 + 27 + 29 = 125 = 5^3$, $31 + 33 + 35 + 37 + 39 + 41 = 216 = 6^3$
7 $1 + 6 + 15 + 20 + 15 + 6 + 1 = 64$, $1 + 7 + 21 + 35 + 35 + 21 + 7 + 1 = 128$
8 $12\,345\,679 \times 45 = 555\,555\,555$, $12\,345\,679 \times 54 = 666\,666\,666$
9 $1^3 + 2^3 + 3^3 + 4^3 = (1 + 2 + 3 + 4)^2 = 100$, $1^3 + 2^3 + 3^3 + 4^3 + 5^3 = (1 + 2 + 3 + 4 + 5)^2 = 225$
10 $36^2 + 37^2 + 38^2 + 39^2 + 40^2 = 41^2 + 42^2 + 43^2 + 44^2$, $55^2 + 56^2 + 57^2 + 58^2 + 59^2 + 60^2 = 61^2 + 62^2 + 63^2 + 64^2 + 65^2$
11 12345678987654321 **12** 999999998000000001 **13** $12^2 + 12$ **14** 8190 **15** $81 = 9^2$ **16** $512 = 8^3$ **17** 512
18 $999\,999\,999$ **19** $(1 + 2 + 3 + 4 + 5 + 6 + 7 + 8 + 9)^2 = 2025$

Exercise 23B

1 a 9, 11, 13: add 2 **b** 10, 12, 14: add 2 **c** 80, 160, 320: double **d** 81, 243, 729: multiply by 3 **e** 28, 34, 40: add 6
f 23, 28, 33: add 5 **g** 20 000, 200 000, 2 000 000: multiply by 10 **h** 19, 22, 25: add 3 **i** 46, 55, 64: add 9
j 405, 1215, 3645: multiply by 3 **k** 18, 22, 26: add 4 **l** 625, 3125, 15 625: multiply by 5 **2 a** 16, 22 **b** 26, 37
c 31, 43 **d** 46, 64 **e** 121, 169 **f** 782, 3907 **g** 22 223, 222 223 **h** 11, 13 **i** 33, 65 **j** 78, 108
3 a 21, 34: add previous 2 terms **b** 49, 64: next square number **c** 47, 76: add previous 2 terms **4** 15, 21, 28, 36
5 61, 91, 127 **6 a** 48, 96, 192 **b** 33, 39, 45 **c** 29, 47, 76 **d** 38, 35, 32 **e** 37, 50, 65 **f** 26, 33, 41
g 14, 16, 17 **h** 19, 22, 25 **i** 28, 36, 45 **j** 5, 6, 7 **k** 0.16, 0.032, 0.0064 **l** 0.0625, 0.031 25, 0.015 625

Exercise 23C

1 a 3, 5, 7, 9, 11 **b** 1, 4, 7, 10, 13 **c** 7, 12, 17, 22, 27 **d** 1, 4, 9, 16, 25, **e** 4, 7, 12, 19, 28 **2 a** 4, 5, 6, 7, 8 **b** 2, 5, 8, 11, 14 **c** 3, 8, 13, 18, 23 **d** 0, 3, 8, 15, 24 **e** 9, 13, 17, 21, 25 **3** $\frac{2}{4}, \frac{3}{5}, \frac{4}{6}, \frac{5}{7}, \frac{6}{8}$ **4 a** 6, 10, 15, 21, 28
b Triangle numbers **5 a** 2, 6, 24, 720 **b** 69

Exercise 23D

1 a 13, 15, $2n + 1$ **b** 25, 29, $4n + 1$ **c** 33, 38, $5n + 3$ **d** 32, 38, $6n - 4$ **e** 20, 23, $3n + 2$ **f** 37, 44, $7n - 5$ **g** 21, 25, $4n - 3$ **h** 23, 27, $4n - 1$ **i** 17, 20, $3n - 1$ **j** 42, 52, $10n - 8$ **k** 24, 28, $4n + 4$ **l** 29, 34, $5n - 1$
2 a $3n + 1$, 151 **b** $2n + 5$, 105 **c** $5n - 2$, 248 **d** $4n - 3$, 197 **e** $8n - 6$, 394 **f** $n + 4$, 54 **g** $5n + 1$, 251
h $8n - 5$, 395 **i** $3n - 2$, 148 **j** $3n + 18$, 168 **k** $7n + 5$, 355 **l** $8n - 7$, 393 **3 a i** $4n + 1$ **ii** 401
b i $2n + 1$ **ii** 201 **c i** $3n + 1$ **ii** 301 **d i** $2n + 6$ **ii** 206 **e i** $4n + 5$ **ii** 405 **f i** $5n + 1$ **ii** 501 **g i** $3n - 3$
ii 297 **h i** $6n - 4$ **ii** 596 **i i** $8n - 1$ **ii** 799 **j i** $2n + 23$ **ii** 223

Exercise 23E

1 b $4n - 3$ **c** 97 **d** 50th diagram **2 b** $2n + 1$ **c** 121 **d** 49th set **3 a** 18 **b** $4n + 2$ **c** 12
4 b $2n + 1$ **c** 101 **d** 149th diagram **5 a i** 20 cm **ii** $(3n + 2)$ cm **iii** 152 cm **b** 332 **6 a i** 20
ii 162 **b** 79.8 km

Examination questions (Chapter 23)

1 a Quantity doubles **b** 1600 ml **2 a i** 11 **ii** 2 **b i** 16 **ii** 154 **c** 6 **3 a** 2, 12 **b** Goes up in steps of 3
4 a 19, $9^2 - 8^2 = 17$ **b** $8^2 - 7^2 = 15$ **5 a i** 19 **ii** 39 **b** 5, −4 **6 a** $3 \times 3 \times 3$, $4 \times 4 \times 4 = 64$ **b** $100 = 10^2$
c $1^3 + 2^3 + 3^3 + 4^3 + 5^3 + 6^3 = 441 = 21^2$ **7** 72 **8 a** **b** 13, 16, 19 **c** Multiply 25 by 3 and add 1

9 a 13, 17, 21 **b** 49: multiply 12 by 4 and add 1 **10 b** 2, 4, 6, 8, 10 **c** 200

Answers

Practice Examination Paper 1

All answers are worth one mark unless otherwise stated. In such cases, there may be marks available for method.
1 a 13 06 **b** 29 min **c** 25 min **d** 27 min **2 a** 24 500 **b** 4000 **c** 47 203 **d** 155 **3 a** About 9 m or 30 ft
[The answer can be given as a range as it is an estimate: 8.5 to 10 m or 28 ft to 33 ft. 1 mark out of 2 if you show that the scoreboard is about 5.3 times as tall as the man, who will be about 2 m or 6 ft.] **b** 23 040 [1 mark if you do part of a long-multiplication method but make one mistake.] **4** Bags of chips. It should be about 7 times original order [1 mark if you show that it is about 7 times bigger.] **5** [You must be within ± 1 mm and within ± 1°. Each part is worth 1 mark.] **6 a** Slab is two equilateral triangles
b i 240 cm **ii** **c–d** For example: **7** Hexagon [1 mark for the face, 1 mark for the name.]
8 a (4, 3), (4, 1), (2, 1), (2, 3), (1, 3). [1 mark off for each wrong answer up to a maximum of two.] **b** 8 cm^2

9 £12.79 [1 mark for getting £487.21.] **10 a** B, C, E and F [1 mark off for each wrong answer up to maximum of two.]
b B: 3 lines along short diagonals, D: 1 vertical line, F:4 lines, G: 1 vertical line [1 mark off for each wrong answer up to a maximum of two.] **11 a** 11, 13, 15, 17 **b** Not an odd number **c** $m = 2t + 1$ [1 mark if you get $2t$] **d** 201 [You can still get these marks following through from a wrong answer in **c**.] **12 a** Top row 9, 10, 11, 12; second row 8, 9, 10, 11; third row 7, 8, 9, 10; fourth row 6, 7, 8, 9 **b** (1, 6), (2, 5), (3, 4), (4, 3), (5, 2), (6, 1) **c i** $\frac{1}{6}$ **ii** $\frac{1}{6}$ **13 a** £9, £15
b Graph goes through (5, 6) and (50, 15) **c** £8 [You must show a line on the graph to get the mark.]
14 a 5 [1 mark for $4x = 20$] **b** $\frac{1}{2}$ [2 marks for $x = \frac{2}{4}$ and 1 mark for $4x = 2$] **15 a** 13 [1 mark for 5 or 8] **b** 32
16 38, 19, 56 [1 mark for two correct]

Practice Examination Paper 2

All answers are worth one mark unless otherwise stated. In such cases, there may be marks available for method.
1 a 71 cm [1 mark for doing 3 − (0.75 + 1.54) or similar.] **b** $\frac{1}{4}$ **2 a** 108° **b** No, because angle a not 106°
3 288 cm^3 [1 mark for working] **4 a** 68 m **b** 294 m^2 [1 mark for area of triangle of 54 m^2] **5 a** 25.1 m [1 mark for using $2\pi r$ or πd.] **b** 50.3 m^2 [1 mark for using πr^2] **6 a** £1.32 [1 mark for 60 × 2.2] **b** 51p [1 mark for 15% of 60p = 9p]
7 a i $\frac{2}{5}$ **ii** 360 **b** 5% [1 mark for $\frac{30}{600} \times 100$] **c** 600 [1 mark for calculating 1500 ÷ (2 + 3).] **d** $\frac{3}{4}$
8 17 m^2 [1 mark for 14 = a − 3] **9 a** 1,2; 1,3; 1,4; 1,5; 1,6; 2,3; 2,4; 2,5; 2,6; 3,4; 3,5; 3,6; 4,5; 4,6; 5,6 [1 mark off for each wrong or missing pair up to a maximum of two.] **b** 0.93 [1 mark for 1 − 0.07] **10** 300 g flour, 75 g sugar, 100 g margarine, 25 g water [1 mark for multiplying by 2.5] **11 a** 35 **b** 87.5% [1 mark for (35 ÷ 40) × 100] **c** $\frac{1}{20}$ [1 mark for $\frac{2}{40}$]
12 a £13.20 [1 mark for $\frac{12}{100} \times$ £15 = £1.80] **b** About $\frac{2}{3}$ shaded [Some tolerance allowed.] **13 a i** 18.6 min [1 mark for 223 ÷ 12]
ii 16 min **b** Mean about the same, but journey times for Dennis are much more consistent [1 mark for comment on mean and 1 mark for comment on range.] **14 a** [1 mark for two correct] **b** Any question about route, for example: 'Where do you live?' Any questions about time, for example: 'What time do you go shopping?' [1 mark for each]
15 a 26.092 307 69 [1mark for 101.76 ÷ 3.9] **b** 25 [1 mark for 100 ÷ 4] **16** 114° [1 mark for finding 66°] **17 a** 60mph [1 mark for 135 ÷ 2.25] **b** 1$\frac{1}{2}$ hours [1 mark for 135 ÷ 90]

Index

This index covers the text from chapters 1 to 23, but does not cover the exercises or examination questions.

The alphabetical order is word-by-word, e.g. 'average speeds' precedes 'averages'.